D1298135

INTERNATIONAL THEOLOGICAL LIBRARY

A HISTORY

OF

THE REFORMATION

BY

THOMAS M. LINDSAY, D.D., LL.D.

PRINCIPAL, THE UNITED FREE CHURCH
COLLEGE, GLASGOW

IN TWO VOLUMES

VOLUME I

*THE REFORMATION IN GERMANY
FROM ITS BEGINNING TO THE
RELIGIOUS PEACE OF AUGSBURG*

SECOND EDITION

EDINBURGH
T. & T. CLARK, 38 GEORGE STREET

PRINTED IN GREAT BRITAIN BY
MORRISON AND GIBB LIMITED
FOR
T. & T. CLARK, EDINBURGH
NEW YORK: CHARLES SCRIBNER'S SONS

FIRST EDITION . . . . *April* 1906
SECOND EDITION . . . . . *November* 1907
Latest Reprint .(*Second Edition, January* 1959)

TO

THE REV. GEORGE CLARK HUTTON, D.D.

PREFACE.

THIS History of the Reformation has been written with the intention of describing a great religious movement amid its social environment. The times were heroic, and produced great men, with striking individualities not easily weighed in modern balances. The age is sufficiently remote to compel us to remember that while the morality of one century can be judged by another, the men who belong to it must be judged by the standard of their contemporaries, and not altogether by ours. The religious revival was set in a framework of political, intellectual, and economic changes, and cannot be disentangled from its surroundings without danger of mutilation. All these things add to the difficulty of description.

My excuse, if excuse be needed, for venturing on the task is that the period is one to which I have devoted special attention for many years, and that I have read and re-read most of the original contemporary sources of information. While full use has been made of the labours of predecessors in the same field, no chapter in the volume, save that on the political condition of Europe, has been written without constant reference to contemporary evidence.

A History of the Reformation, it appears to me, must describe five distinct but related things—the social and religious conditions of the age out of which the great movement came; the Lutheran Reformation down to 1555, when it received legal recognition; the Reformation in countries beyond Germany which did not submit to the guidance of Luther; the issue of certain portions of the religious life of the Middle Ages in Anabaptism, Socinianism, and Anti-Trinitarianism; and, finally, the Counter-Reformation.

The second follows the first in natural succession; but the third was almost contemporary with the second. If the Reformation won its way to legal recognition earlier in Germany than in any other land, its beginnings in France, England, and perhaps the Netherlands, had appeared before Luther had published his *Theses*. I have not found it possible to describe all the five in chronological order.

This volume describes the eve of the Reformation and the movement itself under the guidance of Luther. In a second volume I hope to deal with the Reformation beyond Germany, with Anabaptism, Socinianism, and kindred matters which had their roots far back in the Middle Ages, and with the Counter-Reformation.

The first part of this volume deals with the intellectual, social, and religious life of the age which gave birth to the Reformation. The intellectual life of the times has been frequently described, and its economic conditions are beginning to attract attention. But few have cared to investigate popular and family religious life in the decades before the great revival. Yet for the history of the Reformation movement nothing can be more important. When it is studied, it can be seen that the evangelical revival was not a unique phenomenon, entirely unconnected with the immediate past. There was a continuity in the religious life of the period. The same hymns were sung in public and in private after the Reformation which had been in use before Luther raised the standard of revolt. Many of the prayers in the Reformation liturgies came from the service-books of the mediæval Church. Much of the family instruction in religious matters received by the Reformers when they were children was in turn taught by them to the succeeding generation. The great Reformation had its roots in the simple evangelical piety which had never entirely disappeared in the mediæval Church. Luther's teaching was recognised by thousands to be no startling novelty, but something which they had always at heart believed, though they might not have been able to formulate it. It is true that Luther and his fellow-Reformers taught their generation that Our Lord, Jesus Christ, filled the whole sphere of God, and that other mediators and intercessors were superfluous, and that they also delivered it from the fear of a priestly caste; but men did not receive that teaching as entirely new; they rather accepted it as something they had always felt, though they had not been able to give their feelings due and complete expression. It is true that this simple piety had been set in a framework of superstition, and that the Church had been generally looked upon as an institution within which priests exercised a secret science of redemption through their power over the sacraments; but the old evangelical piety existed, and its traces can be found when sought for.

A portion of the chapter which describes the family and popular religious life immediately preceding the Reformation has already appeared in the *London Quarterly Review* for October 1903.

In describing the beginnings of the Lutheran Reformation, I have had to go over the same ground covered by my chapter on "Luther" contributed to the second volume of the *Cambridge Modern History*, and have found it impossible not to repeat myself. This is specially the case with the account given of the theory and practice of Indulgences. It ought to be said, however, that in view of certain strictures on the earlier work by Roman Catholic reviewers, I have gone over again the statements made about Indulgences by the great mediæval theologians of the thirteenth and fifteenth centuries, and have not been able to change the opinions previously expressed.

My thanks are due to my colleague, Dr. Denney, and to another friend for the care they have taken in revising the proof-sheets, and for many valuable suggestions which have been given effect to.

THOMAS M. LINDSAY

March, 1906.

PUBLISHERS' NOTE TO THE SECOND EDITION.

THIS Second Impression has been carefully revised and corrected by Principal Lindsay. It was his intention to write a new Prefatory Note in acknowledgment of the kindness of many reviewers and friends. But unfortunately a sudden indisposition has rendered that impossible, and the present great demand for the book necessitates its immediate issue.

November 1*st*, 1907.

CONTENTS.

BOOK I.

ON THE EVE OF THE REFORMATION.

CHAPTER I.

The Papacy.

CHAPTER II.

The Political Situation.

CHAPTER III.

The Renaissance.

CHAPTER IV.

Social Conditions.

CHAPTER V.

Family and Popular Religious Life in the Decades before the Reformation.

CHAPTER VI.

HUMANISM AND THE REFORMATION.

BOOK II.

THE REFORMATION.

CHAPTER I.

LUTHER TO THE BEGINNING OF THE CONTROVERSY ABOUT INDULGENCES.

CHAPTER II.

FROM THE BEGINNING OF THE INDULGENCE CONTROVERSY TO THE DIET OF WORMS.

CHAPTER III.

The Diet of Worms.

CHAPTER IV.

From the Diet of Worms to the Close of the Peasants' War.

final overthrow of the last remains of a cultured paganism. It became the sketch outline which the jurists of the Roman Curia gradually filled in with details by their strictly defined and legally expressed claim of the Roman Pontiff to a universal jurisdiction. Its living but poetically indefinite ideas were transformed into clearly defined legal principles found ready-made in the all-embracing jurisprudence of the ancient empire, and were analysed and exhibited in definite claims to rule and to judge in every department of human activity. When poetic thoughts, which from their very nature stretch forward towards and melt in the infinite, are imprisoned within legal formulas and are changed into principles of practical jurisprudence, they lose all their distinctive character, and the creation which embodies them becomes very different from what it was meant to be. The mischievous activity of the Roman canonists actually transformed the *Civitas Dei* of the glorious vision of St. Augustine into that *Civitas Terrena* which he reprobated, and the ideal Kingdom of God became a vulgar earthly monarchy, with all the accompaniments of conquest, fraud, and violence which, according to the great theologian of the West, naturally belonged to such a society. But the glamour of the City of God long remained to dazzle the eyes of gifted and pious men during the earlier Middle Ages, when they contemplated the visible ecclesiastical empire ruled by the Bishop of Rome.

The requirements of the practical religion of everyday life were also believed to be in the possession of this ecclesiastical monarchy to give and to withhold. For it was the almost universal belief of mediæval piety that the mediation of a priest was essential to salvation; and the priesthood was an integral part of this monarchy, and did not exist outside its boundaries. "No good Catholic Christian doubted that in spiritual things the clergy were the divinely appointed superiors of the laity, that this power proceeded from the right of the priests to celebrate the sacraments, that the Pope was the real possessor of this power, and was far superior to all secular authority."[1] In the decades immediately preceding the Reformation, many an educated man might have doubts about this power of the clergy over the spiritual and eternal welfare of men and women; but when it came to the point, almost no one could venture to say that there was nothing in it. And so long as the feeling remained that there might be something in it, the anxieties, to say the least, which Christian men and women could not help having when they looked forward to an unknown future, made kings and peoples hesitate before they offered defiance to the Pope and the clergy. The spiritual powers which were believed to come from the exclusive possession of priesthood and sacraments went for much in increasing the authority of the papal empire and in binding it together in one compact whole.

In the earlier Middle Ages the claims of the Papacy to universal supremacy had been urged and defended by ecclesiastical jurists alone; but in the thirteenth century theology also began to state them from its own point of view. Thomas Aquinas set himself to prove that submission to the Roman Pontiff was necessary for every human being. He declared that, under the law of the New Testament, the king must be subject to the priest to the extent that, if kings proved to be heretics or schismatics, the Bishop of Rome was entitled to deprive them of all kingly authority by releasing subjects from their ordinary obedience.[2]

The fullest expression of this temporal and spiritual supremacy claimed by the Bishops of Rome is to be found in Pope Innocent IV.'s *Commentary on the Decretals*[3] (1243–1254), and in the Bull, *Unam Sanctam*, published by Pope Boniface VIII. in 1302. But succeeding Bishops of Rome

[1] Harnack, *History of Dogma*, vi. 132 n. (Eng. trans.).

[2] Compare his *Opuscula contra errores Græcorum; De regimine principum*. (The first two books were written by Thomas and the other two probably by Tolomeo (Ptolomæus) of Lucca.)

[3] *Apparatus super quinque libris Decretalium* (Strassburg. 1488).

in no way abated their pretensions to universal sovereignty The same claims were made during the Exile at Avignon and in the days of the Great Schism. They were asserted by Pope Pius II. in his Bull, *Execrabilis et pristinis* (1459), and by Pope Leo X. on the very eve of the Reformation, in his Bull, *Pastor Æternus* (1516); while Pope Alexander VI. (Rodrigo Borgia), acting as the lord of the universe, made over the New World to Isabella of Castile and to Ferdinand of Aragon by legal deed of gift in his Bull, *Inter cætera divinæ* (May 4th, 1493).[1]

The power claimed in these documents was a twofold supremacy, temporal and spiritual.

§ 2. *The Temporal Supremacy.*

The former, stated in its widest extent, was the right to depose kings, free their subjects from their allegiance, and bestow their territories on another. It could only be

[1] Full quotations from the Bulls, *Unam Sanctam* and *Inter cætera divinæ*, are to be found in Mirbt's *Quellen zur Geschichte des Papsttums* (Leipzig, 1895), pp. 88, 107. The Bulls, *Execrabilis* and *Pastor Æternus*, are in Denzinger, *Enchiridion* (Würzburg, 1900), 9th ed. pp. 172, 174.

The Deed of Gift of the American Continent to Isabella and Ferdinand is in the 6th section of the Bull, *Inter cætera divinæ*. It is as follows:—"Motu proprio . . . de nostra mera liberalitate et ex certa scientia ac de apostolicæ potestatis plenitudine omnes insulas et terras firmas inventas et inveniendas, detectas et detegendas versus Occidentem et Meridiem fabricando et construendo unam lineam a Polo Artico scilicet Septentrione ad Polum Antarticum scilicet Meridiem, sive terræ firmæ et insulæ inventæ et inveniendæ sint versus Indiam aut versus aliam quamcumque partem, quæ linea distet a qualibet insularum, quæ vulgariter nuncupantur de los Azores y cabo vierde, centum leucis versus Occidentem et Meridiem; ita quod omnes insulæ et terræ firmæ, repertæ et reperiendæ, detectæ et detegendæ, a præfata linea versus Occidentem et Meridiem per alium Regem aut Principem Christianum non fuerint actualiter possessæ usque ad diem nativitatis Domini Nostri Jesu Christi proximi præteritum . . . auctoritate omnipotentis Dei nobis in Beato Petro concessa, ac vicarius Jesu Christi, qua fungimur in terris, cum omnibus illarum dominiis, civitatibus, castris, locis et villis, juribusque et jurisdictionibus ac pertinentiis univeris, vobis hæredibusque et successoribus vestris in perpetuum tenore præsentium donamus. . . . Vosque et hæredes ac successores præfatos illarum dominos cum plena, libera et omnimoda potestate, auctoritate et jurisdictione facimus, constituimus et deputamus."

enforced when the Pope found a stronger potentate willing to carry out his orders, and was naturally but rarely exercised. Two instances, however, occurred not long before the Reformation. George Podiebrod, the King of Bohemia, offended the Bishop of Rome by insisting that the Roman See should keep the bargain made with his Hussite subjects at the Council of Basel. He was summoned to Rome to be tried as a heretic by Pope Pius II. in 1464, and by Pope Paul II. in 1465, and was declared by the latter to be deposed; his subjects were released from their allegiance, and his kingdom was offered to Matthias Corvinus, the King of Hungary, who gladly accepted the offer, and a protracted and bloody war was the consequence. Later still, in 1511, Pope Julius II. excommunicated the King of Navarre, and empowered any neighbouring king to seize his dominions—an offer readily accepted by Ferdinand of Aragon.[1]

It was generally, however, in more indirect ways that this claim to temporal supremacy, *i.e.* to direct the policy and to be the final arbiter in the actions of temporal sovereigns, made itself felt. A great potentate, placed over the loosely formed kingdoms of the Middle Ages, hesitated to provoke a contest with an authority which was able to give religious sanction to the rebellion of powerful feudal nobles seeking a legitimate pretext for defying him, or which could deprive his subjects of the external consolations of religion by laying the whole or part of his dominions under an interdict. We are not to suppose that the exercise of this claim of temporal supremacy was always an evil thing. Time after time the actions and interference of right-minded Popes proved that the temporal supremacy of the Bishop of Rome meant that moral considerations must have due weight attached to them in the international affairs of Europe; and this fact,

[1] This excommunication, with its consequences, was used to threaten Queen Elizabeth by the Ambassador of Philip II. in 1559 (*Calendar of Letters and State Papers relating to English affairs preserved principally in the Archives of Simancas*, i. 62, London, 1892).

recognised and felt, accounted largely for much of the practical acquiescence in the papal claims. But from the time when the Papacy became, on its temporal side, an Italian power, and when its international policy had for its chief motive to increase the political prestige of the Bishop of Rome within the Italian peninsula, the moral standard of the papal court was hopelessly lowered, and it no longer had even the semblance of representing morality in the international affairs of Europe. The change may be roughly dated from the pontificate of Pope Sixtus IV. (1471–1484), or from the birth of Luther (November 10th, 1483). The possession of the Papacy gave this advantage to Sixtus over his contemporaries in Italy, that he "was relieved of all ordinary considerations of decency, consistency, or prudence, because his position as Pope saved him from serious disaster." The divine authority, assumed by the Popes as the representatives of Christ upon earth, meant for Sixtus and his immediate successors that they were above the requirements of common morality, and had the right for themselves or for their allies to break the most solemn treaties when it suited their shifting policy.

§ 3. *The Spiritual Supremacy.*

The ecclesiastical supremacy was gradually interpreted to mean that the Bishop of Rome was the *one* or universal bishop in whom all spiritual and ecclesiastical powers were summed up, and that all other members of the hierarchy were simply delegates selected by him for the purposes of administration. On this interpretation, the Bishop of Rome was the absolute monarch over a kingdom which was called spiritual, but which was as thoroughly material as were those of France, Spain, or England. For, according to mediæval ideas, men were spiritual if they had taken orders, or were under monastic vows; fields, drains, and fences were spiritual things if they were Church property; a house, a barn, or a byre was a spiritual thing, if it stood on land belonging to the Church. This papal kingdom, miscalled spiritual, lay scattered over Europe in diocesan lands, convent estates, and parish glebes—interwoven in the web of the ordinary kingdoms and principalities of Europe. It was part of the Pope's claim to *spiritual* supremacy that his subjects (the clergy) owed no allegiance to the monarch within whose territories they resided; that they lived outside the sphere of civil legislation and taxation; and that they were under special laws imposed on them by their supreme spiritual ruler, and paid taxes to him and to him alone. The claim to spiritual supremacy therefore involved endless interference with the rights of temporal sovereignty in every country in Europe, and things civil and things sacred were so inextricably mixed that it is quite impossible to speak of the Reformation as a purely religious movement. It was also an endeavour to put an end to the exemption of the Church and its possessions from all secular control, and to her constant encroachment on secular territory.

To show how this claim for spiritual supremacy trespassed continually on the domain of secular authority and created a spirit of unrest all over Europe, we have only to look at its exercise in the matter of patronage to benefices, to the way in which the common law of the Church interfered with the special civil laws of European States, and to the increasing burden of papal requisitions of money.

In the case of bishops, the theory was that the dean and chapter elected, and that the bishop-elect had to be confirmed by the Pope. This procedure provided for the selection locally of a suitable spiritual ruler, and also for the supremacy of the head of the Church. The mediæval bishops, however, were temporal lords of great influence in the civil affairs of the kingdom or principality within which their dioceses were placed, and it was naturally an object of interest to kings and princes to secure men who would be faithful to themselves. Hence the tendency was for the civil authorities to interfere more or less in episcopal appointments. This frequently resulted in making these elections a matter of conflict between the head of the Church in Rome and the head of the State in France, England, or Germany; in which case the rights of the dean and chapter were commonly of small account. The contest was in the nature of things almost inevitable even when the civil and the ecclesiastical powers were actuated by the best motives, and when both sought to appoint men competent to discharge the duties of the position with ability. But the best motives were not always active. Diocesan rents were large, and the incomes of bishops made excellent provision for the favourite followers of kings and of Popes, and if the revenues of one see failed to express royal or papal favour adequately, the favourite could be appointed to several sees at once. Papal nepotism became a byword; but it ought to be remembered that kingly nepotism also existed. Pope Sixtus V. insisted on appointing a retainer of his nephew, Cardinal Giuliano della Rovere, to the see of Modrus in Hungary, and after a contest of three years carried his point in 1483; and Matthias Corvinus, King of Hungary, gave the archbishopric of Gran to Ippolito d'Este, a youth under age, and after a two years' struggle compelled the Pope to confirm the appointment in 1487.

During the fourteenth century the Papacy endeavoured to obtain a more complete control over ecclesiastical appointments by means of the system of *Reservations* which figures so largely in local ecclesiastical affairs to the discredit of the Papacy during the years before the Reformation. For at least a century earlier, Popes had been accustomed to declare on various pretexts that certain benefices were *vacantes apud Sedem Apostolicam*, which meant that the Bishop of Rome reserved the appointment for himself. Pope John XXII. (1316–1334), founding on such previous practice, laid down a series of rules stating what benefices were to be reserved for the papal patronage. The ostensible reason for this legislation was to prevent the growing evil of pluralities; but, as in all cases of papal lawmaking, these *Constitutiones Johanninæ* had the effect of binding ecclesiastically all patrons but the Popes themselves. For the Popes always maintained that they alone were superior to the laws which they made. They were *supra legem* or *legibus absoluti,* and their dispensations could always set aside their legislation when it suited their purpose. Under these constitutions of Pope John XXII., when sees were vacant owing to the invalidation of an election they were *reserved* to the Pope. Thus we find that there was a disputed election to the see of Dunkeld in 1337, and after some years' litigation at Rome the election was quashed, and Richard de Pilmor was appointed bishop *auctoritate apostolica.* The see of Dunkeld was declared to be reserved to the Pope for the appointment of the two succeeding bishops at least.[1] This system of *Reservations* was gradually extended under the successors of Pope John XXII., and was applied to benefices of every kind all over Europe, until it would be difficult to say what piece of ecclesiastical preferment escaped the papal net. There exists in the town library in Trier a MS. of the *Rules of the Roman Chancery* on which someone has sketched the head of a Pope, with the legend issuing from the mouth, *Reservamus omnia,* which somewhat roughly represents the contents of the book. In the end, the assertion was made that the Holy See owned all benefices, and, in the universal secularisation of the Church which the half century before the Reformation witnessed, the very Rules of the Roman Chancery contained the lists of prices to be charged for various benefices, whether with or without cure of souls; and in completing the bargain the purchaser could always procure a clause setting aside the civil rights of patrons.

On the other hand, ecclesiastical preferments always implied the holders being liferented in lands and in monies, and the right to bestow these temporalities was protected by the laws of most European countries. Thus the ever-extending papal *reservations* of benefices led to continual conflicts between the laws of the Church—in this case latterly the Rules of the Roman Chancery—and the laws of the European States. Temporal rulers sought to

[1] *Scottish Historical Review,* i. 318–320.

protect themselves and their subjects by statutes of *Præmunire* and others of a like kind,[1] or else made bargains with the Popes, which took the form of *Concordats*, like that of Bourges (1438) and that of Vienna (1448). Neither statutes nor bargains were of much avail against the superior diplomacy of the Papacy, and the dread which its supposed possession of spiritual powers inspired in all classes of people. A Concordat was always represented by papal lawyers to be binding only so long as the goodwill of the Pope maintained it; and there was a deep-seated feeling throughout the peoples of Europe that the Church was, to use the language of the peasants of Germany, "the Pope's House," and that he had a right to deal freely with its property. Pious and patriotic men, like Gascoigne in England, deplored the evil effects of the papal *reservations*; but they saw no remedy unless the Almighty changed the heart of the Holy Father; and, after the failures of the Conciliar attempts at reform, a sullen hopelessness seemed to have taken possession of the minds of men, until Luther taught them that there was nothing in the indefinable power that the Pope and the clergy claimed to possess over the spiritual and eternal welfare of men and women.

To Pope John XXII. (1316–1334) belongs the credit or discredit of creating for the Papacy a machinery for gathering in money for its support. His situation rendered this almost inevitable. On his accession he found himself with an empty treasury; he had to incur debts in order to live; he had to provide for a costly war with the Visconti; and he had to leave money to enable his successors to carry out his temporal policy. Few Popes lived so plainly; his money-getting was not for personal luxury, but for the supposed requirements of the papal policy. He was the first Pope who systematically made the dispensation of grace, temporal and eternal, a source of revenue. Hitherto the charges made by the papal Chancery had

[1] The two English statutes of *Præmunire* are printed in Gee and Hardy, *Documents illustrative of English Church History* (London, 1896), pp. 103, 122.

been, ostensibly at least, for actual work done—fees for clerking and registration, and so on. John made the fees proportionate to the grace dispensed, or to the power of the recipient to pay. He and his successors made the *Tithes*, the *Annates*, *Procurations*, Fees for the bestowment of the *Pallium*, the *Medii Fructus*, *Subsidies*, and *Dispensations*, regular sources of revenue.

The *Tithe*—a tenth of all ecclesiastical incomes for the service of the Papacy—had been levied occasionally for extraordinary purposes, such as crusades. It was still supposed to be levied for special purposes only, but necessary occasions became almost continuous, and the exactions were fiercely resented. When Alexander VI. levied the *Tithe* in 1500, he was allowed to do so in England. The French clergy, however, refused to pay; they were excommunicated; the University of Paris declared the excommunication unlawful, and the Pope had to withdraw.

The *Annates* were an ancient charge. From the beginning of the twelfth century the incoming incumbent of a benefice had to pay over his first year's income for local uses, such as the repairs on ecclesiastical buildings, or as a solatium to the heirs of the deceased incumbent. From the beginning of the thirteenth century prelates and princes were sometimes permitted by the Popes to exact it of entrants into benefices. One of the earliest recorded instances was when the Archbishop of Canterbury was allowed to use the *Annates* of his province for a period of seven years from 1245, for the purpose of liquidating the debts on his cathedral church. Pope John XXII. began to appropriate them for the purposes of the Papacy. His predecessor Clement V. (1305–1314) had demanded all the *Annates* of England and Scotland for a period of three years from 1316. In 1316 John made a much wider demand, and in terms which showed that he was prepared to regard the *Annates* as a permanent tax for the general purposes of the Papacy. It is difficult to trace the stages of the gradual universal enforcement of this tax; but in the decades before the Reformation it was commonly imposed, and averages had been struck as to its amount.[1] "They consisted of a portion, usually computed at one-half, of the estimated revenue of all benefices worth more than 25 florins. Thus the archbishopric of Rouen was taxed at 12,000 florins, and the little see of Grenoble at 300; the great abbacy of St. Denis at 6000, and the little St. Ciprian Poictiers at 33; while all the parish cures in France were uniformly rated at 24 ducats, equivalent to about 30 florins." Archbishoprics were subject to a special tax as the price of the *Pallium,* and this was often very large.

The *Procurationes* were the charges, commuted to money payments, which bishops and archdeacons were authorised to make for their personal expenses while on their tours of visitation throughout their dioceses. The Popes began by demanding a share, and ended by often claiming the whole of these sums.

Pope John XXII. was the first to require that the incomes of vacant benefices (*medii fructus*) should be paid over to the papal treasury during the vacancies. The earliest instance dates from 1331, when a demand was made for the income of the vacant archbishopric of Gran in Hungary; and it soon became the custom to insist that the stipends of all vacant benefices should be paid into the papal treasury.

Finally, the Popes declared it to be their right to require special *subsidies* from ecclesiastical provinces, and great pressure was put on the people to pay these so-called free-will offerings.

Besides the sums which poured into the papal treasury from these regular sources of income, irregular sources afforded still larger amounts of money. Countless dispensations were issued on payment of fees for all manner of breaches of canonical and moral law—dispensations for marriages within the prohibited degrees, for holding plural-

[1] For information about the English *annates* and the *valor ecclesiasticus,* cf. Bird, *Handbook to the Public Records,* pp. 100, 106.

ities, for acquiring unjust gains in trade or otherwise. This demoralising traffic made the Roman treasury the partner in all kinds of iniquitous actions, and Luther, in his address *To the Nobility of the German Nation respecting the Reformation of the Christian Estate*, could fitly describe the Court of the Roman Curia as a place "where vows were annulled, where the monk gets leave to quit his Order, where priests can enter the married life for money, where bastards can become legitimate, and dishonour and shame may arrive at high honours; all evil repute and disgrace is knighted and ennobled." "There is," he adds, "a buying and a selling, a changing, blustering and bargaining, cheating and lying, robbing and stealing, debauchery and villainy, and all kinds of contempt of God that Antichrist could not reign worse."

The vast sums of money obtained in these ways do not represent the whole of the funds which flowed from all parts of Europe into the papal treasury. The Roman Curia was the highest court of appeal for the whole Church of the West. In any case this involved a large amount of law business, with the inevitable legal expenses; but the Curia managed to attract to itself a large amount of business which might have been easily settled in the episcopal or metropolitan courts. This was done in pursuance of a double policy—an ecclesiastical and a financial one. The half century before the Reformation saw the overthrow of feudalism and the consolidation of kingly absolutism, and something similar was to be seen in the Papacy as well as among the principalities of Europe. Just as the kingly absolutism triumphed when the hereditary feudal magnates lost their power, so papal absolutism could only become an accomplished fact when it could trample upon an episcopate deprived of its ecclesiastical independence and inherent powers of ruling and judging. The Episcopate was weakened in many ways,—by exempting abbacies from episcopal control, by encouraging the mendicant monks to become the rivals of the parish clergy, and so on,—but the most potent method of degrading it was by encouraging people with ecclesiastical complaints to pass by the episcopal courts and to carry their cases directly to the Pope. Nationalities, men were told, had no place within the Catholic Church. Rome was the common fatherland, and the Pope the universal bishop and judge ordinary. His judgment, which was always final, could be had directly. In this way men were enticed to take their pleas straight to the Pope. No doubt this involved sending a messenger to Italy with a statement of the plea and a request for a hearing; but it did not necessarily involve that the trial should take place at Rome. The central power could delegate its authority, and the trial could take place wherever the Pope might appoint. But the conception undoubtedly did increase largely the business of the courts actually held in Rome, and caused a flow of money to the imperial city. The Popes were also ready to lend monies to impoverished litigants, for which, of course, heavy interest was charged.

The immense amount of business which was thus directed into the papal chancery from all parts of Europe required a horde of officials, whose salaries were provided partly from the incomes of *reserved* benefices all over Europe, and partly from the fees and bribes of the litigants. The papal law-courts were notoriously dilatory, rapacious, and venal. Every document had to pass through an incredible number of hands, and pay a corresponding number of fees; and the costs of suits, heavy enough according to the prescribed rule of the chancery, were increased immensely beyond the regular charges by others which did not appear on the official tables. Cases are on record where the *briefs* obtained cost from twenty-four to forty-one times the amount of the legitimate official charges. The Roman Church had become a law-court, not of the most reputable kind, — an arena of rival litigants, a chancery of writers, notaries, and tax-gatherers,—where transactions about privileges, dispensations, buying of benefices, etc., were carried on, and where suitors went wandering with their petitions from the door of one office to another.

During the half century which preceded the Reformation, things went from bad to worse. The fears aroused by the attempts at a reform through General Councils had died down, and the Curia had no desire to reform itself. The venality and rapacity increased when Popes began to sell offices in the papal court. Boniface IX. (1389–1404) was the first to raise money by selling these official posts to the highest bidders. "In 1483, when Sixtus IV. (1471–1484) desired to redeem his tiara and jewels, pledged for a loan of 100,000 ducats, he increased his secretaries from six to twenty-four, and required each to pay 2600 florins for the office. In 1503, to raise funds for Cæsar Borgia, Alexander VI. (1492–1503) created eighty new offices, and sold them for 760 ducats apiece. Julius II. formed a 'college' of one hundred and one scriveners of papal briefs, in return for which they paid him 74,000 ducats. Leo X. (1513–1521) appointed sixty chamberlains and a hundred and forty squires, with certain perquisites, for which the former paid him 90,000 ducats and the latter 112,000. Places thus paid for were personal property, transferable on sale. Burchard tells us that in 1483 he bought the mastership of ceremonies from his predecessor Patrizzi for 450 ducats, which covered all expenses; that in 1505 he vainly offered Julius II. (1503–1513) 2000 ducats for a vacant scrivenership, and that soon after he bought the succession to an abbreviatorship for 2040."[1] When Adrian VI. (1522–1523) honestly tried to cleanse this Augean stable, he found himself confronted with the fact that he would have to turn men adrift who had spent their capital in buying the places which any reform must suppress.

The papal exactions needed to support this luxurious Roman Court, especially those taken from the clergy of Europe, were so obnoxious that it was often hard to collect them, and devices were used which in the end increased the burdens of those who were required to provide the money. The papal court made bargains with the temporal

[1] H. C. Lea, *Cambridge Modern History*, i. 670.

rulers to share the spoils if they permitted the collection.[1] The Popes agreed that the kings or princes could seize the *Tithes* or *Annates* for a prescribed time provided the papal officials had their authority to collect them, as a rule, for Roman use. In the decades before the Reformation it was the common practice to collect these dues by means of agents, often bankers, whose charges were enormous, amounting sometimes to fifty per cent. The collection of such extraordinary sources of revenue as the Indulgences was marked by even worse abuses, such as the employment of pardon-sellers, who overran Europe, and whose lies and extortions were the common theme of the denunciations of the greatest preachers and patriots of the times.

The unreformed Papacy of the closing decades of the fifteenth and of the first quarter of the sixteenth century was the open sore of Europe, and the object of execrations by almost all contemporary writers. Its abuses found no defenders, and its partisans in attacking assailants contented themselves with insisting upon the necessity for the spiritual supremacy of the Bishops of Rome.

> "Sant Peters schifflin ist im schwangk
> Ich sorge fast den untergangk,
> Die wallen schlagen allsit dran,
> Es würt vil sturm und plagen han."[2]

---

[1] J. Haller, *Papsttum und Kirchen-Reform* (1903), i. 116, 117.

[2] Sebastian Brand, *Das Narrenschiff*, cap. ciii. l. 63–66. Barclay paraphrases these lines:

> "Suche counterfayte the kayes that Jesu dyd commyt
> Unto Peter: brekynge his Shyppis takelynge,
> Subvertynge the fayth, beleuynge theyr owne wyt
> Against our perfyte fayth in euery thynge,
> *So is our Shyp without gyde wanderynge,*
> *By tempest dryuen, and the mayne sayle of torne,*
> *That without gyde the Shyp about is borne.*"

—*The Ship of Fools*, translated by Alexander Barclay, ii. 225 (Edinburgh 1874).

CHAPTER II.

THE POLITICAL SITUATION.[1]

§ 1. *The small extent of Christendom.*

DURING the period of the Reformation a small portion of the world belonged to Christendom, and of that only a part was affected, either really or nominally, by the movement. The Christians belonging to the Greek Church were entirely outside its influence.

Christendom had shrunk greatly since the seventh century. The Saracens and their successors in Moslem sovereignty had overrun and conquered many lands which had formerly been inhabited by a Christian population and governed by Christian rulers. Palestine, Syria, Asia Minor, Egypt, and North Africa westwards to the Straits of Gibraltar, had once been Christian, and had been lost to Christendom during the seventh and eighth centuries. The Moslems had invaded Europe in the West, had conquered the Spanish Peninsula, had passed the Pyrenees, and had invaded France. They were met and defeated in a three days' battle at Tours (732) by the Franks under Charles the Hammer, the grandfather of Charles the Great. After they had been thrust back beyond the Pyrenees, the Spanish Peninsula was the scene of a struggle between Moslem and Christian which lasted for more than seven hundred years, and Spain did not become wholly Christian until the last decade of the fifteenth century.

If the tide of Moslem conquest had been early checked in the West, in the East it had flowed steadily if slowly.

[1] *Cambridge Modern History,* I. iii, vii, viii, ix, xi, xii, xiv; Lavisse, *Histoire de France depuis les Origines jusqu' à la Révolution.* IV. i. ii.

In 1338, Orchan, Sultan of the Ottoman Turks, seized on Gallipoli, the fortified town which guarded the eastern entrance to the Dardanelles, and the Moslems won a footing on European soil. A few years later the troops of his son Murad I. had seized a portion of the Balkan peninsula, and had cut off Constantinople from the rest of Christendom. A hundred years after, Constantinople (1453) had fallen, the Christian population had been slain or enslaved, the great church of the *Holy Wisdom* (St. Sophia) had been made a Mohammedan mosque, and the city had become the metropolis of the wide-spreading empire of the Ottoman Turks. Servia, Bosnia, Herzogovina (the Duchy, from *Herzog*, a Duke), Greece, the Peloponnesus, Roumania, Wallachia, and Moldavia were incorporated in the Moslem Empire. Belgrade and the island of Rhodes, the two bulwarks of Christendom, had fallen. Germany was threatened by Turkish invasions, and for years the bells tolled in hundreds of German parishes calling the people to pray against the coming of the Turk. It was not until the heroic defence of Vienna, in 1529, that the victorious advance of the Moslem was stayed. Only the Adriatic separated Italy from the Ottoman Empire, and the great mountain wall with the strip of Dalmatian coast which lies at its foot was the bulwark between civilisation and barbarism.

§ 2. *Consolidation.*

In Western Europe, and within the limits affected directly or indirectly by the Reformation, the distinctive political characteristic of the times immediately preceding the movement was consolidation or coalescence. Feudalism, with its liberties and its lawlessness, was disappearing, and compact nations were being formed under monarchies which tended to become absolute. If the Scandinavian North be excluded, five nations included almost the whole field of Western European life, and in all of them the principle of consolidation is to be seen at work. In three, England, France, and Spain, there emerged great united kingdoms; and if in two, Germany and Italy, there was no clustering of the people round one dynasty, the same principle of coalescence showed itself in the formation of permanent States which had all the appearance of modern kingdoms.

It is important for our purpose to glance at each and show the principle at work.

§ 3. *England*

By the time that the Earl of Richmond had ascended the English throne and ruled with "politic governance" as Henry VII., the distinctively modern history of England had begun. Feudalism had perished on the field of the battle of Bosworth. The visitations of the Black Death, the gigantic agricultural labour strike under Wat Tyler and priest Ball, and the consequent transformation of peasant serfs into a free people working for wages, had created a new England ready for the changes which were to bridge the chasm between mediæval and modern history. The consolidation of the people was favoured by the English custom that the younger sons of the nobility ranked as commoners, and that the privileges as well as the estates went to the eldest sons. This kept the various classes of the population from becoming stereotyped into castes, as in Germany, France, and Spain, It tended to create an ever-increasing middle class, which was not confined to the towns, but permeated the country districts also. The younger sons of the nobility descended into this middle class, and the transformation of the serfs into a wage-earning class enabled some of them to rise into it. England was the first land to become a compact nationality.

The earlier portion of the reign of Henry VII. was not free from attempts which, if successful, would have thrown the country back into the old condition of disintegration. Although the king claimed to unite the rival lines of York and Lancaster, the Yorkists did not cease to raise difficulties at home which were eagerly fostered from abroad. Ireland was a Yorkist stronghold, and Margaret, the dowager Duchess of Burgundy, the sister of Edward IV., exercised a sufficiently powerful influence in Flanders to make that land a centre of Yorkist intrigue.

Lambert Simnel, a pretender who claimed to be either the son or the nephew of Edward IV. (his account of himself varied), appeared in Ireland, and the whole island gathered round him. He invaded England, drew to his standard many of the old Yorkists, but was defeated at Stoke-on-Trent in 1487 This was really a formidable rebellion. The rising under Perkin Warbeck, a young Burgundian from Tournay, though supported by Margaret of Burgundy and James IV. of Scotland, was more easily suppressed. A popular revolt against severe taxation was subdued in 1497, and it may be said that Henry's home difficulties were all over by the year 1500. England entered the sixteenth century as a compact nation.

The foreign policy of Henry VII. was alliance with Spain and a long-sighted attempt to secure Scotland by peaceful means. It had for consequences two marriages which had far-reaching results. The marriage of Henry's daughter Margaret with James IV. of Scotland led to the union of the two crowns three generations later; and that between Katharine, the third daughter of Ferdinand and Isabella of Spain, and the son of Henry VII. came to be the occasion, if not the cause, of the revolt of England from Rome. Katharine was married to Arthur, Prince of Wales, in 1501 (November 14th). Prince Arthur died on January 14th, 1502. After protracted negotiation, lengthened by the unwillingness of the Pope (Pius III.) to grant a dispensation, Katharine was contracted to Henry, and the marriage took place in the year of Prince Henry's accession to the crown. Katharine and Henry were crowned together at Westminster on June 28th, 1509.

England had prospered during the reign of the first Tudor sovereign. The steady increase in wool-growing and wool-exporting is in itself testimony to the fact that the period of internal wars had ceased, for sheep speedily become extinct when bands of raiders disturb the country. The growth in the number of artisan capitalists shows that money had become the possession of all classes in the community. The rise of the companies of merchant adventurers proves that England was taking her share in the world-trade of the new era. English scholars like Grocyn and Linacre (tutor in Italy of Pope Leo X. and in England of the Prince of Wales) had imbibed the New Learning in Italy, and had been followed there by John Colet, who caught the spirit of the Renaissance from the Italian Humanists and the fervour of a religious revival from Savonarola's work in Florence. The country had emerged from Mediævalism in almost everything when Henry VIII., the hope of the English Humanists and reformers, ascended the throne in 1509.

§ 4. *France.*

If England entered on the sixteenth century as the most compact kingdom in Europe, in the sense that all classes of its society were welded together more firmly than anywhere else, it may be said of France at the same date that nowhere was the central authority of the sovereign more firmly established. Many things had worked for this state of matters. The Hundred Years' War with England did for France what the wars against the Moors had done for Spain. It had created a sense of nationality. It had also made necessary national armies and the raising of national taxes. During the weary period of anarchy under Charles VI. every local and provincial institution of France had seemed to crumble or to display its inefficiency to help the nation in its sorest need. The one thing which was able to stand the storms and stress of the time was the kingly authority, and this in spite of the incapacity of the man who possessed it. The reign of Charles VII. had made it plain that England was not destined to remain in possession of French territory; and the succeeding reigns had seen the central authority slowly acquiring irresistible strength. Charles VII. by his policy of yielding slightly to pressure and sitting still when he could—by his inactivity, perhaps masterly,—Louis XI. by his restless, unscrupulous craft, Anne of Beaujeu (his daughter) by her clear insight and prompt decision, had not only laid the foundations, but built up and consolidated the edifice of absolute monarchy in France. The kingly power had subdued the great nobles and feudatories; it had to a large extent mastered the Church; it had consolidated the towns and made them props to its power; and it had made itself the direct lord of the peasants.

The work of consolidation had been as rapid as it was complete. In 1464, three years after his succession, Louis XI. was confronted by a formidable association of the great feudatories of France, which called itself the *League of Public Weal.* Charles of Guyenne, the king's brother, the Count of Charolais (known as Charles the Bold of Burgundy), the Duke of Brittany, the two great families of the Armagnacs, the elder represented by the Count of Armagnac, and the younger by the Duke of Nemours, John of Anjou, Duke of Calabria, and the Duke of Bourbon, were allied in arms against the king. Yet by 1465 Normandy had been wrested from the Duke of Guyenne; Guyenne itself had become the king's in 1472; the Duke of Nemours had been crushed and slain in 1476; the Count of Charolais, become Duke of Burgundy, had been overthrown, his power shattered, and himself slain by the Swiss peasant confederates, and almost all his French *fiefs* had been incorporated by 1480; and on the death of King René (1480) the provinces of Anjou and Provence had been annexed to the Crown of France. The great feudatories were so thoroughly broken that their attempt to revolt during the earlier years of the reign of Charles VIII. was easily frustrated by Anne of Beaujeu acting on behalf of the young king.

The efforts to secure hold on the Church date back from the days of the Council of Basel, when Pope Eugenius was at hopeless issue with the majority of its members. In 1438 a deputation from the Council waited upon the king and laid before him the conciliar plans of reform. Charles VII. summoned an assembly of the French clergy to meet at Bourges. He was present himself with his principal nobles; and the meeting was also attended by members of the Council and by papal delegates. There the celebrated Pragmatic Sanction of Bourges was formally presented and agreed upon.

This Pragmatic Sanction embodied most of the cherished conciliar plans of reform. It asserted the ecclesiastical supremacy of Councils over Popes. It demanded a meeting of a Council every ten years. It declared that the selection of the higher ecclesiastics was to be left to the Chapters and to the Convents. It denied the Pope's general claim to the reservation of benefices, and greatly limited its use in special cases. It did away with the Pope's right to act as Ordinary, and insisted that no ecclesiastical cases should be appealed to Rome without first having exhausted the lower courts of jurisdiction. It abolished the *Annates*, with some exceptions in favour of the present Pope. It also made some attempts to provide the churches with an educated ministry. All these declarations simply carried out the proposals of the Council of Basel; but they had an important influence on the position of the French clergy towards the king. The Pragmatic Sanction, though issued by an assembly of the French clergy, was nevertheless a royal ordinance, and thereby gave the king indefinite rights over the Church within France. The right to elect bishops and abbots was placed in the hands of Chapters and Convents, but the king and nobles were expressly permitted to bring forward and recommend candidates, and this might easily be extended to enforcing the election of those recommended. Indefinite rights of patronage on the part of the king and of the nobles over benefices in France could not fail to be the result, and the French Church could scarcely avoid assuming the appearance of a national Church controlled by the king as the head of the State. The abolition of the Pragmatic Sanction was always a bait which the French king could dangle before the eyes of the Pope, and the promise to maintain the Pragmatic Sanction was always a bribe to secure the support of the clergy and the *Parlements* of France.

In 1516, Francis I. and Leo X. agreed on a Concordat, the practical effect of which was that the king received the right to nominate to almost all the higher vacant benefices in France, while the Popes received the *Annates.* The results were not beneficial to the Church. It left the clergy a prey to papal exactions, and it compelled them to seek for promotion through subserviency to the king and the court; but it had the effect of ranging the monarch on the side of the Papacy when the Reformation came.

It can scarcely be said that France was a compact nation. The nobility were separated from the middle and lower classes by the fact that all younger sons retained the status and privileges of nobles. In ancient times they had paid no share of the taxes raised for war, on the ground that they rendered personal service, and the privilege of being free from taxation was retained long after the services of a feudal militia had disappeared. The nobility in France became a caste, numerous, poor in many instances, and too proud to belittle themselves by entering any of the professions or engaging in commerce.

Louis XI. had done his best to encourage trade, and had introduced the silkworm industry into France. But as the whole weight of taxation fell upon the rural districts, the middle classes took refuge in the towns, and the peasantry, between the dues they had to pay to their lords and the taxation for the king, were in an oppressed condition. Their grievances were set forth in the petition they addressed, in the delusive hope of amelioration, to the States-General which assembled on the accession of Charles VIII. "During the past thirty-four years," they say, "troops have been ever passing through France and living on the poor people. When the poor man has managed, by the sale of the coat on his back, and after hard toil, to pay his *taille*, and hopes he may live out the year on the little he has left, then come fresh troops to his cottage, eating him up. In Normandy, multitudes have died of hunger. From want of cattle, men and women have to yoke themselves to the carts; and others, fearing that if seen in the daytime they will be seized for not having paid their *taille*, are compelled to work at night. The king should have pity on his poor people, and relieve them from the said *tailles* and charges." This was in 1483, before the Italian wars had further increased the burdens which the poorest class of the community had to pay.

The New Learning had begun to filter into France at a comparatively early date. In 1458 an Italian of Greek descent had been appointed to teach Greek by the University of Paris. But that University had been for long the centre of mediæval scholastic study, and it was not until the Italian campaigns of Charles VIII., who was in Italy when the Renaissance was at its height, that France may be said to have welcomed the Humanist movement. A Greek Press was established in Paris in 1507, a group of French Humanists entered upon the study of the authors of classical antiquity, and the new learning gradually displaced the old scholastic disciplines. French Humanists were perhaps the earliest to make a special study of Roman Law, and to win distinction as eminent jurists. Francis, like Henry VIII. of England, was welcomed on his accession as a Humanist king. Such was the condition of France in the beginning of the sixteenth century.

§ 5. *Spain.*

Spain had for centuries been under Mohammedan domination. The Moslems had overrun almost the whole country, and throughout its most fertile provinces the Christian peasantry lived under masters of an alien faith. At the beginning of the tenth century the only independent Christian principalities were small states lying along the southern shore of the Bay of Biscay and the south-western slopes of the Pyrenees. The Gothic and Vandal chiefs slowly recovered the northern districts, while the Moors retained the more fertile provinces of the south. The political conditions of the country at the close of the fifteenth century inevitably reflected this gradual reconquest, which had brought the Christian principalities into existence. In 1474, when Isabella (she had been married in 1469 to Ferdinand, the heir to Aragon) succeeded her brother Henry IV. in the sovereignty of Castile, Spain was divided into five separate principalities: Castile, with Leon, containing 62 per cent.; Aragon, with Valentia and Catalonia, containing 15 per cent.; Portugal, containing 20 per cent.; Navarre, containing 1 per cent.; and Granada, the only remaining Moslem State, containing 2 per cent. of the entire surface of the country.

Castile had grown by almost continuous conquest of lands from the Moslems, and these additions were acquired in many ways. If they had been made in what may be termed a national war, the lands seized became the property of the king, and could be retained by him or granted to his lords spiritual and temporal under varying conditions. In some cases these grants made the possessors almost independent princes. On the other hand, lands might be wrested from the aliens by private adventurers, and in such cases they remained in possession of the conquerors, who formed municipalities which had the right of choosing and of changing their overlords, and really formed independent communities. Then there were, as was natural in a period of continuous warfare, waste lands. These became the property of those who settled on them. Lastly, there were the dangerous frontier lands, which it was the policy of king or great lord who owned them to people with settlers, who could only be induced to undertake the perilous occupation provided they received charters (*fueros*), which guaranteed their practical independence. In such a condition of things the central authority could not be strong. It was further weakened by the fact that the great feudatories claimed to have both civil administration and military rule over their lands, and assumed an almost regal state. Military religious orders abounded, and were possessed of great wealth. Their Grand Masters, in virtue of their office, were independent military commanders, and had great gifts, in the shape of rich commandries, to bestow on their followers. Their power overshadowed that of the sovereign. The great ecclesiastics, powerful feudal lords in virtue of their lands, claimed the rights of civil administration and military rule like their lay compeers, and, being personally protected by the indefinable sanctity of the priestly character, were even more turbulent. Almost universal anarchy had prevailed during the reigns of the two weak kings who preceded Isabella on the throne of Castile, and the crown lands, the support and special protection of the sovereign, had been alienated by lavish gifts to the great nobles. This was the situation which faced the young queen when she came into her inheritance. It was aggravated by a rebellion on behalf of Juanna, the illegitimate daughter of Henry IV. The rebellion was successfully crushed. The queen and her consort, who was not yet in possession of the throne of Aragon, then tried to give the land security. The previous anarchy had produced its usual results. The country was infested with bands of brigands, and life was not safe outside the walls of the towns. Isabella instituted, or rather revived, the Holy Brotherhood (*Hermandad*), a force of cavalry raised by the whole country (each group of one hundred houses was bound to provide one horseman). It was an army of mounted police. It had its own judges, who tried criminals on the scene of their crimes, and those convicted were punished by the troops according to the sentences pronounced. Its avowed objects were to put down all crimes of violence committed outside the cities, and to hunt criminals who had fled from the towns' justice. Its judges superseded the justiciary powers of the nobles, who protested in vain. The Brotherhood did its work very effectively, and the towns and the common people rallied round the monarchy which had given them safety for limb and property.

The sovereigns next attacked the position of the nobles, whose mutual feuds rendered them a comparatively easy foe to rulers who had proved their strength of government. The royal domains, which had been alienated during the previous reign, were restored to the sovereign, and many of the most abused privileges of the nobility were curtailed.

One by one the Grand Masterships of the Crusading Orders were centred in the person of the Crown, the Pope acquiescing and granting investiture. The Church was stripped of some of its superfluous wealth, and the civil powers of the higher ecclesiastics were abolished or curtailed. In the end it may be said that the Spanish clergy were made almost as subservient to the sovereign as were those of France.

The pacification and consolidation of Castile was followed by the conquest of Granada. The Holy Brotherhood served the purpose of a standing army, internal feuds among the Moors aided the Christians, and after a protracted struggle (1481–1492) the city of Granada was taken, and the Moorish rule in the Peninsula ceased. All Spain, save Portugal and Navarre (seized by Ferdinand in 1512), was thus united under Ferdinand and Isabella, the Catholic Sovereigns as they came to be called, and the civil unity increased the desire for religious uniformity. The Jews in Spain were numerous, wealthy, and influential. They had intermarried with many noble families, and almost controlled the finance of the country. It was resolved to compel them to become Christians, by force if necessary. In 1478 a Bull was obtained from Pope Sixtus IV. establishing the Inquisition in Spain, it being provided that the inquisitors were to be appointed by the sovereign. The Holy Office in this way became an instrument for establishing a civil despotism, as well as a means for repressing heresy. It did its work with a ruthless severity hitherto unexampled. Sixtus himself and some of his successors, moved by repeated complaints, endeavoured to restrain its savage energy; but the Inquisition was too useful an instrument in the hands of a despotic sovereign, and the Popes were forced to allow its proceedings, and to refuse all appeals to Rome against its sentences. It was put in use against the Moorish subjects of the Catholic kings, notwithstanding the terms of the capitulation of Granada, which provided for the exercise of civil and religious liberty. The result was that, in spite of fierce rebellions, all the Moors, save small groups of families under the special protection of the Crown, had become nominal Christians by 1502, although almost a century had to pass before the Inquisition had rooted out the last traces of the Moslem faith in the Spanish Peninsula.

The death of Isabella in 1504 roughly dates a formidable rising against this process of repression and consolidation. The severities of the Inquisition, the insistence of Ferdinand to govern personally the lands of his deceased wife, and many local causes led to widespread conspiracies and revolts against his rule. The years between 1504 and 1522 were a period of revolutions and of lawlessness which was ended when Charles v., the grandson of Ferdinand and Isabella, overcame all resistance and inaugurated a reign of personal despotism which long distinguished the kingdom of Spain. Spanish troubles had something to do with preventing Charles from putting into execution in Germany, as he wished to do, the ban issued at Worms against Martin Luther.

§ 6. *Germany and Italy.*

Germany and Italy, in the beginning of the sixteenth century, had made almost no progress in becoming united and compact nations. The process of national consolidation, which was a feature of the times, displayed itself in these lands in the creation of compact principalities rather than in a great and effective national movement under one sovereign power. It is a commonplace of history to say that the main reason for this was the presence within these two lands of the Pope and the Emperor, the twin powers of the earlier mediæval ideal of a dual government, at once civil and ecclesiastical. Machiavelli expressed the common idea in his clear and strenuous fashion. He says that the Italians owe it to Rome that they are divided into factions and not united as were Spain and France. The Pope, he explains, who claimed temporal as well as spiritual jurisdiction, though not strong enough to rule all Italy by himself, was powerful enough to prevent any other Italian dynasty from taking his place. Whenever he saw any Italian power growing strong enough to have a future before it, he invited the aid of some foreign potentate, thus making Italy a prey to continual invasions. The shadowy lordship of the Pope was sufficient, in the opinion of Machiavelli, to prevent any real lordship under a native dynasty within the Italian peninsula. In Germany there was a similar impotency. The German king was the Emperor, the mediæval head of the Holy Roman Empire, the "king of the Romans." Some idea of what underlay the thought and its expression may be had when one reads across Albert Dürer's portrait of Maximilian, "Imperator Cæsar Divus Maximilianus Pius Felix Augustus," just as if he had been Trajan or Constantine. The phrase carries us back to the times when the Teutonic tribes swept down on the Roman possessions in Western Europe and took possession of them. They were barbarians with an unalterable reverence for the wider civilisation of the great Empire which they had conquered. They crept into the shell of the great Empire and tried to assimilate its jurisprudence and its religion. Hence it came to pass, in the earlier Middle Ages, as Mr. Freeman says, "The two great powers in Western Europe were the Church and the Empire, and the centre of each, in imagination at least, was Rome. Both of these went on through the settlements of the German nations, and both in a manner drew new powers from the change of things. Men believed more than ever that Rome was the lawful and natural centre of the world. For it was held that there were of divine right two Vicars of God upon earth, the Roman Emperor,

His Vicar in temporal things, and the Roman Bishop, His Vicar in spiritual things. This belief did not interfere with the existence either of separate commonwealths principalities, or of national Churches. But it was held that the Roman Emperor, who was the Lord of the World, was of right the head of all temporal States, and the Roman Bishop, the Pope, was the head of all the Churches." This idea was a devout imagination, and was never actually and fully expressed in fact. No Eastern nation or Church ever agreed with it; and the temporal lordship of the Emperors was never completely acknowledged even in the West. Still it ruled in men's minds with all the force of an ideal. As the modern nations of Europe came gradually into being, the real headship of the Emperor became more and more shadowy. But both headships could prevent the national consolidation of the countries, Germany and Italy, in which the possessors dwelt. All this is, as has been said, a commonplace of history, and, like all commonplaces, it contains a great deal of truth. Still it may be questioned whether the mediæval idea was solely responsible for the disintegration of either Germany or Italy in the sixteenth century. A careful study of the conditions of things in both countries makes us see that many causes were at work besides the mediæval idea—conditions geographical, social, and historical. Whatever the causes, the disintegration of these two lands was in marked contrast to the consolidation of the three other nations.

§ 7. *Italy.*

In the end of the fifteenth century, Italy contained a very great number of petty principalities and five States which might be called the great powers of Italy—Venice, Milan, and Florence in the north, Naples in the south, and the States of the Church in the centre. Peace was kept by a delicate and highly artificial balance of powers. Venice was a commercial republic, ruled by an oligarchy of nobles. The city in the lagoons had been founded by trembling fugitives fleeing before Attila's Huns, and was more than a thousand years old. It had large territories on the mainland of Italy, and colonies extending down the east coast of the Adriatic and among the Greek islands. It had the largest revenue of all the Italian States, but its expenses were also much the heaviest. Milan came next in wealth, with its yearly income of over 700,000 ducats. At the close of the century it was in the possession of the Sforza family, whose founder had been born a ploughman, and had risen to be a formidable commander of mercenary soldiers. It was claimed by Maximilian as a fief of the Empire, and by the Kings of France as a heritage of the Dukes of Orleans. The disputed heritage was one of the causes of the invasion of Italy by Charles VIII. Florence, the most cultured city in Italy, was, like Venice, a commercial republic; but it was a democratic republic, wherein one family, the Medici, had usurped almost despotic power while preserving all the external marks of republican rule.

Naples was the portion of Italy where the feudal system of the Middle Ages had lingered longest. The old kingdom of the Two Sicilies (Naples and Sicily) had, since 1458, been divided, and Sicily had been politically separated from the mainland. The island belonged to the King of Aragon; while the mainland had for its ruler the illegitimate son of Alphonso of Aragon, Ferdinand, or Ferrante, who proved a despotic and masterful ruler. He had crushed his semi-independent feudal barons, had brought the towns under his despotic rule, and was able to hand over a compact kingdom to his son Alphonso in 1494.

The feature, however, in the political condition of Italy which illustrated best the general tendency of the age towards coalescence, was the growth of the States of the Church. The dominions which were directly under the temporal power of the Pope had been the most disorganised in all Italy. The vassal barons had been turbulently independent, and the Popes had little power even within the city of Rome. The helplessness of the Popes to control their vassals perhaps reached its lowest stage in the days of Innocent VIII. His successors Alexander VI. (Rodrigo Borgia, 1492–1503), Julius II. (Cardinal della Rovere, 1503–1513), and Leo X. (Giovanni de Medici, 1513–1521), strove to create, and partly succeeded in forming, a strong central dominion, the States of the Church. The troubled times of the French invasions, and the continual warfare among the more powerful States of Italy, furnished them with the occasion. They pursued their policy with a craft which brushed aside all moral obligations, and with a ruthlessness which hesitated at no amount of bloodshed. In their hands the Papacy appeared to be a merely temporal power, and was treated as such by contemporary politicians. It was one of the political States of Italy, and the Popes were distinguished from their contemporary Italian rulers only by the facts that their spiritual position enabled them to exercise a European influence which the others could not aspire to, and that their sacred character placed them above the obligations of ordinary morality in the matter of keeping solemn promises and maintaining treaty obligations made binding by the most sacred oaths. In one sense their aim was patriotic. They were Italian princes whose aim was to create a strong Italian central power which might be able to maintain the independence of Italy against the foreigner; and in this they were partially successful, whatever judgment may require to be passed on the means taken to attain their end. But the actions of the Italian prince placed the spiritual Head of the Church outside all those influences, intellectual, artistic, and religious (the revival under Savonarola in Florence), which were working in Italy for the regeneration of European society. The Popes of the Renaissance set the example, only too faithfully followed by almost every prince of the age, of believing that political far outweighed all moral and religious motives.

§ 8. *Germany.*

Germany, or the Empire, as it was called, included, in the days of the Reformation, the Low Countries in the north-west and a large part of what are now the Austro-Hungarian lands in the east. It was in a strange condition. On the one hand a strong popular sentiment for unity had arisen in all the German-speaking portions, and on the other the country was cut into sections and slices, and was more hopelessly divided than was Italy itself.

Nominally the Empire was ruled over by one supreme lord, with a great feudal assembly, the Diet, under him.

The Empire was elective, though for generations the rulers chosen had always been the heads of the House of Hapsburg, and since 1356 the election had been in the hands of seven prince-electors—three on the Elbe and four on the Rhine. On the Elbe were the King of Bohemia, the Elector of Saxony, and the Elector of Brandenburg; on the Rhine, the Count Palatine of the Rhine and the Archbishops of Mainz, Trier, and Köln.

This Empire, nominally one, and full of the strongest sentiments of unity, was hopelessly divided, and—for this was the peculiarity of the situation—all the elements making for peaceful government, which in countries like France or England supported the central power, were on the side of disunion.

A glance at the map of Germany in the times of the Reformation shows an astonishing multiplicity of separate principalities, ecclesiastical and secular, all the more bewildering that most of them appeared to be composed of patches lying separate from each other. Almost every ruling prince had to cross some neighbour's land to visit the outlying portions of his dominions. It must also be remembered that the divisions which can be represented on a map but faintly express the real state of things. The territories of the imperial cities—the lands outside the walls ruled by the civic fathers—were for the most part too small to figure on any map, and for the same reason the tiny principalities of the hordes of free nobles are also invisible. So we have to imagine all those little mediæval republics and those infinitesimal kingdoms camped on the territories of the great princes, and taking from them even the small amount of unity which the map shows.

The greater feudal States, Electoral and Ducal Saxony, Brandenburg, Bavaria, the Palatinate, Hesse, and many others, had meetings of their own Estates,—Councils of subservient nobles and lawyers,—their own Supreme Courts of Justice, from which there was no appeal, their own fiscal system, their own finance and coinage, and largely controlled their clergy and their relations to powers outside Germany. Their princes, hampered as they were by the great Churchmen, thwarted continually by the town republics, defied by the free nobles, were nevertheless actual kings, and profited by the centralising tendencies of the times. They alone in Germany represented settled central government, and attracted to themselves the smaller units lying outside and around them.

Yet with all these divisions, having their roots deep down in the past, there was pervading all classes of society, from princes to peasants, the sentiment of a united Germany, and no lack of schemes to convert the feeling into fact. The earliest practical attempts began with the union of German Churchmen at Constance and the scheme for a National Church of Germany; and the dream of ecclesiastical unity brought in its train the aspiration after political oneness.

The practical means proposed to create a German national unity over lands which stretched from the Straits of Dover to the Vistula, and from the Baltic to the Adriatic, were the proclamation of a universal Land's Peace, forbidding all internecine war between Germans; the establishment of a Supreme Court of Justice to decide quarrels within the Empire; a common coinage, and a common Customs Union. To bind all more firmly together there was needed a Common Council or governing body, which, under the Emperor, should determine the Home and Foreign Policy of the Empire. The only authorities which could create a governmental unity of this kind were the Emperor on the one hand and the great princes on the other, and the two needed to be one in mutual confidence and in intention. But that is what never happened, and all through the reign of Maximilian and in the early years of Charles we find two different conceptions of what the central government ought to be—the one oligarchic and the other autocratic. The princes were resolved to keep their independence, and their plans for unity always implied a governing oligarchy with serious restraint placed on the power of the Emperor; while the Emperors, who would never submit to be controlled by an oligarchy of German princes, and who found that they could not carry out their schemes for an autocratic unity, were at least able to wreck any other.

The German princes have been accused of preferring the security and enlargement of their dynastic possessions to the unity of the Empire, but it can be replied that in doing so they only followed the example set them by their Emperors. Frederick III., Maximilian, and Charles V. invariably neglected imperial interests when they clashed with the welfare of the family possessions of the House of Hapsburg. When Maximilian inherited the imperial Burgundian lands, a fief of the Empire, through his marriage with Mary, the heiress of Charles the Bold, he treated the inheritance as part of the family estates of his House. The Tyrol was absorbed by the House of Hapsburg when the Swabian League prevented Bavaria seizing it (1487). The same fate fell on the Duchy of Austria when Vienna was recovered, and on Hungary and Bohemia; and when Charles V. got hold of Würtemberg on the outlawry of Duke Ulrich, it, too, was detached from the Empire and absorbed into the family possessions of the Hapsburgs. There was, in short, a persistent policy pursued by three successive Emperors, of despoiling the Empire in order to increase the family possessions of the House to which they belonged.

The last attempt to give a constitutional unity to the German Empire was made at the Diet of Worms (1521) —the Diet before which Luther appeared. There the Emperor, Charles v., agreed to accept a *Reichsregiment*, which was in all essential points, though differing in some details, the same as his grandfather Maximilian had proposed to the Diet of 1495. The Central Council was composed of a President and four members appointed by the Emperor, six Electors (the King of Bohemia being excluded), who might sit in person or by deputies, and twelve members appointed by the rest of the Estates. The cities were not represented. This *Reichsregiment* was to govern all German lands, including Austria and the Netherlands, but excluding Bohemia. Switzerland, hitherto nominally within the Empire, formally withdrew and ceased to form part of Germany. The central government needed funds to carry on its work, and especially to provide an army to enforce its decisions; and various schemes for raising the money required were discussed at its earlier meetings. It was resolved at last to raise the necessary funds by imposing a tax of four per cent. on all imports and exports, and to establish custom-houses on all the frontiers. The practical effect of this was to lay the whole burden of taxation upon the mercantile classes, or, in other words, to make the cities, who were not represented in the *Reichsregiment*, pay for the whole of the central government. This *Reichsregiment* was to be simply a board of advice, without any decisive control so long as the Emperor was in Germany. When he was absent from the country it had an independent power of government. But all important decisions had to be confirmed by the absent Emperor, who, for his part, promised to form no foreign leagues involving Germany without the consent of the Council.

As soon as the *Reichsregiment* had settled its scheme of taxation, the cities on which it was proposed to lay the whole burden of providing the funds required very naturally objected. They met by representatives at Speyer (**1523**), and sent delegates to Spain, to Valladolid, where

Charles happened to be, to protest against the scheme of taxation. They were supported by the great German capitalists. The Emperor received them graciously, and promised to take the government into his own hands. In this way the last attempt to give a governmental unity to Germany was destroyed by the joint action of the Emperor and of the cities. It is unquestionable that the Reformation under Luther did seriously assist in the disintegration of Germany, but it must be remembered that a movement cannot become national where there is no nation, and that German nationality had been hopelessly destroyed just at the time when it was most needed to unify and moderate the great religious impulses which were throbbing in the hearts of its citizens.

Maximilian had been elected King of the Romans in 1486, and had succeeded to the Empire on the death of his father, Frederick III., in 1493. His was a strongly fascinating personality—a man full of enthusiasms, never lacking in ideas, but singularly destitute of the patient practical power to make them workable. He may almost be called a type of that Germany over which he was called to rule. No man was fuller of the longing for German unity as an ideal; no man did more to perpetuate the very real divisions of the land.

He was the patron of German learning and of German art, and won the praises of the German Humanists: no ruler was more celebrated in contemporary song. He protected and supported the German towns, encouraged their industries, and fostered their culture. In almost everything ideal he stood for German nationality and unity. He placed himself at the head of all those intellectual and artistic forces from which spread the thought of a united Germany for the Germans. On the other hand, his one persistent practical policy, and the only one in which he was almost uniformly successful, was to unify and consolidate the family possessions of the House of Hapsburg. In this policy he was the leader of those who broke up Germany into an aggregate of separate and independent principalities. The greater German princes followed his example, and did their best to transform themselves into the civilised rulers of modern States.

Maximilian died somewhat unexpectedly on January 12th, 1519, and five months were spent in intrigues by the partisans of Francis of France and young Charles, King of Spain, the grandson of Maximilian. The French party believed that they had secured by bribery a majority of the Electors; and when this was whispered about, the popular feeling in favour of Charles, on account of his German blood, soon began to manifest itself. It was naturally strongest in the Rhine provinces. Papal delegates could not get the Rhine skippers to hire boats to them for their journey, as it was believed that the Pope favoured the French king. The Imperial Cities accused Francis of fomenting internecine war in Germany, and displayed their hatred of his candidature. The very Landsknechten clamoured for the grandson of their "Father" Maximilian. The eyes of all Germany were turned anxiously enough to the venerable town of Frankfurt-on-the-Main, where, according to ancient usage, the Electors met to select the ruler of the Holy Roman Empire. On the 28th of June (1519) the alarm bell of the town gave the signal, and the Electors assembled in their scarlet robes of State in the dim little chapel of St. Bartholomew, where the conclave was always held. The manifestation of popular feeling had done its work. Charles was unanimously chosen, and all Germany rejoiced,—the good burghers of Frankfurt declaring that if the Electors had chosen Francis they would have been "playing with death."

It was a wave of national excitement, the desire for a *German* ruler, that had brought about the unanimous election; and never were a people more mistaken and, in the end, disappointed. Charles was the heir of the House of Hapsburg, the grandson of Maximilian, his veins full of German blood. But he was no German. Maximilian was the last of the real German Hapsburgs. History scarcely shows another instance where the mother's blood has so completely changed the character of a race. Charles was his mother's son, and her Spanish characteristics showed themselves in him in greater strength as the years went on. When he abdicated, he retired to end his days in a Spanish convent. It was the Spaniard, not the German, who faced Luther at Worms.

CHAPTER III.

THE RENAISSANCE.[1]

§ 1. *The Transition from the Mediæval to the Modern World.*

THE movement called the Renaissance, in its widest extent, may be described as the transition from the mediæval to the modern world. All our present conceptions of life and thought find their roots within this period.

It saw the beginnings of modern science and the application of true scientific methods to the investigation of nature. It witnessed the astronomical discoveries of

[1] SOURCES: Boccaccio, *Lettere edite e inedite, tradotte et commentate con nuovi documenti da Corrazzini* (Florence, 1877); *Francisci Petrarchæ, Epistolæ familiares et variæ* (Florence, 1859); Cusani, *Opera* (Basel, 1565); Böcking, *Ulrici Hutteni Opera*, 5 vols. (Leipzig, 1871); Supplement containing *Epistolæ Obscurorum Virorum*, 2 vols. (Leipzig, 1864, 1869); Gillert, *Der Briefwechsel des Konrad Mutianus* (Halle, 1890); Reuchlin, *De Verbo Mirifico* (1552).

LATER BOOKS: Jacob Burckhardt, *The Civilisation of the Period of the Renaissance* (Eng. trans., London, 1892); Geiger, *Humanismus und Renaissance in Italien und Deutschland* (Berlin, 1882); Michelet, *Histoire de France*, vol. vii., *Renaissance* (Paris, 1855); Lavisse, *Histoire de France*, v. i. p. 287 ff.; Symonds, *The Renaissance in Italy* (London, 1877); H. Hallam, *Introduction to the Literature of Europe during the Fifteenth, Sixteenth, and Seventeenth Centuries*, 6th ed. (London, 1860); Kamptschulte, *Die Universität Erfurt in ihrem Verhältniss zu dem Humanismus und der Reformation*, 2 vols. (Trier, 1856, 1860); Krause, *Helius Eobanus Hessus, sein Leben und seine Werke*, 2 vols. (Gotha, 1879); Geiger, *Johann Reuchlin* (Leipzig, 1871); Binder, *Charitas Pirkheimer, Aebtissin von St. Clara zu Nürnberg* (Freiburg i. B., 1893); Höfler, *Denkwürdigkeiten der Charitas Pirkheimer* (*Quellensamml. z. fränk. Gesch.* iv., 1858); Roth, *Willibald Pirkheimer* (Halle, 1874); Scott, *Albert Dürer, his Life and Works* (London, 1869); Thausing, *Dürer's Briefe, Tagebücher, Reime* (Vienna, 1884); *Cambridge Modern History*, I. xvi, xvii; II. i.

Copernicus and Galileo, and the foundation of anatomy under Vessalius.

It was the age of geographical explorations. The discoveries of the telescope, the mariner's compass, and gunpowder gave men mastery over previously unknown natural forces, and multiplied their powers, their daring, and their capacities for adventure. When these geographical discoveries had made a world-trade a possible thing, there began that change from mediæval to modern methods in trade and commerce which lasted from the close of the fourteenth to the beginning of the seventeenth century, when the modern commercial conditions were thoroughly established. The transition period was marked by the widening area of trade, which was no longer restricted to the Mediterranean, the Black and the North Seas, to the Baltic, and to the east coasts of Africa. The rigid groups of artisans and traders—the guild system of the Middle Ages—began to dissolve, and to leave freer space for individual and new corporate effort. Prices were gradually freed from official regulation, and became subject to the natural effects of bargaining. Adventure companies were started to share in the world-trade, and a beginning was made of dealing on commissions. All these changes belong to the period of transition between the mediæval and the modern world.

In the art of governing men the Renaissance was the age of political concentration. In two realms—Germany and Italy—the mediæval conceptions of Emperor and Pope, world-king and world-priest, were still strong enough to prevent the union of national forces under one political head; but there, also, the principle of coalescence may be found in partial operation,—in Germany in the formation of great independent principalities, and in Italy in the growth of the States of the Church,—and its partial failure subjected both nationalities to foreign oppression. Everywhere there was the attempt to assert the claims of the secular powers to emancipate themselves from clerical tutelage and ecclesiastical usurpation. While, underlying all, there was the beginning of the assertion of the supreme right of individual revolt against every custom, law, or theory which would subordinate the man to the caste or class. The Swiss peasantry began it when they made pikes by tying their scythes to their alpenstocks, and, standing shoulder to shoulder at Morgarten and Sempach, broke the fiercest charges of mediæval knighthood. They proved that man for man the peasant was as good as the noble, and individual manhood asserted in this rude and bodily fashion soon began to express itself mentally and morally.

In jurisprudence the Renaissance may be described as the introduction of historical and scientific methods, the abandonment of legal fictions based upon collections of false decretals, the recovery of the true text of the Roman code, and the substitution of civil for canon law as the basis of legislation and government. There was a complete break with the past. The substitution of civil law based upon the lawbooks of Justinian for the canon law founded upon the Decretum of Gratian, involved such a breach in continuity that it was the most momentous of all the changes of that period of transition. For law enters into every human relation, and a thorough change of legal principles must involve a revolution which is none the less real that it works almost silently. The codes of Justinian and of Theodosius completely reversed the teachings of the canonists, and the civilian lawyers learned to look upon the Church as only a department of the State.

In literature there was the discovery of classical manuscripts, the introduction of the study of Greek, the perception of the beauties of language in the choice and arrangement of words under the guidance of classical models. The literary powers of modern languages were also discovered,—Italian, English, French, and German,—and with the discovery the national literatures of Europe came into being.

In art a complete revolution was effected in architecture, painting, and sculpture by the recovery of ancient models and the study of the principles of their construction.

The manufacture of paper, the discovery of the arts of printing and engraving, multiplied the possession of the treasures of the intelligence and of artistic genius, and combined to make art and literature democratic. What was once confined to a favoured few became common property. New thoughts could act on men in masses, and began to move the multitude. The old mediæval barriers were broken down, and men came to see that there was more in religion than the mediæval Church had taught, more in social life than feudalism had manifested, and that knowledge was a manifold unknown to their fathers.

If the Renaissance be the transition from the mediæval to the modern world,—and it is scarcely possible to regard it otherwise,—then it is one of those great movements of the mind of mankind that almost defy exact description, and there is an elusiveness about it which confounds us when we attempt definition. "It was the emancipation of the reason," says Symonds, "in a race of men, intolerant of control, ready to criticise canons of conduct, enthusiastic of antique liberty, freshly awakened to the sense of beauty, and anxious above all things to secure for themselves free scope in spheres outside the region of authority. Men so vigorous and independent felt the joy of exploration. There was no problem they feared to face, no formula they were not eager to recast according to their new conceptions."[1] It was the blossoming and fructifying of the European intellectual life; but perhaps it ought to be added that it contained a new conception of the universe in which religion consisted less in a feeling of dependence on God, and more in a faith on the possibilities lying in mankind.

[1] Symonds, *Renaissance in Italy, Revival of Letters* (London, 1877) p. 13.

§ 2. *The Revival of Literature and Art.*

But the Renaissance has generally a more limited meaning, and one defined by the most potent of the new forces which worked for the general intellectual regeneration. It means the revival of learning and of art consequent on the discovery and study of the literary and artistic masterpieces of antiquity. It is perhaps in this more limited sense that the movement more directly prepared the way for the Reformation and what followed, and deserves more detailed examination. It was the discovery of a lost means of culture and the consequent awakening and diffusion of a literary, artistic, and critical spirit.

A knowledge of ancient Latin literature had not entirely perished during the earlier Middle Ages. The Benedictine monasteries had preserved classical manuscripts —especially the monastery of Monte Cassino for the southern, and that of Fulda for the northern parts of Europe. These monasteries and their sister establishments were schools of learning as well as libraries, and we read of more than one where the study of some of the classical authors was part of the regular training. Virgil, Horace, Terence and Martial, Livy, Suetonius and Sallust, were known and studied. Greek literature had not survived to anything like the same extent, but it had never entirely disappeared from Southern Europe, and especially from Southern Italy. Ever since the days of the Roman Republic in that part of the Italian peninsula once called Magna Græcia, Greek had been the language of many of the common people, as it is to this day, in districts of Calabria and of Sicily; and the teachers and students of the mediæval University of Salerno had never lost their taste for its study.[1] But with all this, the fourteenth century, and notably the age of Petrarch, saw the begin-

[1] There is evidence that Thomas Aquinas was not dependent, as is commonly supposed, for his acquaintance with Greek philosophy on translations into Latin of the Arabic translations of portions of Aristotle, but that he procured Latin versions made directly from the original Greek.

nings of new zeal for the literature of the past, and was really the beginning of a new era.

Italy was the first land to become free from the conditions of mediæval life, and ready to enter on the new life which was awaiting Europe. There was an Italian language, the feeling of distinct nationality, a considerable advance in civilisation, an accumulation of wealth, and, during the age of the despots, a comparative freedom from constant changes in political conditions.

Dante's great poem, interweaving as it does the imagery and mysticism of Giacchino di Fiore, the deepest spiritual and moral teaching of the mediæval Church, and the insight and judgment on men and things of a great poet, was the first sign that Italy had wakened from the sleep of the Middle Ages. Petrarch came next, the passionate student of the lives, the thoughts, and emotions of the great masters of classical Latin literature. They were real men for him, his own Italian ancestors, and they as he had felt the need of Hellenic culture to solace their souls, and serve for the universal education of the human race. Boccaccio, the third leader in the awakening, preached the joy of living, the universal capacity for pleasure, and the sensuous beauty of the world. He too, like Petrarch, felt the need of Hellenic culture. For both there was an awakening to the beauty of literary form, and the conviction that a study of the ancient classics would enable them to achieve it. Both valued the vision of a new conception of life derived from the perusal of the classics, freer, more enlarged and joyous, more rational than the Middle Ages had witnessed. Petrarch and Boccaccio yearned after the life thus disclosed, which gave unfettered scope to the play of the emotions, to the sense of beauty, and to the manifold activity of the human intelligence.

Learned Greeks were induced to settle in Italy—men who were able to interpret the ancient Greek poets and prose writers—Manuel Chrysoloras (at Florence, 1397–1400), George of Trebizond, Theodore Gaza (whose Greek *Grammar* Erasmus taught from while in England), Gemistos

Plethon, a distinguished Platonist, under whom the Christian Platonism received its impulse, and John Argyropoulos, who was the teacher of Reuchlin. The men of the early Renaissance were their pupils.

§ 3. *Its earlier relation to Christianity.*

There was nothing hostile to Christianity or to the mediæval Church in the earlier stages of this intellectual revival, and very little of the neo-paganism which it developed afterwards. Many of the instincts of mediæval piety remained, only the objects were changed. Petrarch revered the MS. of Homer, which he could not read, as an ancestor of his might have venerated the scapulary of a saint.[1] The men of the early Renaissance made collections of MSS. and inscriptions, of cameos and of coins, and worshipped them as if they had been relics. The Medicean Library was formed about 1450, the Vatican Library in 1453, and the age of passionate collection began.

The age of scholarship succeeded, and Italian students began to interpret the ancient classical authors with a mysticism all their own. They sought a means of reconciling Christian thought with ancient pagan philosophy, and, like Clement of Alexandria and Origen, discovered it in Platonism. Platonic academies were founded, and Cardinal Bessarion, Marsiglio Ficino, and Pico della Mirandola became the Christian Platonists of Italy. Of course, in their enthusiasm they went too far. They appropriated the whole intellectual life of a pagan age, and adopted its ethical as well as its intellectual perceptions, its basis of sensuous pleasures, and its joy in sensuous living. Still their main thought was to show that Hellenism as well as Judaism was a pathway to Christianity, and that the Sibyl as well as David was a witness for Christ.

The Papacy lent its patronage to the revival of litera-

[1] He embraced it, sighed over it, and told it how he longed to hear it speak: Fracasetti, *Francisci Petrarchæ, Epistolæ familiares et variæ*, ii. 472–475.

ture and art, and put itself at the head of the movement of intellectual life. Pope Nicolas v. (1447–1455) was the first Bishop of Rome who fostered the Renaissance, and he himself may be taken as representing the sincerity, the simplicity, and the lofty intellectual and artistic aims of its earliest period. Sprung from an obscure family belonging to Sarzana a small town near Spezzia, and cast on his own resources before he had fairly quitted boyhood, he had risen by his talents and his character to the highest position in the Church. He had been private tutor, secretary, librarian, and through all a genuine lover of books. They were the only personal luxury he indulged in, and perhaps no one in his days knew more about them. He was the confidential adviser of Lorenzo de Medici when he founded his great library in San Marco. He himself began the Vatican Library. He had agents who ransacked the monasteries of Europe, and he collected the literary relics which had escaped destruction in the sack of Constantinople. Before his death his library in the Vatican contained more than 5000 MSS. He gathered round him a band of illustrious artists and scholars. He filled Rome with skilled and artistic artisans, with decorators, jewellers, workers in painted glass and embroidery. The famous Leo Alberti was one of his architects, and Fra Angelico one of his artists. Laurentius Valla and Poggio Bracciolini, Cardinal Bessarion and George of Trebizond, were among his scholars. He directed and inspired their work. Valla's critical attacks on the Donation of Constantine, and on the tradition that the Twelve had dictated the Apostles' Creed, did not shake his confidence in the scholar. The principal Greek authors were translated into Latin by his orders. Europe saw theology, learning, and art lending each other mutual support under the leadership of the head of the Church. Perhaps Julius ii. (1503–1513) conceived more definitely than even Nicolas had done that one duty of the head of the Church was to assume the leadership of the intellectual and artistic movement which was making wider the thought of Europe,—only his restless energy never permitted him leisure to give effect to his conception. "The instruction which Pope Julius II. gave to Michelangelo to represent him as Moses can bear but one interpretation: that Julius set himself the mission of leading forth Israel (the Church) from its state of degradation, and showing it—though he could not grant possession—the Promised Land at least from afar, that blessed land which consists in the enjoyment of the highest intellectual benefits, and the training and consecration of all the faculties of man's mind to union with God."[1]

The classical revival in Italy soon exhausted itself. Its sensuous perceptions degenerated into sensuality, its instinct for the beauty of expression into elegant trifling, and its enthusiasm for antiquity into neo-paganism. It failed almost from the first in real moral earnestness; scarcely saw, and still less understood how to cure, the deep-seated moral evils of the age.

Italy had given birth to the Renaissance, but it soon spread to the more northern lands. Perhaps Germany first felt the impulse, then France and England last of all. In dealing with the Reformation, the movement in Germany is the most important.

The Germans, throughout the Middle Ages, had continuous and intimate relations with the southern peninsula, and in the fifteenth century these were stronger than ever. German merchants had their factories in Venice and Genoa; young German nobles destined for a legal or diplomatic career studied law at Italian universities; students of medicine completed their studies in the famous southern schools; and the German wandering student frequently crossed the Alps to pick up additional knowledge. There was such constant scholarly intercourse between Germany and Italy, that the New Learning could not fail to spread among the men of the north.

[1] Professor Krauss, *Cambridge Modern History*, ii. 6.

§ 4. *The Brethren of the Common Lot.*

Germany and the Low Countries had been singularly prepared for that revival of letters, art, and science which had come to Italy. One of the greatest gifts bestowed by the Mystics of the fourteenth and fifteenth centuries on their native land had been an excellent system of school education. Gerard Groot, a disciple of the Flemish mystic Jan van Rysbroeck, had, after long consultations with his Master, founded a brotherhood called the *Brethren of the Common Life*,[1] whose aim was to better the religious condition of their fellow-men by the multiplication of good books and by the careful training of the young. They were to support themselves by copying and selling manuscripts. All the houses of the Brethren had a large room, where a number of scribes sat at tables, a reader repeated slowly the words of the manuscript, and books were multiplied as rapidly as was possible before the invention of printing. They filled their own libraries with the best books of Christian and pagan antiquity. They multiplied small tracts containing the mystical and practical theology of the *Friends of God*, and sent them into circulation among the people. One of the intimate followers of Groot, Florentius Radewynsohn, proved to be a distinguished educationalist, and the schools of the Order soon became famous. The Brethren, to use the words of their founder, employed education for the purpose of "raising spiritual pillars in the Temple of the Lord." They insisted on a study of the Vulgate in their classes; they placed German translations of Christian authors in the hands of their pupils; they took pains to give them a good knowledge of Latin, and read with them selections from the best known ancient authors; they even taught a little Greek; and their scholars learned to sing the simpler, more evangelical Latin hymns.

The mother school was at Deventer, a town situated at

[1] C. H. Delprot, *Verhandeling over de Brœderschap van Gerard Groote* (Arnheim, 1856).

the south-west corner of the great episcopal territory of Utrecht, now the Dutch province of Ober-Yessel. It lies on the bank of that branch of the Rhine (the Yessel) which flowing northwards glides past Zutphen, Deventer, Zwolle, and loses itself in the Zuyder Zee at Kampen. A large number of the more distinguished leaders of the fifteenth century owed their early training to this great school at Deventer. During the last decades of the fifteenth century the headmaster was Alexander Hegius (Haage, 1433–1498), who came to Deventer in 1471 and remained there until his death.[1] The school reached its height of fame under this renowned master, who gathered 2000 pupils around him, —among them Erasmus, Conrad Mutti (Mutianus Rufus), Hermann von Busch, Johann Murmellius,—and, rejecting the older methods of grammatical instruction, taught them to know the niceties of the Latin tongue by leading them directly to the study of the great writers of classical antiquity. He was such an indefatigable student that he kept himself awake during the night-watches, it is said, by holding in his hands the candle which lighted him, in order to be wakened by its fall should slumber overtake him. The glory of Deventer perished with this great teacher, who to the last maintained the ancient traditions of the school by his maxim, that learning without piety was rather a curse than a blessing.

Other famous schools of the Brethren in the second half of the fifteenth century were Schlettstadt,[2] in Elsass, some miles from the west bank of the Rhine, and about half-way between Strassburg and Basel; Munster on the Ems, the Monasterium of the earlier Middle Ages; Emmerich, a town on the Rhine near the borders of Holland, and Altmarck, in the north-west. Schlettstadt, under its master Ludwig Dringenberg, almost rivalled the fame of Daventer, and many of the members of the well-known Strassburg circle which gathered round Jacob Wimpheling, Sebastian Brand,

[1] H. Hartfelder, *Der Zustand der deutschen Hochschulen am Ende des Mittelalters. Hist. Zeitschr.* lxiv. 50–107, 1890.

[2] Struver, *Die Schule von Schlettstadt* (Leipzig, 1880).

and the German Savonarola, John Geiler von Keysersberg, had been pupils in this school. Besides these more famous establishments, the schools of the Brethren spread all over Germany. The teachers were commonly called the *Roll-Brueder*, and under this name they had a school in Magdeburg to which probably Luther was sent when he spent a year in that town. Their work was so pervading and their teaching so effectual, that we are informed by chroniclers, who had nothing to do with the Brethren, that in many German towns, girls could be heard singing the simpler Latin hymns, and that the children of artisans could converse in Latin.

§ 5. *German Universities, Schools, and Scholarship.*

The desire for education spread all over Germany in the fifteenth century. Princes and burghers vied with each other in erecting seats of learning. Within one hundred and fifty years no fewer than seventeen new universities were founded. Prag, a Bohemian foundation, came into existence in 1348. Then followed four German foundations, Vienna, in 1365 or 1384; Heidelberg, in 1386; Köln, in 1388; and Erfurt, established by the townspeople, in 1392. In the fifteenth century there were Leipzig, in 1409; Rostock, on the shore of what was called the East Sea, almost opposite the south point of Sweden, in 1419; Cracow, a Polish foundation, in 1420; Greifswald, in 1456; Freiburg and Trier, in 1457; Basel, in 1460; Ingolstadt, founded with the special intention of training students in obedience to the Pope, a task singularly well accomplished, in 1472; Tübingen and Mainz, in 1477; Wittenberg, in 1502; and Frankfurt-on-the-Oder, in 1507. Marburg, the first Reformation University, was founded in 1527.

The craving for education laid hold on the burgher class, and towns vied with each other in providing superior schools, with teachers paid out of the town's revenues. Some German towns had several such foundations. Breslau, "the student's paradise," had seven. Nor was the education of girls neglected. Frankfurt-on-the-Main founded a high school for girls early in the fifteenth century, and insisted that the teachers were to be learned ladies who were not nuns.[1] Besides the classrooms, the towns usually provided hostels, where the boys got lodging and sometimes firewood (they were expected to obtain food by begging through the streets of the town), and frequently hospitals where the scholars could be tended in illness.[2]

These possibilities of education attracted boys from all parts of the country, and added a new class of vagrants to the tramps of all kinds who infested the roads during the later Middle Ages. The wandering scholar, with his yellow scarf, was a feature of the era, and frequently not a reputable one. He was usually introduced as a character into the *Fastnachtspiele*, or rude popular carnival comedies, and was almost always a rogue and often a thief. Children of ten and twelve years of age left their villages, in charge of an older student, to join some famous school. But these older students were too often mere vagrants, with just learning enough to impose upon the simple peasantry, to whom they sold charms against toothache and other troubles. The young children entrusted to them by confiding parents were often treated with the greatest cruelty, employed by them to beg or steal food, and sent round to the public-houses with cans to beg for beer. The small unfortunates were the prisoners, the slaves, of their disreputable masters, and many of them died by the roadside. We need not wonder that Luther, with his memory full of these wandering students, in after days denounced the system by which men spent sometimes "twenty and even forty years" in a so-called student life, which was often one of the lowest vagrancy and debauchery, and in the end knew neither German nor Latin, "to say nothing," he adds with honest indignation, "of the shameful and vicious life by which our worthy youth have been so grievously cor-

[1] Kriegk, *Deutsches Bürgerthum im Mittelalter*, neue Folge (Frankfurt a. M. 1868), pp. 77 ff.

[2] Boos, *Thomas und Felix Platter* (Leipzig, 1878), pp. 20 ff.

rupted." Two or three of the autobiographies of these wandering students have survived; and two of them, those of Thomas Platter and of Johann Butzbach, belong to Luther's time, and give a vivid picture of their lives.[1]

Germany had no lack of schools and universities, but it can scarcely be said that they did more than serve as a preparation for the entrance of the Renaissance movement. During the fifteenth century all the Universities were under the influence of the Church, and Scholasticism prescribed the methods of study. Very little of the New Learning was allowed to enter. It is true that if Köln and perhaps Ingolstadt be excepted, the Scholastic which was taught represented what were supposed to be the more advanced opinions—those of John Duns Scotus, William of Occam, and Gabriel Biel, rather than the learning of Thomas Aquinas and other great defenders of papal traditions; but it lent itself as thoroughly as did the older Scholastic to the discussion of all kinds of verbal and logical subtleties. Knowledge of every kind was discussed under formulæ and phrases sanctioned by long scholastic use. It is impossible to describe the minute distinctions and the intricate reasoning based upon them without exceeding the space at our disposal. It is enough to say that the prevailing course of study furnished an imposing framework without much solid content, and provided an intellectual gymnastic without much real knowledge. A survival can be seen in the Formal Logic still taught. The quantity of misspent ingenuity called forth to produce the figures and moods, and bestowed on discovering and arranging all possible moods under each figure and in providing all with mnemonic names,—*Barbara, Celarent, Darii, Ferioque prioris,* etc.,—affords some insight into the scholastic methods in use in these universities of the fifteenth century.

Then it must be remembered that the scholarship

[1] H. Boos, *Thomas und Felix Platter* (Leipzig, 1876); Becker, *Chronica des fahrenden Schulers oder Wanderbüchlein des Johannes Butzbach* (Ratisbon, 1869).

took a quasi-ecclesiastical form. The universities were all monastic institutions, where the teachers were professional and the students amateur celibates. The scholars were gathered into hostels in which they lived with their teachers, and were taught to consider themselves very superior persons. The statutes of mediæval Oxford declare that God created "clerks" with gifts of intelligence denied to mere lay persons; that it behoved "clerks" to exhibit this difference by their outward appearance; and that the university tailors, whose duty it was to make men *extrinsecus* what God had made them *intrinsecus*, were to be reckoned as members of the University. Those mediæval students sometimes assumed airs which roused the passions of the laity, and frequently led to tremendous riots. Thus in 1513 the townsfolk of Erfurt battered in the gates of the University with cannon, and after the flight of the professors and students destroyed almost all the archives and library. About the same time some citizens of Vienna having jeered at the sacred student dress, there ensued the "Latin war," which literally devastated the town. This pride of separation between "clerks" and laity culminated in the great annual procession, when the newly capped graduates, clothed in all the glory of new bachelors' and masters' gowns and hoods, marched through the principal streets of the university town, in the midst of the university dignitaries and frequently attended by the magistrates in their robes. Young Luther confessed that when he first saw the procession at Erfurt he thought that no position on earth was more enviable than that of a newly capped graduate.

Mediæval ecclesiastical tradition brooded over all departments of learning; and the philosophy and logic, or what were supposed to be the philosophy and logic, of Aristotle ruled that tradition. The reverence for the name of Aristotle almost took the form of a religious fervour. In a curious mediæval *Life of Aristotle* the ancient pagan thinker is declared to be a forerunner of Christ. All who refused to accept his guidance were heretics, and his formal scheme of thought was supposed to justify the refined sophisms of mediæval dialectic. His system of thought was the fortified defence which preserved the old and protected it from the inroads of the New Learning. Hence the hatred which almost all the German Humanists seem to have had for the name of Aristotle. The attitudes of the partisans of the old and of the new towards the ancient Greek thinker are represented in two pictures, each instinct with the feeling of the times. In one, in the church of the Dominicans in Pisa, Aristotle is represented standing on the right with Plato on the left of Thomas Aquinas, and rays streaming from their opened books make a halo round the head of the great mediæval theologian and thinker. In the other, a woodcut published by Hans Holbein the younger in 1527, Aristotle with the mediæval doctors is represented descending into the abodes of darkness, while Jesus Christ stands in the foreground and points out the true light to a crowd of people, among whom the artist has figured peasants with their flails.

§ 6. *The earlier German Humanists.*

When the beginnings of the New Learning made their appearance in Germany, they did not bring with them any widespread revival of culture. There was no outburst, as in Italy, of the artistic spirit, stamping itself upon such arts as painting, sculpture, and architecture, which could appeal to the whole public intelligence. The men who first felt the stirrings of the new intellectual life were, for the most part, students who had been trained in the more famous schools of the *Brethren of the Common Life*, all of whom had a serious aim in life. The New Learning appealed to them not so much a means of self-culture as an instrument to reform education, to criticise antiquated methods of instruction, and, above all, to effect reforms in the Church and to purify the social life. One of the most conspicuous of such scholars was Cardinal Nicolas Cusanus [1]

[1] Scharpff, *Der Cardinal und Bischof Nicolaus von Cusa als Reformator in Kirche, Reich und Philosophie* (Tübingen, 1871).

(1401–1464). He was a man of singularly open mind, who, while he was saturated with the old learning, was able to appreciate the new. He had studied the classics in Italy. He was an expert mathematician and astronomer. Some have even asserted that he anticipated the discoveries of Galileo. The instruments with which he worked, roughly made by a village tinsmith, may still be seen preserved in the Brother-house which he founded at his birthplace, Cues, on the Mosel; and there, too, the sheets, covered with his long calculations for the reform of the calendar, may still be studied.

Another scholar, sent out by the same schools, was John Wessel of Gröningen (1420–1489), who wandered in search of learning from Köln to Paris and from Paris to Italy. He finally settled down as a canon in the Brotherhood of Mount St. Agnes. There he gathered round him a band of young students, whom he encouraged to study Greek and Hebrew. He was a theologian who delighted to criticise the current opinions on theological doctrines. He denied that the fire of Purgatory could be material fire, and he theorised about indulgences in such a way as to be a forerunner of Luther.[1] "If I had read his books before," said Luther, "my enemies might have thought that Luther had borrowed everything from Wessel, so great is the agreement between our spirits. I feel my joy and my strength increase, I have no doubt that I have taught aright, when I find that one who wrote at a different time, in another clime, and with a different intention, agrees so entirely in my view and expresses it in almost the same words."

Other like-minded scholars might be mentioned, Rudolph Agricola[2] (1442–1485), Jacob Wimpheling[3] (1450–1528), and Sebastian Brand (1457–1521), who

[1] Wessel's most important Theses on Indulgences are given in Ullmann, *Reformers before the Reformation* (Edinburgh, 1855), ii. 546 f.

[2] Tresling, *Vita et Merita Rudolphi Agricolæ* (Gröningen, 1830).

[3] Wiskowatoff, *Jacob Wimpheling, sein Leben und seine Schriften* (Berlin, 1867).

was town-clerk of Strassburg from 1500, and the author of the celebrated *Ship of Fools*, which was translated into many languages, and was used by his friend Geiler of Keysersberg as the text for one of his courses of popular sermons.

All these men, and others like-minded and similarly gifted, are commonly regarded as the precursors of the German Renaissance, and are classed among the German Humanists. Yet it may be questioned whether they can be taken as the representatives of that kind of Humanism which gathered round Luther in his student days, and of which Ulrich von Hutten, the stormy petrel of the times of the Reformation, was a notable example. Its beginnings must be traced to other and less reputable pioneers. Numbers of young German students, with the talent for wandering and for supporting themselves by begging possessed by so many of them, had tramped down to Italy, where they contrived to exist precariously while they attended, with a genuine thirst for learning, the classes taught by Italian Humanists. There they became infected with the spirit of the Italian Renaissance, and learned also to despise the ordinary restraints of moral living. There they imbibed a contempt for the Church and for all kinds of theology, and acquired the genuine temperament of the later Italian Humanists, which could be irreligious without being anti-religious, simply because religion of any sort was something foreign to their nature.

Such a man was Peter Luders (1415–1474). He began life as an ecclesiastic, wandered down into Italy, where he devoted himself to classical studies, and where he acquired the irreligious disposition and the disregard for ordinary moral living which disgraced a large part of the later Italian Humanists. While living at Padua (1444), where he acted as private tutor to some young Germans from the Palatinate, he was invited by the Elector to teach Latin in the University of Heidelberg. The older professors were jealous of him: they insisted on reading and revising his introductory lecture: they refused him the use of the library; and in general made his life a burden. He struggled on till 1460. Then he spent many years in wandering from place to place, teaching the classics privately to such scholars as he could find. He was not a man of reputable life, was greatly given to drink, a free liver in every way, and thoroughly irreligious, with a strong contempt for all theology. He seems to have contrived when sober to keep his heretical opinions to himself, but to have betrayed himself occasionally in his drinking bouts. When at Basel he was accused of denying the doctrine of Three Persons in the Godhead, and told his accusers that he would willingly confess to four if they would only let him alone. He ended his days as a teacher of medicine in Vienna.

History has preserved the names of several of these wandering scholars who sowed the seeds of classical studies in Germany, and there were, doubtless, many who have been forgotten. Loose living, irreligious, their one gift a genuine desire to know and impart a knowledge of the ancient classical literature, careless how they fared provided only they could study and teach Latin and Greek, they were the disreputable apostles of the New Learning, and in their careless way scattered it over the northern lands.

§ 7. *The Humanist Circles in the Cities.*

The seed-beds of the German Renaissance were at first not so much the Universities, as associations of intimates in some of the cities. Three were pre-eminent,—Strassburg, Augsburg, and Nürnberg, — all wealthy imperial cities, having intimate relations with the imperial court on the one hand and with Italy on the other.

The Humanist circle at Nürnberg was perhaps the most distinguished, and it stood in closer relations than any other with the coming Reformation. Its best known member was Willibald Pirkheimer[1] (1470–1528), whose training had been more that of a young Florentine patrician

[1] Roth, *Willibald Pirkheimer* (Halle, 1887).

than of the son of a German burgher. His father, a wealthy Nürnberg merchant of great intellectual gifts and attainments, a skilled diplomatist, and a confidential friend of the Emperor Maximilian, superintended his son's education. He took the boy with him on the journeys which trade or the diplomatic business of his city compelled him to make, and initiated him into the mysteries of commerce and of German politics. The lad was also trained in the knightly accomplishments of horsemanship and the skilful use of weapons. He was sent, like many a young German patrician, to Padua and Pavia (1490–1497) to study jurisprudence and the science of diplomacy, and was advised not to neglect opportunities to acquire the New Learning. When he returned, in his twenty-seventh year, he was appointed one of the counsellors of the city, and was entrusted with an important share in the management of its business. In this capacity it was necessary for him to make many a journey to the Diet or to the imperial court, and he soon became a favourite with the Emperor Maximilian, who rejoiced in converse with a mind as versatile as his own. No German so nearly approached the many-sided culture of the leading Italian Humanists as did this citizen of Nürnberg. On the other hand, he possessed a fund of earnestness which no Italian seems to have possessed. He was deeply anxious about reformation in Church and State, and after the Leipzig disputation had shown that Luther's quarrel with the Pope was no mere monkish dispute, but went to the roots of things, he was a sedate supporter of the Reformation in its earlier stages. His sisters Charitas and Clara, both learned ladies, were nuns in the Convent of St. Clara at Nürnberg. The elder, who was the abbess of her convent, has left an interesting collection of letters, from which it seems probable that she had great influence over her brother, and prevented him from joining the Lutheran Church after it had finally separated from the Roman obedience.

Pirkheimer gave the time which was not occupied with public affairs to learning and intercourse with scholars.

His house was a palace filled with objects of art. His library, well stocked with MSS. and books, was open to every student who came with an introduction to its owner. At his banquets, which were famous, he delighted to assemble round his table the most distinguished men of the day. He was quite at home in Greek, and made translations from the works of Plato, Xenophon, Plutarch, and Lucian into Latin or German. The description which he gives, in his familiar letters to his sisters and intimate friends, of his life on his brother-in-law's country estate is like a picture of the habits of a Roman patrician of the fifth century in Gaul. The morning was spent in study, in reading Plato or Cicero; and in the afternoon, if the gout chanced to keep him indoors, he watched from his windows the country people in the fields, or the sportsman and the fisher at their occupations. He was fond of entertaining visitors from the neighbourhood. Sometimes he gathered round him his upper servants or his tenants, with their wives and families. The evening was usually devoted to the study of history and archæology, in both of which he was greatly interested. He was in the habit of sitting up late at night, and when the sky was clear he followed the motions of the planets with a telescope; for, like many others in that age, he had faith in astrology, and believed that he could read future events and the destinies of nations in the courses of the wandering stars.

In all those civic circles, poets and artists were found as members—Hans Holbein at Augsburg; Albert Dürer, with Hans Sebaldus Beham, at Nürnberg. The contemporary Italian painters, when they ceased to select their subjects from Scripture or from the Lives of the Saints, turned instinctively to depict scenes from the ancient pagan mythology. The German artists strayed elsewhere. They turned for subjects to the common life of the people. But the change was gradual. The Virgin ceased to be the Queen of Heaven and became the purest type of homely human motherhood, and the attendant angels, sportive children plucking flowers, fondling animals, playing with fruit. In Lucas Cranach's "Rest on the Flight to Egypt" two cherubs have climbed a tree to rob a bird's nest, and the parent birds are screaming at them from the branches. In one of Albert Dürer's representations of the Holy Family, the Virgin and Child are seated in the middle of a farmyard, surrounded by all kinds of rural accessories. Then German art plunged boldly into the delineation of the ordinary commonplace life—knights and tournaments, merchant trains, street scenes, pictures of peasant life, and especially of peasant dances, university and school scenes, pictures of the camp and of troops on the march. The coming revolution in religion was already proclaiming that all human life, even the most commonplace, could be sacred; and contemporary art discovered the picturesque in the ordinary life of the people—in the castles of the nobles, in the markets of the cities, and in the villages of the peasants.

§ 8. *Humanism in the Universities.*

The New Learning made its way gradually into the Universities. Classical scholars were invited to lecture or settle as private teachers in university towns, and the students read Cicero and Virgil, Horace and Propertius, Livy and Sallust, Plautus and Terence. One of the earliest signs of the growing Humanist feeling appeared in changes in one of the favourite diversions of German students. In all the mediæval Universities at carnival time the students got up and performed plays. The subjects were almost invariably taken from the Scriptures or from the Apocrypha. Chaucer says of an Oxford student, that

> "Sometimes to shew his lightnesse and his mastereye
> He played Herod on a gallows high."

At the end of the fifteenth century the subjects changed, and students' plays were either reproductions from Plautus or Terence, or original compositions representing the common life of the time.

The legal recognition of Humanism within a University

commonly showed itself in the institution of a lectureship of Poetry or Oratory—for the German Humanists were commonly known as the "Poets." Freiburg established a chair of Poetry in 1471, and Basel in 1474; in Tübingen the stipend for an Orator was legally sanctioned in 1481, and Conrad Celtis was appointed to a chair of Poetry and Eloquence in 1492.

Erfurt, however, was generally regarded as the special nursery of German university Humanism ever since Peter Luders had taught there in 1460. From that date the University never lacked Humanist teachers, and a Humanist circle had gradually grown up among the successive generations of students. The permanent chief of this circle was a German scholar, whose name was Conrad Mut (Mudt, Mutta, and Mutti are variations), who Latinised his name into Mutianus, and added Rufus because he was red-haired. This Mutianus Rufus was in many respects a typical German Humanist. He was born in 1472 at Homburg in Hesse, had studied at Deventer under Alexander Hegius, had attended the University of Erfurt, and had then gone to Italy to study law and the New Learning. He became a Doctor of Laws of Bologna, made friends among many of the distinguished Italian Humanists, and had gained many patrons among the cardinals in Rome. He finally settled in Gotha, where he had received a canonry in the Church. He did not win any distinction as an author, but has left behind him an interesting collection of letters. His great delight was to gather round him promising young students belonging to the University of Erfurt, to superintend their reading, and to advise them in all literary matters. While in Italy he had become acquainted with Pico della Mirandola, and had adopted the conception of combining Platonism and Christianity in an eclectic mysticism, which was to be the esoteric Christianity for thinkers and educated men, while the popular Christianity, with its superstitions, was needed for the common herd. Christianity, he taught, had its beginnings long before the historical advent of our Lord. "The true Christ," he said, "was not a man, but the Wisdom of God; He was the Son of God, and is equally imparted to the Jews, the Greeks, and the Germans."[1] "The true Christ is not a man, but spirit and soul, which do not manifest themselves in outward appearance, and are not to be touched or seized by the hands."[2] "The law of God," he said in another place, "which enlightens the soul, has two heads: to love God, and to love one's neighbour as one's self. This law makes us partakers of Heaven. It is a natural law; not hewn in stone, as was the law of Moses; not carved in bronze, as was that of the Romans; not written on parchment or paper, but implanted in our hearts by the highest Teacher." "Whoever has eaten in pious manner this memorable and saving Eucharist, has done something divine. For the true Body of Christ is peace and concord, and there is no holier Host than neighbourly love."[3] He refused to believe in the miraculous, and held that the Scriptures were full of fables, meant, like those of Æsop, to teach moral truths. He asserted that he had devoted himself to "God, the saints, and the study of all antiquity"; and the result was expressed in the following quotation from a letter to Urban (1505), one of his friends and pupils at Erfurt: "There is but one god and one goddess; but there are many forms and many names—Jupiter, Sol, Apollo, Moses, Christ, Luna, Ceres, Proserpina, Tellus, Mary. But do not spread it abroad; we must keep silence on these Eleusinian mysteries. In religious matters we must employ fables and enigmas as a veil. Thou who hast the grace of Jupiter, the best and greatest God, shouldst in secret despise the little gods. When I say Jupiter, I mean Christ and the true God. But enough of these things, which are too high for us."[4] Such a man looked with contempt on the Church of his age, and lashed it with his scorn. "I do not revere the coat or the beard of Christ; I revere the true and living God, who has neither beard nor coat."[5] In private he denounced the fasts of the Church, confession,

[1] Krause, *Briefwechsel des Mutianus Rufus* (Cassel, 1855), p. 32.
[2] *Ibid.* p. 94. [3] *Ibid.* p. 93. [4] *Ibid.* p. 28. [5] *Ibid.* p. 427.

and masses for the dead, and called the begging friars "cowled monsters." He says sarcastically of the Christianity of his times: "We mean by faith not the conformity of what we say with fact, but an opinion about divine things founded on credulity and a persuasion which seeks after profit. Such is its power that it is commonly believed that to us were given the keys of the kingdom of heaven. Whoever, therefore, despises our keys, shall feel our nails and our clubs (*quisquis claves contemserit clavum et clavam sentiet*). We have taken from the breast of Serapis a magical stamp to which Jesus of Galilee has given authority. With that figure we put our foes to flight, we cozen money, we consecrate God, we shake hell, and we work miracles; whether we be heavenly minded or earthly minded makes no matter, provided we sit happily at the banquet of Jupiter."[1] But he did not wish to revolt from the external authority of the Church of the day. "He is impious who wishes to know more than the Church. We bear on our forehead," he says, "the seal of the Cross, the standard of our King. Let us not be deserters; let nothing base be found in our camp."[2] The authority which the Humanists revolted against was merely intellectual, as was the freedom they fought for. It did not belong to their mission to proclaim a spiritual freedom or to free the common man from his slavish fear of the mediæval priesthood; and this made an impassable gulf between their aspirations and those of Luther and the real leaders of the Reformation movement.[3]

The Erfurt circle of Humanists had for members Heinrich Urban, to whom many of the letters of Mutianus were addressed, Petreius Alperbach, who won the title of "mocker of gods and men" (*derisor deorum et hominum*), Johann Jaeger of Dornheim (Crotus Rubeanus), George Burkhardt from Spalt (Spalatinus), Henry and Peter Eberach. Eoban of Hesse (Helius Eobanus Hessus), the

[1] Krause, *Briefwechsel des Mutianus Rufus* (Cassel, 1855), p. 79.

[2] *Ibid.* p. 175: "Non sit vobiscum in castris (nostris) ulla turpitudo."

[3] *Ibid.*; cf. especially Letter to Urban, pp. 352, 353, and pp. 153, 190.

most gifted of them all, and the hardest drinker, joined the circle in 1494.

Similar university circles were formed elsewhere: at Basel, where Heinrich Loriti from Glarus (Glareanus), and afterwards Erasmus, were the attractions; at Tübingen, where Heinrich Bebel, author of the *Facetiæ*, encouraged his younger friends to study history; and even at Köln, where Hermann von Busch, a pupil of Deventer, and Ortuin Gratius, afterwards the butt of the authors of the *Epistolæ obscurorum virorum*, were looked upon as leaders full of the New Learning.

As in Italy Popes and cardinals patronised the leaders of the Renaissance, so in Germany the Emperor and some princes gave their protection to Humanism. To German scholars, who were at the head of the new movement, Maximilian seemed to be an ideal ruler. His coffers no doubt were almost always empty, and he had not lucrative posts at his command to bestow upon them; the position of court poet given to Conrad Celtes and afterwards to Ulrich von Hutten brought little except coronation in presence of the imperial court with a tastefully woven laurel crown;[1] but the character of Maximilian attracted peasantry and scholars alike. His romanticism, his abiding youthfulness, his amazing intellectual versatility, his knight-errantry, and his sympathy fascinated them. Maximilian lives in the folk-song of Germany as no other ruler does. The scheme of education sung in the *Weisskunig*, and illustrated by Hans Burgmaier, entitled him to the name "the Humanist Emperor."

§ 9. *Reuchlin.*

The German Humanists, whether belonging to the learned societies of the cities or to the groups in the Universities, were too full of individuality to present the

[1] Geiger in his *Renaissance und Humanismus in Italien und Deutschland* (Berlin, 1882, Oncken's Series) has given a picture of the insignia of the poet laureate on p. 457, and one of Conrad Celtes crowned on p. 459.

appearance of a body of men leagued together under the impulse of a common aim. The Erfurt band of scholars was called "the Mutianic Host"; but the partisans of the New Learning could scarcely be said to form a solid phalanx. Something served, however, to bring them all together. This was the persecution of Reuchlin.

Johann Reuchlin (1455–1522), like Erasmus after him, was very much a man by himself. He entered history at first dramatically enough. A party of Italian Humanists had met in the house of John Argyropoulos in Rome in 1483. Among them was a young unknown German, who had newly arrived with letters of introduction to the host. He had come, he explained, to study Greek. Argyropoulos gave him a Thucydides and asked him to construe a page or two into Latin. Reuchlin construed with such ease and elegance, that the company exclaimed that Greece had flown across the Alps to settle in Germany. The young German spent some years in Italy, enjoying the friendship of the foremost Italian scholars. He was an ardent student of the New Learning, and on his return was the first to make Greek thoroughly popular in Germany. But he was a still more ardent student of Hebrew, and it may almost be said of him that he introduced that ancient language to the peoples of Europe. His *De Rudimentis Hebraicis* (1506), a grammar and dictionary in one, was the first book of its kind. His interest in the language was more than that of a student. He believed that Hebrew was not only the most ancient, but the holiest of languages. God had spoken in it. He had revealed Himself to men not merely in the Hebrew writings of the Old Testament, but had also imparted, through angels and other divine messengers, a hidden wisdom which has been preserved in ancient Hebrew writings outside of the Scriptures, —a wisdom known to Adam, to Noah, and to the Patriarchs. He expounded his strange mystical theosophy in a curious little book, *De Verbo Mirifico* (1494), full of out-of-the-way learning, and finding sublime mysteries in the very points of the Hebrew Scriptures. Perhaps his central thought is expressed in the sentence, "God is love; man is hope; the bond between them is faith. . . . God and man may be so combined in an indescribable union that the human God and the divine man may be considered as one being."[1] The book is a *Symposium* where Sidonius, Baruch, and Capnion (Reuchlin) hold prolonged discourse with each other.

Reuchlin was fifty-four years of age when a controversy began which gradually divided the scholars of Germany into two camps, and banded the Humanists into one party fighting in defence of free inquiry.

John Pfefferkorn (1469–1522), born a Jew and converted to Christianity (1505), animated with the zeal of a convert to bring the Jews wholesale to Christianity, and perhaps stimulated by the Dominicans of Köln (Cologne), with whom he was closely associated, conceived an idea that his former co-religionists might be induced to accept Christianity if all their peculiar books, the Old Testament excepted, were confiscated. During the earlier Middle Ages the Jews had been continually persecuted, and their persecution had always been popular; but the fifteenth century had been a period of comparative rest for them; they had bought the imperial protection, and their services as physicians had been gratefully recognised in Frankfurt and many other cities.[2] Still the popular hatred against them as usurers remained, and manifested itself in every time of social upheaval. It was always easy to arouse the slumbering antipathy.

Pfefferkorn had written four books against the Jews (*Judenspiegel*, *Judenbeichte*, *Osternbuch*, *Judenfeind*) in the years 1507–1509, in which he had suggested that the Jews should be forbidden to practise usury, that they should be compelled to listen to sermons, and that their Hebrew books should be confiscated. He actually got a mandate from the Emperor Maximilian, probably through some corrupt secretary, empowering him to seize upon all

[1] *De Verbo Mirifico* (ed. 1552), p. 71.
[2] Kriegk, *Deutsches Bürgerthum im Mittelalter*, pp. 1 ff., 38–53.

such books. He began his work in the Rhineland, and had already confiscated the books of many Jews, when, in the summer of 1509, he came to Reuchlin and requested his aid. The scholar not only refused, but pointed out some irregularities in the imperial mandate. The doubtful legality of the imperial order had also attracted the attention of Uriel, the Archbishop of Mainz, who forbade his clergy from rendering Pfefferkorn any assistance.

Upon this Pfefferkorn and the Dominicans again applied to the Emperor, got a second mandate, then a third, which was the important one. It left the matter in the hands of the Archbishop of Mainz, who was to collect evidence on the subject of Jewish books. He was to ask the opinions of Reuchlin, of Victor von Karben (1422–1515), who had been a Jew but was then a Christian priest, of James Hochstratten (1460–1527), a Dominican and Inquisitor to the diocese of Köln, a strong foe to Humanism, and of the Universities of Heidelberg, Erfurt, Köln, and Mainz. They were to write out their opinions and send them to Pfefferkorn, who was to present them to the Emperor. Reuchlin was accordingly asked by the Archbishop to advise the Emperor "whether it would be praiseworthy and beneficial to our holy religion to destroy such books as the Jews used, excepting only the books of the Ten Commandments of Moses, the Prophets, and the Psalter of the Old Testament?" Reuchlin's answer was ready by November 1510. He went into the matter very thoroughly and impartially. He divided the books of the Jews into several classes, and gave his opinion on each. It was out of the question to destroy the Old Testament. The Talmud was a collection of expositions of the Jewish law at various periods; no one could express an opinion about it unless he had read it through; Reuchlin had only been able to procure portions; judging from these, it was likely that the book did contain many things contrary to Christianity, but that was the nature of the Jewish religion which was protected by law; it did contain many good things, and ought not to be destroyed. The Cabala was, according to

Reuchlin, a very precious book, which assured us as no other did of the divinity of Christ, and ought to be carefully preserved. The Jews had various commentaries on the books of the Old Testament which were very useful to enable Christian scholars to understand them rightly, and they ought not to be destroyed. They had also sermons and ceremonial books belonging to their religion which had been guaranteed by imperial law. They had books on arts and sciences which ought to be destroyed only in so far as they taught such forbidden arts as magic. Lastly, there were books of poetry and fables, and some of them might contain insults to Christ, the Virgin, and the Apostles, and might deserve burning, but not without careful and competent examination. He added that the best way to deal with the Jews was not to burn their books, but to engage in reasonable, gentle, and kindly discussion.

Reuchlin's opinion stood alone: all the other authorities suggested the burning of Jewish books, and the University of Mainz would not exempt the Old Testament until it had been shown that it had not been tampered with by Jewish zealots.

The temperate and scholarly answer of Reuchlin was made a charge against him. The controversy which followed, and which lasted for six weary years, was so managed by the Dominicans, that Reuchlin, a Humanist and a layman, was made to appear as defying the theologians of the Church on a point of theology. Like all mediæval controversies, it was conducted with great bitterness and no lack of invective, frequently coarse enough. The Humanists saw, however, that it was the case of a scholar defending genuine scholarship against obscurantists, and, after a fruitless endeavour to get Erasmus to lead them, they joined in a common attack. Artists also lent their aid. In one contemporary engraving, Reuchlin is seated in a car decked with laurels, and is in the act of entering his native town of Pforzheim. The Köln theologians march in chains before the car; Pfefferkorn lies on the ground with an executioner ready to decapitate him; citizens and their wives in gala costume await the hero, and the town's musicians salute him with triumphant melody; while one worthy burgher manifests his sympathy by throwing a monk out of a window. The other side of the controversy is represented by a rough woodcut, in which Pfefferkorn is seen breaking the chair of scholarship in which a double-tongued Reuchlin is sitting.[1] The most notable contribution to the dispute, however, was the publication of the famous *Epistolæ Obscurorum Virorum*, inseparably connected with the name of Ulrich von Hutten.

§ 10. *The "Epistolæ Obscurorum Virorum."*

While the controversy was raging (1514), Reuchlin had collected a series of testimonies to his scholarship, and had published them under the title of *Letters from Eminent Men.*[2] This suggested to some young Humanist the idea of a collection of letters in which the obscurantists could be seen exposing themselves and their unutterable folly under the parodied title of *Epistolæ Obscurorum Virorum.* The book bears the same relation to the scholastic disputations of the later fifteenth century that *Don Quixote* does to the romances of mediæval chivalry. It is a farrago of questions on grammar, etymology, graduation precedence, life in a country parsonage, and scholastic casuistry. Magister Henricus Schaffsmulius writes from Rome that he went one Friday morning to breakfast in the Campo dei Fiori,

[1] A chronicle and the details of the Reuchlin controversy are to be found in the second volume of the supplement to Böcking's edition of the works of Ulrich von Hutten. Good accounts are to be found in Geiger's *Renaissanc und Humanismus in Italien und Deutschland*, pp. 510 ff. (Berlin, 1882, Oncken's Series); in Strauss' *Ulrich von Hutten: His Life and Times*, pp. 100–140 (English translation by Mrs. Sturge, London, 1874); and in Creighton's *History of the Papacy from the Great Schism to the Sack of Rome*, vol. vi. pp. 37 ff. (London, 1897).

[2] The second edition is entitled *Illustrium Virorum Epistolæ Hebraicæ, Græcæ, et Latinæ ad Jo. Reuchlinum*; the first edition was entitled *Clarorum Virorum*, etc. The letters are forty-three in number—the first being from Erasmus, "the most learned man of the age."

ordered an egg, which on being opened contained a chicken. "Quick," said his companion, "swallow it, or the landlord will charge the chicken in the bill." He obeyed, forgetting that the day was Friday, on which no flesh could be eaten lawfully. In his perplexity he consulted one theologian, who told him to keep his mind at rest, for an embryo chicken within an egg was like the worms or maggots in fruit and cheese, which men can swallow without harm to their souls even in Lent. But another, equally learned, had informed him that maggots in cheese and worms in fruit were to be classed as fish, which everyone could eat lawfully on fast days, but that an embryo chicken was quite another thing—it was flesh. Would the learned Magister Ortuin, who knew everything, decide for him and relieve his burdened conscience? The writers send to their dear Magister Ortuin short Latin poems of which they are modestly proud. They confess that their verses do not scan; but that matters little. The writers of secular verse must be attentive to such things; but their poems, which relate the lives and deeds of the saints, do not need such refinements. The writers confess that at times their lives are not what they ought to be; but Solomon and Samson were not perfect; and they have too much Christian humility to wish to excel such honoured Christian saints. The letters contain a good deal of gossip about the wickedness of the poets (Humanists). These evil men have been speaking very disrespectfully about the Holy Coat at Trier (Treves); they have said that the Blessed Relics of the Three Kings at Köln are the bones of three Westphalian peasants. The correspondents exchange confidences about sermons they dislike. One preacher, who spoke with unseemly earnestness, had delivered a plain sermon without any learned syllogisms or intricate theological reasoning; he had spoken simply about Christ and His salvation, and the strange thing was that the people seemed to listen to him eagerly: such preaching ought to be forbidden. Allusions to Reuchlin and his trial are scattered all through the letters, and the writers reveal artlessly their hopes and fears about the result. It is possible, one laments, that the rascal may get off after all: the writer hears that worthy Inquisitor Hochstratten's money is almost exhausted, and that he has scarcely enough left for the necessary bribery at Rome; it is to be hoped that he will get a further supply. It is quite impossible to translate the epistles and retain the original flavour of the language,—a mixture of ecclesiastical phrases, vernacular idioms and words, and the worst mediæval Latin. Of course, the letters contain much that is very objectionable: they attack the character of men, and even of women; but that was an ordinary feature of the Humanism of the times. They were undoubtedly successful in covering the opponents of Reuchlin with ridicule, more especially when some of the obscurantists failed to see the satire, and looked upon the letters as genuine accounts of the views they sympathised with. Some of the mendicant friars in England welcomed a book against Reuchlin, and a Dominican prior in Brabant bought several copies to send to his superiors.

The authorship of these famous letters is not thoroughly known; probably several Humanist pens were at work. It is generally admitted that they came from the Humanist circle at Erfurt, and that the man who planned the book and wrote most of the letters was John Jaeger of Dornheim (Crotus Rubeanus). They were long ascribed to Ulrich von Hutten; some of the letters may have come from his pen—one did certainly. These *Epistolæ Obscurorum Virorum*, when compared with the *Encomium Moriæ* of Erasmus, show how immeasurably inferior the ordinary German Humanist was to the scholar of the Low Countries.[1]

[1] The best edition of the *Epistolæ Obscurorum Virorum* is to be found in vol. i. of the Supplement to Böcking's *Ulrici Hutteni Opera*, 5 vols., with 2 vols. of Supplement (Leipzig, 1864, 1869). The first edition was published in 1515, and consisted of forty-one letters; the second, in 1516, contained the same number; in the third edition an appendix of seven additional letters was added. In 1517 a second part appeared containing sixty-two letters, and an appendix of eight letters was added to the second edition of the second part.

§ 11. *Ulrich von Hutten.*

Ulrich von Hutten,[1] the stormy petrel of the Reformation period in Germany, was a member of one of the oldest families of the Franconian nobles—a fierce, lawless, turbulent nobility. The old hot family blood coursed through his veins, and accounts for much in his adventurous career. He was the eldest son, but his frail body and sickly disposition marked him out in his father's eyes for a clerical life. He was sent at the age of eleven to the ancient monastery of Fulda, where his precocity in all kinds of intellectual work seemed to presage a distinguished position if he remained true to the calling to which his father had destined him. The boy, however, soon found that he had no vocation for the Church, and that, while he was keenly interested in all manner of studies, he detested the scholastic theology. He appealed to his father, told him how he hated the thought of a clerical life, and asked him to be permitted to look forward to the career of a scholar and a man of letters. The old Franconian knight was as hard as men of his class usually were. He promised Ulrich that he could take as much time as he liked to educate himself, but that in the end he was to enter the Church. Upon this, Ulrich, an obstinate chip of an obstinate block, determined to make his escape from the monastery and follow his own life. How he managed it is unknown. He fell in with John Jaeger of Dornheim, and the two wandered, German student fashion, from University to University; they were at Köln together, then at Erfurt. The elder Hutten refused to assist his son in any way. How the young student maintained himself no one knows. He had wretched health; he was at least twice robbed and half-murdered by ruffians as he tramped along the unsafe highways; but his indomitable purpose to live the life of a literary man or to die sustained him. At last family friends patched up a half-hearted reconciliation between father and

[1] Strauss, *Ulrich von Hutten*, 2 vols. (2nd ed., Leipzig, 1874), translated and slightly abridged by Mrs. George Sturge (London, 1874).

son. They pointed out that the young man's abilities might find scope in a diplomatic career since the Church was so distasteful to him, and the father was induced to permit him to go to Italy, provided he applied himself to the study of law. Ulrich went gladly to the land of the New Learning, reached Pavia, struggled on to Bologna, found that he liked law no better than theology, and began to write. It is needless to follow his erratic career. He succeeded frequently in getting patrons; but he was not the man to live comfortably in dependence; he always remembered that he was a Franconian noble; he had an irritable temper,—his wretched health furnishing a very adequate excuse.

It is probable that his sojourn in Italy did as much for him as for Luther, though in a different way. The Reformer turned with loathing from Italian, and especially from Roman wickedness. The Humanist meditated on the greatness of the imperial idea, now, he thought, the birthright of his Germany, which was being robbed of it by the Papacy. Henceforward he was dominated by one persistent thought.

He was a Humanist and a poet, but a man apart, marked out from among his fellows, destined to live in the memories of his nation when their names had been forgotten. They might be better scholars, able to write a finer Latinity, and pen trifles more elegantly; but he was a man with a purpose. His erratic and by no means pure life was ennobled by his sincere, if limited and unpractical, patriotism. He wrought, schemed, fought, flattered, and apostrophised to create a united Germany under a reformed Emperor. Whatever hindered this was to be attacked with what weapons of sarcasm, invective, and scorn were at his command; and the *one* enemy was the Papacy of the close of the fifteenth century, and all that it implied. It was the Papacy that drained Germany of gold, that kept the Emperor in thraldom, that set one portion of the land against the other, that gave the separatist designs of the princes their promise of success. The Papacy was his Carthage, which must be destroyed.

Hutten was a master of invective, fearless, critically destructive; but he had small constructive faculty. It is not easy to discover what he meant by a reformation of the Empire—something loomed before him vague, grand, a renewal of an imagined past. Germany might be great, it is suggested in the *Inspicientes* (written in 1520), if the Papacy were defied, if the princes were kept in their proper place of subordination, if a great imperial army were created and paid out of a common imperial fund,—an army where the officers were the knights, and the privates a peasant infantry (*landsknechts*). It is the passion for a German Imperial Unity which we find in all Hutten's writings, from the early *Epistola ad Maximilianum Cæsarem Italiæ fictitia*, the *Vadiscus, or the Roman Triads*, down to the *Inspicientes*—not the means whereby this is to be created. He was a born foeman, one who loved battle for battle's sake, who could never get enough of fighting,—a man with the blood of his Franconian ancestors coursing hotly through his veins. Like them, he loved freedom in all things—personal, intellectual, and religious. Like them, he scorned ease and luxury, and despised the burghers, with their love of comfort and wealth. He thought much more highly of the robber-knights than of the merchants they plundered. Germany, he believed, would come right if the merchants and the priests could be got rid of. The robbers were even German patriots who intercepted the introduction of foreign merchandise, and protected the German producers in securing the profits due to them for their labour.

Hutten is usually classed as an ally of Luther's, and from the date of the Leipzig Disputation (1519), when Luther first attacked the Roman Primacy, he was an ardent admirer of the Reformer. But he had very little sympathy with the deeper religious side of the Reformation movement. He regarded Luther's protest against Indulgences in very much the same way as did Pope Leo X. It was a contemptible monkish dispute, and all sensible men, he thought, ought to delight to see monks devour one another. "I lately said to a friar, who was telling me about it," he writes, "'Devour one another, that ye may be consumed one of another.' It is my desire that our enemies (the monks) may live in as much discord as possible, and may be always quarrelling among themselves." He attached himself vehemently to Luther (and Hutten was always vehement) only when he found that the monk stood for freedom of conscience (*The Liberty of a Christian Man*) and for a united Germany against Rome (*To the Christian Nobility of the German Nation respecting the Reformation of the Christian Estate*). As we study his face in the engravings which have survived, mark his hollow cheeks, high cheek-bones, long nose, heavy moustache, shaven chin, whiskers straggling as if frayed by the helmet, and bold eyes, we can see the rude Franconian noble, who by some strange freak of fortune became a scholar, a Humanist, a patriot, and, in his own way, a reformer.

CHAPTER IV.

SOCIAL CONDITIONS.[1]

§ 1. *Towns and Trade.*

It has been already said that the times of the Renaissance were a period of transition in the social as well as in the intellectual condition of the peoples of Europe. The economic changes were so great, that no description of the environment of the Reformation would be complete without some account of the social revolution which was slowly progressing. It must be remembered, however, that there is some danger in making the merely general statements

[1] Sources: Barack, *Zimmerische Chronik*, 4 vols. (2nd ed., Freiburg i. B. 1881–1882); *Chroniken der deutschen Städte*, 29 vols. (in progress); Grimm, *Weisthümer*, 7 vols. (Göttingen, 1840–1878); Haetzerlin, *Liederbuch* (Quedlinburg, 1840); Liliencron, *Die historischen Volkslieder der Deutschen vom dreizehnten bis zum sechzehnten Jahrhundert* (Leipzig, 1865–1869); Sebastian Brand's *Narrenschiff* (Leipzig, 1854); Geiler von Keysersberg's *Ausgewählte Schriften* (Trier, 1881); Hans Sachs, *Fastnachspiele* (*Neudrucke deutschen Litteraturwerke*, Nos. 26, 27, 31, 32, 39, 40, 42, 43, 51, 52, 60, 63, 64); Hans von Schweinichen, *Leben und Abenteuer des schlessischen Ritters, Hans v. Schweinichen* (Breslau, 1820–1823); Vandam, *Social Life in Luther's Time* (Westminster, 1902); Trithemius, *Annales Hirsaugienses* (St. Gallen, 1590).

Later Books: Alwyn Schulz, *Deutsches Leben im 14ten und 15ten Jahrhundert* (Prague, 1892); Kriegk, *Deutsches Bürgerthum im Mittelalter* (Frankfurt, 1868, 1871); Freytag, *Bilder aus der deutschen Vergangenheit*, II. ii. (Leipzig, 1899—translation by Mrs. Malcolm of an earlier edition, London, 1862); the series of *Monographien zur deutschen Kulturgeschichte* edited by Steinhausen (Leipzig, 1899–1905), are full of valuable information and illustrations; Aloys Schulte, *Die Fugger in Rom* (Leipzig, 1904); Gothein, *Politische und religiöse Volksbewegungen vor der Reformation* (Breslau, 1878); *Cambridge Modern History*, I. i. xv; v. Bezold, *Geschichte der deutschen Reformation* (Berlin, 1890); Genée, *Hans Sachs und seine Zeit* (Leipzig, 1902); Janssen, *Geschichte des deutschen Volkes, seil dem Ausgang des Mittelalters*, i. (1897); Roth v. Schreckenstein, *Das Patriziat in den deutschen Städten* (Freiburg i. B., no date).

which alone are possible in this chapter. The economic forces at work were modified and changed in countries and in districts, and during decades, by local conditions. Any general description is liable to be qualified by numerous exceptions.

Beneath the whole mediæval system lay the idea that the land was the only economic basis of wealth. During the earlier Middle Ages this was largely true everywhere, and was specially so in Germany. Each little district produced almost all that it needed for its own wants; and the economic value of the town consisted in its being a corporation of artisans exchanging the fruits of their industries for the surplus of farm produce which the peasants brought to their market-place. But the increasing trade of the towns, developed at first along the greater rivers, the arteries of the countries, gradually produced another source of wealth; and this commerce made great strides after the Crusades had opened the Eastern markets to European traders. Trade, commerce, and manufactures were the life of the towns, and were rapidly increasing their importance.

In mediæval times each town was an independent economic centre, and the regulation of industry and of trade was an exclusively municipal affair. This state of matters had changed in some countries before the time of the Reformation, and statesmen had begun to recognise the importance of a national trade, and to take steps to further it; but in Germany, chiefly owing to its hopeless divisions, the old state of matters remained, and the municipalities continued to direct and control all commercial and industrial affairs.

The towns had originally grown up under the protection of the Emperor, or of some great lord of the soil, or of an ecclesiastical prince or foundation, and the early officials were the representatives of these fostering powers. The descendants of this early official class became known as the "patricians" of the city, and they regarded all the official positions as the hereditary privileges of their class. The town population was thoroughly organised in associations of workmen, commonly called "gilds," which at first concerned themselves simply with the regulation and improvement of the industry carried on, and with the education and recreations of the workers. But these "gilds" soon assumed a political character. The workmen belonging to them formed the fighting force needed for the independence and protection of the city. Each "gild" had its fighting organisation, its war banner, its armoury; and its members were trained to the use of arms, and practised it in their hours of recreation. The "gilds" therefore began to claim some share in the government of the town, and in most German cities, in the decades before the Reformation, the old aristocratic government of the "patricians" had given place to the more democratic rule of the "gilds." The chief offices connected with the "gilds" insensibly tended to become hereditary in a few leading families, and this created a second "patriciat," whose control was resented by the great mass of the workmen. Nürnberg was one of the few great German cities where the old "patricians" continued to rule down to the times of the Reformation.

These "gilds" were for the most part full of business energy, which showed itself in the twofold way of making such regulations as they believed would insure good workmanship, and of securing facilities for the sale of their wares. All the workmen, it was believed, were interested in the production of good articles, and the bad workmanship of one artisan was regarded as bringing discredit upon all. Hence, as a rule, every article was tested in private before it was exposed for public sale, and various punishments were devised to check the production of inferior goods. Thus in Bremen every badly made pair of shoes was publicly destroyed at the pillory of the town. Such regulations belonged to the private administration of the towns, and differed in different places. Indeed, the whole municipal government of the German cities presents an endless variety, due to the local history and other conditions affecting the individual towns. While the production was a matter for private regulation in each centre of industry, distribution involved the towns in something like a common policy. It demanded safe means of communication between one town and another, between the towns and the rural districts, and safe outlets to foreign lands. It needed roads, bridges, and security of travel. The towns banded themselves together, and made alliances with powerful feudal nobles to secure these advantages. Such was the origin of the great Hanseatic League, which had its beginnings in Flanders, spread over North Germany, included the Scandinavian countries, and grew to be a European power.[1] The less known leagues among the cities of South Germany did equally good service, and they commonly secured outlets to Venice, Florence, and Genoa, by alliances with the peasantry in whose hands were the chief passes of the Alps. All this meant an opposition between the burghers and the nobles—an opposition which was continuous, which on occasion flamed out into great wars, and which compelled the cities to maintain civic armies, composed partly of their citizens and partly of hired troops. It was reckoned that Strassburg and Augsburg together could send a fighting force of 40,000 men into the field.

The area of trade, though, according to modern ideas, restricted, was fairly extensive. It included all the countries in modern Europe and the adjacent seas. The sea-trade was carried on in the Mediterranean and Black Seas, in the Baltic and North Seas, and down the western coasts of France and Spain. The North Sea was the great fishing ground, and large quantities of dried fish, necessary for the due keeping of Lent, were despatched in coasting vessels, and by the overland routes to the southern countries of Europe. Furs, skins, and corn came from Russia and the northern countries. Spain, some parts of Germany, and above all England, were the wool-exporting countries. The eastern counties of England, many towns in Germany and France, and especially the Low Countries, were the centres of the woollen manufactures. The north of France was

[1] Daenell, *Geschichte der deutschen Hanse in der zweiten Hälfte des 14 Jahrhunderts* (Leipzig, 1897).

the great flax-growing country. In Italy, at Barcelona in Spain, and at Lyons in France, silk was produced and manufactured. The spices and dried fruits of the East, and its silks and costly brocades and feathers, came from the Levant to Venice, and were carried north through the great passes which pierce the range of the Alps.

Civic statesmen did their best, by mutual bargains and the establishment of factories, to protect and extend trading facilities for their townsmen. The German merchant had his magnificent *Fondaco dei Tedeschi* in Venice, his factories of the Hanseatic League in London, Bruges, Bergen, and even in far-off Novgorod; and Englishmen had also their factories in foreign parts, within which they could buy and sell in peace.

The perils of the German merchant, in spite of all civic leagues, were at home rather than abroad. His country swarmed with Free Nobles, each of whom looked upon himself as a sovereign power, with full right to do as he pleased within his own dominions, whether these were an extensive principality or a few hundred acres surrounding his castle. He could impose what tolls or customs dues he pleased on the merchants whose heavily-laden waggons entered his territories. He had customary rights which made bad roads and the lack of bridges advantages to the lord of the soil. If an axle or wheel broke, if a waggon upset in crossing a dangerous ford, the bales thrown on the path or stranded on the banks of the stream could be claimed by the proprietor of the land. Worse than all were the perils from the robber-knights—men who insisted on their right to make private war even when that took the form of highway robbery, and who largely subsisted on the gains which came, as they said, from making their "horses bite off the purses of travellers."

In spite of all these hindrances, a capitalist class gradually arose in Germany. Large profits, altogether apart from trade, could be made by managing, collecting, and forwarding the money coming from the universal system of Indulgences. It was in this way that the

Fuggers of Augsburg first rose to wealth. Money soon bred money. During the greater part of the Middle Ages there was no such thing as lending out money on interest, save among the Italian merchants of North Italy or among the Jews. The Church had always prohibited what it called usury. But Churchmen were the first to practise the sin they had condemned. The members of ecclesiastical corporations began to make useful advances, charging an interest of from 7 to 12 per cent.—moderate enough for the times. Gradually the custom spread among the wealthy laity, who did not confine themselves to these reasonable profits, and we find Sebastian Brand inveighing against the "Christian Jews," who had become worse oppressors than the Israelite capitalists whom they copied.

But the great alteration in social conditions, following change in the distribution of wealth, came when the age of geographical discovery had made a world commerce a possible thing.

§ 2. *Geographical Discoveries and the beginning of a World Trade.*

The fifteenth century from its beginning had seen one geographical discovery after another. Perhaps we may say that the sailors of Genoa had begun the new era by reaching the Azores and Madeira. Then Dom Henrique of Portugal, Governor of Ceuta, organised voyages of trade and discovery down the coast of Africa. Portuguese, Venetian, and Genoese captains commanded his vessels. From 1426, expedition after expedition was sent forth, and at his death in 1460 the coast of Africa as far as Guinea had been explored. His work was carried on by his countrymen. The Guinea trade in slaves, gold, and ivory was established as early as 1480; the Congo was reached in 1484; and Portuguese ships, under Bartholomew Diaz, rounded the Cape of Good Hope in 1486. During these later years a new motive had prompted the voyages of exploration. The growth of the

Turkish power in the east of Europe had destroyed the commercial colonies and factories on the Black Sea; the fall of Constantinople had blocked the route along the valley of the Danube; and Venice had a monopoly of the trade with Egypt and Syria, the only remaining channels by which the merchandise from the East reached Europe. The great commercial problem of the times was how to get some hold of the direct trade with the East. It was this that inspired Bristol skippers, familiar with Iceland, with the idea that by following old Norse traditions they might find a path by way of the North Atlantic; that sent Columbus across the Mid-Atlantic to discover the Bahamas and the continent of America; and that drove the more fortunate Portuguese round the Cape of Good Hope. Young Vasco da Gama reached the goal first, when, after doubling the Cape, he sailed up the eastern coast of Africa, reached Mombasa, and then boldly crossed the Indian Ocean to Calicut, the Indian emporium for that rich trade which all the European nations were anxious to share. The possibilities of a world commerce led to the creation of trading companies; for a larger capital was needed than individual merchants possessed, and the formation of these companies overshadowed, discredited, and finally destroyed the gild system of the mediæval trading cities. Trade and industry became capitalised to a degree previously unknown. One great family of capitalists, the Welser, had factories in Rome, Milan, Genoa, and Lyons, and tapped the rich Eastern trade by their houses in Antwerp, Lisbon, and Madeira. They even tried, unsuccessfully, to establish a German colony on the new continent—in Venezuela. Another, the Fuggers of Augsburg, were interested in all kinds of trade, but especially in the mining industry. It is said that the mines of Thuringia, Carinthia, and the Tyrol within Germany, and those of Hungary and Spain outside it, were almost all in their hands. The capital of the family was estimated in 1546 at sixty-three millions of gulden. This increase of wealth does not seem to have been confined to a few favourites of fortune. It belonged to the mass of the members of the great trading companies. Von Bezold instances a "certain native of Augsburg" whose investment of 500 gulden in a merchant company brought him in seven years 24,500 gulden. Merchant princes confronted the princes of the State and those of the Church, and their presence and power dislocated the old social relations. The towns, the abodes of these rich merchants, acquired a new and powerful influence among the complex of national relations, until it is not too much to say, that if the political future of Germany was in the hands of the secular princes, its social condition came to be dominated by the burgher class.

§ 3. *Increase in Wealth and luxurious Living.*

Culture, which had long abandoned the cloisters, came to settle in the towns. We have already seen that they were the centres of German Humanism and of the New Learning. The artists of the German Renaissance belonged to the towns, and their principal patrons were the wealthy burghers. The rich merchants displayed their civic patriotism in aiding to build great churches; in erecting magnificent chambers of commerce, where merchandise could be stored, with halls for buying and selling, and rooms where the merchants of the town could consult about the interests of the civic trade; in building *Artushöfe* or assembly rooms, where the patrician burghers had their public dances, dinners, and other kinds of social entertainments; in raising great towers for the honour of the town. They built magnificent private houses. Æneas Sylvius tells us that in Nürnberg he saw many burgher houses that befitted kings, and that the King of Scotland was not as nobly housed as a Nürnberg burgher of the second rank. They filled these dwellings with gold and silver plate, and with costly Venetian glass; their furniture was adorned with delicate wood-carving; costly tapestries, paintings, and engravings decorated the walls; and the reception-room or *stube* was the place of greatest display. The towns in which all this wealth was accumulated were neither populous nor powerful. They cannot be compared with the city republics of Italy, where the town ruled over a large territory: the lands belonging to the imperial cities of Germany were comparatively of small extent. Nor could they boast of the population of the great cities of the Netherlands. Nürnberg, it is said, had a population of a little over 20,000 in the middle of the fifteenth century. Strassburg, a somewhat smaller one. The population of Frankfurt-on-the-Main was about 10,000 in 1440.[1] The number of inhabitants had probably increased by one-half more in the decades immediately preceding the Reformation. But all the great towns, with their elaborate fortifications, handsome buildings, and massive towers, had a very imposing appearance in the beginning of the sixteenth century.

There was, however, another side to all this. There was very little personal "comfort" and very little personal refinement among the rich burghers and nobles of Germany —much less than among the corresponding classes in Italy, the Netherlands, and France. The towns were badly drained, if drained at all; the streets were seldom paved, and mud and filth accumulated in almost indescribable ways; the garbage was thrown out of the windows; and troops of swine were the ordinary scavengers. The increase of wealth showed itself chiefly in all kinds of sensual living. Preachers, economists, and satirists denounce the luxury and immodesty of the dress both of men and women, the gluttony and the drinking habits of the rich burghers and of the nobility of Germany. We learn from Hans von Schweinichen that noblemen prided themselves on having men among their retainers who could drink all rivals

[1] These figures have been taken from Dr. F. von Bezold (*Geschichte der deutschen Reformation,* Berlin, 1890, p. 36). When the *Chron. Episc. Hildesheim.* says that during a visitation of the plague 10,000 persons died in Nürnberg alone, the territory as well as the city must be included.

beneath the table, and that noble personages seldom met without such a drinking contest.[1] The wealthy, learned, and artistic city of Nürnberg possessed a public waggon, which every night was led through the streets to pick up and convey to their homes drunken burghers found lying in the filth of the streets. The *Chronicle of the Zimmer Family* relates that at the castle of Count Andrew of Sonnenberg, at the conclusion of a carnival dance and after the usual "sleeping drink" had been served round, one of the company went to the kennels and carried to the ball-room buckets of scraps and slops gathered to feed the hounds, and that the lords and ladies amused themselves by flinging the contents at each other, "to the great detriment," the chronicler adds, "of their clothes and of the room."[2] A like licence pervaded the relations between men and women, of which it will perhaps suffice to say that the public baths, where, be it noted, the bathing was often promiscuous, were such that they served Albert Dürer and other contemporary painters the purpose of a "life school" to make drawings of the nude.[3] The conversation and behaviour of the nobles and wealthy burghers of Germany in the decades before the Reformation displayed a coarseness which would now be held to disgrace the lowest classes of the population in any country.[4]

The gradual capitalising of industry had been sapping the old "gild" organisation within the cities; the extension of commerce, and especially the shifting of the centre of external trade from Venice to Antwerp, in consequence of the discovery of the new route to the Eastern markets, and

[1] *Hans von Schweinichen*, i. 185.

[2] *Zimmerische Chronik*, ii. 68, 69.

[3] Ephrussi, *Les Bains des Femmes d'Albert Dürer* (Nürnberg, no date).

[4] It has recently become a fashion among some Anglican and Roman Catholic writers to dwell on the "coarseness" of Luther displayed in his writings. One is tempted to ask whether these writers have ever read the *Zimmer Chronicle*, if they know anything about the *Fastnachtspiele* in the beginning of the sixteenth century, of the *Rollwagen*, of Thomas Murner and Bebel, Humanists; above all, if they have ever heard of the parable of the mote and the beam?

above all, the growth of the great merchant companies, whose world-trade required enormous capital, overshadowed the "gilds" and destroyed their influence. The rise and power of this capitalist order severed the poor from the rich, and created, in a sense unknown before, a proletariat class within the cities, which was liable to be swollen by the influx of discontented and ruined peasants from the country districts. The corruption of morals, which reached its height in the city life of the first quarter of the sixteenth century, intensified the growing hatred between the rich burgher and the poor workman. The ostentatious display of burgher wealth heightened the natural antipathy between merchant and noble. The universal hatred of the merchant class is a pronounced feature of the times. "They increase prices, make hunger, and slay the poor folk," was a common saying. Men like Ulrich von Hutten were prepared to justify the robber-knights because they attacked the merchants, who, he said, were ruining Germany. Yet the merchant class increased and flourished, and with them, the towns which they inhabited.

§ 4. *The Condition of the Peasantry.*

The condition of the peasantry in Germany has also to be described. The folk who practise husbandry usually form the most stable element in any community, but they could not avoid being touched by the economic movements of the time. The seeds of revolution had long been sown among the German peasantry, and peasant risings had taken place in different districts of south-central Europe from the middle of the fourteenth down to the opening years of the sixteenth centuries. It is difficult to describe accurately the state of these German peasants. The social condition of the nobles and the burghers has had many an historian, and their modes of life have left abundant traces in literature and archæology; but peasant houses and implements soon perished, and the chronicles seldom refer to the world to which the "land-folk" belonged, save when some local peasant rising or the tragedy of the Peasants' War thrust them into history. Our main difficulty, however, does not arise so much from lack of descriptive material—for that can be found when diligently sought for—as from the varying, almost contradictory statements that are made. Some contemporary writers condescend to describe the peasant class. A large number of collections of *Weisthümer*, the consuetudinary laws which regulated the life of the village communities, have been recovered and carefully edited;[1] folk-songs preserve the old life and usages; many of the *Fastnachtspiele* or rude carnival dramas deal with peasant scenes; and Albert Dürer and other artists of the times have sketched over and over again the peasant, his house and cot-yard, his village and his daily life. We can, in part, reconstruct the old peasant life and its surroundings. Only it must be remembered that the life varied not only in different parts of Germany, but in the same districts and decades under different rural proprietors; for the peasant was so dependent on his over-lord that the character of the proprietor counted for much in the condition of the people.

The village artisan did not exist. The peasants lived by themselves apart from all other classes of the population. That is the universal statement. They carried the produce of their land and their live-stock to the nearest town, sold it in the market-place, and bought there what they needed for their life and work.

They dwelt in villages fortified after a fashion; for the group of houses was surrounded sometimes by a wall, but usually by a stout fence, made with strong stakes and interleaved branches. This was entered by a gate that could be locked. Outside the fence, circling the whole was

[1] The most complete collection of the *Weisthümer* is in seven volumes. Volumes i.–iv. edited by J. Grimm, and volumes v.–vii. edited by R. Schroeder, Göttingen, 1840–1842, 1866, 1869, 1878. Important extracts are given by Alwin Schultz in his *Deutsches Leben im 14 und 15 Jahrhundert*, Vienna, 1892, pp. 145–178 (Grosse Ausgabe).

a deep ditch crossed by a "falling door" or drawbridge. Within the fence among the houses there was usually a small church, a public-house, a house or room (*Spielhaus*) where the village council met and where justice was dispensed. In front stood a strong wooden stake, to which criminals were tied for punishment, and near it always the stocks, sometimes a gallows, and more rarely the pole and wheel for the barbarous mediæval punishment "breaking on the wheel."

The houses were wooden frames filled in with sun-dried bricks, and were thatched with straw; the chimneys were of wood protected with clay. The cattle, fuel, fodder, and family were sheltered under the one large roof. The timber for building and repairs was got from the forest under regulations set down in the *Weisthümer*, and the peasants had leave to collect the fallen branches for fire-wood, the women gathering and carrying, and the men cutting and stacking under the eaves. All breaches of the forest laws were severely punished (in some of the *Weisthümer* the felling of a tree without leave was punished by beheading); so was the moving of landmarks; for wood and soil were precious.

Most houses had a small fenced garden attached, in which were grown cabbages, greens, and lettuce; small onions (cibölle, *Scotticé* syboes), parsley, and peas; poppies, garlic, and hemp; apples, plums, and, in South Germany, grapes; as well as other things whose mediæval German names are not translatable by me. Wooden beehives were placed in the garden, and a pigeon-house usually stood in the yard.

The scanty underclothing of the peasants was of wool and the outer dress of linen—the men's, girt with a belt from which hung a sword, for they always went armed. Their furniture consisted of a table, several three-legged stools, and one or two chests. Rude cooking utensils hung on the walls, and dried pork, fruits, and baskets of grain on the rafters. The drinking-cups were of coarse clay; and we find regulations that the table-cloth or covering ought to be washed at least once a year! Their ordinary food was "some poor bread, oatmeal porridge, and cooked vegetables; and their drink, water and whey." The live-stock included horses, cows, goats, sheep, pigs, and hens.[1]

The villagers elected from among themselves four men, the *Bauernmeister*, who were the Fathers of the community. They were the arbiters in disputes, settled quarrels, and arranged for an equitable distribution of the various feudal assessments and services. They had no judicial or administrative powers; these belonged to the over-lord, or a representative appointed by him. This official sat in the justice room, heard cases, issued sentences, and exercised all the mediæval powers of "pit and gallows." The whole list of mediæval punishments, ludicrous and gruesome, were at his command. It was he who ordered the scolding wife to be carried round the church three times while her neighbours jeered; who set the unfortunate charcoal-burner, who had transgressed some forest law, into the stocks, with his bare feet exposed to a slow fire till his soles were thoroughly burnt; who beheaded men who cut down trees, and ordered murderers to be broken on the wheel. He saw that the rents, paid in kind, were duly gathered. He directed the forced services of ploughing, sowing, and harvesting the over-lord's fields, what wood was to be hewn for the castle, what ditches dug, and what roads repaired. He saw that the peasants drank no wine

[1] In the interesting collection of mediæval songs, of date 1470 or 1471, *Liederbuch der Clara Hätzlerin* (Quedlinburg and Leipzig, 1840), No. 67 (p. 259), entitled *Von Mair Betzen*, describes a peasant wedding, and tells us what each of the pair contributed to the "plenishing." The bridegroom, Betze or Bartholomew Mair, gave to his bride an acre (*juchart*) of land well sown with flax, eight bushels of oats, two sheep, a cock and fourteen hens, and a small sum of money (*fünff pfunt pfenning*); while Metze Nodung, the bride, brought to the common stock two wooden beehives, a mare, a goat, a calf, a dun cow, and a young pig. It is perhaps worth remarking that, according to the almost universal custom in mediæval Germany, and in spite of ecclesiastical commands and threats, the actual marriage ceremony consisted in the father of the bride demanding from the young people whether they took each other for man and wife, and in their promising themselves to each other before witnesses. It was not until the morning after the marriage had been consummated that the wedded pair went to church to get the priest's blessing on a marriage that had taken place.

but what came from the proprietor's vineyards, and that they drank it in sufficient quantity; that they ground their grain at the proprietor's mill, and fired their bread at the estate bakehouse. He exacted the two most valuable of the moveable goods of a dead peasant—the hated "death-tax." There was no end to his powers. Of course, according to the *Weisthümer,* these powers were to be exercised in *customary* ways; and in some parts of Germany the indefinite "forced services" had been commuted to twelve days' service in the year, and in others to the payment of a fixed rate in lieu of service.

This description of the peasant life has been taken entirely from the *Weisthümer*, and, for reasons to be seen immediately, it perhaps represents rather a "golden past" than the actual state of matters at the beginning of the sixteenth century. It shows the peasants living in a state of rude plenty, but for the endless exactions of their lords and the continual robberies to which they were exposed from bands of sturdy rogues which swarmed through the country, and from companies of soldiers, who thought nothing of carrying off the peasant's cows, slaying his swine, maltreating his womenkind, and even firing his house.

The peasants had their diversions, not always too seemly. On the days of Church festivals, and they were numerous, the peasantry went to church and heard Mass in the morning, talked over the village business under the lime-trees, or in some open space near the village, and spent the afternoon in such amusements as they liked best—eating and drinking at the public-house, and dancing on the village green. In one of his least known poems, Hans Sachs describes the scene—the girls and the pipers waiting at the dancing-place, and the men and lads in the public-house eating calf's head, tripe, liver, black puddings, and roast pork, and drinking whey and the sour country wine, until some sank under the benches; and there was such a jostling, scratching, shoving, bawling, and singing, that not a word could be heard. Then three young men came to the dancing-place, his sweetheart had a garland ready for one of them, and the dancing began; other couples joined, and at last sixteen pairs of feet were in motion. Rough jests, gestures, and caresses went round.

> "Nach dem der Messner von Hirschau,
> Der tanzet mit des Pfarrhaus Frau
> Von Budenheim, die hat er lieb,
> Viel Scherzens am Tanz mit ihr trieb."

The men whirled their partners off their feet and spun them round and round, or seized them by the waist and tossed them as high as they could; while they themselves leaped and threw out their feet in such reckless ways that Hans Sachs thought they would all fall down.

The winter amusements gathered round the spinning house. For it was the custom in most German villages for the young women to resort to a large room in the mill, or to the village tavern, or to a neighbour's house, with their wool and flax, their distaffs and spindles, some of them old heirlooms and richly ornamented, to spin all evening. The lads came also to pick the fluff off the lasses' dresses, they said; to hold the small beaker of water into which they dipped their fingers as they span; and to cheer the spinsters with songs and recitations. After work came the dancing. On festival evenings, and especially at carnival times, the lads treated their sweethearts to a late supper and a dance; and escorted them home, carrying their distaffs and spindles.[1] All the old German love folk-songs are full of allusions to this peasant courtship, and it is not too much to say that from the singing in the spinning house have come most of the oldest folk-songs.

These descriptions apply to the German peasants of Central and South Germany. In the north and north-east, the agricultural population, which was for the most part of Slavonic descent, had been reduced by their conquerors to a serfdom which had no parallel in the more favoured districts.

[1] Barack, *Zeitschrift für deutsche Culturgeschichte*, iv. (1859) 36 ff.

§ 5. *Earlier Social Revolts.*

It was among the peasants of German descent that there had been risings, successful and unsuccessful, for more than a century. The train for revolution had been laid not where serfdom was at its worst, but where there was ease enough in life to allow men to think, and where freedom was nearest in sight. It may be well to refer to the earlier peasant revolts, before attempting to investigate the causes of that permanent unrest which was abundantly evident at the beginning of the sixteenth century.

The first great successful peasant rebellion was the fight for freedom made by the people of the four forest cantons in Switzerland. The weapons with which they overthrew the chivalry of Europe, rude pikes made by tying their scythes to their alpenstocks, may still be seen in the historical museums of Basel and Constance. They proved that man for man the peasant was as good as the noble. The free peasant soldier had come into being. These free peasants did not really secede from the Empire till 1499, and were formally connected with it till 1648. The Emperor was still their over-lord. But they were his free peasants, able to form leagues for their mutual defence and for the protection of their rights. Other cantons and some neighbouring cities joined them, and the Swiss Confederacy, with its flag, a white cross on a red ground, and its motto, "Each for all and all for each," became a new nation in Europe. During the next century (1424–1471) the peasants of the Rhætian Alps also won their freedom, and formed a confederacy similar to the Swiss, though separate from it. It was called the *Graubund.*

The example of these peasant republics, strong in the protection which their mountains gave them, fired the imagination of the German peasantry of the south and the south-west of the Empire, and the leaders of lost popular causes found a refuge in the Alpine valleys while they meditated on fresh schemes to emancipate their followers. We have evidence of the popularity of the Swiss in the towns and country districts of Germany all through the fifteenth and into the sixteenth century.[1]

But while the social tumults and popular uprisings against authority, which are a feature of the close of the Middle Ages, are usually and rightly enough called peasant insurrections, the name tends to obscure their real character. They were rather the revolts of the poor against the rich, of debtors against creditors, of men who had scanty legal rights or none at all against those who had the protection of the existing laws, and they were joined by the poor of the towns as well as by the peasantry of the country districts. The peasants generally began the revolt and the townsmen followed; but this was not always the case. Sometimes the mob of the cities rose first and the peasants joined afterwards. In many cases, too, the poorer nobles were in secret or open sympathy with the insurrectionary movement. On more than one occasion they led the insurgents and fought at their head. The union of poor nobles and peasants had made the Bohemian revolt successful.

It must also be remembered that from the end of the fourteenth century on to the beginning of the sixteenth, however varied the cries and watchwords of the insurgents may be, one persistent note of detestation of the priests (the *pfaffen*) is always heard; and, from the way in which Jews and priests are continually linked together in one common denunciation, it may be inferred that the hatred arose more from the intolerable pressure of clerical extortion than from any feeling of irreligion. The tithes, great and small, and the means taken to exact them, were a galling burden. "The priests," says an English writer, "have their tenth part of all the corn, meadows, pasture, grass, wood, colts, lambs, geese, and chickens. Over and besides the tenth part of every servant's wages, wool, milk, honey, wax, cheese, and butter; yea, and they look so narrowly after their profits that the poor wife must be

[1] Droysen, *Geschichte der preussischen Politik*, II. i. p. 309 ff. (5 vols., Berlin, 1855–1886); Boos, *Thomas und Felix Platter* (Leipsic, 1876), p. 21

countable to them for every tenth egg, or else she getteth not her rights at Easter, and shall be taken as a heretic." As matter of fact, many of these tithes, extorted in the name of the Church, did not go into the pockets of the clergy at all, but were seized by the feudal superior and went to increase his revenues. Popular feeling, however, seldom discriminates, and feudal and clerical dues were regarded as belonging to one system of intolerable oppression. Besides, the rapacity of Churchmen went far beyond the exaction of the tithes. "I see," said a Spaniard, "that we can scarcely get anything from Christ's ministers but for money; at baptism money, at bishoping money, at marriage money, for confession money—no, not extreme unction without money! They will ring no bells without money, no burial in the church without money; so that it seemeth that Paradise is shut up from them that have no money. The rich is buried in the church, the poor in the churchyard. The rich man may marry with his nearest kin, but the poor not so, albeit he be ready to die for love of her. The rich may eat flesh in Lent, but the poor may not, albeit fish perhaps be much dearer. The rich man may readily get large Indulgences, but the poor none, because he wanteth money to pay for them."[1]

In spite of this hatred of the priests, it will be found that almost every insurrectionary movement was impregnated by some sentiment of enthusiastic religion, with which was blended some confused dream that the kingdom of God might be set up on earth, if only the priests were driven out of the land. This religious element drew some of its strength from the Lollard movement in England and from the Taborite in Bohemia, but after 1476 it had a distinctly German character. Its connection with what may almost be called the epidemic of pilgrimages, the strongly increased veneration for the Blessed Virgin, and the injunctions laid upon the confederates in some of the revolutionary movements to repeat so many *Pater Nosters*

[1] These quotations have been taken from Seebohm, *The Era of the Protestant Revolution*, pp. 57, 58 (London, 1875).

and *Ave Marias*, seem to lead to the conclusion that much of that revival of an enthusiastic and superstitious religion which marked the last half of the fifteenth century may be regarded as an attempt to create a popular religion apart from priests and clergy of all kinds.

One of the earliest of these popular uprisings occurred at Gotha in 1391, when the peasantry of the neighbourhood and many of the burghers of the town rose against the exactions of the Jews, and demanded their expulsion. It was an insurrection of debtors against usurers, and was in the end put down by the majority of the citizens. From this date onwards to 1470 similar risings took place in many parts of Germany, prompted by the same or like causes—the exactions of Jews, priests, or nobles. The years 1431–1432 saw a great Hussite propaganda carried on all over Europe. Countries were flooded with Hussite proclamations, and traversed by Hussite emissaries. Paul Crawar was sent to Scotland, and others like him to Spain, to the Netherlands, and to East Prussia. They taught among other things that the Old Testament law about tithes had no place within the Christian Church, and that Christian tithes were originally free-will offerings,—a statement peculiarly acceptable to the German peasantry. All Germany had learnt by this time how Bohemian peasants, trained and led by men belonging to the lesser nobility, had routed in two memorable campaigns the imperial armies led by the Emperor himself, and how they had begun even to invade Germany. The chroniclers speak of the anxiety of the governing classes, civic and rural, when they recognised the strength of the feelings excited by this propaganda. The Hussite doctrine of tithes appears hereafter in most of the peasant programmes.

A still more powerful impulse to revolts was given by the tragic fate of Charles the Bold of Burgundy. Charles was the ideal feudal autocrat. He was looked up to and imitated by the feudal princes of Germany in the fifteenth as was Louis XIV. by their descendants in the end of the seventeenth century. The common people regarded him as the typical feudal tyrant, and the hateful impression which his arrogance, his vindictiveness, and his oppression of the poor made upon them comes out in the folk-songs of the period:

> "Er schazt sich künig Alexander gleich;
> Er wolt bezwingen alle Reich,
> Das wante Got in kurzer stund."

He even came to be considered by them as one of the Antichrists who were to appear, and for years after his death at Nancy (1477) many believed that he was alive, expiating his sins on a prolonged pilgrimage.

When this great potentate, who was believed to have boasted that there were three rulers—God in heaven, Lucifer in hell, and himself on earth—was defeated at Granson, routed at Morat, routed and slain at Nancy, and that by Swiss peasants, the exultation was immense, and it was believed that the peasantry might inherit the earth.[1]

§ 6. *The religious Socialism of Hans Böhm.*

During the last years of this memorable Burgundian war a strange movement arose in the very centre of Germany, within the district which may be roughly defined as the triangle whose points were the towns of Aschaffenburg, Würzburg, and Crailsheim, in the secluded valleys of the Spessart and the Taubergrund. A young man, Hans Böhm (Böheim, Böhaim), belonging to the very lowest class of society, below the peasant, who wandered from one country festival or church ale to another, and played on the small drum or on the dudelsack (rude bagpipes), or

[1] Liliencron, *Die historischen Volkslieder der Deutschen vom dreizehnten bis zum sechzehnten Jahrhundert*, ii. No. 146 (Leipzig, 1865–1869); cf. also 131, 132, 133, 136, 137, 138–147. Konrad Stolle, pastor at Erfurt, collected all the information he could from "priests, clerical and lay students, merchants, burghers, peasants, pilgrims, knights and other good people," and wove it all into a *Thuringian Chronicle* which forms the 33rd volume of the *Bibliothek des literarischen Vereins in Stuttgart*. It reflects the opinions of the time almost as faithfully as the folk-songs do, and contains the above quoted saying of Charles; cf. pp. 61 ff.

sang songs for the dancers, was suddenly awakened to a sense of spiritual things by the discourse of a wandering Franciscan. He was utterly uneducated. He did not even know the Creed. He had visions of the Blessed Virgin, who appeared to him in the guise of a lady dressed in white, called him to be a preacher, and promised him further revelations, which he received from time to time. His home was the village of Helmstadt in the Tauber valley; and the most sacred spot he knew was a chapel dedicated to the Virgin at the small village of Niklashausen on the Tauber. The chapel had been granted an indulgence, and was the scene of small pilgrimages. Hans Böhm appeared suddenly on the Sunday in Mid-Lent (March 24th, 1476), solemnly burnt his rude drum and bagpipes before the crowd of people, and declared that he had hitherto ministered to the sins and vanities of the villagers, but that henceforth he was going to be a preacher of grace. He had been a lad of blameless life, and his character gave force to his words. He related his visions, and the people believed him. It was a period when an epidemic of pilgrimage was sweeping over Europe, and the pilgrims spread the news of the prophet far and wide. Crowds came to hear him from the neighbouring valleys. His fame spread to more distant parts, and chroniclers declare that on some days he preached to audiences of from twenty to thirty thousand persons. His pulpit was a barrel set on end, or the window of a farmhouse, or the branch of a tree. He assured his hearers that the holiest spot on earth, holier by far than Rome, was the chapel of Our Lady at Niklashausen, and that true religion consisted in doing honour to the Blessed Virgin. He denounced all priests in unmeasured terms: they were worse than Jews; they might be converted for a while, but as soon as they went back among their fellows they were sure to become backsliders. He railed against the Emperor: he was a miscreant, who supported the whole vile crew of princes, over-lords, tax-gatherers, and other oppressors of the poor. He scoffed at the Pope. He denied the existence of Purgatory: good men went directly to heaven and bad men went to hell. The day was coming, he declared, when every prince, even the Emperor himself, must work for his day's wages like all poor people. He asserted that taxes of all kinds were evil, and should not be paid; that fish, game, and meadow lands were common property; that all men were brethren, and should share alike. When his sermon was finished the crowd of devotees knelt round the "holy youth," and he, blessing them, pardoned their sins in God's name. Then the crowd surged round him, tearing at his clothes to get some scrap of cloth to take home and worship as a relic; and the Niklashausen chapel became rich with the offerings of the thousands of pilgrims.

The authorities, lay and clerical, paid little attention to him at first. Some princes and some cities (Nürnberg, for example) prohibited their subjects from going to Niklashausen; but the prophet was left untouched. He came to believe that his words ought to be translated into actions. One Sunday he asked his followers to meet him on the next Sunday, bringing their swords and leaving their wives and children at home. The Bishop of Würzburg, hearing this, sent a troop of thirty-four horsemen, who seized the prophet, flung him on a horse, and carried him away to the bishop's fortress of Frauenberg near Würzburg. His followers had permitted his capture, and seemed dazed by it. In a day or two they recovered their courage, and, exhorted by an old peasant who had received a vision, and headed by four Franconian knights, they marched against Frauenberg and surrounded it. They expected its walls to fall like those of Jericho; when they were disappointed they lingered for some days, and then gradually dispersed. Hans himself, after examination, was condemned to be burnt as a heretic. He died singing a folk-hymn in praise of the Blessed Virgin.

His death did not end the faith of his followers. In spite of severe prohibitions, the pilgrimages went on and the gifts accumulated. A neighbouring knight sacked the chapel and carried away the treasure, which he was forced to share with his neighbours. Still the pilgrimages continued, until at last the ecclesiastical authorities removed the priest and tore down the building, hoping thereby to destroy the movement.

The memory of Hans Böhm lived among the common people, peasants and artisans; for the lower classes of Würzburg and the neighbouring towns had been followers of the movement. A religious social movement, purely German, had come into being, and was not destined to die soon. The effects of Hans Böhm's teaching appear in almost all subsequent peasant and artisan revolts.[1] Even Sebastian Brand takes the Niklashausen pilgrims as his type of those enthusiasts who are not contented with the revelations of the Old and New Testaments, but must seek a special prophet of their own:

> "Man weis doch aus der Schrift so viel,
> Aus altem und aus neuem Bunde,
> Es braucht nicht wieder neuer Kunde.
> Dennoch wallfahrten sie zur Klausen
> Des Sackpfeifers von Nicklashausen."[2]

And the Niklashausen pilgrimage was preserved in the memories of the people by a lengthy folk-song which Liliencron has printed in his collection.[3]

From this time onwards there was always some tinge of religious enthusiasm in the social revolts, where peasant and poor burgher stood shoulder to shoulder against the ruling powers in country and in town.

The peasants within the lands of the Abbot of Kempten, north-east of the Lake of Constance, had for two generations protested against the way in which the authorities

[1] The best account of this movement is to be found in an article contributed to the *Archiv des historischen Vereins von Unterfranken und Aschaffenburg*, XIV. iii. 1, where Hans Böhm's sayings have been carefully collected. Pastor Konrad Stolle's *Chronicle*, published in the library of the Stuttgart Literary Society (*Bibliothek des literarischen Vereins in Stuttgart*, xxxiii.), is also valuable. A list of authorities may also be found in Ullmann's *Reformers before the Reformation* (Eng. trans.), i. 377 ff.

[2] *Narrenschiff*, c. xi. l. 14–18.

[3] *Die historischen Volkslieder der Deutschen vom 13 bis 16 Jahrhundert*, ii. No. 148.

were treating them (1420–1490). They rose in open revolt in 1491–1492. It was a purely agrarian rising to begin with, caused by demands made on them by their over-lord not sanctioned by the old customs expressed in the *Weisthümer*; but the lower classes of the town of Kempten made common cause with the insurgents. Yet there are distinct traces of impregnation with religious enthusiasm not unlike that which inspired the Hans Böhm movement. The rising was crushed, and the leaders who escaped took refuge in Switzerland.

§ 7. *Bundschuh Revolts.*

In the widespread social revolt which broke out in Elsass in 1493, the peasants were supported by the towns; demands were made for the abolition of the imperial and the ecclesiastical courts of justice, for the reduction of ecclesiastical property, for the plundering of Jews who had been fattening upon usury, and for the curbing of the power of the priests. The Germans had a proverb, "The poor man must tie his shoes with string," and the "tied shoe" (*Bundschuh*), the poor man's shoe, became the emblem of this and subsequent social revolts, while their motto was, "Only what is just before God." This rebellion, which was prematurely betrayed, did not lack prominent leaders. One of them was Hans Ulman, the burgomeister of Schlettstadt, who died on the scaffold affirming the justice of the demands which he and his companions had made, and predicting their future triumph.

In 1501 the peasants of Kempten and the neighbouring districts again rose in rebellion, and were again joined by the poorer townspeople. In the year following, 1502, a revolt was planned having for its headquarters the village of Untergrombach, near Speyer; it spread into Elsass, along the Neckar and down the Rhine. The *Bundschuh* banner was again unfurled. It was made of blue silk, with a white cross, the emblem of Switzerland, in the centre. It was adorned with a picture of the crucified Christ, a *Bund-*

schuh on the one side, and a kneeling peasant on the other. The motto was again, "Only what is just before God." Every associate promised to repeat five times a day the Lord's Prayer and the *Ave Maria.* The patron saints were declared to be the Blessed Virgin and St. John. The movement was strongly anti-clerical. The leaders taught that there could be no deliverance from oppression until the priests were driven from the land, and until the property of the nobles and the priests was confiscated and their power broken. Tithes, feudal exactions of all kinds, and all social inequalities were denounced; water, forest and pasture lands were declared to be the common property of all. The leaders recognised the rule of the Emperor as over-lord, but denounced all intermediate jurisdictions. The plan was to raise the peasants and the townspeople throughout all Germany, and to call upon the Swiss to aid them in winning their deliverance from oppression. The revolt was put down with savage cruelty; most of the leaders were quartered. Many escaped to Switzerland, and lay hid among the Alpine valleys.

One of these was Joss Fritz, who had been a soldier (*landsknecht*)—a man with many qualities of leadership He had tenacity of purpose, great powers of organisation, and gifts of persuasion. He vowed to restore the *Bundschuh* League. He remained years in hiding in Switzerland, maturing his plans. Then he returned secretly to his own people. He seems to have secured an appointment as forester to a nobleman whose lands lay near the town of Freiburg in the Breisgau; and there, in the small village of Lehen, he began to weave together again the broken threads of the *Bundschuh* League. He mingled with the poorer people in the taverns, at church ales, on the village greens on festival days. He spoke of the justice of God and the wickedness of the world. He expounded the old principles of the *Bundschuh* with some few variations. Indiscriminate hatred of priests seems to have been abandoned. Most of the village priests were peasants, and suffered, like them, from overbearing superiors. The parish priest of Lehen became a strong supporter of the *Bundschuh*, and told his parishioners that all its ideas could be proved from the word of God. Joss Fritz won over to his side the "gilds" of beggars, strolling musicians, all kinds of vagrants who could be useful. They carried his messages, summoned the people to his meetings in quiet spaces in the woods, and were active assistants. At these meetings Joss Fritz and his lieutenant Jerome, a journeyman baker, expounded the Scriptures "under the guidance of the Holy Spirit simply," and proved all the demands of the *Bundschuh* from the word of God.

When the country seemed almost ripe for the rising, Joss Fritz resolved to prepare the banner as secretly as possible. It was easy to get the blue silk and sew the white cross on its ground; the difficulty was to find an artist sympathetic enough to paint the emblems, and courageous enough to keep the secret. The banner was at last painted. The crucified Christ in the centre, a peasant kneeling in prayer on the one side and the *Bundschuh* on the other, the figures of the Virgin Mary and St. John, and the pictures of the Pope and the Emperor. The motto, "O Lord, help the righteous," was added, and the banner with its striking symbolism was complete. The League had the old programme with some alterations:—no masters but God, the Pope, and the Emperor, no usury, all debts to be cancelled, and the clauses mentioned above. The leaders boasted that their league extended as far as the city of Köln (Cologne), and that the Swiss would march at their head. But the secret leaked out before the date planned for the general rising; and the revolt was mercilessly stamped out (1512–1513). Its leader escaped with the *Bundschuh* banner wound round his body under his clothes. In four years he was back again at his work (1517). In a very short time his agents, the "gild" of beggars, wandering minstrels, poor priests, pilgrims to local shrines, pardon-sellers, begging friars, and even lepers, had leagued the peasantry and the poorer artisans in the towns in one vast conspiracy which permeated the entire district between the Vosges and the Black Forest, including the whole of Baden and Elsass. The plot was again betrayed before the plans of the leaders were matured, and the partial risings were easily put down; but when the authorities set themselves to make careful investigations, they were aghast at the extent of the movement. The peasants of the country districts and the populace of the towns had been bound together to avenge common wrongs. The means of secret communication had been furnished by country innkeepers, old *landsknechts*, pedlars, parish priests, as well as by the vagrants above mentioned; and the names of some of the subordinate leaders—"long" John, "crooked" Peter, "old" Kuntz—show the classes from which they were drawn. It was discovered that the populace of Weisenburg had come to an agreement with the people of Hagenau (both towns were in Elsass) to slay the civic councillors and judges and all the inhabitants of noble descent, to refuse payment of all imperial and ecclesiastical dues, and that the Swiss had promised to come to their assistance.

One might almost say that between the years 1503 and 1517 the social revolution was permanently established in the southern districts of the Empire, from Elsass in the west to Carinthia and the Steiermarck in the east. It is needless to describe the risings in detail. They were not purely peasant rebellions, for the townspeople were almost always involved; but they all displayed that mingling of communist ideas and religious enthusiasm of which the *Bundschuh* banner had become the emblem, and which may be traced back to the movement under Hans Böhm as its German source, and perhaps to the earlier propaganda of the Hussite revolutionaries or Taborites. The later decades of the fifteenth and the earlier years of the sixteenth century were a time of permanent social unrest.

§ 8. *The Causes of the continuous Revolts.*

If we ask why it was that the peasants, whose lot, according to the information given in the *Weisthümer*, could not have been such a very hard one, were so ready to rise in rebellion during the last quarter of the fifteenth century, the answer seems to be that there must have been a growing change in their circumstances. Some chroniclers have described the condition of the peasants in the end of the fifteenth and in the beginning of the sixteenth century, and they always dwell upon their misery. John Böhm, who wrote in the beginning of the sixteenth century, says that "their lot was hard and pitiable," and calls them "slaves."[1] Sebastian Frank (1534), Sebastian Munster (1546), H. Pantaleone (1570), an Italian who wrote a description of Germany, all agree with Böhm. Frank adds that the peasants hate every kind of cleric, good or bad, and that their speech is full of gibes against priests and monks; while Pantaleone observes that many skilled workmen, artisans, artists, and men of learning have sprung from this despised peasant class. There must have been a great change for the worse in the condition of the poorer dwellers both in town and in country.

So far as the townsmen are concerned, nothing need be added to what has already been said; but the causes of the growing depression of the peasantry were more complicated. The universal testimony of contemporaries is that the gradual introduction of Roman law brought the greatest change, by placing a means of universal oppression in the hands of the over-lords. There is no need to suppose that the lawyers who introduced the new jurisprudence meant to use it to degrade and oppress the peasant class. A slight study of the *Weisthümer* shows how complicated and varied was this consuetudinary law which regulated the relations between peasant and overlord. It was natural, when great estates grew to be principalities, whether lay or clerical, that the over-lords should seek for some principle of codification or reduction to uniformity. It had been the custom for centuries to attempt to simplify the ruder and involved German codes by bringing them into harmony with the principles of

[1] *Omnium Gentium Mores*, III. xii. (first printed in 1576).

Roman law, and this idea had received a powerful impetus from the Renaissance movement. But when the bewildering multiplicity of customary usages which had governed the relations of cultivators to over-lords was simplified according to the ideas of Roman law, the result was in the highest degree dangerous to the free peasantry of Germany. The conception of strict individual proprietorship tended to displace the indefinite conception of communal proprietorship, and the peasants could only appear in the guise of tenants on long leases, or serfs who might have some personal rights but no rights of property, or slaves who had no rights at all. The new jurisprudence began by attacking the common lands, pastures, and forests. The passion for the chase, which became the more engrossing as the right to wage private war grew more and more dangerous, led to the nobles insisting on the individual title to all forest lands, and to the publication of such forest laws as we find made in Würtemberg, where anyone found trespassing with gun or cross-bow was liable to lose one eye. The attempt to reduce a free peasantry in possession of communal property to tenants on long lease, then to serfs, and, lastly, to slaves, may be seen in the seventy years' struggle between the Abbots of Kempten and their peasants. These spiritual lords carried on the contest with every kind of force and chicanery they could command. They enlarged illegally the jurisdiction of their spiritual courts; they prevented the poor people who opposed them from coming to the Lord's Table; they actually falsified their title-deeds, inserting provisions which were not originally contained in them.

The case of the Kempten lands was, no doubt, an extreme one, though it could be matched by others. But the point to be noticed is the immense opportunities for oppression which were placed in the hands of the over-lords by the new jurisprudence, and the temptation to make use of them when their interests seemed to require it, or when their peasantry began to grow refractory or became too prosperous. The economic changes which were at work throughout the fifteenth century gave occasion for the use of the powers which the new jurisdiction had placed at the disposal of landlords. The economic revolution from the first impoverished the nobles of Germany, while, in its beginnings and until after the great rise in prices, it rather helped the peasantry. They had a better market for their produce, and they so profited by it that the burghers spoke of denying them the right of free markets, on the ground that they had begun to usurp the place of the merchants and were trafficking in gold by lending money on interest. The competition in luxurious dress and living, which the impoverished nobles carried on with the rich burghers, made the former still poorer and more reckless. We read of a noble lady in Swabia who, rather than be outshone at a tournament, sold a village and all her rights over it in order to buy a blue velvet dress. The nobles, becoming poorer and poorer, saw their own peasants making money to such an extent that they were, comparatively speaking, much better off than themselves, so that in Westphalia it was said that a peasant could get credit more easily than five nobles.

Moreover, the peasants did not appear to be as submissive to their lords as they once had been. Nor was it to be wondered at. The creation of the *landsknechts* had put new thoughts into their heads. The days of the old fighting chivalry were over, and the strength of armies was measured by the number and discipline of the infantry. The victories of the Swiss over Charles the Bold had made the peasant or artisan soldier a power. Kings and princes raised standing armies, recruited from the country districts or from among the wilder and more restless of the town population. The folk-songs are full of the doings of these plebeian soldiers. When the *landsknecht* visited his relations in village or in town, swaggered about in his gorgeous parti-coloured clothes, his broad hat adorned with huge feathers, his great gauntlets and his weapons; when he showed a gold chain or his ducats, or a jewel he had won as his share of the booty; when his old neighbours saw his dress and gait imitated by the young burghers,—he became a centre of admiration, and his relations began to hold themselves high on his account. They acquired a new independence of character, a new impatience against all that prevented them from rising in the world. It has scarcely been sufficiently noted how most of the leaders in the plebeian risings were disbanded *landsknechts*.[1]

The new jurisprudence was a very effectual instrument in the hands of an impoverished landlord class to ease the peasant of his superfluous wealth, and to keep him in his proper place. It was used almost universally, and the peasant rebellions were the natural consequences. But the more determined peasant revolts, which began with the *Bundschuh* League, arose at a time when life was hard for peasant and artisan alike.

The last decade of the fifteenth century and the first of the sixteenth contained a number of years in which the harvest failed almost entirely over all or in parts of Germany. They began with 1490, and in that year contemporary writers, like Trithemius, declare that the lot of the poor was almost unbearable. The bad harvests of 1491 and 1492 made things worse. In 1493, the year which saw the foundation of the *Bundschuh*, the state of matters may be guessed from the fact that men came all the way from the Tyrol to the upper reaches of the Main, where the harvest was comparatively good, bought barley

[1] *Landsknecht* or *lanzknecht* (for the words are the same) is often transliterated *lance-knight* in English State Papers of the sixteenth century. The English word, suggesting as it does cavalry armed with lances, is very misleading. The victories of the Swiss peasants, and their reputation as soldiers, suggested to the Emperor Frederick, and especially to his son, the Emperor Maximilian, the formation of troops of infantry recruited from the peasantry and from the lower classes of townsmen. Troops of cavalry of a like origin were also formed, and they were called *reiters* or *reisiger*. These mercenaries frequently gained much money both from pay and from plunder, and were regarded as heroes by the members of the classes from whom they had sprung. Liliencron's *Die historischen Volkslieder vom 13ten bis zum 16ten Jahrhundert* contains many folk-songs celebrating their prowess. The history of the gradual rise and growing importance of these peasant soldiers is given in Schultz, *Deutsches Leben im 14ten und 15ten Jahrhundert*, pp. 589 f. (Grosse Ausgabe), and in the authorities there quoted.

there for five times its usual price, carried it on pack-horses by little frequented paths to their own country, and sold it at a profit.

In 1499 the Swiss refused to submit to the imperial proposals for consolidating the Empire. Maximilian or his government in the Tyrol resolved to punish them, and the Swabian League were to be the executioners. The Swiss, highly incensed, had declared that if they were forced into war it would be a war of extermination. They were as bad as their word. An eye-witness saw whole villages in the wasted districts forsaken by the men, and the women gathered in troops, feeding on herbs and roots, and seeing with the apathy of despair their ranks diminish day by day.[1] The Swiss war was worse than many bad harvests for the Hegau and other districts in South Germany.

In 1500 the harvest failed over all Germany; 1501 and 1502 were years when the crops failed in a number of districts; and in 1503 there was another universally bad harvest. These years of scarcity pressed most heavily on the peasant class. In some districts of Brandenburg, peasants were found in the woods dead of starvation, with the grass which they had been trying to eat still in their mouths. Cities like Augsburg and Strassburg bought grain, stored it in magazines, and kept the poor alive by periodical distributions. This cycle of famine years from 1490 to 1503 was the period when the most determined and desperate social risings took place, and largely explains them.[2]

Our description of the social conditions existing during the period which ushered in the Reformation has been confined to Germany. The great religious movement took its origin in that land, and it is of the utmost importance to study the environment there. But the universal economic

[1] Willibald Pirkheimer in his book on the Swiss war, chap. ii. (German ed., Basel, 1826).

[2] Gothein, *Politische und religiöse Volksbewegungen vor der Reformation* (Breslau, 1878), p. 78.

changes were producing social disturbances everywhere, modified in appearance and character by the special conditions of the various countries of Europe. The popular risings in England, which began with the gigantic labour strike under Wat Tyler and priest Ball, and ended with the disturbances during the reign of Edward VI., were the counterpart of the social revolt in Germany.

From all that has been said, it will be evident that on the eve of the Reformation the condition of Europe, and of Germany in particular, was one of seething discontent and full of bitter class hatreds,—the trading companies and the great capitalists against the "gilds," the poorer classes against the wealthier, and the nobles against the towns. This state of things is abundantly reflected in the folk-songs of the period, which best reveal the intimate feelings of the people. For it was an age of song everywhere, and especially in Germany. Nobles and knights, burghers and peasants, *landsknechts* and Swiss soldiers, priests and clerks, lawyers and merchants—all expressed the feelings of their class when they sang; and the folk-songs give us a wonderful picture of the class hatreds which were rending asunder the old conditions of mediæval life, and preparing the way for a new world.

This social ferment was increased by a sudden and mysterious rise in prices, affecting first the articles of foreign produce, to which the wealthier classes had become greatly addicted, and at last the ordinary necessaries of life. The cause, it is now believed, was not the debasing of the coinage, for that affected a narrow circle only; nor was it the importation of precious metals from America, for that came later; it was rather the increased output of the mines in Europe. Whatever the cause, the thing was to contemporaries an irritating mystery, and each class in society was disposed to blame the others for it. We have thus at the beginning of the sixteenth century a restless social condition in Germany, caused in great measure by economic causes which no one understood, but whose results were painfully manifest in the crowds of sturdy beggars who thronged the roads—the refuse of all classes in society, from the broken noble and the disbanded mercenary soldier to the ruined peasant, the workman out of employment, the begging friar, and the "wandering student." It was into this mass of seething discontent that the spark of religious protest fell—the one thing needed to fire the train and kindle the social conflagration. This was the society to which Luther spoke, and its discontent was the sounding-board which made his words reverberate.

CHAPTER V.

FAMILY AND POPULAR RELIGIOUS LIFE IN THE DECADES BEFORE THE REFORMATION.[1]

§ 1. *The Devotion of Germany to the Roman Church.*

THE real roots of the spiritual life of Luther and of the other Reformers ought to be sought for in the family and in the popular religious life of the times. It is the duty of the historian to discover, if possible, what religious instruction was given by parents to children in the pious homes out of which most of the Reformers came, and what religious influences confronted and surrounded pious lads after they had left the family circle. Few have cared to

[1] To Sources given to Chapter IV. add: Wackernagel, *Das deutsche Kirchenlied von der ältesten Zeit bis zum Anfang des 17 Jahrhunderts* (Leipzig, 1864–1877) vols. i. ii.; "Rainerii Sachoni Summa de Catharis et Leonistis" in the *Magna Bibliotheca Patrum*, vol. xiii. (Col. Agrip. 1618), cf. "Comm. Crit. de Rainerii Sachoni Summa" (*Göttingen Osterprogramm* of 1834); Habler, *Das Wallfahrtbuch des Hermann von Vach, und die Pilgerreisen der Deutschen nach Santiago de Compostella* (Strassburg, 1899); *Mirabilia Romæ* (reprint by Parthey, Berlin, 1869); Munzenberger, *Frankfurter und Magdeburger Beichtbuchlein* (Mainz, 1883); Hasak, *Die letzte Rose*, etc. (Ratisbon, 1883); Hasak, *Der christliche Glaube des deutschen Volkes beim Schluss des Mittelalters* (Ratisbon, 1868); Höfler, *Denkwürdigkeiten der Charitas Pirckheimer* (*Quellensamml. z. fränk. Gesch.* iv., 1858); Konrad Stolle, *Thüringische Chronik* (in *Bibliothek d. lit. Vereins* (Stuttgardt), xxxiii.).

LATER BOOKS: v. Bezold, *Geschichte der deutschen Reformation* (Berlin, 1890); Janssen, *Geschichte des deutschen Volkesseit dem Ausgang des Mittelalters* (17th ed., 1897), vol. i.; Brück, *Der religiöse Unterricht für Jugend und Volk in Deutschland in der zweiten Hälfte des fünfzehnten Jahrhunderts;* Cruel, *Geschichte der deutschen Predigt im Mittelalter* (Detwold, 1879); Dacheux, *Jean Geiler de Keysersberg* (Paris, 1876); Walther, *Die deutsche Bibelübersetzung des Mittelalters* (Brunswick, 1889); Uhlhorn, *Die christliche Liebesthätigkeit im Mittelalter* (Stuttgart, 1887); Wilken, *Geschichte der geistlichen Spiele in Deutschland* (Göttingen, 1872).

prosecute the difficult task; and it is only within late years that the requisite material has been accumulated. It has to be sought for in autobiographies, diaries, and private letters; in the books of popular devotion which the patience of ecclesiastical archæologists is exhuming and reprinting; in the references to the pious confraternities of the later Middle Ages, and more especially to the *Kalands* among the artisans, which appear in town chronicles, and whose constitutions are being slowly unearthed by local historical societies; in the police regulations of towns and country districts which aim at curbing the power of the clergy, and in the edicts of princes attempting to enforce some of the recommendations of the Councils of Constance and Basel; in the more popular hymns of the time, and in the sermons of the more fervent preachers; in the pilgrim songs and the pilgrim guide-books; and in a variety of other sources not commonly studied by Church historians.

On the surface no land seemed more devoted to the mediæval Church and to the Pope, its head, than did Germany in the half century before the Reformation. A cultivated Italian, Aleander, papal nuncio at the Diet of Worms, was astonished at the signs of disaffection he met with in 1520.[1] He had visited Germany frequently, and he was intimately acquainted with many of the northern Humanists; and his opinion was that down to 1510 (the date of his last visit) he had never been among a people so devoted to the Bishop of Rome. No nation had exhibited such signs of delight at the ending of the Schism and the re-establishment of the "Peace of the Church." The Italian Humanists continually express their wonder at the strength of the religious susceptibilities of the Germans; and the papal Curia looked upon German devotion as a never-failing source of Roman revenue. The Germans displayed an almost feverish anxiety to profit by all the ordinary and extraordinary means of grace. They built innumerable churches; their towns were full of conventual

[1] Kalkoff, *Die Depeschen des Nuntius Aleander*, etc. (Halle a. S. 1897), pp. 26, 45–48.

foundations; they bought Indulgences, went on pilgrimages, visited shrines, reverenced relics in a way that no other nation did. The piety of the Germans was proverbial.

The number of churches was enormous for the population. Almost every tiny village had its chapel, and every town of any size had several churches. Church building and decoration was a feature of the age. In the town of Dantzig 8 new churches had been founded or completed during the fifteenth century. The "holy" city of Köln (Cologne) at the close of the fifteenth century contained 11 great churches, 19 parish churches, 22 monasteries, 12 hospitals, and 76 convents; more than a thousand Masses were said at its altars every day. It was exceptionally rich in ecclesiastical buildings, no doubt; but the smaller town of Brunswick had 15 churches, over 20 chapels, 5 monasteries, 6 hospitals, and 12 Beguine-houses, and its great church, dedicated to St. Blasius, had 26 altars served by 60 ecclesiastics. So it was all over Germany.

Besides the large numbers of monks and nuns who peopled the innumerable monasteries and convents, a large part of the population belonged to some semi-ecclesiastical association. Many were tertiaries of St. Francis; many were connected with the Beguines: Köln (Cologne) had 106 Beguine-houses; Strassburg, over 60, and Basel, over 30.

The churches and chapels, monasteries and religious houses, received all kinds of offerings from rich and poor alike. In those days of unexampled burgher prosperity and wealth, the town churches became "museums and treasure-houses." The windows were filled with painted glass; weapons, armour, jewels, pictures, tapestries were stored in the treasuries or adorned the walls. Ancient inventories have been preserved of some of these ecclesiastical accumulations of wealth. In the cathedral church in Bern, to take one example, the head of St. Vincentius, the patron, was adorned with a great quantity of gold, and with one jewel said to be priceless; the treasury contained 70 gold and 50 silver cups, 2 silver coffers, and 450 costly sacramental robes decked with jewels of great value. The luxury, the artistic fancy, and the wealth which could minister to both, all three were characteristic of the times, were lavished by the Germans on their churches.

§ 2. *Preaching.*

On the other hand, preaching took a place it had never previously held in the mediæval Church. Some distinguished Churchmen did not hesitate to say that it was the most important duty the priest could perform—more important than saying Mass. It was recognised that when the people began to read the Bible and religious books in the vernacular, it became necessary for the priests to be able to instruct their congregations intelligently and sympathetically in sermons. Attempts were made to provide the preachers with material for their sermon-making. The earliest was the *Biblia Pauperum* (the Bible for the *Pauperes Christi*, or the preaching monks), which collects on one page pictures of Bible histories fitted to explain each other, and adds short comments. Thus, on the twenty-fifth leaf there are three pictures—in the centre the Crucifixion; on the left Abraham about to slay Isaac, with the lamb in the foreground; and on the left the Brazen Serpent and the healing of the Plague. More scholarly preachers found a valuable commentary in the *Postilla* of the learned Franciscan Nicolas de Lyra (Lira or Lire, a village in Normandy), who was the first real exegetical scholar, and to whom Luther was in later days greatly indebted.[1]

Manuals of Pastoral Theology were also written and published for the benefit of the parish priests,—the most famous, under the quaint title, *Dormi Secure* (sleep in safety). It describes the more important portions of the service, and what makes a good sermon; it gives the Lessons for the Sunday services, the chief articles of the Christian faith, and adds directions for pastoral work and the cure of souls.

[1] No fewer than six editions of his *Postilla* were published between 1471 and 1508.

It is somewhat difficult to describe briefly the character of the preaching. Some of it was very edifying and deservedly popular. The sermons of John Herolt were printed, and attained a very wide circulation. No fewer than forty-one editions appeared. Much of the preaching was the exposition of themes taken from the Scholastic Theology treated in the most technical way. Many of the preachers seem to have profaned their office in the search after popularity, and mingled very questionable stories and coarse jokes with their exhortations. The best known of the preachers who flourished at the close of the fifteenth century was John Geiler of Keysersberg (in Elsass near Colmar), the friend of Sebastian Brand, and a member of the Humanist circle of Strassburg. The position he filled illustrates the eagerness of men of the time to encourage preaching. A burgher of Strassburg, Peter Schott, left a sum of money to endow a preacher, who was to be a doctor of theology, one who had not taken monk's vows, and who was to preach to the people in the vernacular; a special pulpit was erected in the Strassburg Minster for the preacher provided by this foundation, who was John Geiler. His sermons are full of exhortations to piety and correct living. He lashed the vices and superstitions of his time. He denounced relic worship, pilgrimages, buying indulgences, and the corruptions in the monasteries and convents. He spoke against the luxurious living of Popes and prelates, and their trafficking in the sale of benefices. He made sarcastic references to the papal decretals and to the quibblings of Scholastic Theology. He paints the luxuries and vices he denounced so very clearly, that his writings are a valuable mine for the historian of popular morals. He was a stern preacher of morals, but his sermons contain very little of the gospel message. As we read them we can understand Luther's complaint, that while he had listened to many a sermon on the sins of the age, and to many a discourse expounding scholastic themes, he had never heard one which declared the love of God to man in the mission and work of Jesus Christ.

§ 3. *Church Festivals.*

The Church itself, recognising the fondness of the people for all kinds of scenic display, delighted to gratify the prevailing taste by magnificent processions, by gorgeous church ceremonial, by Passion and Miracle Plays. Such scenes are continually described in contemporary chronicles. The processions were arranged for Corpus Christi Day, for Christmas, for Harvest Thanksgivings, when the civic fathers requested the clergy to pray for rain, or when a great papal official visited the town. We hear of one at Erfurt which began at five o'clock in the morning, and, with its visits to the stations of the Cross and the services at each, did not end till noon. The school children of the town, numbering 948, headed the procession, then came 312 priests, then the whole University,—in all, 2141 persons,—and the monks belonging to the five monasteries followed. The Holy Sacrament carried by the chief ecclesiastics, and preceded by a large number of gigantic candles, occupied the middle of the procession. The town council followed, then all the townsmen, then the women and maidens. The troop of maidens was 2316 strong. They had garlands on their heads, and their hair flowed down over their shoulders; they carried lighted candles in their hands, and they marched modestly looking to the ground. Two beautiful girls walked at their head with banners, followed by four with lanterns. In the centre was the fairest, clad in black and barefoot, carrying a large and splendid cross, and by her side one of the town councillors chosen for his good looks. Everything was arranged with a view to artistic effect.[1]

The Passion and Miracle Plays[2] were of great use in instructing the people in the contents of Scripture, being almost always composed of biblical scenes and histories.

[1] v. Bezold, *Geschichte der deutschen Reformation*, p. 91 f.

[2] Heinzel, *Beschreibung des geistlichen Schauspiels im deutschen Mittelalter* (Hamburg and Leipzig, 1898); F. J. Mone, *Schauspiele des Mittelalters*, 2 vols. (Karlsruhe, 1846).

They were often very elaborate; sometimes more than one hundred actors were needed to fill the parts; and the plays were frequently so lengthy that they lasted for two or three days. The ecclesiastical managers felt that the continuous presentation of grave and lofty scenes and sentiments might weary their audiences, and they mixed them with lighter ones, which frequently degenerated into buffoonery and worse. The sacred and severe pathos of the Passion was interlarded with coarse jokes about the devil; and the most solemn conceptions were profaned. These Mysteries were generally performed in the great churches, and the buildings dedicated to sacred things witnessed scenes of the coarsest humour, to the detriment of all religious feeling. The more serious Churchmen felt the profanation, and tried to prohibit the performance of plays interlarded with rude and indecent scenes within the churches and churchyards. Their interference came too late; the rough popular taste demanded what it had been accustomed to; sacred histories and customs coming down from a primitive heathenism were mixed together, and the people lost the sense of sacredness which ought to attach itself to the former. The Feast of the Ass, to mention one, was supposed to commemorate the Flight to Egypt. A beautiful girl, holding a child in her lap, was seated on an ass decked with splendid trappings of gold cloth, and was led in procession by the clergy through the principal streets of the town to the parish church. The girl on her ass was conducted into the church and placed near the high altar, and the Mass and other services were each concluded by the whole congregation braying. There is indeed an old MS. extant with a rubric which orders the priest to bray thrice on elevating the Host.[1] At other seasons of popular licence, all the parts of the church service, even the most solemn, were parodied by the profane youth of the towns.[2]

[1] Hampsen, *Medii Ævi Kalendarium* (London, 1841), i. 140 f.

[2] Tilliot, *Mémoires pour servir à l'histoire de la fête des fous* (Lausanne, 1751); cf. Floegel's *Geschichte des Grotesk-Komischen* (3rd ed., Leipzig, 1886), pp. 199–242.

All this, however, tells us little about the intimate religious life and feelings of the people, which is the important matter for the study of the roots of the great ecclesiastical revolt.

When the evidence collected from the sources is sifted, it will be found that the religious life of the people at the close of the fifteenth and beginning of the sixteenth centuries is full of discordant elements, and makes what must appear to us a very incongruous mosaic. If classification be permissible, which it scarcely is (for religious types always refuse to be kept distinct, and always tend to run into each other), one would be disposed to speak of the simple homely piety of the family circle—the religion taught at the mother's knee, the *Kinderlehre*, as Luther called it; of a certain flamboyant religion which inspired the crowds; of a calm anti-clerical religion which grew and spread silently throughout Germany; of the piety of the praying-circles, the descendants of the fourteenth century Mystics.

§ 4. *The Family Religious Life.*

The biographies of some of the leaders of the Reformation, when they relate the childish reminiscences of the writers, bear unconscious witness to the kind of religion which was taught to the children in pious burgher and peasant families. We know that Luther learned the Creed, the Ten Commandments, and the Lord's Prayer. He knew such simple evangelical hymns as "Ein kindelein so lobelich,"[1] "Nun bitten wir den heiligen Geist," and "Crist ist erstanden." Children were rocked to sleep while the mothers sang:

> "Ach lieber Heere Jhesu Christ
> Sid Du ein Kind gewesen bist,
> So gib ouch disem Kindelin
> Din Gnod und ouch den Segen den.
> Ach Jhesu, Heere min,
> Behüt diz Kindelin.

[1] The old Scottish version is, "To us is borne a barne of bliss," *Gude and Godlie Ballates* (Scot. Text Society, Edinburgh, 1897), pp. 51, 250.

Nun sloff, nun sloff, min Kindelin,
Jhesus der sol din bülli sin,
Der well, daz dir getroume wol
Und werdest aller Tugent vol.
Ach Jhesus, Heere min,
Behüt diz Kindelin." [1]

These songs or hymns, common before the Reformation, were sung as frequently after the break with Rome. The continuity in the private devotional life before and after the advent of the Reformation is a thing to be noted. Few hymns were more popular during the last decade of the fifteenth century than the "In dulci Jubilo" in which Latin and German mingled. The first and last verses were:

"In dulci jubilo,
Nun singet und seid froh!
Unsers Herzens Wonne
Leit in præsepio,
Und leuchtet als die Sonne
Matris in gremio.
Alpha es et O,
Alpha es et O!

Ubi sunt gaudia?
Nirgends mehr denn da,
Da die Engel singen
Nova cantica,
Und die Schellen klingen
In regis curia.
Eya, wär'n wir da,
Eya, wär'n wir da!"

---

[1] This may be translated:

"Oh Jesus, Master, meek and mild,
Since Thou wast once a little child,
Wilt Thou not give this baby mine
Thy Grace and every blessing thine?
Oh Jesus, Master mild,
Protect my little child.

Now sleep, now sleep, my little child,
He loves thee, Jesus, meek and mild:
He'll never leave thee nor forsake,
He'll make thee wise and good and great.
Oh Jesus, Master mild,
Protect my little child."

This hymn continued to enjoy a wonderful popularity in the German Protestant churches and families until quite recently, and during the times of the Reformation it spread far beyond Germany.[1] In the fifteenth-century version it contained one verse in praise of the Virgin:

"Mater et filia
Du bist, Jungfraw Maria.
Wir weren all verloren
Per nostra crimina,
So hat sy uns erworben
Celorum gaudia.
Eya, wär'n wir da,
Eya, wär'n wir da!"

---

[1] The old Scotch version was:

"In dulci jubilo,
Now let us sing with mirth and jo!
Our hartis consolation
Lies in præsepio;
And schynis as the Sonne
Matris in gremio.
Alpha es et O,
Alpha es et O!

O Jesu parvule,
I thirst sair after Thee;
Comfort my hart and mind,
O Puer optime!
God of all grace so kind,
Et Princeps Gloriæ,
Trahe me post Te,
Trahe me post Te!

Ubi sunt gaudia
In any place but there,
Where that the angels sing
Nova cantica,
But and the bellis ring
In Regis curia!
God gif I were there,
God gif I were there!"

—(*Gude and Godlie Ballates* (Scot. Text Society, Edinburgh, 1897), pp. 53. 250.)

There is a variety of English versions: "Let Jubil trumpets blow, and hearts in rapture flow"; "In dulci jubilo, to the House of God we'll go"; "In dulci jubilo, sing and shout all below." Cf. Julian, *Dictionary of Hymnology*, p. 564.

which was either omitted in the post-Reformation versions, or there was substituted:

"O Patris charitas,
O Nati lenitas!
Wir weren all verloren
Per nostra crimina,
So hat Er uns erworben
Cœlorum gaudia.
Eya, wär'n wir da,
Eya, wär'n wir da."[1]

Nor was direct simple evangelical instruction lacking. Friedrich Mecum (known better by his Latinised name of Myconius), who was born in 1491, relates how his father, a substantial burgher belonging to Lichtenfels in Upper Franconia, instructed him in religion while he was a child. "My dear father," he says, "had taught me in my childhood the Ten Commandments, the Lord's Prayer, and the Creed, and constrained me to pray always. For, said he, 'Everything comes to us from God alone, and that *gratis*, free of cost, and He will lead us and rule us, if we only diligently pray to Him.'" We can trace this simple evangelical family religion away back through the Middle Ages. In the wonderfully interesting Chronicle of Brother Salimbene of the Franciscan Convent of Parma, which comes from the thirteenth century, we are told how many of the better-disposed burghers of the town came to the convent frequently to enjoy the religious conversation of Brother Hugh. On one occasion the conversation turned upon the mystical theology of Abbot Giaocchino di Fiore. The burghers professed to be greatly edified, but said that they hoped that on the next evening Brother Hugh would confine himself to telling them the *simple words of Jesus.*

The central thought in all evangelical religion is that the believer does not owe his position before God, and his assurance of salvation, to the good deeds which he really can do, but to the grace of God manifested in the mission and the work of Christ; and the more we turn

[1] Wackernagel, *Das deutsche Kirchenlied*, etc., ii. 483 ff.

from the thought of what we can do to the thought of what God has done for us, the stronger will be the conviction that simple trust in God is that by which the pardoning grace of God is appropriated. This double conception—God's grace coming down upon us from above, and the believer's trust rising from beneath to meet and appropriate it—was never absent from the simplest religion of the Middle Ages. It did not find articulate expression in mediæval theology, for, owing to its enforced connection with Aristotelian philosophy, that theology was largely artificial; but the thought itself had a continuous and constant existence in the public consciousness of Christian men and women, and appeared in sermons, prayers, and hymns, and in the other ways in which the devotional life manifested itself. It is found in the sermons of the greatest of mediæval preachers, Bernard of Clairvaux, and in the teaching of the most persuasive of religious guides, Francis of Assisi. The one, Bernard, in spite of his theological training, was able to rise above the thought of human merit recommending the sinner to God; and the other, Francis, who had no theological training at all, insisted that he was fitted to lead a life of imitation simply because he had no personal merits whatsoever, and owed everything to the marvellous mercy and grace of God given freely to him in the work of Christ. The thought that all the good we can do comes from the wisdom and mercy of God, and that without these gifts of grace we are sinful and worthless—the feeling that all pardon and all holy living are free gifts of God's grace, was the central thought round which in mediæval, as in all times, the faith of simple and pious people twined itself. It found expression in the simpler mediæval hymns, Latin and German. The utter need for sin-pardoning grace is expressed and taught in the prayer of the *Canon of the Mass.* It found its way, in spite of the theology, even into the official agenda of the Church, where the dying are told that they must repose their confidence upon Christ and His Passion as the sole ground of confidence in their salvation. If we take the fourth book of Thomas à Kempis' *Imitatio Christi*, it is impossible to avoid seeing that his ideas about the sacrament of the Supper (in spite of the mistakes in them) kept alive in his mind the thought of a free grace of God, and that he had a clear conception that God's grace was freely given, and not merited by what man can do. For the main thought with pious mediæval Christians, however it might be overlaid with superstitious conceptions, was that they received in the sacrament a *gift* of overwhelming greatness. Many a modern Christian seems to think that the main idea is that in this sacrament one *does* something —makes a profession of Christianity. The old view went a long way towards keeping people right in spite of errors, while the modern view does a great deal towards leading them wrong in spite of truth.

All these things combine to show us how there was a simple evangelical faith among pious mediæval Christians, and that their lives were fed upon the same divine truths which lie at the basis of Reformation theology. The truths were all there, as poetic thoughts, as earnest supplication and confession, in fervent preaching or in fireside teaching. When mediæval Christians knelt in prayer, stood to sing their Redeemer's praises, spoke as a dying man to dying men, or as a mother to the children about her knees, the words and thoughts that came were what Luther and Zwingli and Calvin wove into Reformation creeds, and expanded into that experimental theology which was characteristic of the Reformation.

When the printing-press began in the last decades of the fifteenth century to provide little books to aid private and family devotion, it is not surprising, after what has been said, to find how full many of them were of simple evangelical piety. Some contained the Lord's Prayer, the Ten Commandments, the Apostles' Creed, and occasionally a translation or paraphrase of some of the Psalms, notably the 51st Psalm. Popular religious instructions and catechisms for family use were printed. The Catechism of Dietrich Koelde (written in 1470) says: "Man must place his faith and hope and love on God alone, and not in any creature; he must trust in nothing but in the work of Jesus Christ." The *Seelenwurzgartlein*, a widely used book of devotion, instructs the penitent: "Thou must place all thy hope and trust on nothing else than on the work and death of Jesus Christ." The *Geistliche Streit* of Ulrich Krafft (1503) teaches the dying man to place all his trust on the "mercy and goodness of God, and not on his own good works." Quotations might be multiplied, all proving the existence of a simple evangelical piety, and showing that the home experience of Friedrich Mecum (Myconius) was shared in by thousands, and that there was a simple evangelical family religion in numberless German homes in the end of the fifteenth century.

§ 5. *A superstitious Religion based on Fear.*

When sensitive, religiously disposed boys left pious homes, they could not fail to come in contact with a very different kind of religion. Many did not need to quit the family circle in order to meet it. Near Mansfeld, Luther's home, were noted pilgrimage places. Pilgrims, singly or in great bands, passed to make their devotions before the wooden cross at Kyffhäuser, which was supposed to effect miraculous cures. The Bruno Quertfort Chapel and the old chapel at Welfesholz were pilgrimage places. Sick people were carried to spots near the cloister church at Wimmelberg, where they could best hear the sound of the cloister bells, which were believed to have a healing virtue.

The latter half of the fifteenth century witnessed a great and widespreading religious revival, which prolonged itself into the earlier decades of the sixteenth, though the year 1475 may perhaps be taken as its high-water mark. Its most characteristic feature was the impulse to make pilgrimages to favoured shrines; and these pilgrimages were always considered to be something in the nature of satisfactions made to God for sins. With some of the earlier phenomena we have nothing here to do.

The impetus to pilgrimages given after the great Schism by the celebration in 1456 of the first Jubilee "after healing the wounds of the Church"; the relation of these pilgrimages to the doctrines of Indulgences which, formulated by the great Schoolmen of the thirteenth century, had changed the whole penitential system of the mediæval Church, must be passed over; the curious socialist, anti-clerical, and yet deeply superstitious movement led by the cowherd and village piper, Hans Böhm, has been described. But one movement is so characteristic of the times, that it must be noticed. In the years 1455–1459 all the chroniclers describe great gatherings of children from every part of Germany, from town and village, who, with crosses and banners, went on pilgrimage to St. Michael in Normandy. The chronicler of Lübeck compares the spread of the movement to the advance of the plague, and wonders whether the prompting arose from the inspiration of God or from the instigation of the devil. When a band of these child-pilgrims reached a town, carrying aloft crosses and banners blazoned with a rude image of St. Michael, singing their special pilgrim song,[1] the town's children were impelled to join them. How this strange epidemic arose, and what put an end to it, seems altogether doubtful; but the chronicles of almost every important town in Germany attest the facts, and the contemporary records of North France describe the bands of youthful pilgrims who traversed the country to go to St. Michael's Mount.

During these last decades of the fifteenth century, a great fear seems to have brooded over Central Europe

[1] The song began:

"Wöllent ir geren hören
Von sant Michel's wunn;
In Gargau ist er gsessen
Drei mil im meresgrund.

'O heilger man, sant Michel.
Wie hastu dass gesundt,
Dass du so tief hast buwen
Wol in des meres grund?'"

—(Wackernagel, *Das deutsche Kirchenlied*, etc. ii. 1003.)

The countries were scourged by incessant visits of the plague; new diseases, never before heard of, came to swell the terror of the people. The alarm of a Turkish invasion was always before their eyes. Bells tolled at midday in hundreds of German parishes, calling the parishioners together for prayer against the incoming of the Turks, and served to keep the dread always present to their minds. Mothers threatened their disobedient children by calling on the Turk to come and take them. It was fear that lay at the basis of this crude revival of religion which marks the closing decades of the fifteenth century. It gave rise to an urgent restlessness. Prophecies of evil were easily believed in. Astrologers assumed a place and wielded a power which was as new as it was strange. The credulous people welcomed all kinds of revelations and proclamations of miraculous signs. At Wilsnack, a village in one of the divisions of Brandenburg (Priegnitz), it had been alleged since 1383 that a consecrated wafer secreted the Blood of Christ. Suddenly, in 1475, people were seized with a desire to make a pilgrimage to this shrine. Swarms of child-pilgrims again filled the roads—boys and girls, from eight to eighteen years of age, bareheaded, clad only in their shirts, shouting, "O Lord, have mercy upon us"—going to Wilsnack. Sometimes schoolmasters headed a crowd of pilgrims; mothers deserted their younger children; country lads and maids left their work in the fields to join the processions. These pilgrims came mostly from Central Germany (1100 from Eisleben alone), but the contagion spread to Austria and Hungary, and great bands of youthful pilgrims appeared from these countries. They travelled without provisions, and depended on the charity of the peasants for food. Large numbers of these child-pilgrims did not know why they had joined the throng; they had never heard of the *Bleeding Host* towards which they were journeying; when asked why they had set out, they could only answer that they could not help it, that they saw the red cross at the head of their little band, and had to follow it. Many of them could not speak, all went weeping and groaning, shivering as if they had a fit of ague. An unnatural strength supported them. Little boys and girls, some of them not eight years old, from a small village near Bamberg, were said to have marched, on their first setting forth, all day and the first night the incredible distance of not less than eighty miles! Some towns tried to put a stop to these pilgrimages. Erfurt shut its gates against the youthful companies. The pilgrimages ended as suddenly as they had begun.[1]

Succeeding years witnessed similar astonishing pilgrimages—in 1489, to the "black Mother of God" in Altötting; in 1492, to the "Holy Blood" at Sternberg; in the same year, to the "pitiful Bone" at Dornach; in 1499, to the picture of the Blessed Virgin at Grimmenthal; in 1500, to the head of St. Anna at Düren; and in 1519, to the "Beautiful Mary" at Regensburg.

Apart altogether from these sporadic movements, the last decades of the fifteenth century were pre-eminently a time of pilgrimages. German princes and wealthy merchants made pilgrimages to the Holy Land, visited the sacred places there, and returned with numerous relics, which they stored in favourite churches. Frederick the Wise, the Elector of Saxony, to be known afterwards as the protector of Luther, made such a pilgrimage, and placed the relics he had acquired in the Castle Church (the Church of All Saints) in Wittenberg. He became an assiduous collector of relics, and had commissioners on the Rhine, in the Netherlands, and at Venice, with orders to procure him any sacred novelties they met with for sale.[2] He procured from the Pope an Indulgence for all who visited the collection and took part in the services of the church on All Saints' Day; for it is one of the ironies of history that the church on whose door Luther nailed his theses against Indulgences was one of the sacred edifices on which an Indulgence had been bestowed, and that the day selected

[1] Konrad Stolle, *Thüringische Chronik*, pp. 128–131 (*Bibliothek des literarischen Vereins in Stuttgart*, xxxiii.).

[2] Kolde, *Friedrich der Weise und die Anfänge der Reformation*, p. 14.

by Luther was the yearly anniversary, which drew crowds to benefit by it.[1]

A pilgrimage to the Holy Land was too costly and dangerous to be indulged in by many. The richer Germans made pilgrimages to Rome, and the great pilgrimage place for the middle-class or poorer Germans was Compostella in Spain. Einsiedeln, in Switzerland, also attracted yearly swarms of pilgrims.

Guide-books were written for the benefit of these pious travellers, and two of them, the most popular, have recently been reprinted. They are the *Mirabilia Romæ* for Roman pilgrims, and the *Walfart und Strasse zu Sant Jacob* for travellers to Compostella. These little books had a wonderful popularity. The *Mirabilia Romæ* went through nineteen Latin and at least twelve German editions before the year 1500; it was also translated into Italian and Dutch. It describes the various shrines at Rome where pilgrims may win special gifts of grace by visiting and worshipping at them. Who goes to the Lateran Church and worships there has "forgiveness of all sins, both guilt and penalty." There is "a lovely little chapel" (probably what is now called the Lateran Baptistry) near the Lateran, where the same privileges may be won. The pilgrim who goes with good intention to the High Altar of St. Peter's Church, "even if he has murdered his father or his mother," is freed from all sin, "guilt as well as penalty," provided he repents. The virtues of St. Croce seem to have been rated even higher. If a man leaves his house with the intention of going to the shrine, even if he die by the way, all his sins are forgiven him; and if he visits the church he wins a thousand years' relief from Purgatory.[2]

Compostella in Spain was the people's pilgrimage place. Before the invention of printing we find traces of manu-

[1] Lucas Cranach, *Wittenberger Heiligenthumsbuch vom Jahre 1509*, in Hirth's *Liebhaber-Bibliothek alter Illustratoren in Facsimilien-Reproduktion*, No. vii. (Munich, 1896).

[2] *Mirabilia Romæ*, ed. by G. Parthey: the quotations are from an old German translation.

script guides to travellers, which were no doubt circulated among intending pilgrims, and afterwards the services of the printing-press were early called in to assist. In the Spanish archives at Simancas there are two single sheets, one of which states the numerous Indulgences for the benefit of visitors at the shrine of St. James, while the other enumerates the relics which are to be seen and visited there. It mentions thirty-nine great relics—from the bones of St. James, which lay under the great altar of the cathedral, to those of St. Susanna, which were interred in a church outside the walls of the town.[1] These leaflets were sold to the pilgrims, and were carried back by them to Germany, where they stimulated the zeal and devotion of those who intended to make the pilgrimage. Our pilgrim's guide-book, the *Walfart und Strasse zu Sant Jacob*,[2] deals almost exclusively with the road. The author was a certain Hermann Künig of Vach, who calls himself a *Mergen-knecht*, or servant of the Virgin Mary. The well-known pilgrim song, "Of Saint James" (*Von Sant Jacob*), told how those who reached the end of their journey got, through the intercession of St. James, forgiveness from the guilt and penalty (*von Pein und Schuldt*) of all their sins; it tells the pilgrims to provide themselves with two pairs of shoes, a water-bottle and spoon, a satchel and staff, a broad-brimmed hat and a cloak, both trimmed with leather in the places likeliest to be frayed, and both needed as a protection against wind and rain and snow.[3] It

[1] The title is *Hæ sunt reliquiæ quæ habentur in hac sanctissima ecclesia Compostellana in qua corpus Beati Jacobi Zebedei in integrum.*

[2] No. i. of *Drucke und Holzschnitte des 15 und 16 Jahrhunderts* (Strassburg, 1899).

[3] "Zway par schuech der darff er wol,
Ein schüssel bei der flaschen;
Ein breiten huet den sol er han,
Und an mantel sol er nit gan
Myt leder wol besezet;
Es schnei oder regn oder wehe der wint,
Dass in die lufft nicht nezet;
Sagkh und stab ist auch dar bey."

—(Wackernagel, *Das deutsche Kirchenlied von der aeltesten Zeit bis zu Anfang des 17 Jahrhunderts*, ii. 1009.)

charges them to take permits from their parish priests to dispense with confession, for they were going to foreign lands where they would not find priests who spoke German. It warns them that they might die far from home and find a grave on the pilgrimage route. Our guide-book omits all these things. It is written by a man who has made the pilgrimage on foot; who had observed minutely all the turns of the road, and could warn fellow-pilgrims of the difficulties of the way. He gives the itinerary from town to town; where to turn to the right and where to the left; what conspicuous buildings mark the proper path; where the traveller will find people who are generous to poor pilgrims, and where the inhabitants are uncharitable and food and drink must be paid for; where hostels abound, and those parts of the road on which there are few, and where the pilgrims must buy their provisions beforehand and carry them in their satchels; where sick pilgrims can find hospitals on the way, and what treatment they may expect there;[1] at what hostels they must change their money into French and Spanish coin. In brief, the booklet is a mediæval "Baedeker," compiled with German accuracy for the

[1] The hospital at Romans is much praised:

> "Da selbst eyn gutter spital ist,
> Dar inne gybt mann brot und wyn
> Auch synt die bett hubsch und fyn."

On the other hand, although the hospital at Montpelier was good enough, its superintendent was a sworn enemy to Germans, and the pilgrims of that nation suffered much at his hands. These hospitals occupy a good deal of space in the pilgrimage song, and the woes of the Germans are duly set forth. If the pilgrim asks politely for more bread:

> "Spitelmeister, lieber spitelmeister meyn,
> Die brot sein vil zu kleine";

or suggests that the beds are not very clean:

> "Spitelmeister, lieber spitelmeister meyn,
> Die bet sein nit gar reine,"

the superintendent and his daughter (der spitelmeister het eyn tochterlein es mocht recht vol eyn schelckin seyn) declared that they were not going to be troubled with "German dogs."—Wackernagel, *Das deutsche Kirchenlied*, etc., ii. 1009–1010.

benefit of German pilgrims to the renowned shrine of St. James of Compostella. This little book went through several editions between 1495 and 1521, and is of itself a proof of the popularity of this pilgrimage place. In the last decades of the fifteenth century there arose a body of men and women who might be called professional pilgrims, and who were continually on the road between Germany and Spain. A pilgrimage was one of the earliest so-called "satisfactions" which might be done vicariously, and the Brethren of St. James (*Jacobs-Brueder*) made the pilgrimage regularly, either on behalf of themselves or of others.

Many of these pilgrims were men and women of indifferent character,[1] who had been sent on a pilgrimage as an ecclesiastical punishment for their sins. The *Chronicles of the Zimmer Family*[2] gives several cases of criminals, who had committed murder or theft or other serious crimes between 1490 and 1520, who were sent to Santiago as a punishment. Even in the last decades of the fifteenth century, when the greater part of the pilgrims were devout in their way, it was known only too well that pilgrimages were not helpful to a moral life. Stern preachers of righteousness like Geiler of Keysersberg and Berchtold of Regensburg denounced pilgrimages, and said that they created more sins than they yielded pardons.[3] Parish priests continually forbade their women penitents, especially if they were unmarried, from going on a pilgrimage. But these warnings and rebukes were in vain. The prevailing terror had possessed the people, and they journeyed from shrine to shrine seeking some relief for their stricken consciences.

A marked characteristic of this revival which found such striking outcome in these pilgrimages was the thought that Jesus was to be looked upon as the Judge who was to come to punish the wicked. His saving and intercessory work was thrust into the background. Men forgot that He was the Saviour and the Intercessor; and

[1] *Zimmerische Chronik* (Freiburg i. B. 1881–1882), ii. 314.
[2] *Ibid.* iii. 474–475 iv. 201.
[3] *Predigten*, i. 448.

as the human heart craves for someone to intercede for it, another intercessor had to be found. This gracious personality was discovered in the Virgin Mother, who was to be entreated to intercede with her Son on behalf of poor sinning human creatures. The last half of the fifteenth century saw a deep-seated and widely-spread craving to cling to the protection of the Virgin Mother with a strength and intensity hitherto unknown in mediæval religion. It witnessed the furthest advance that had yet been made towards what must be called Mariolatry. This devotion expressed itself, as religious emotion continually does, in hymns; a very large proportion of the mediæval hymns in praise of the Virgin were written in the second half of the fifteenth century—the period of this strange revival based upon fear. Dread of the Son as Judge gave rise to the devotion to the Mother as the intercessor. Little books for private and family devotion were printed, bearing such titles as the *Pearl of the Passion* and the *Little Gospel*, containing, with long comments, the words of our Lord on the cross to John and to Mary. She became the ideal woman, the ideal mother, the "Mother of God," the *mater dolorosa*, with her heart pierced by the sword, the sharer in the redemptive sufferings of her Son, retaining her sensitive woman's heart, ready to listen to the appeals of a suffering, sorrowful humanity. We can see this devotion to the Virgin Mother impregnating the social revolts from Hans Böhm to Joss Fritz. The theology of the schools followed in the wake of the popular sentiment, and the doctrine of the Immaculate Conception was more strictly defined and found its most strenuous supporters during the later decades of this fifteenth century.

The thought of motherly intercession went further; the Virgin herself had to be interceded with to induce her to plead with her Son for men sunk in sin, and *her* mother (St. Anna) became the object of a cult which may almost be said to be quite new. Hymns were written in her praise.[1] Confraternities, modelled on the confraternities

[1] Wackernagel, *Das deutsche Kirchenlied*, etc., ii. 554, 1016–1022.

dedicated to the Blessed Virgin, were formed in order to bring the power of the prayers of numbers to bear upon her. These confraternities spread all over Germany and beyond it.[1] It is almost possible to trace the widening area of the cult from the chronicles of the period. The special cult of the Virgin seems to have begun, at least in its extravagant popular form, in North France, and to have spread from France through Germany and Spain; but so far as it can be traced, this cult of St. Anna, "the Grandmother," had a German origin, and the devotion manifested itself most deeply on German soil. Even the Humanist poets sang her praises with enthusiasm, and such collectors of relics as Frederick of Saxony and the Cardinal Archbishop of Mainz rejoiced when they were able to add a thumb of St. Anna to their store. Luther himself tells us that "St. Anna was his idol"; and Calvin speaks of his mother's devotion to the saint. Her name was graven on many a parish church bell, and every pull at the ropes and clang of the bell was supposed to be a prayer to her to intercede. The Virgin and St. Anna brought in their train other saints who were also believed to be the true intercessors. The three bells of the church in which Luther was baptized bore the following inscriptions carved deeply in the brass:—"God help us; Mary have mercy. 1499." "Help us Anna, also St. Peter, St. Paul. 1509." "Help us God, Mary, Anna, St. Peter, Paul, Arnold, Stephan, Simon. 1509." The popular religion always represented Jesus, Mecum (Myconius) tells us, as the stern Judge who would convict and punish all those who had not secured righteousness by the intercession of the saints or by their own good works.

This revival of religion, crude as it was, and based on fear, had a distinct effect for good on a portion of the clergy, and led to a great reformation of morals among those who came under its influence. The papal Schism, which had lasted till 1449, had for one of its results the

[1] Schwaumkell, *Der Cultus der heiligen Anna am Ausgange des Mittelalters* (Freiburg, 1893).

weakening of all ecclesiastical discipline, and its consequences were seen in the growing immorality which pervaded all classes of the clergy. So far as one can judge, the revival of religion described above had not very much effect on the secular clergy. Whether we take the evidence from the chronicles of the time or from visitations of the bishops, the morals of the parish priests were extremely low, and the private lives of the higher clergy in Germany notoriously corrupt. The occupants of episcopal sees were for the most part the younger brothers of the great princes, and had been placed in the religious life for the sake of the ecclesiastical revenues. The author of the *Chronicles of the Zimmer Family* tells us that at the festive gatherings which accompanied the meetings of the Diet, the young nobles, lay and clerical, spent most of their time at dice and cards. As he passed through the halls, picking his way among groups of young nobles lying on the floor (for tables and chairs were rare in these days), he continually heard the young count call out to the young bishop, "Play up, parson; it is your turn." The same writer describes the retinue of a great prelate, who was always accompanied to the Diet by a concubine dressed in man's clothes. Nor were the older Orders of monks, the Benedictines and their offshoots, greatly influenced by the revival. It was different, however, with those Orders of monks who came into close contact with the people, and caught from them the new fervour. The Dominicans, the great preaching Order, were permeated by reform. The Franciscans, who had degenerated sadly from their earlier lives of self-denial, partook of a new life. Convent after convent reformed itself, and the inmates began to lead again the lives their founder had contemplated. The fire of the revival, however, burnt brightest among the Augustinian Eremites, the Order which Luther joined, and they represented, as none of the others did, all the characteristics of the new movement.

These Augustinian Eremites had a somewhat curious

history. They had nothing in common with St. Augustine save the name, and the fact that a Pope had given them the rule of St. Augustine as a basis for their monastic constitution. They had originally been hermits, living solitary lives in mountainous parts of Italy and of Germany. Many Popes had desired to bring them under conventual rule, and this was at last successfully done. They shared as no other Order had done in the revival of the second half of the fifteenth century, and exhibited in their lives all its religious characteristics. No Order of monks contained such devoted servants of the Virgin Mother. She was the patron along with St. Augustine. Her image stood in the chapter-house of every convent. The theologians of the Augustinian Eremites vied with those of the Franciscans in spreading the doctrine of the Immaculate Conception. They did much to spread the cult of the "Blessed Anna." They were devoted to the Papacy. One of their learned men, John of Palz, one of the two professors of theology in the Erfurt Convent when Luther entered it as a novice, was the most strenuous defender of the doctrine of Attrition and of the religious value of Indulgences. With all this their lives were more self-denying than those of most monks. They cultivated theological learning, and few Universities in Germany were without an Augustinian Eremite who acted as professor of philosophy or of theology. They also paid great attention to the art of preaching, and every large monastery had a special preacher who attracted crowds of the laity to the convent chapel. Their monasteries were usually placed in large towns; and their devout lives, their learning, and the popular gifts of their preachers, made them favourites with the townspeople. They were the most esteemed Order in Germany.

These last decades of the fifteenth century were the days of the resuscitation of the mendicant Orders and the revival of their power over the people. The better disposed among the princes and among the wealthier burghers invariably selected their confessors from the monks of the mendicant Orders, and especially from the Augustinian Eremites. The chapels of the Franciscans and of the Eremites were thronged, and those of the parish clergy were deserted. The common people took for their religious guides men who shared the new revival, and who proved their sincerity by self-denying labours. It was in vain that the Roman Curia published regulations insisting that every parishioner must confess to the priest of the parish at least once a year, and that it explained again and again that the personal character of the ministrant did not affect the efficacy of the sacraments administered by him. So long as poorly clad, emaciated, clean-living Franciscan or Eremite priests could be found to act as confessors, priests, or preachers, the people deserted the parish clergy, flocked to their confessionals, waited on their serving the Mass, and thronged their chapels to listen to their sermons. These decades were the time of the last revival of the mendicant monks, who were the religious guides in this flamboyant popular religion which is so much in evidence during our period.

§ 6. *A non-Ecclesiastical Religion.*

The third religious movement which belongs to the last decades of the fifteenth and the earlier decades of the sixteenth century was of a kind so different from, and even contrary to, what has just been described, that it is with some surprise that the student finds he must recognise its presence alongside of the other. It was the silent spread of a quiet, sincere, but non-ecclesiastical religion. Historians usually say nothing about this movement, and it is only a minute study of the town chronicles and of the records of provincial and municipal legislation that reveals its power and extent. It has always been recognised that Luther's father was a man of a deeply religious turn of mind, although he commonly despised the clergy, and thought that most monks were rogues or fools; but what is not recognised is that in this he represented thousands of quiet and pious Germans in all classes of society. We find traces of the silent, widespreading movement in the ecclesiastical legislation of German princes; in the police regulations, and in the provisions for the support of the poor among the burghers; in the constitutions and practices of the confraternities among the lower classes, and especially among the artisans in the towns; and in the numerous translations of the Vulgate into the vernacular.

The reforms sketched by the Councils of Constance and of Basel had been utterly neglected by the Roman Curia, and in consequence several German princes, while they felt the hopelessness of insisting on a general purification of the Church, resolved that these reforms should be carried out within their own dominions. As early as 1446, Duke William of Saxony had published decrees which interfered with the pretensions of the Church to be quite independent of the State. His regulations about the observance of the Sunday, his forbidding ecclesiastical courts to interfere with Saxon laymen, his stern refusal to allow any Saxon to appeal to a foreign jurisdiction, were all more or less instances of the interference of the secular power within what had been supposed to be the exclusive province of the ecclesiastical. He went much further, however. He enacted that it belonged to the secular power to see that parish priests and their superiors within his dominions lived lives befitting their vocation—a conception which was entirely at variance with the ecclesiastical pretensions of the Middle Ages. He also declared it to be within the province of the secular power to visit officially and to reform all the convents within his dominions. So far as proofs go, it is probable that these declarations about the rights of the civil authorities to exercise discipline over the parish priests and their superiors remained a dead letter. We hear of no such reformation being carried out. But the visitation of the Saxon monasteries was put in force in spite of the protests of the ecclesiastical powers. Andreas Proles would never have been able to carry out his proposals of reform in the convents of the Augustinian Eremites but for the support he received from the secular princes against his ecclesiastical superiors in Rome. The Dukes Ernest and Albrecht carried out Duke William's conceptions about the relation of the civil to the ecclesiastical authorities in their ordinances of 1483, and the Elector Frederick the Wise was heir to this ecclesiastical policy of his family.

The records of the Electorate of Brandenburg, investigated by Priebatsch and described by him in the *Zeitschrift für Kirchengeschichte*,[1] testify to the same ideas at work there. A pious prince like Frederick II. of Brandenburg removed unworthy Church dignitaries and reinstituted them, thus taking upon himself the oversight of the Church. Appeals to Rome were forbidden under penalties. Gradually under Frederick and his successors there arose what was practically a national Church of Brandenburg, which was almost completely under the control of the civil power and almost entirely separated from Roman control.

The towns also interfered in what had hitherto been believed to be within the exclusive domain of the ecclesiastical authorities. They recognised the harm which the numerous Church festivals and saints' days were doing to the people, and passed regulations about their observance, all of them tending to lessen the number of the days on which men were compelled by ecclesiastical law to be idle. When Luther pleaded in his *Address to the Nobility of the German Nation* for the abolition of the ecclesiastical laws enforcing idleness on the numerous ecclesiastical holy days, he only suggested an extension and wider application of the police regulations which were in force within his native district of Mansfeld.

This non-ecclesiastical feeling appears strongly in the change of view about Christian charity which marks the close of the fifteenth century.

Nothing shows how the Church of the thirteenth and fourteenth centuries had instilled the mind of Jesus into the peoples of Europe like the zeal with which they tried to do their duty by the poor, the sick, and the helpless.

[1] xix. p. 397 ff., xx. p. 159 ff., 329 ff., xxi. p. 43 ff.

Institutions, founded by individuals or by corporations, for the purpose of housing the destitute abounded, and men and women willingly dedicated themselves to the service of the unfortunate.

> "The Beguins crowned with flapping hats,
> O'er long-drawn bloodless faces blank,
> And gowns unwashed to wrap their lank
> Lean figures,"[1]

were sisters of mercy in every mediæval town. Unfortunately the lessons of the Church included the thought that begging was a Christian virtue; while the idea that because charity is taught by the law of Christ, its exercise must be everywhere superintended by ecclesiastics, was elevated to a definite principle of action, if not to something directly commanded by the law of God. The Reformation protested against these two ideas, and the silent anticipation of this protest is to be found in the non-ecclesiastical piety of the close of the fifteenth century.

The practice of begging, its toleration and even encouragement, was almost universal. In some of the benevolent institutions the sick and the pensioners were provided from the endowment with all the necessaries of life, but it was generally thought becoming that they should beg them from the charitable. The very fact of begging seemed to raise those who shared in it to the level of members of a religious association. St. Francis, the "imitator of Christ," had taught his followers to beg, and this great example sanctified the practice. It is true that the begging friars were always the butt of the satirists of the close of the fifteenth century. They delighted to portray the mendicant monk, with his sack, into which he seemed able to stuff everything: honey and spice, nutmegs, pepper, and preserved ginger, cabbage and eggs, poultry, fish, and new clothes, milk, butter, and cheese; cheese especially, and of all kinds—ewe's milk and goat's milk, hard cheese and soft cheese, large cheeses and small cheeses—were greedily

[1] *The Romance of the Rose*, ii. p. 168 (Temple Classics edition).

demanded by these "cheese hunters," as they were satirically called. On their heels tramped a host of semi-ecclesiastical beggars, all of them with professional names—men who begged for a church that was building, or for an altar-cloth, or to hansel a young priest at his first Mass; men who carried relics about for the charitable to kiss—some straw from the manger of Bethlehem, or a feather from the wing of the angel Gabriel; the Brethren of St. James, who performed continual and vicarious pilgrimages to Compostella, and sometimes robbed and murdered on the road; the Brethren of St. Anthony, who had the special privilege of wearing a cross and carrying a bell on their begging visits. These were all ecclesiastical beggars. The ordinary beggars did their best to obtain some share of the sanctity which surrounded the profession; they carried with them the picture of some saint, or placed the cockle-shell, the badge of a pilgrim, in their hats, and secured a quasi-ecclesiastical standing.[1] Luther expressed not merely his own opinion on this plague of beggars in his *Address to the Nobility of the German Nation*, but what had been thought and partially practised by quiet laymen for several decades. Some towns began to make regulations against promiscuous begging by able-bodied persons, provided work for them, seized their children, and taught them trades—all of which sensible doings were against the spirit of the mediæval Church.

The non-ecclesiastical religious feeling, however, appears much more clearly when the history of the charitable foundations is examined. The invariable custom during the earlier Middle Ages was that charitable bequests were left to the management of the Church and the clergy. At the close of the fifteenth century the custom began to alter. The change from clerical to lay management was at first probably due mainly to the degeneracy of the clergy, and to the belief that the funds set apart for the poor were not properly administered. The evidences of this are to be found in numerous instances of the civic

[1] v. Bezold, *Geschichte der deutschen Reformation*, pp. 95 f.

authorities attempting, and successfully, to take the management of charitable foundations out of the hands of ecclesiastical authorities, and to vest them in lay management. But this cannot have been the case always. We should rather say that it began to dawn upon men that although charity was part of the law of Christ, this did not necessarily mean that all charities must be placed under the control of the clergy or other ecclesiastical administrators. Hence we find during the later years of the fifteenth century continual instances of bequests for the poor placed in the hands of the town council or of boards of laymen. That this was done without any animus against the Church is proved by the fact that the same testator is found giving benefactions to foundations which are under clerical and to others under lay management. Out of the funds thus accumulated the town councils began a system of caring for the poor of the city, which consisted in giving tokens which could be exchanged for so much bread or woollen cloth, or shoes, or wood for firing, at the shops of dealers who were engaged for the purpose. How far this new and previously unheard of lay management, in what had hitherto been the peculiar possession of the clergy, had spread before the close of the fifteenth century, it is impossible to say. No archæologist has yet made an exhaustive study of the evidence lying buried in archives of the mediæval towns of Germany; but enough has been collected by Kriegk[1] and others to show that it had become very extensive. The laity saw that they were quite able to perform this peculiarly Christian work apart from any clerical direction.

Another interesting series of facts serves also to show the growth of a non-ecclesiastical religious sentiment. The later decades of the fifteenth century saw the rise of innumerable associations, some of them definitely religious,

[1] Kriegk, *Deutsches Bürgerthum im Mittelalter. Nach urkundlichen Forschungen und mit besonderer Beziehung auf Frankfurt a. M.*, pp. 161 ff. (Frankfurt, 1868). Uhlhorn, *Die christliche Liebesthätigkeit im Mittelalter*, pp. 431 ff. (Stuttgart, 1854).

and all of them with a religious side, which are unlike what we meet with earlier. They did not aim to be, like the praying circles of the Mystics or of the *Gottesfreunde*, *ecclesiolæ in ecclesia*, strictly non-clerical or even anti-clerical. They had no difficulty in placing themselves under the protection of the Church, in selecting the ordinary ecclesiastical buildings for their special services, and in employing priests to conduct their devotions; but they were distinctively lay associations, and lived a religious life in their own way, without any regard to the conceptions of the higher Christian life which the Church was accustomed to present to its devout disciples. Some were associations for prayer; others for the promotion of the "cult" of a special saint, like the confraternities dedicated to the Virgin Mother or the associations which spread the "cult" of the Blessed Anna; but by far the largest number were combinations of artisans, and resembled the workmen's "gilds" of the Roman Empire.

Perhaps one of the best known of these associations formed for the purpose of encouraging prayer was the "Brotherhood of the Eleven Thousand Virgins," commonly known under the quaint name of *St. Ursula's Little Ship*. The association was conceived by a Carthusian monk of Cologne, and it speedily became popular. Frederick the Wise was one of its patrons, his secretary, Dr. Pfeffinger, one of its supporters; it numbered its associates by the thousand; its praises were sung in a quaint old German hymn.[1] No money dues were exacted from its members. The only duty exacted was to pray regularly, and to learn to better one's life through the power of prayer. This was one type of the pious brotherhoods of the fifteenth century.

[1] Wackernagel, *Das deutsche Kirchenlied*, ii. 768–769; it began:

"Ein zeyt hort ich mit gütter mer
von einem schyfflin sagen,
Wie es mit tugenden also gar
kostlichen war beladen:
Zu dem schyfflin gewan ich ein hertz.
Ich fand dar yn vil güter gemertz
in mancher hande gaden."

It was the best known of its kind, and there were many others. But among the brotherhoods which bear testimony to the spread of a non-ecclesiastical piety none are more important than the confraternities which went by the names of *Kalands* or *Kalandsgilden* in North Germany and *Zechen* in Austria. These associations were useful in a variety of ways. They were unions for the practice of religion; for mutual aid in times of sickness; for defence in attack; and they also served the purpose of insurance societies and of burial clubs. It is with their religious side that we have here to do. It was part of the bond of association that all the brethren and sisters (for women were commonly admitted) should meet together at stated times for a common religious service. The brotherhood selected the church in which this was held, and so far as we can see the chapels of the Franciscans or of the Augustinian Eremites were generally chosen. Sometimes an altar was relegated to their exclusive use; sometimes, if the church was a large one, a special chapel. The interesting thing to be noticed is that the rules and the modes of conducting the religious services of the association were entirely in the hands of the brotherhood itself, and that these laymen insisted on regulating them in their own way. Luther has a very interesting sermon, entitled *Sermon upon the venerable Sacrament of the holy true Body of Christ and of the Brotherhoods*, the latter half of which is devoted to a contrast between good brotherhoods and evil ones. Those brotherhoods are evil, says Luther, in which the religion of the brethren is expressed in hearing a Mass on one or two days of the year, while by guzzling and drinking continually at the meetings of the brotherhood, they contrive to serve the devil the greater part of their time. A true brotherhood spreads its table for its poorer members, it aids those who are sick or infirm, it provides marriage portions for worthy young members of the association. He ends with a comparison between the true brotherhood and the Church of Christ. Theodore Kolde remarks that a careful monograph on the brotherhoods of the end of the fifteenth century in the light of this sermon of Luther's would afford great information about the popular religion of the period. Unfortunately, no one has yet attempted the task, but German archæologists are slowly preparing the way by printing, chiefly from MS. sources, accounts of the constitution and practices of many of these Kalands.

From all this it may be seen that there was in these last decades of the fifteenth and in the earlier of the sixteenth centuries the growth of what may be called a non-ecclesiastical piety, which was quietly determined to bring within the sphere of the laity very much that had been supposed to belong exclusively to the clergy. The *jus episcopale* which Luther claimed for the civil authorities in his tract on the *Liberty of the Christian Man*, had, in part at least, been claimed and exercised in several of the German principalities and municipalities; the practice of Christian charity and its management were being taken out of the hands of the clergy and entrusted to the laity; and the brotherhoods were making it apparent that men could mark out their religious duties in a way deemed most suitable for themselves without asking any aid from the Church, further than to engage a priest whom they trusted to conduct divine service and say the Masses they had arranged for.

The appearance of numerous translations of the Scriptures into the vernacular, unauthorised by the officials of the mediæval Church, and jealously suspected by them, appears to confirm the growth and spread of this non-ecclesiastical piety. The relation of the Church of the Middle Ages, earlier and later, to vernacular translations of the Vulgate is a complex question. The Scriptures were always declared to be the supreme source and authority for all questions of doctrines and morals, and in the earlier stages of the Reformation controversy the supreme authority of the Holy Scriptures was not supposed to be one of the matters in dispute between the contending parties. This is evident when we remember that the *Augsburg*

Confession, unlike the later confessions of the Reformed Churches, does not contain any article affirming the supreme authority of Scripture. That was not supposed to be a matter of debate. It was reserved for the Council of Trent, for the first time, to place *traditiones sine Scripto* on the same level of authority with the Scriptures of the Old and New Testaments. Hence, many of the small books, issued from convent presses for the instruction of the people during the decades preceding the Reformation, frequently declare that the whole teaching of the Church is to be found within the books of the Holy Scriptures.

It is, of course, undoubted that the mediæval Church forbade over and over again the reading of the Scriptures in the Vulgate and especially in the vernacular, but it may be asserted that these prohibitions were almost always connected with attempts to suppress heretical or schismatic revolts.[1]

On the other hand, no official encouragement of the reading of the Scriptures in the vernacular by the people can be found during the whole of the Middle Ages, nor any official patronage of vernacular translations. The utmost that was done in the way of tolerating, it can scarcely be said of encouraging, a knowledge of the vernacular Scriptures was the issue of Psalters in the vernacular, of Service-Books, and, in the fifteenth century, of the *Plenaria*—little books which contained translations of some of the paragraphs of the Gospels and Epistles read in the Church service accompanied with legends and popular tales. Translations of the Scriptures were continually reprobated

[1] The strongest prohibition of the vernacular Scriptures comes from the time of the Albigenses: "Prohibemus etiam, ne libros veteris Testamenti aut novi permittantur habere; nisi forte psalterium, vel brevarium pro divinis officiis, aut horas B. Mariæ aliquis ex devotione habere velit. Sed ne præmissos libros habeant in vulgari translatos, arctissime inhibemus" (*Conc. of Toulouse* of 1229, c. xiv.). The *Constitutiones Thomæ Arundel*, for the mediæval Church of England, declared: "Ordinamus ut nemo deinceps aliquem textum S. Scripturæ auctoritate sua in linguam Anglicanam vel aliam transferat per viam libri, libelli aut tractatus" (Art. VII., 1408 A.D.).

by Popes and primates for various reasons.[1] It is also unquestionable that a knowledge of the Scriptures in the vernacular, especially by uneducated men and women, was almost always deemed a sign of heretical tendency. "The third cause of heresy," says an Austrian inquisitor, writing about the end of the thirteenth century, "is that they translate the Old and New Testaments into the vulgar tongue; and so they learn and teach. I have heard and seen a certain country clown who repeated the Book of Job word for word, and several who knew the New Testament perfectly."[2] A survey of the evidence seems to lead to the conclusion that the rulers of the mediæval Church regarded a knowledge of the vernacular Scriptures with grave suspicion, but that they did not go the length of condemning entirely their possession by persons esteemed trustworthy, whether clergy, monks, nuns, or distinguished laymen.

Yet we have in the later Middle Ages, ever since Wiclif produced his English version, the gradual publication of the Scriptures in the vernaculars of Europe. This was specially so in Germany; and when the invention of printing had made the diffusion of literature easy, it is noteworthy that the earliest presses in Germany printed many more books for family and private devotion, many more *Plenaria,* and many more editions of the Bible than of the classics. Twenty-two editions of the Psalter in German appeared before 1509, and twenty-five of the Gospels and Epistles before 1518. No less than fourteen (some say seventeen) versions of the whole Bible were printed in High-German and three in Low-German during the last decades of the fifteenth and the earlier decades of the sixteenth century—all translations from the

[1] Pope Innocent III. reprobated the translation of the Scriptures into the vernacular, because ordinary laymen, and especially women, had not sufficient intelligence to understand them (*Epistolæ,* ii. 141); and Berthold, Archbishop of Mainz, in his diocesan edict of 1486, asserted that vernaculars were unable to express the profundity of the thoughts contained in the original languages of the Scriptures or in the Latin of the Vulgate.

[2] *Magna Bibliotheca Patrum* (Coloniæ Agrippinæ, 1618), xiii. 299.

Vulgate. The first was issued by John Metzel in Strassburg in 1466. Then followed another Strassburg edition in 1470, two Augsburg editions in 1473, one in the Swiss dialect in 1474, two in Augsburg in 1477, one in Augsburg in 1480, one in Nürnberg in 1483, one in Strassburg in 1485, and editions in Augsburg in 1487, 1490, 1507, and 1518. A careful comparison of these printed vernacular Bibles proves that the earlier editions were independent productions; but as edition succeeded edition the text became gradually assimilated until there came into existence a German Vulgate, which was used indiscriminately by those who adhered to the mediæval Church and those who were dissenters from it. These German versions were largely, but by no means completely, displaced by Luther's translation. The Anabaptists, for example, retained this German Vulgate long after the publication of Luther's version, and these pre-Reformation German Bibles were to be found in use almost two hundred years after the Reformation.[1]

Whence sprang the demand for these vernacular versions of the Holy Scriptures? That the leaders of the mediæval Church viewed their existence with alarm is evident from the proclamation of the Primate of Germany, Berthold of Mainz, issued in 1486, ordering a censorship of books with special reference to vernacular translations of the Scriptures.[2] On the other hand, there is no evidence that these versions were either wholly or in great part the work of enemies of the mediæval Church. The mediæval *Brethren*, as they called themselves (Waldenses, Picards, Wiclifites, Hussites, etc., were names given to them very indiscriminately by the ecclesiastical authorities), had translations of the Scriptures both in the Romance and in the Teutonic languages as early as the close of the thirteenth century. The records of inquisitors and of councils prove it. But there is no evidence to connect any of these German versions, save, perhaps, one at Augs-

[1] Walther, *Die deutsche Bibelübersetzung des Mittelalters* (Brunswick, 1889).
[2] Gudenus, *Codex Diplomatic. Anecdota*, iv. 469–475 (1758).

burg, and that issued by the Koburgers in Nürnberg, with these earlier translations. The growing spread of education in the fifteenth century, and, above all, the growth of a non-ecclesiastical piety which claimed to examine and to judge for itself, demanded and received these numerous versions of the Holy Scriptures in the vulgar tongue.[1] The "common man" had the word of God in his hands, could read, meditate, and judge for himself. The effect of the presence of these vernacular Scriptures is apt to be exaggerated.[2] The Humanist, Conrad Celtes, might threaten the priests that the Bible would soon be seen in every village tavern; but we know that in these days of early printing a complete Bible must have been too expensive to be purchased by a poor man. Still he could get the Gospels or the Epistles, or the Psalter; and there is evidence, apart from the number of editions, that the people were buying and were studying the Scriptures. Preachers were exhorted to give the meaning of the passages of Scripture read in Church to prevent the people being confused by the different ways in which the text was translated in the Bibles in their possession. Stories were told of peasants, like Hans Werner, who worsted their parish priests in arguments drawn from Scripture. The ecclesiastical authorities were undoubtedly anxious, and their anxiety was shared by many who desired a reformation in life and manners, but dreaded any revolutionary movement. It was right that the children should be fed with the Bread of Life, but Mother Church ought to keep the bread-knife in her hands lest the children cut their fingers. Some publishers of the translations inserted prefaces saying that the contents of the volumes should be understood in the way taught by the Church, as was done in the *Book of the Gospels*,

[1] Walther, *Die deutsche Bibelübersetzungen des Mittelalters* (Brunswick, 1889).

[2] Sebastian Brand, *Narrenschiff*, Preface, lines 1–4:

> "Alle Land ist jetz voll heilger Schrift,
> Und was der seelen Heil betrifft
> Bibel und heilger Vater Lehr
> Und andrer frommen Bücher mehr."

published at Basel in 1514. But in spite of all a lay religion had come into being, and laymen were beginning to think for themselves in matters where ecclesiastics had hitherto been considered the sole judges.

§ 7. *The "Brethren."*

There was another type of religious life and pious association which existed, and which seems in one form or other to have exercised a great influence among the better class of artisans, and more especially among the printers of Augsburg, Nürnberg, and Strassburg.

It is probable that this type of piety had at least three roots.

(*a*) We can trace as far back as the closing years of the thirteenth century, in many parts of Germany, the existence of nonconformists who, on the testimony of inquisitors, lived pious lives, acted righteously towards their neighbours, and believed in all the articles of the Christian faith, but repudiated the Roman Church and the clergy. Their persecutors gave them a high character. "The heretics are known by their walk and conversation: they live quietly and modestly; they have no pride in dress; their learned men are tailors and weavers; they do not heap up riches, but are content with what is necessary; they live chastely; they are temperate in eating and drinking; they never go to taverns, nor to public dances, nor to any such vanities; they refrain from all foul language, from backbiting, from thoughtless speech, from lying and from swearing." The list of objections which they had to usages of the mediæval Church are those which would occur to any evangelical Protestant of this century. They professed a simple evangelical creed; they offered a passive resistance to the hierarchical and priestly pretensions of the clergy; they were careful to educate their children in schools which they supported; they had vernacular translations of the Scriptures, and committed large portions to memory; they conducted their religious service in the vernacular, and it was one of the accusations made against them that they alleged that the word of God was as profitable when read in the vernacular as when studied in Latin. It is also interesting to know that they were accused of visiting the leper-houses to pray with the inmates, and that in some towns they had schools for the leper children.[1] They called themselves the *Brethren*. The societies of the *Brethren* had never died out. During the fourteenth and fifteenth centuries they were continually subject to local and somewhat spasmodic persecutions, when the ecclesiastical could secure the aid of the secular authorities to their schemes of repression, which was not always possible. They were strongly represented among the artisans in the great cities, and there are instances when the civic authorities gave them one of the churches of the towns for their services. The liability to intermittent persecution led to an organisation whereby the *Brethren*, who were for the time being living in peace, made arrangements to receive and support those who were able to escape from any district where the persecution raged. These societies were in correspondence with their brethren all over Europe, and were never so active as during the last decades of the fifteenth and the first quarter of the sixteenth century.

(*b*) As early as the times of Meister Eckhart (d. 1327), of his disciples Tauler (d. 1361) and Suso (d 1366), of the mysterious "Friend of God in the Oberland" and his associates (among them the Strassburg merchant Rulman Merswin (d. 1382)), and of the Brussels curate John Ruysbroeck (d. 1381), the leaders of the mediæval Mystics had been accustomed to gather their followers together into praying circles; and the custom was perpetuated long after their departure. How these pious associations continued to exist in the half century before the Reformation, and what forms their organisation took, it seems impossible to say with any accuracy. The school system of the *Brethren*

[1] *Magna Bibliotheca Patrum* (Coloniæ Agrippinæ, 1618), vol. xiii. pp. 299-301.

of the Common Lot, which always had an intimate connection with the *Gottesfreunde*, in all probability served to spread the praying circles which had come down from the earlier Mystics. It seems to have been a custom among these *Brethren of the Common Lot* to invite their neighbours to meet in their schoolrooms or in a hall to listen to religious discourses. There they read and expounded the New Testament in the vernacular. They also read extracts from books written to convey popular religious instruction. They questioned their audience to find out how far their hearers understood their teaching, and endeavoured by question and answer to discover and solve religious difficulties. These schools and teachers had extended all over Germany by the close of the fifteenth century, and their effect in quickening and keeping alive personal religion must have been great.

(*c*) Then, altogether apart from the social and semi-political propaganda of the Hussites, there is evidence that ever since the circulation of the encyclic letter addressed by the Taborites in November 1431 to all Christians in all lands, and more especially since the foundation of the *Unitas Fratrum* in 1452, there had been constant communication between Bohemia and the scattered bodies of evangelical dissenters throughout Germany. Probably historians have credited the Hussites with more than their due influence over their German sympathisers. The latter had arrived at the conclusion that tithes ought to be looked upon as free-will offerings, that the cup should be given to the laity, etc., long before the movements under the leadership of Wiclif and of Huss. But the knowledge that they had sympathisers and brethren beyond their own land must have been a source of strength to the German nonconformists.

Our knowledge of the times is still too obscure to warrant us in making very definite statements about the proportionate effect of these three religious sources of influence on the small communities of *Brethren* or evangelical dissenters from the mediæval Church which maintained a precarious existence at the close of the Middle Ages. There is one curious fact, however, which shows that there must have been an intimate connection between the Waldenses of Savoy and France, the *Brethren* of Germany, and the *Unitas Fratrum* of Bohemia. They all used the same catechism for the instruction of their children in divine things. So far as can be ascertained, this small catechism was first printed in 1498, and editions can be traced down to 1530. It exists in French, Italian, German, and Bohemian. The inspiration drawn from the earlier Mystics and *Gottesfreunde* is shown by the books circulated by the *Brethren*. They made great use of the newly discovered art of printing to spread abroad small mystical writings on personal religion, and translations of portions of the Holy Scriptures. They printed and circulated books which had been used in manuscript among the Mystics of the fourteenth century, such as the celebrated *Masterbook*, single sermons by Tauler, Prayers and Rules for holy living extracted from his writings, as well as short tracts taken from the later Mystics, like the *Explanation of the Ten Commandments*. It is also probable that some of the many translations of the whole or portions of the Bible which were in circulation in Germany before the days of Luther came from these praying circles. The celebrated firm of Nürnberg printers, the Koburgers, who published so many Bibles, were the German printers of the little catechism used by the *Brethren*; and, as has been said, the Anabaptists, who were the successors of these associations, did not use Luther's version, but a much older one which had come down to them from their ancestors.

The members of these praying circles welcomed the Lutheran Reformation when it came, but they can scarcely be said to have belonged to it. Luther has confessed how much he owed to one of their publications, *Die deutsche Theologie*; and what helped him must have benefited others. The organisation of a Lutheran Church, based on civil divisions of the Empire, gave the signal for a thorough reorganisation of the members of these old associations who refused to have anything to do with a State Church They formed the best side of the very mixed and very much misunderstood movement which later was called Anabaptism, and thus remained outside of the two great divisions into which the Church of the Reformation separated. This religious type existed and showed itself more especially among the artisans in the larger towns of Germany.

It must not be supposed that these four classes of religious sentiment which have been found existing during the later decades of the fifteenth and the early decades of the sixteenth centuries can always be clearly distinguished from each other. Religious types cannot be kept distinct, but continually blend with each other in the most unexpected way. Humanism and Anabaptism seem as far apart as they can possibly be; yet some of the most noted Anabaptist leaders were distinguished members of the Erasmus circle at Basel. Humanism and delicate clinging to the simple faith of childhood blended in the exquisite character of Melanchthon. Luther, *after* his stern wrestle with self-righteousness in the convent at Erfurt, believed that, had his parents been dead, he could have delivered their souls from purgatory by his visits to the shrines of the saints at Rome. The boy Mecum (Myconius) retained only so much of his father's teaching about the *free* Grace of God that he believed an Indulgence from Tetzel would benefit him if he could obtain it without paying for it. There is everywhere and at all times a blending of separate types of religious faith, until a notable crisis brings men suddenly face to face with the necessity of a choice. Such a crisis occurred during the period we call the Reformation, with the result that the leaders in that great religious revival found that the truest theology after all was what had expressed itself in hymns and prayers, in revivalist sermons and in fireside teaching, and that they felt it to be their duty as theologians to give articulate dogmatic expression to what their fathers had been content to find inarticulately in the devotional rather than in the intellectual sphere of the mediæval religious life.

Such was the religious atmosphere into which Luther was born, and which he breathed from his earliest days. Every element seems to have shared in creating and shaping his religious history, and had similar effects doubtless on his most distinguished and sympathetic followers.

CHAPTER VI.

HUMANISM AND REFORMATION.[1]

§ 1. *Savonarola.*

WHEN the Italian Humanism seemed about to become a mere revival of ancient Paganism, with its accompaniments of a cynical sensualism on the one hand, and the blindest trust in the occult sciences on the other, a great preacher arose in Florence who recalled men to Christianity and to Christian virtue.

Girolamo Savonarola was an Italian, a countryman of Giaocchino di Fiore, of Arnold of Brescia, of Francis of Assisi, of John of Parma, and, like them, he believed himself to be favoured with visions apocalyptic and other. He belonged to a land over which, all down through the Middle Ages, had swept popular religious revivals, sudden, consuming, and transient as prairie fires. When a boy, he

[1] SOURCES: Casanova and Guasti, *Poesie di G. Savonarola* (Florence, 1862); *Scella di Prediche e Scritti di Frà G. Savonarola, con nuovi Documenti intorno alla sua Vita*, by Villari and Casanova (Florence, 1898); Bayonne, *Œuvres Spirituelles choisies de Jerome Savonarola* (Paris, 1879); *The Workes of Sir Thomas More . . . written by him in the Englyshe tonge* (London, 1557); Erasmus, *Opera Omnia*, ed. Le Clerc (Leyden, 1703–1706); Nichols, *The Epistles of Erasmus from his earliest letters to his fifty-first year, arranged in order of time* (London, 1901); *Enchiridion Militis Christiani* (Cambridge, 1685); *The whole Familiar Colloquies of Erasmus* (London, 1877); Sir Thomas More, *Utopia* (Temple Classics Series).

LATER WORKS: Villari, *Girolamo Savonarola*, 2 vols. (Florence, 1887–1888; Eng. trans., London, 1890); Seebohm, *The Oxford Reformers: John Colet, Erasmus, and Thomas More*, etc. (London, 1887); Drummond, *Erasmus, his life and character* (London, 1873); Woltmann, *Holbein and his Time* (London, 1872); Froude, *Life and Letters of Erasmus* (London, 1894); Amiel, *Un libre penseur du 16 siècle: Érasme* (Paris, 1889); Emerton, *Desiderius Erasmus of Rotterdam* (New York, 1899); *The Cambridge History of English Literature*, III. i. and vii., with bibliographies (Cambridge, 1909).

had quivered at seeing the pain in the world around him; he had shuddered as he passed the great grim palaces of the Italian despots, where the banqueting hall was separated from the dungeon by a floor so thin that the groans of the prisoners mingled with the tinkle of the silver dishes and the wanton conversation of the guests. He had been destined by his family for the medical profession, and the lad was set to master the writings of Thomas Aquinas and the Arabian commentaries on Aristotle—the gateway in those days to a knowledge of the art of healing. The *Summa* of the great Schoolman entranced him, and insensibly drew him towards theology; but outwardly he did not rebel against the lot in life marked out for him. A glimpse of a quiet resting-place in this world of pain and evil had come to him, but it vanished, swallowed up in the universal gloom, when Roberto Strozzi refused to permit him to marry his daughter Laodamia. There remained only rest on God, study of His word, and such slight solace as music and sonnet-writing could bring. His devotion to Thomas Aquinas impelled him to seek within a Dominican convent that refuge which he passionately yearned for, from a corrupt world and a corrupt Church. There he remained buried for long years, reading and re-reading the Scriptures, poring over the *Summa*, drinking in the New Learning, almost unconsciously creating for himself a philosophy which blended the teachings of Aquinas with the Neo-Platonism of Marsiglio Ficino and of the Academy, and planning how he could best represent the doctrines of the Christian religion in harmony with the natural reason of man.

When at last he became a great preacher, able to sway heart and conscience, it should not be forgotten that he was mediæval to the core. His doctrinal teaching was based firmly on the theology of Thomas Aquinas. His intellectual conception of faith, his strong belief in the divine predestination and his way of expressing it, his view of Scripture as possessing manifold meanings, were all defined for him by the great Dominican Schoolman.

He held strongly the mediæval idea that the Church was an external political unity, ruled by the Bishop of Rome, to whom every human soul must be subject, and whom everyone must obey save only when commands were issued contrary to a plain statement of the evangelical law. He expounded the fulness of and the slight limitations to the authority of the Pope exactly as Thomas and the great Schoolmen of the thirteenth century had done, though in terms very different from the canonists of the Roman Curia at the close of the Middle Ages. Even his appreciation of the Neo-Platonist side of Humanism could be traced back to mediæval authorities; for at all times the writings of the pseudo-Dionysius had been a source of inspiration to the greater Schoolmen.

His scholarship brought him into relation with the Humanist leaders in Florence, the earnest tone of his teaching and the saintliness of his character attracted them, his deep personal piety made them feel that he possessed something which they lacked; while no Neo-Platonist could be repelled by his claim to be the recipient of visions from on high.

The celebrated Humanists of Florence became the disciples of the great preacher. Marsiglio Ficino himself, the head of the Florentine Academy, who kept one lamp burning before the bust of Plato and another before an image of the Virgin, was for a time completely under his spell. Young Giovanni Pico della Mirandola's whole inner life was changed through his conversations with the Prior of San Marco. He reformed his earlier careless habits. He burnt five books of wanton love-songs which he had composed before his conversion.[1] He prayed daily at fixed hours, and he wrote earnestly to his nephew on the importance of prayer for a godly life:

"'I stir thee not,' he says, 'to that prayer that standeth in many words, but to that prayer which in the secret chamber of the mind, in the privy-closet of the soul, with

[1] *The Workes of Sir Thomas More, Knyght, sometyme Lorde Chancellour of England, Wrytten by him in the Englysh tonge* (London, 1557), p. 6 C.

every affect speaketh to God; which in the most lightsome darkness of contemplation not only presenteth the mind to the Father, but also uniteth it with Him by unspeakable ways which only they know who have assayed. Nor care I how long or how short thy prayer be; but how effectual, how ardent, and rather interrupted and broken between with sighs, than drawn on length with a number of words. . . . Let no day pass but thou once at the leastwise present thyself to God in prayer. . . . What thou shalt in thy prayer ask of God, both the Holy Spirit which prayeth for us and also thine own necessity shall every hour put in thy mind.'"[1]

He studied the writings of Thomas Aquinas, which contained the favourite theology of Savonarola, and spoke of the great Schoolman as a "pillar of truth."[2] He handed over the third part of his estates to his nephew, and lived plainly on what remained, that he might give largely in charity.[3] He made Savonarola his almoner, who on his behalf gave alms to destitute people and marriage portions to poor maidens.[4] He had frequent thoughts of entering the Dominican Order, and

"On a time as he walked with his nephew, John Francis, in a garden at Ferrara, talking of the love of Christ, he broke out with these words: 'Nephew,' said he, 'this will I show thee; I warn thee keep it secret; the substance I have left after certain books of mine are finished, I intend to give out to poor folk, and, fencing myself with the crucifix, barefoot, walking about the world, in every town and castle I purpose to preach of Christ.'"[5]

It is also recorded that he made a practice of scourging himself; especially "on those days which represent unto us the Passion and Death that Christ suffered for our sake, he beat and scourged his own flesh in remembrance of that great benefit, and for cleansing his old offences."[6] But above all things he devoted himself to a diligent study of

[1] *The Workes of Sir Thomas More, Knyght, sometyme Lorde Chancellour of England, Wrytten by him in the Englysh tonge* (London, 1557), p. 13 C.
[2] *Ibid.* 5 A. [3] *Ibid.* 6 B. [4] *Ibid.* 6 C.
[5] *Ibid.* 8 D. [6] *Ibid.* 6 D.

the Holy Scriptures, and commended the practice to his nephew:

"'Thou mayest do nothing more pleasing to God, nothing more profitable to thyself, than if thine hand cease not day and night to turn and read the volumes of Holy Scripture. There lieth privily in them a certain heavenly strength, quick and effectual, which, with a marvellous power, transformeth and changeth the readers' mind into the love of God, if they be clean and lowly entreated.'"[1]

The great Platonist forsook Plato for St. Paul, whom he called the "glorious Apostle."[2] When he died he left his lands to one of the hospitals in Florence, and desired to be buried in the hood of the Dominican monks and within the Convent of San Marco.

Another distinguished member of the Florentine Academy, Angelo Poliziano, was also one of Savonarola's converts. We find him exchanging confidences with Pico, both declaring that love and not knowledge is the faculty by which we learn to know God:

"'But now behold, my well-beloved Angelo,' writes Pico, 'what madness holdeth us. Love God (while we be in this body) we rather may, than either know Him, or by speech utter Him. In loving Him also we more profit ourselves; we labour less and serve Him more. And yet had we rather always by knowledge never find that thing we seek, than by love possess that thing which also without love were in vain found.'"[3]

Poliziano, like Pico, had at one time some thoughts of joining the Dominican Order. He too was buried at his own request in the cowl of the Dominican monk in the Convent of San Marco.

Lorenzo de Medici, who during his life had made many attempts to win the support of Savonarola, and had always been repulsed, could not die without entreating the great preacher to visit him on his deathbed and grant him absolution.

[1] *The Workes of Sir Thomas More, Knyght, sometyme Lorde Chancellour of England, Wrytten by him in the Englysh tonge* (London, 1557), 13 F.

[2] *Ibid.* 12 D.

[3] *Ibid.* 7 D.

Italian Humanism was for the moment won over to Christianity by the Prior of San Marco. Had the poets and the scholars, the politicians and the ecclesiastics, the State and the Church, not been so hopelessly corrupt, there might have been a great renovation of mankind, under the leadership of men who had no desire to break the political unity of the mediæval Church. For it can scarcely be too strongly insisted that Savonarola was no Reformation leader in the more limited sense of the phrase. The movement he headed has much more affinity with the crude revival of religion in Germany in the end of the fifteenth century, than with the Reformation itself; and the aim of the reorganisation of the Tuscan congregation of the Dominicans under Savonarola has an almost exact parallel in the creation of the congregation of the Augustinian Eremites under Andreas Proles and Johann Staupitz. The whole Italian movement, as might be expected, was conducted by men of greater intelligence and refinement. It had therefore less sympathy than the German with pilgrimages, relics, the niceties of ceremonial worship, and the cult of the vulgarly miraculous; but it was not the less mediæval on these accounts. It was the death rather than the life and lifework of Savonarola that was destined to have direct effect on the Reformation soon to come beyond the Alps; for his martyrdom was a crowning evidence of the impossibility of reforming the Church of the Middle Ages apart from the shock of a great convulsion. "Luther himself," says Professor Villari, "could scarcely have been so successful in inaugurating his Reform, had not the sacrifice of Savonarola given a final proof that it was hopeless to hope in the purification of Rome."[1]

§ 2. *John Colet.*

While Savonarola was at the height of his influence in Florence, there chanced to be in Italy a young Englishman,

[1] *Life and Times of Girolamo Savonarola*, p. 771 (Eng. trans., London, 1897).

John Colet, son of a wealthy London merchant who had been several times Lord Mayor. He had gone there, we may presume, like his countrymen Grocyn and Linacre, to make himself acquainted with the New Learning at its fountainhead. There is no proof that he went to Florence or ever saw the great Italian preacher; but no stranger could have visited Northern Italy in 1495 without hearing much of him and of his work. Colet's whole future life in England bears evidence that he did receive a new impulse while he was in Italy, and that of such a kind as could have come only from Savonarola. What Erasmus tells us of his sojourn there amply confirms this. Colet gave himself up to the study of the Holy Scriptures; he read carefully those theologians of the ancient Church specially acceptable to the Neo-Platonist Christian Humanists; he studied the pseudo-Dionysius, Origen, and Jerome. What is more remarkable still in a foreign Humanist come to study in Italy, he read diligently such English classics as he could find in order to prepare himself for the work of preaching when he returned to England. The words of Erasmus imply that the impulse to do all this came to him when he was in Italy, and there was no one to impart it to him but the great Florentine.

When Colet returned to England in 1496, he began to lecture at Oxford on the Epistles of St. Paul. His method of exposition, familiar enough after Calvin had introduced it into the Reformed Church, was then absolutely new, and proves that he was an original and independent thinker. His aim was to find out the *personal* message which the writer (St. Paul) had sent to the Christians at Rome; and this led him to seek for every trace which revealed the personality of the Apostle to the Gentiles. It was equally imperative to know what were the surroundings of the men to whom the Epistle was addressed, and Colet studied Suetonius to find some indications of the environment of the Roman Christians. He had thus completely freed himself from the Scholastic habit of using the Scriptures as a mere collection of isolated texts to be employed in proving doctrines or moral rules constructed or imposed by the Church, and it is therefore not surprising to find that he never lards his expositions with quotations from the Fathers. It is a still greater proof of his daring that he set aside the allegorising methods of the Schoolmen,—methods abundantly used by Savonarola,—and that he did so in spite of his devotion to the writings of the pseudo-Dionysius. He was the first to apply the critical methods of the New Learning to discover the exact meaning of the books of the Holy Scriptures. His treatment of the Scriptures shows that however he may have been influenced by Savonarola and by the Christian Humanists of Italy, he had advanced far beyond them, and had seen, what no mediæval theologian had been able to perceive, that the Bible is a personal and not a dogmatic revelation. They were mediæval: he belongs to the Reformation circle of thinkers. Luther, Calvin, and Colet, whatever else separates them, have this one deeply important thought in common. Further, Colet discarded the mediæval conception of a mechanical inspiration of the text of Scripture, in this also agreeing with Luther and Calvin. The inspiration of the Holy Scriptures was something mysterious to him. "The Spirit seemed to him by reason of its majesty to have a peculiar method of its own, singularly, absolutely free, blowing where it lists, making prophets of whom it will, yet so that the spirit of the prophets is subject to the prophets."[1]

Colet saw clearly, and denounced the abounding evils which were ruining the Church of his day. The Convocation of the English Church never listened to a bolder

[1] Seebohm, *The Oxford Reformers: John Colet, Erasmus, and Thomas More; being a history of their fellow-work*, 2nd ed. p. 125 (London, 1869). Mr. Seebohm seems to think that the Reformers clung to the mediæval conception of the inspiration of Scripture. Calvin held the same ideas as Colet, and expressed them in the same way. Cf. his comments on Matt. xxvii. 9: "Quomodo Hieremiæ nomen obrepserit, me nescire fateor, *nec anxie laboro*: certe Hieremiæ nomen *errore* positum esse pro Zacharia, res ipsa ostendit"; and his comment on Acts vii. 16: "quare hic locus corrigendus est."

sermon than that preached to them by the Dean of St. Paul's in 1512—the same year that Luther addressed an assembly of clergy at Leitzkau. The two addresses should be compared. The same fundamental thought is contained in both—that every true reformation must begin with the individual man. Colet declared that reform must begin with the bishops, and that once begun it would spread to the clergy and thence to the laity; "for the body follows the soul; and as are the rulers in a State, such will the people be." He urged that what was wanted was the enforcement of ecclesiastical laws which were already in existence. Ignorant and wicked men were admitted to holy orders, and there were laws prohibiting this. Simony was creeping "like a cancer through the minds of priests, so that most are not ashamed in these days to get for themselves great dignities by petitions and suits at court, rewards and promises"; and yet strict laws against the evil were in existence. He proceeded to enumerate the other flagrant abuses—the non-residence of clergy, the worldly pursuits and indulgences of the clergy; the scandals and vices of the ecclesiastical law-courts; the infreqency of provincial councils to discuss and remedy existing evils; the wasting of the patrimony of the Church on sumptuous buildings, on banquets, on enriching kinsfolk, or on keeping hounds. The Church had laws against all these abuses, but they were not enforced, and could not be until the bishops amended their ways. His scheme of reform was to put in operation the existing regulations of Canon Law. "The diseases which are now in the Church were the same in former ages, and there is no evil for which the holy fathers did not provide excellent remedies; there are no crimes in prohibition of which there are not laws in the body of Canon Law." Such was his definite idea of reform in this famous Convocation sermon.

But he had wider views. He desired the diffusion of a sound Christian education, and did the best that could be done by one man to promote it, by spending his private fortune in founding St. Paul's school, which he characteristically left in charge of a body of laymen. He longed to see a widespread preaching in the vernacular, and believed that the bishops should show an example in this clerical duty. It is probable that he wished the whole service to be in the vernacular, for it was made a charge against him that he taught his congregation to repeat the Lord's Prayer in English. Besides, he had clearly grasped the thought, too often forgotten by theologians of all schools, that the spiritual facts and forces which lie at the roots of the Christian life are one thing, and the intellectual conceptions which men make to explain these facts and forces are another, and a much less important thing; that men are able to be Christians and to live the Christian life because of the former and not because of the latter. He saw that, while dogma has its place, it is at best the alliance of an immortal with a mortal, the union between that which is unchangeably divine and the fashions of human thought which change from one age to another. For this reason he thought little of the Scholastic Theology of his days, with its forty-three propositions about the nature of God and its forty-five about the nature of man before and after the Fall, each of which had to be assented to at the risk of a charge of heresy. "Why do you extol to me such a man as Aquinas? If he had not been so very arrogant, indeed, he would not surely so rashly and proudly have taken upon himself to define all things. And unless his spirit had been somewhat worldly, he would not surely have corrupted the whole teaching of Christ by mixing it with his profane philosophy." The Scholastic Theology might have been scientific in the thirteenth century, but the "scientific" is the human and changing element in dogma, and the old theology had become clearly unscientific in the sixteenth. Therefore he was accustomed to advise young theological students to keep to the Bible and the Apostles' Creed, and let divines, if they liked, dispute about the rest; and he taught Erasmus to look askance at Luther's reconstruction of the Augustinian theology.

But no thinking man, however he may flout at philosophy and dogma, can do without either; and Colet was no exception to the general rule. He has placed on record his detestation of Aquinas and his dislike of Augustine, and we may perhaps see in this a lack of sympathy with a prominent characteristic of the theology of Latin Christianity from Tertullian to Aquinas and Occam, to say nothing of developments since the Reformation. The great men who built up the Western Church were almost all trained Roman lawyers. Tertullian, Cyprian, Augustine, Gregory the Great (whose writings form the bridge between the Latin Fathers and the Schoolmen) were all men whose early training had been that of a Roman lawyer,—a training which moulded and shaped all their thinking, whether theological or ecclesiastical. They instinctively regarded all questions as a great Roman lawyer would. They had the lawyer's craving for exact definitions. They had the lawyer's idea that the primary duty laid upon them was to enforce obedience to authority, whether that authority expressed itself in external institutions or in the precise definitions of the correct ways of thinking about spiritual truths. No branch of Western Christendom has been able to free itself from the spell cast upon it by these Roman lawyers of the early centuries of the Christian Church.

If the ideas of Christian Roman lawyers, filtering slowly down through the centuries, had made the Bishops of Rome dream that they were the successors of Augustus, at once Emperor and Pontifex Maximus, master of the bodies and of the souls of mankind, they had also inspired the theologians of the Mediæval Church with the conception of an intellectual imperialism, where a system of Christian thought, expressed with legal precision, could bind into a comprehensive unity the active intelligence of mankind. Dogmas thus expressed can become the instruments of a tyranny much more penetrating than that of an institution, and so Colet found. In his revolt he turned from the Latins to the Greeks, and to that thinker who was furthest removed from the legal precision of statement which was characteristic of Western theology.

It is probable that his intercourse with the Christian Humanists of Italy, and his introduction to Platonists and to Neo-Platonism, made him turn to the writings of the pseudo-Dionysius; but it is certain that he believed at first that the author of these quaint mystical tracts was the Dionysius who was one of the converts of St. Paul at Athens, and that these writings embodied much of the teaching of the Apostle to the Gentiles, and took the reader back to the first generation of the Christian Church. After he had learned from Grocyn that the author of the *Celestial* and the *Terrestrial Hierarchies* could not have been the convert of St. Paul, and that the writings could not be earlier than the sixth century, he still regarded them as evidence of the way in which a Christian philosopher could express the thoughts which were current in Christianity one thousand years before Colet's time. The writings could be used as a touchstone to test usages and opinions prevalent at the close of the Middle Ages, when men were still subject to the domination of the Scholastic Theology, and as justification for rejecting them.

They taught him two things which he was very willing to learn: that the human mind, however it may be able to feel after God, can never comprehend Him, nor imprison His character and attributes in propositions—stereotyped aspects of thoughts—which can be fitted into syllogisms; and that such things as hierarchy and sacraments are to be prized not because they are in themselves the active sources and centres of mysterious powers, but because they faintly symbolise the spiritual forces by which God works for the salvation of His people. Colet applied to the study of the writings of the pseudo-Dionysius a mind saturated with simple Christian truth gained from a study of the Holy Scriptures, and especially of the Epistles of St. Paul; and the very luxuriance of imagination and bewildering confusion of symbolism in these writings, their elusiveness as opposed to the precision of Thomas Aquinas or of John Duns the Scot, enabled him the more easily to find in them the germs of his own more definite opinions.

When one studies the abstracts of the *Hierarchies*[1]—which Colet wrote out from memory—with the actual text of the books themselves, it is scarcely surprising to find how much there is of Colet and how little of Dionysius.[2]

While it is impossible to say how far Colet, and the Christian Humanists who agreed with him, would have welcomed the principles of a Reformation yet to come, it can be affirmed that he held the same views on two very important points. He did not believe in a priesthood in the mediæval nor in the modern Roman sense of the word, and his theory of the efficacy and meaning of the sacraments of the Christian Church was essentially Protestant.

According to Colet, there was no such thing as a mediatorial priesthood whose essential function it was to approach God on men's behalf and present their offerings to Him. The duty of the Christian priesthood was ministerial; it was to declare the love and mercy of God to their fellowmen, and to strive for the purification, illumination, and salvation of mankind by constant preaching of the truth and diffusion of gospel light, even as Christ strove. He did not believe that priests had received from God the power of absolving from sins. "It must be heedfully remarked," he says, "lest bishops be presumptuous, that it is not the part of men to loose the bonds of sins; nor does the power belong to them of loosing or binding anything,"—the truth Luther set forth in his Theses against Indulgences.

[1] Colet's abstracts of the *Celestial* and of the *Terrestrial Hierarchies* have been published by the Rev. J. H. Lupton (London, 1869), from the MS. at St. Paul's School. Mr. Lupton has also published Colet's treatise *On the Sacraments of the Church* (London, 1867). The best edition of the works of the pseudo-Dionysius is that of Balthasar Corderius, S.J., published at Venice in 1755. The actual writings of the pseudo-Dionysius are not extensive; the editor has added translations, notes, scholia, commentaries, etc., and his folio edition contains more than one thousand pages.

[2] "The radical conception is most often due to Dionysius; the passages represent the effervescence produced by the Dionysian conceptions in Colet's mind. . . . The fire was indeed very much Colet's. I find passages which burn in Colet's abstract, freeze in the original."—Seebohm, *The Oxford Reformers*, p. 76 (2nd ed., London, 1869).

Colet is even more decided in his repudiation of the sacramental theories of the mediæval Church. The Eucharist is not a sacrifice, but a commemoration of the death of our Lord, and a symbol of the union and communion which believers have with Him, and with their fellow-men through Him. Baptism is a ceremony which symbolises the believer's change of heart and his vow of service to his Master, and signifies "the more excellent baptism of the inner man"; and the duty of sponsors is to train children in the knowledge and fear of God.[1]

We are told that the Lollards delighted in Colet's preaching; that they advised each other to go to hear him; and that attendance at the Dean's sermons was actually made a charge against them. Colet was no Lollard himself; indeed, he seems to have once sat among ecclesiastical judges who condemned Lollards to death;[2] but the preacher who taught that tithes were voluntary offerings, who denounced the evil lives of the monks and the secular clergy; who hated war, and did not scruple to say so; whose sermons were full of simple Bible instruction, must have recalled many memories of the old Lollard doctrines. For Lollardy had never died out in England: it was active in Colet's days, leavening the country for the Reformation which was to come.

Nor should it be forgotten, in measuring the influence of Colet's personality on the coming Reformation, that William Tyndale was one of his favourite pupils, and that he persuaded Erasmus to turn from purely classical studies to edit the New Testament and the early Christian Fathers.

[1] Cf. Mr. Lupton's translation of the *Ecclesiastical Hierarchies*, c. ii. If it be permissible to adduce evidence from the *Utopia* of Sir Thomas More, the anti-sacerdotal views of the Oxford Reformers went much further. In *Utopia* confession was made to the head of the family and not to the priests; women could be priests; divorce from bed and board was permitted. Cf. the Temple Classics edition, p. 116 (divorce), p. 148 (women-priests), p. 152 (confession).

[2] Seebohm, *The Oxford Reformers*, p. 221 (2nd ed. 1869).

§ 3. *Erasmus.*

Erasmus, as has often been said, was a "man by himself"; yet he may be regarded as representing one, and perhaps the most frequent, type of Christian Humanism. His character will always be matter of controversy; and his motives may, without unfairness, be represented in an unfavourable light,—a "great scholar but a petty-minded man," is a verdict for which there is abundant evidence. Such was the final judgment of his contemporaries, mainly because he refused to take a definite side in the age when the greatest controversy which has convulsed Western Europe since the downfall of the old Empire seemed to call on every man to range himself with one party or other. Our modern judgment must rest on a different basis. In calmer days, when the din of battle has almost died away, it is possible to recognise that to refuse to be a partisan *may* indicate greatness instead of littleness of soul, a keener vision, and a calmer courage. We cannot judge the man as hastily as his contemporaries did. Still there is evidence enough and to spare to back their verdict. Every biographer has admitted that it is hopeless to look for truth in his voluminous correspondence. His feelings, hopes, intentions, and actual circumstances are described to different correspondents at the same time in utterly different ways. He was always writing for effect, and often for effect of a rather sordid kind. He seldom gave a definite opinion on any important question without attempting to qualify it in such a manner that he might be able, if need arose, to deny that he had given it. No man knew better how to use "if" and "but" so as to shelter himself from all responsibility. He had the ingenuity of the cuttle-fish to conceal himself and his real opinions, and it was commonly used to protect his own skin. All this may be admitted; it can scarcely be denied.

Yet from his first visit to England (1498) down to his practical refusal of a Cardinal's Hat from Pope Adrian VI., on condition that he would reside at Rome and assist in fighting the Reformation, Erasmus had his own conception of what a reformation of Christianity really meant, and what share in it it was possible for him to take. It must be admitted that he held to this idea and kept to the path he had marked out for himself with a tenacity of purpose which did him honour. It was by no means always that of personal safety, still less the road to personal aggrandisement. It led him in the end where he had never expected to stand. It made him a man despised by both sides in the great controversy; it left him absolutely alone, friendless, and without influence. He frequently used very contemptible means to ward off attempts to make him diverge to the right or left; he abandoned many of his earlier principles, or so modified them that they were no longer recognisable. But he was always true to his own idea of a reformation and of his life-work as a reformer.

Erasmus was firmly convinced that Christianity was above all things something practical. It had to do with the ordinary life of mankind. It meant love, humility, purity, reverence,—every virtue which the Saviour had made manifest in His life on earth. This early "Christian philosophy" had been buried out of sight under a Scholastic Theology full of sophistical subtleties, and had been lost in the mingled Judaism and Paganism of the popular religious life, with its weary ceremonies and barbarous usages. A true reformation, he believed, was the moral renovation of mankind, and the one need of the age was to return to that earlier purer religion based on a real inward reverence for and imitation of Christ. The man of letters, like himself, he conceived could play the part of a reformer, and that manfully, in two ways. He could try, by the use of wit and satire, to make contemptible the follies of the Schoolmen and the vulgar travesty of religion which was in vogue among the people. He could also bring before the eyes of all men that earlier and purer religion which was true Christianity. He could edit the New Testament, and enable men to read the very words which Jesus spoke and

Paul preached, make them see the deeds of Jesus and hear the apostolic explanations of their meaning. He could say:

"Only be teachable, and you have already made much way in this (the Christian) Philosophy. It supplies a spirit for a teacher, imparted to none more readily than to the simple-minded. Other philosophies, by the very difficulty of their precepts, are removed out of the range of most minds. No age, no sex, no condition of life is excluded from this. The sun itself is not more common and open to all than the teaching of Christ. For I utterly dissent from those who are unwilling that the Sacred Scriptures should be read by the unlearned translated into their vulgar tongue, as though Christ had taught such subtleties that they can scarcely be understood even by a few theologians, or as though the strength of the Christian religion consisted in men's ignorance of it. The mysteries of kings it may be safer to conceal, but Christ wished His mysteries to be published as openly as possible. I wish that even the weakest woman should read the Gospel—should read the Epistles of Paul. And I wish these were translated into all languages, so that they might be read and understood, not only by Scots and Irishmen, but also by Turks and Saracens. To make them understood is surely the first step. It may be that they might be ridiculed by many, but some would take them to heart. I long that the husbandman should sing portions of them to himself as he follows the plough, that the weaver should hum them to the tune of his shuttle, that the traveller should beguile with their stories the tedium of his journey."[1]

The scholar who became a reformer could further make plain, by editing and publishing the writings of the earlier Christian Fathers, what the oldest Christian Theology had been before the Schoolmen spoiled it.

The conception that a reformation of Christianity was mainly a renovation of morals, enabled the Christian Humanist to keep true to the Renaissance idea that the writers of classical antiquity were to be used to aid the work of ameliorating the lot of mankind. The Florentine circle spoke of the inspiration of Homer, of Plato, and of

[1] Erasmus, *Opera Omnia* (Leyden, 1703–1706), v. 140.

Cicero, and saw them labouring as our Lord had done to teach men how to live better lives. Pico and Reuchlin had gone further afield, and had found illuminating anticipations of Christianity, in this sense and in others, among the Hebrews, the Egyptians, and perhaps the Brahmins. Erasmus was too clear-sighted to be drawn into any alliance with Oriental mysticism or cabalistic speculations; but he insisted on the aid which would come from the Christian reformer making full use of the ethical teaching of the wise men of Greece and Rome in his attempt to produce a moral renovation in the lives of his fellows. Socrates and Cicero, each in his own day and within his own sphere, had striven for the same moral renovation that Christianity promised, and, in this sense at least, might be called Christians before Christ. So persuaded was Erasmus of their affinity with the true spirit of Christianity, that he declared that Cicero had as much right to a high place in heaven as many a Christian saint, and that when he thought of the Athenian martyr he could scarcely refrain from saying, *Sancte Socrates, Ora pro nobis.*

It must be remembered also that Erasmus had a genuine and noble horror of war, which was by no means the mere shrinking of a man whose nerves were always quivering. He preached peace as boldly and in as disinterested a fashion as did his friend John Colet. He could not bear the thought of a religious war. This must not be forgotten in any estimate of his conduct and of his relation to the Reformation. No man, not even Luther, scattered the seeds of revolution with a more reckless hand, and yet a thorough and steadfast dislike to all movements which could be called revolutionary was one of the most abiding elements in his character. He hated what he called the "tumult." He had an honest belief that all public evils in State and Church must be endured until they dissolve away quietly under the influence of sarcasm and common sense, or until they are removed by the action of the responsible authorities. He was clear-sighted enough to see that an open and avowed attack on the papal supremacy, or on any of the more cherished doctrines and usages of the mediæval Church, must end in strife and in bloodshed, and he therefore honestly believed that no such attack ought to be made.

When all these things are kept in view, it is possible to see what conception Erasmus had about his work as a reformer, with its possibilities and its limitations. He adhered to it tenaciously all his life. He held it in the days of his earlier comparative obscurity. He maintained it when he had been enthroned as the prince of the realm of learning. He clung to it in his discredited old age. No one can justify the means he sometimes took to prevent being drawn from the path he had marked out for himself; but there is something to be said for the man who, through good report and evil, stuck resolutely to his view of what a reformation ought to be, and what were the functions of a man of letters who felt himself called to be a reformer. Had Luther been gifted with that keen sense of prevision with which Erasmus was so fatally endowed, would he have stood forward to attack Indulgences in the way he did? It is probable that it would have made no difference in his action; but he did not think so himself. He said once, "No good work comes about by our own wisdom; it begins in dire necessity. I was forced into mine; but had I known then what I know now, ten wild horses would not have drawn me into it." The man who leads a great movement of reform may see the distant, but has seldom a clear vision of the nearer future. He is one who feels the slow pressure of an imperious spiritual power, who is content with one step at a time, and who does not ask to see the whole path stretching out before him.

Erasmus lost both his parents while he was a child, and never enjoyed the advantages of a home training. He was driven by deceit or by self-deception into a monastery when he was a lad. He escaped from the clutches of the monastic life when he was twenty years of age, broken in health, and having learned to know human nature on its bad side and to trade on that knowledge. He was one of the loneliest of mortals, and trusted in no one but himself. With one great exception, he had no friendship which left an enduring influence on his character. From childhood he taught himself in his own way; when he grew to manhood he planned and schemed for himself; he steadfastly refused to be drawn into any kind of work which he did not like for its own sake; he persistently shunned every entanglement which might have controlled his action or weighted him with any responsibility. He stands almost alone among the Humanists in this. All the others were officials, or professors, or private teachers, or jurists, or ecclesiastics. Erasmus was nothing, and would be nothing, but a simple man of letters.

Holbein has painted him so often that his features are familiar. Every line of the clearly cut face suggests demure sarcasm—the thin lips closely pressed together, the half-closed eyelids, and the keen glance of the scarcely seen blue eyes. The head is intellectual, but there is nothing masculine about the portrait—nothing suggesting the massiveness of the learned burgher Pirkheimer; or the jovial strength of the Humanist *landsknecht* Eobanus Hessus; or the lean wolf-like tenacity of Hutten, the descendant of robber-knights; or the steadfast homely courage of Martin Luther. The dainty hands, which Holbein drew so often, and the general primness of his appearance, suggest a descent from a long line of maiden aunts. The keen intelligence was enclosed in a sickly body, whose frailty made continuous demands on the soul it imprisoned. It needed warm rooms with stoves that sent forth no smell, the best wines, an easy-going horse, and a deft servant; and to procure all these comforts Erasmus wrote the sturdiest of begging letters and stooped to all kinds of flatteries.

The visit which Erasmus paid to England in 1499 was the turning-point in his life. He found himself, for the first time, among men who were his equals in learning and his superiors in many things. "When I listen to my friend Colet," he says, "it seems to me like listening to Plato himself. Who does not marvel at the complete mastery of the sciences in Grocyn? What could be keener, more profound, and more searching than the judgment of Linacre? Has Nature ever made a more gentle, a sweeter, or a happier disposition than Thomas More's?" He made the acquaintance of men as full of the New Learning as he was himself, who hated the Scotist theology more bitterly than he did, and who nevertheless believed in a pure, simple Christian philosophy, and were earnest Christians. They urged him to join them in their work, and we can trace in the correspondence of Erasmus the growing influence of Colet. The Dean of St. Paul's made Erasmus the decidedly Christian Humanist he became, and impressed on him that conception of a reformation which, leaving external things very much as they were, undertook a renovation of morals. He never lost the impress of Colet's stamp.

It would appear from one of Erasmus' letters that Colet urged him to write commentaries on some portions of the New Testament; but Erasmus would only work in his own way; and it is probable that his thoughts were soon turned to preparing an edition of the New Testament in Greek. The task was long brooded over; and he had to perfect himself in his knowledge of the language.

This determination to undertake no work for which he was not supremely fitted, together with his powers of application and acquisition, gave Erasmus the reputation of being a strong man. He was seen to be unlike any other Humanist, whether Italian or German. He had no desire merely to reproduce the antique, or to confine himself within the narrow circle in which the "Poets" of the Renaissance worked. He put ancient culture to modern uses. Erasmus was no arm-chair student. He was one of the keenest observers of everything human—the Lucian or the Voltaire of the sixteenth century. From under his half-closed eyelids his quick glance seized and retained the salient characteristics of all sorts and conditions of men and women. He described theologians, jurists and philosophers, monks and parish priests, merchants and soldiers.

husbands and wives, women good and bad, dancers and diners, pilgrims, pardon-sellers, and keepers of relics; the peasant in the field, the artisan in the workshop, and the vagrant on the highway. He had studied all, and could describe them with a few deft phrases, as incisive as Dürer's strokes, with an almost perfect style, and with easy sarcasm.

This application of the New Learning to portray the common life, combined with his profound learning, made Erasmus the idol of the young German Humanists. They said that he was more than mortal, that his judgment was infallible, and that his work was perfect. They made pilgrimages to visit him. An interview was an event to be talked about for years; a letter, a precious treasure to be bequeathed as an heirloom. Some men refused to render the universal homage accorded by scholars and statesmen, by princes lay and clerical. Luther scented Pelagian theology in his annotations; he scorned Erasmus' wilful playing with truth; he said that the great Humanist was a mocker who poured ridicule upon everything, even on Christ and religion. There was some ground for the charge. His sarcasm was not confined to his *Praise of Folly* or to his *Colloquies.* It appears in almost everything that he wrote—even in his Paraphrases of the New Testament.

That such a man should have felt himself called upon to be a reformer, that this Saul should have appeared among the prophets, is in itself testimony that he lived during a great religious crisis, and that the religious question was the most important one in his days.

The principal literary works of Erasmus meant to serve the reformation he desired to see are:—two small books, *Enchiridion militis christiani* (*A Handbook of the Christian Soldier*, or *A Pocket Dagger for the Christian Soldier*—it may be translated either way), first printed in 1503, and *Institutio Principis Christiani* (1518); his *Encomium Moriæ* (*Praise of Folly*, 1511); his edition of the *New Testament*, or *Novum Instrumentum* (1516), with prefaces and paraphrases; and perhaps many of the dialogues in his *Colloquia* (1519).

Erasmus himself explains that in the *Enchiridion* he wrote to counteract the vulgar error of those who think that religion consists in ceremonies and in more than Jewish observances, while they neglect what really belongs to piety. The whole aim of the book is to assert the individual responsibility of man to God apart from any intermediate human agency. Erasmus ignores as completely as Luther would have done the whole mediæval thought of the mediatorial function of the Church and its priestly order. In this respect the book is essentially Protestant and thoroughly revolutionary. It asserts in so many words that much of the popular religion is pure paganism:

"One worships a certain Rochus, and why? because he fancies he will drive away the plague from his body. Another mumbles prayers to Barbara or George, lest he fall into the hands of his enemy. This man fasts to Apollonia to prevent the toothache. That one gazes upon an image of the divine Job, that he may be free from the itch. . . . In short, whatever our fears and our desires, we set so many gods over them, and these are different in different nations. . . . This is not far removed from the superstition of those who used to vow tithes to Hercules in order to get rich, or a cock to Æsculapius to recover from an illness, or who slew a bull to Neptune for a favourable voyage. The names are changed, but the object is the same."[1]

In speaking of the monastic life, he says:

"'Love,' says Paul, 'is to edify your neighbour,' . . . and if this only were done, nothing could be more joyous or more easy than the life of the 'religious'; but now this life seems

[1] Erasmus, *Opera Omnia* (Leyden, 1703–1706), v. 26. The sarcasm of Erasmus finds ample confirmation in Kerler's *Die Patronate der Heiligen* (Ulm, 1905), where St. Rochus, with fifty-nine companion saints, is stated to be ready to hear the prayers of those who dread the plague; St. Apollonia, with eighteen others, takes special interest in all who are afflicted with toothache; the holy Job, with thirteen companions, is ready to cure the itch; and St. Barbara with St. George figure as protectors against a violent death; cf. pp. 266–273, 419–422, 218–219, 358–359. The translations are taken from Emerton's *Erasmus.*

gloomy, full of Jewish superstitions, not in any way free from the vices of laymen and in some ways more corrupt. If Augustine, whom they boast of as the founder of their order, came to life again, he would not recognise them; he would exclaim that he had never approved of this sort of life, but had organised a way of living according to the rule of the Apostles, not according to the superstition of the Jews."[1]

The more one studies the *Praise of Folly*, the more evident it becomes that Erasmus did not intend to write a satire on human weakness in general: the book is the most severe attack on the mediæval Church that had, up to that time, been made; and it was meant to be so. The author wanders from his main theme occasionally, but always to return to the insane follies of the religious life sanctioned by the highest authorities of the mediæval Church. Popes, bishops, theologians, monks, and the ordinary lay Christians, are all unmitigated fools in their ordinary religious life. The style is vivid, the author has seen what he describes, and he makes his readers see it also. He writes with a mixture of light mockery and bitter earnestness. He exposes the foolish questions of the theologians; the vices and temporal ambitions of the Popes, bishops, and monks; the stupid trust in festivals, pilgrimages, indulgences, and relics. The theologians, the author says, are rather dangerous people to attack, for they come down on one with their six hundred conclusions and command him to recant, and if he does not they declare him a heretic forthwith. The problems which interest them are:

"Whether there was any instant of time in the divine generation? . . . Could God have taken the form of a woman, a devil, an ass, a gourd, or a stone? How the gourd could have preached, wrought miracles, hung on the cross?"[2]

He jeers at the Popes and higher ecclesiastics:

"Those supreme Pontiffs who stand in the place of Christ, if they should try to imitate His life, that is, His

[1] Erasmus, *Opera Omnia*, v. 35-36. [2] *Ibid.* iv. 465.

poverty, His toil, His teaching, His cross, and His scorn of this world . . . what could be more dreadful! . . . We ought not to forget that such a mass of scribes, copyists, notaries, advocates, secretaries, mule-drivers, grooms, money-changers, procurers, and gayer persons yet I might mention, did I not respect your ears,—that this whole swarm which now burdens—I beg your pardon, honours—the Roman See would be driven to starvation."[1]

As for the monks:

"The greater part of them have such faith in their ceremonies and human traditions, that they think one heaven is not reward enough for such great doings. . . . One will show his belly stuffed with every kind of fish; another will pour out a hundred bushels of psalms; another will count up myriads of fasts, and make up for them all again by almost bursting himself at a single dinner. Another will bring forward such a heap of ceremonies that seven ships would hardly hold them; another boast that for sixty years he has never touched a penny except with double gloves on his hands. . . . But Christ will interrupt their endless bragging, and will demand—'Whence this new kind of Judaism?'

"They do all things by rule, by a kind of sacred mathematics; as, for instance, how many knots their shoes must be tied with, of what colour everything must be, what variety in their garb, of what material, how many straws'-breadth to their girdle, of what form and of how many bushels' capacity their cowl, how many fingers broad their hair, and how many hours they sleep. . . ."[2]

He ridicules men who go running about to Rome, Compostella, or Jerusalem, wasting on long and dangerous journeys money which might be better spent in feeding the hungry and clothing the naked. He scoffs at those who buy Indulgences, who sweetly flatter themselves with counterfeit pardons, and who have measured off the duration of Purgatory without error, as if by a water-clock, into ages, years, months, and days, like the multiplication table.[3] Is it religion to believe that if any one pays a penny out of

[1] Erasmus, *Opera Omnia*, iv. 481–484. [2] *Ibid.* iv. 471–474.
[3] *Ibid.* iv. 445.

what he has stolen, he can have the whole slough of his life cleaned out at once, and all his perjuries, lusts, drunkennesses, all his quarrels, murders, cheats, treacheries, falsehoods, bought off in such a way that he may begin over again with a new circle of crimes? The reverence for relics was perhaps never so cruelly satirised as in the Colloquy, *Peregrinatio Religionis Ergo.*

It must be remembered that this bitter satire was written some years before Luther began the Reformation by an attack on Indulgences. It may seem surprising how much liberty the satirist allowed himself, and how much was permitted to him. But Erasmus knew very well how to protect himself. He was very careful to make no definite attack, and to make no mention of names. He was always ready to explain that he did not mean to attack the Papacy, but only bad Popes; that he had the highest respect for the monastic life, and only satirised evil-minded monks; or that he reverenced the saints, but thought that reverence ought to be shown by imitating them in their lives of piety. He could say all this with perfect truth. Indeed, it is likely that with all his scorn against the monks, Erasmus, in his heart, believed that a devout Capuchin or Franciscan monk lived the ideal Christian life. He seems to say so in his Colloquy, *Militis et Carthusiani.* He wrote, moreover, before the dignitaries of the mediæval Church had begun to take alarm. Liberal Churchmen who were the patrons of the New Learning had no objection to see the vices of the times and the Church life of the day satirised by one who wrote such exquisite latinity. In all his more serious work Erasmus was careful to shelter himself under the protection of great ecclesiastics.

Erasmus was not the only scholar who had proposed to publish a correct edition of the Holy Scriptures. The great Spaniard, Cardinal Ximenes, had announced that he meant to bring out an edition of the Holy Scriptures in which the text of the Vulgate would appear in parallel columns along with the Hebrew and the Greek. The prospectus of this Complutensian Polyglot was issued as early as 1502; the work was finished in 1517, and was published in Spain in 1520 and in other lands in 1522. Erasmus was careful to dedicate the first edition of his *Novum Instrumentum* (1516) to Pope Leo X., who graciously received it. He sent the second edition to the same Pope in 1519, accompanied by a letter in which he says:

"I have striven with all my might to kindle men from those chilling argumentations in which they had been so long frozen up, to a zeal for theology which should be at once more pure and more serious. And that this labour has so far not been in vain I perceive from this, that certain persons are furious against me, who cannot value anything they are unable to teach and are ashamed to learn. But, trusting to Christ as my witness, whom my writings above all would guard, to the judgment of your Holiness, to my own sense of right and the approval of so many distinguished men, I have always disregarded the yelpings of these people. Whatever little talent I have, it has been, once for all, dedicated to Christ: it shall serve His glory alone; it shall serve the Roman Church, the prince of that Church, but especially your Holiness, to whom I owe more than my whole duty."

He dedicated the various parts of the *Paraphrases* of the New Testament to Cardinal Campeggio, to Cardinal Wolsey, to Henry VIII., to Charles V., and to Francis I. of France. He deliberately placed himself under the protection of those princes, ecclesiastical and secular, who could not be suspected of having any revolutionary designs against the existing state of things in Church or in State.

In all this he was followed for the time being by the most distinguished Christian Humanists in England, France, and Germany. They were full of the brightest hopes. A Humanist Pope sat on the throne of St. Peter, young Humanist kings ruled France and England, the Emperor Maximilian had long been the patron of German Humanism, and much was expected from his grandson Charles, the young King of Spain. Erasmus, the acknowledged prince of Christian learning, was enthusiastically supported by Colet and More in England, by Buddæus and Lefèvre in

France by Johann Staupitz, Cochlæus, Thomas Murner, Jerome Emser, Conrad Mutianus, and George Spalatin in Germany. They all believed that the golden age was approaching, when the secular princes would forbid wars, and the ecclesiastical lay aside their rapacity, and when both would lead the peoples of Europe in a reformation of morals and in a re-establishment of pure religion. Their hopes were high that all would be effected without the "tumult" which they all dreaded, and when the storm burst, many of them became bitter opponents of Luther and his action. Luther found no deadlier enemies than Thomas Murner and Jerome Emser. Others, like George Spalatin, became his warmest supporters. Erasmus maintained to the end his attitude of cautious neutrality. In a long letter to Marlianus, Bishop of Tuy in Spain, he says that he does not like Luther's writings, that he feared from the first that they would create a "tumult," but that he dare not altogether oppose the reformer, "because he feared that he might be fighting against God." The utmost that he could be brought to do after the strongest persuasions, was to attack Luther's Augustinian theology in his *De Libero Arbitrio*, and to insinuate a defence of the principle of ecclesiastical authority in the interpretation of Scripture, and a proof that Luther had laid too much stress on the element of "grace" in human actions. He turned away from the whole movement as far as he possibly could, protesting that for himself he would ever cling to the Roman See.

The last years of his life were spent in excessive literary work—in editing the earlier Christian Fathers; he completed his edition of Origen in 1536, the year of his death. He settled at Louvain, and found it too hotly theological for his comfort; went to Basel; wandered off to Freiburg; then went back to Basel to die. After his death he was compelled to take the side he had so long shrunk from. Pope Paul IV. classed him as a notorious heretic, and placed on the first papal "Index" "all his commentaries, notes, scholia, dialogues, letters, translations, books, and writings, even when they contain nothing against religion or about religion."

We look in vain for any indication that those Christian Humanists perceived that they were actually living in a time of revolution, and were really standing on the edge of a crater which was about to change European history by its eruption. Sir Thomas More's instincts of religious life were all mediæval. Colet had persuaded him to abandon his earlier impulse to enter a monastic order, but More wore a hair shirt next his skin till the day of his death. Yet in his sketch of an ideal commonwealth, he expanded St. Paul's thought of the equality of all men before Christ into the conception that no man was to be asked to work more than six hours a day, and showed that religious freedom could only flourish where there was nothing in the form of the mediæval Church. The lovable and pious young Englishman never imagined that his academic dream would be translated into rude practical thoughts and ruder actions by leaders of peasant and artisan insurgents, and that his *Utopia* (1515), within ten years after its publication, and ten years before his own death (1535), would furnish texts for communist sermons, preached in obscure public-houses or to excited audiences on village greens. The satirical criticisms of the hierarchy, the monastic orders, and the popular religious life, which Erasmus flung broadcast so recklessly in his lighter and more serious writings, furnished the weapons for the leaders in that "tumult" which he had dreaded all his days; and when he complained that few seemed to care for the picture of a truly pious life, given in his *Enchiridion*, he did not foresee that it would become a wonderfully popular book among those who renounced all connection with the See of Rome to which the author had promised a life-long obedience. The Christian Humanists, one and all, were strangely blind to the signs of the times in which they lived.

No one can fail to appreciate the nobility of the purpose to work for a great moral renovation of mankind which the Christian Humanists ever kept before them, or refuse to see that they were always and everywhere preachers of righteousness. When we remember the century and a half of wars, so largely excited by ecclesiastical motives, which desolated Europe during the sixteenth and seventeenth centuries, few can withhold their sympathy from the Christian Humanist idea that the path of reformation lay through a great readjustment of the existing conditions of the religious life, rather than through ecclesiastical revolution to a thorough-going reconstruction; although we may sadly recognise that the dynastic struggles of secular princes, the rapacity and religious impotence of Popes and ecclesiastical authorities, and the imperious pressure of social and industrial discontent, made the path of peace impossible. But what must fill us with surprise is that the Christian Humanists seemed to believe with a childlike innocence that the constituted authorities, secular and ecclesiastical, would lead the way in this peaceful reform, mainly because they were tinged with Humanist culture, and were the patrons of artists and men of learning. Humanism meant to Pope Leo x. and to the young Archbishop of Mainz additional sources of enjoyment, represented by costly pictures, collections of MSS., and rare books, the gratification of their taste for jewels and cameos, to say nothing of less harmless indulgences, and the adulation of the circle of scholars whom they had attracted to their courts; and it meant little more to the younger secular princes.

It is also to be feared that the Christian Humanists had no real sense of what was needed for that renovation of morals, public and private, which they ardently desired to see. Pictures of a Christian life lived according to the principles of reason, sharp polemic against the hierarchy, and biting mockery of the stupidity of the popular religion, did not help the masses of the people. The multitude in those early decades of the sixteenth century were scourged by constant visitations of the plague and other new and strange diseases, and they lived in perpetual dread of a

Turkish invasion. The fear of death and the judgment thereafter was always before their eyes. What they wanted was a sense of God's forgiveness for their sins, and they greedily seized on Indulgences, pilgrimages to holy places, and relic-worship to secure the pardon they longed for. The aristocratic and intellectual reform, contemplated by the Christian Humanists, scarcely appealed to them. Their longing for a certainty of salvation could not be satisfied with recommendations to virtuous living according to the rules of Neo-Platonic ethics. It is pathetic to listen to the appeals made to Erasmus for something more than he could ever give:

"'Oh! Erasmus of Rotterdam, where art thou?' said Albert Dürer. 'See what the unjust tyranny of earthly power, the power of darkness, can do. Hear, thou knight of Christ! Ride forth by the side of the Lord Christ; defend the truth, gain the martyr's crown! As it is, thou art but an old man. I have heard thee say that thou hast given thyself but a couple more years of active service; spend them, I pray, to the profit of the gospel and the true Christian faith, and believe me the gates of Hell, the See of Rome, as Christ has said, will not prevail against thee.'"[1]

The Reformation needed a man who had himself felt that commanding need of pardon which was sending his fellows travelling from shrine to shrine, who could tell them in plain homely words, which the common man could understand, how each one of them could win that pardon for himself, who could deliver them from the fear of the priest, and show them the way to the peace of God. The Reformation needed Luther.

[1] Leitschuh, *Albrecht Dürer's Tagebuch der Reise in die Niederlande* (Leipzig, 1884), p. 84.

BOOK II.

THE REFORMATION.

CHAPTER I.

LUTHER TO THE BEGINNING OF THE CONTROVERSY ABOUT INDULGENCES.[1]

§ 1. *Why Luther was successful as the Leader in a Reformation.*

REFORMATION had been attempted in various ways. Learned ecclesiastical Jurists had sought to bring it about in the fifteenth century by what was called *Conciliar Reform.*

[1] SOURCES: Melanchthon, *Historia de vita et actis Lutheri* (Wittenberg, 1545, in the *Corpus Reformatorum,* vi.); Mathesius, *Historien von . . . Martini Lutheri, Anfang, Lere, Leben und Sterben* (Prague, 1896); Myconius, *Historia Reformationis 1517–1542* (Leipzig, 1718); Ratzeberger, *Geschichte über Luther und seine Zeit* (Jena, 1850); Killian Leib, *Annales von 1503–1523* (vols. vii. and ix. of v. Aretin's *Beiträge zur Geschichte und Litteratur,* Munich, 1803–1806); Wrampelmeyer, *Tagebuch über Dr. Martin Luther, geführt von Dr. Conrad Cordatus, 1537* (Halle, 1885); Caspar Cruciger, *Tabulæ chronologicæ actorum M. Lutheri* (Wittenberg, 1553); Förstemann, *Neues Urkundenbuch zur Geschichte der evangelischen Kirchenreformation* (Hamburg, 1842); Kolde, *Analecta Lutherana* (Gotha, 1883); G. Loesche, *Analecta Lutherana et Melanchthoniana* (Gotha, 1892); Löscher. *Vollständige Reformations-Acta und Documenta* (Leipzig, 1720–1729); Enders, *Dr. Martin Luther's Briefwechsel,* 5 vols. (Frankfurt, 1884–1893); De Wette, *Dr. Martin Luther's Briefe, Sendschreiben und Bedenken,* 5 vols. (Berlin, 1825–1828); J. Cochlæus (Rom. Cath.), *Commentarius de actis et scriptis M. Lutheri . . . ab anno 1517 usque ad annum 1537* (St. Victor prope Moguntiam, 1549); V. L. Seckendorf, *Commentarius . . . de Lutheranismo* (Frankfurt, 1692); *Constitutiones Fratrum Heremitarum Sancti Augustini* (Nürnberg, 1504).

LATER BOOKS: J. Köstlin, *Martin Luther, sein Leben und seine*

The sincerity and ability of the leaders of the movement are unquestioned; but they had failed ignominiously, and the Papacy with all its abuses had never been so powerful ecclesiastically as when its superior diplomacy had vanquished the endeavour to hold it in tutelage to a council.

The Christian Humanists had made their attempt—preaching a moral renovation and the application of the existing laws of the Church to punish ecclesiastical wrongdoers. Colet eloquently assured the Anglican Convocation that the Church possessed laws which, if only enforced, contained provisions ample enough to curb and master the ills which all felt to be rampant. Erasmus had held up to scorn the debased religious life of the times, and had denounced its Judaism and Paganism. Both were men of scholarship and genius; but they had never been able to move society to its depths, and awaken a new religious life, which was the one thing needful.

History knows nothing of revivals of moral living apart from some new religious impulse. The motive power needed has always come through leaders who have had communion with the unseen. Humanism had supplied a superfluity of teachers; the times needed a prophet. They received one; a man of the people; bone of their bone, and flesh of their flesh; one who had himself lived that popular religious life with all the thoroughness of a strong, earnest nature, who had sounded all its depths and tested its capacities, and gained in the end no relief for his

Schriften, 2 vols. (Berlin, 1889); Th. Kolde, *Martin Luther. Eine Biographie*, 2 vols. (Gotha, 1884, 1893); A. Hausrath, *Luther's Leben*, 2 vols. (Berlin, 1904); Lindsay, *Luther and the German Reformation* (Edinburgh, 1900); Kolde, *Friedrich der Weise und die Anfänge der Reformation mit archivalischen Beilagen* (Erlangen, 1881), and *Die deutsche Augustiner-Congregation und Johann v. Staupitz* (Gotha, 1879); A. Hausrath, *M. Luther's Romfahrt nach einem gleichzeitigen Pilgerbuche* (Berlin, 1894); Oergel, *Vom jungen Luther* (Erfurt, 1899); Jürgens, *Luther von seiner Geburt bis zum Ablassstreit*, 3 vols. (Leipzig, 1846–1847); Krumhaar, *Die Grafschaft Mansfeld im Reformationszeitalter* (Eisleben, 1845); Buchwald, *Zur Wittenberg Stadt- und Universitätsgeschichte in der Reformationszeit* (Leipzig, 1893); Kampschulte, *Die Universität Erfurt in ihrem Verhältniss zu dem Humanismus und der Reformation* (Trier, 1856–1860); *Cambridge Modern History*, II. iv; Smith's *Luther's Table-Talk: A Critical Study* (New York, 1907); Currie, *The Letters of Martin Luther* (London, 1908).

burdened conscience; who had at last found his way into the presence of God, and who knew, by his own personal experience, that the living God was accessible to every Christian. He had won the freedom of a Christian man, and had reached through faith a joy in living far deeper than that which Humanism boasted. He became a leader of men, because his joyous faith made him a hero by delivering him from all fear of Church or of clergy—the fear which had weighed down the consciences of men for generations. Men could *see* what faith was when they looked at Luther.

It must never be forgotten that to his contemporaries Luther was the embodiment of personal piety. All spoke of his sensitiveness to religious impressions of all kinds in his early years. While he was inside the convent, whether before or after he had found deliverance for his troubles of soul, his fellows regarded him as a model of piety. In later days, when he stood forth as a Reformer, he became such a power in the hearts of men of all sorts and ranks, because he was seen to be a thoroughly pious man. Albert Dürer may be taken as a type. In the great painter's diary of the journey he made with his wife and her maid Susanna to the Netherlands (1520),—a mere summary of the places he visited and the persons he saw, of what he paid for food and lodging and travel, of the prices he got for his pictures, and what he paid for his purchases, literary and artistic,—he tells how he heard of Luther's condemnation at Worms, of the Reformer's disappearance, of his supposed murder by Popish emissaries (for so the report went through Germany), and the news compelled him to that pouring forth of prayers, of exclamations, of fervent appeals, and of bitter regrets, which fills three out of the whole forty-six pages. The Luther he almost worships is the "pious man," the "follower of the Lord and of the true Christian faith," the "man enlightened by the Holy Spirit," the man who had been done to death by the Pope and the priests of his day, as the Son of God had been murdered by the priests of Jerusalem. The one thing which fills the great painter's mind is the personal religious life of the man Martin Luther.[1]

Another source of Luther's power was that he had been led step by step, and that his countrymen could follow him deliberately without being startled by any too sudden changes. He was one of themselves; he took them into his confidence at every stage of his public career; they knew him thoroughly. He had been a monk, and that was natural for a youth of his exemplary piety. He had lived a model monastic life; his companions and his superiors were unwearied in commending him. He had spoken openly what almost all good men had been feeling privately about Indulgences in plain language which all could understand; and he had gradually taught himself and his countrymen, who were following his career breathlessly, that the man who trusted in God did not need to fear the censures of Pope or of the clergy. He emancipated not merely the learned and cultivated classes, but the common people, from the fear of the Church; and this was the one thing needful for a true reformation. So long as the people of Europe believed that the priesthood had some mysterious powers, no matter how vague or indefinite, over the spiritual and eternal welfare of men and women, freedom of conscience and a renovation of the public and private moral life was impossible. The spiritual world will always have its anxieties and terrors for every Christian soul, and the greatest achievement of Luther was that by teaching and, above all, by example, he showed the common man that he was in God's hands, and not dependent on the blessing or banning of a clerical caste. For Luther's doctrine of Justification by Faith, as he himself showed in his tract on the *Liberty of a Christian Man* (1520), was simply that there was nothing in the indefinite claim which the mediæval Church had always made. From the moment the common people, simple men and women, knew and

[1] *Albrecht Dürer's Tagebuch der Reise in die Niederlande.* Edited by Dr. Fr. Leitschuh (Leipzig, 1884), pp. 28–84.

felt this, they were freed from the mysterious dread of Church and priesthood; they could look the clergy fairly in the face, and could care little for their threats. It was because Luther had freed himself from this dread, because the people, who knew him to be a deeply pious man, saw that he was free from it, and therefore that they need be in no concern about it, that he became the great reformer and the popular leader in an age which was compelled to revise its thoughts about spiritual things.

Hence it is that we may say without exaggeration that the Reformation was embodied in Martin Luther, that it lived in him as in no one else, and that its inner religious history may be best studied in the record of his spiritual experiences and in the growth of his religious convictions.

§ 2. *Luther's Youth and Education.*

Martin Luther was born in 1483 (Nov. 10th) at Eisleben, and spent his childhood in the small mining town of Mansfeld. His father, Hans Luther, had belonged to Möhra (Moortown), a small peasant township lying in the north-east corner of the Thuringian Wald, and his mother, Margarethe Ziegler, had come from a burgher family in Eisenach. It was a custom among these Thuringian peasants that only one son, and that usually the youngest, inherited the family house and the croft. The others were sent out one by one, furnished with a small store of money from the family strong-box, to make their way in the world. Hans Luther had determined to become a miner in the Mansfeld district, where the policy of the Counts of Mansfeld, of building and letting out on hire small smelting furnaces, enabled thrifty and skilled workmen to rise in the world. The father soon made his way. He leased one and then three of these furnaces. He won the respect of his neighbours, for he became, in 1491, one of the four members of the village council, and we are told that the Counts of Mansfeld held him in esteem.

In the earlier years, when Luther was a child, the

family life was one of grinding poverty, and Luther often recalled the hard struggles of his parents. He had often seen his mother carrying the wood for the family fire from the forest on her poor shoulders. The child grew up among the hard, grimy, coarse surroundings of the German working-class life, protected from much that was evil by the wise severity of his parents. He imbibed its simple political and ecclesiastical ideas. He learned that the Emperor was God's ruler on earth, who would protect poor people against the Turk, and that the Church was the "Pope's House," in which the Bishop of Rome was the house-father. He was taught the Creed, the Ten Commandments, and the Lord's Prayer. He sang such simple evangelical hymns as "Ein Kindelein so lobelich," "Nun bitten wir den heiligen Geist," and "Crist ist erstanden." He was a dreamy, contemplative child; and the unseen world was never out of his thoughts. He knew that some of the miners practised sorcery in dark corners below the earth. He feared an old woman who lived near; she was a witch, and the priest himself was afraid of her. He was taught about Hell and Purgatory and the Judgment to come. He shivered whenever he looked at the stained-glass window in the parish church and saw the frowning face of Jesus, who, seated on a rainbow and with a flaming sword in His hand, was coming to judge him, he knew not when. He saw the crowds of pilgrims who streamed past Mansfeld, carrying their crucifixes high, and chanting their pilgrim songs, going to the Bruno Quertfort chapel or to the old church at Wimmelberg. He saw paralytics and maimed folk carried along the roads, going to embrace the wooden cross at Kyffhaüser, and find a miraculous cure; and sick people on their way to the cloister church at Wimmelberg to be cured by the sound of the blessed bells.

The boy Luther went to the village school in Mansfeld, and endured the cruelties of a merciless pedagogue. He was sent for a year, in 1497, to a school of the Brethren of the Common Lot in Magdeburg. Then he went to St

George's school in Eisenach, where he remained three years. He was a "poor scholar," which meant a boy who received his lodging and education free, was obliged to sing in the church choir, and was allowed to sing in the streets, begging for food. The whole town was under the spell of St. Elizabeth, the pious landgravine, who had given up family life and all earthly comforts to earn a mediæval saintship. It contained nine monasteries and nunneries, many of them dating back to the days of St. Elizabeth; her good deeds were emblazoned on the windows of the church in which Luther sang as choir-boy; he had long conversations with the monks who belonged to her foundations. The boy was being almost insensibly attracted to that revival of the mediæval religious life which was the popular religious force of these days. He had glimpses of the old homely evangelical piety, this time accompanied by a refinement of manners Luther had hitherto been unacquainted with, in the house of a lady who is identified by biographers with a certain Frau Cotta. The boy enjoyed it intensely, and his naturally sunny nature expanded under its influence. But it did not touch him religiously. He has recorded that it was with incredulous surprise that he heard his hostess say that there was nothing on earth more lovely than the love of husband and wife, when it is in the fear of the Lord.

After three years' stay at Eisenach, Luther entered the University of Erfurt (1501), then the most famous in Germany. It had been founded in 1392 by the burghers of the town, who were intensely proud of their own University, and especially of the fact that it had far surpassed other seats of learning which owed their origin to princes. The academic and burgher life were allied at Erfurt as they were in no other University town. The days of graduation were always town holidays, and at the graduation processions the officials of the city walked with the University authorities. Luther tells us that when he first saw the newly made graduates marching in their new graduation robes in the middle of the procession, he thought that they had attained to the summit of earthly felicity. The University of Erfurt was also strictly allied to the Church. Different Popes had enriched it with privileges; the Primate of Germany. the Archbishop of Mainz, was its Chancellor; many of its professors held ecclesiastical prebends, or were monks; each faculty was under the protection of a tutelary saint; the teachers had to swear to teach nothing opposed to the doctrines of the Roman Church; and special pains were taken to prevent the rise and spread of heresy.

Its students were exposed to a greater variety of influences than those of any other seat of learning in Germany. Its theology represented the more modern type of scholastic, the Scotist; its philosophy was the nominalist teaching of William of Occam, whose great disciple, Gabriel Biel (d. 1495), had been one of its most celebrated professors; the system of biblical interpretation, first introduced by Nicholas de Lyra[1] (d. 1340), had been long taught at Erfurt by a succession of able masters; Humanism had won an early entrance, and in Luther's time the Erfurt circle of "Poets" was already famous. The strongly anti-clerical teaching of John of Wessel, who had lectured in Erfurt for fifteen years (1445–1460), had left its mark on the University, and was not forgotten. Hussite propagandists, Luther tells us, appeared from time to time, whispering among the students their strange, anti-clerical Christian socialism. While, as if by way of antidote, there came Papal Legates, whose magnificence bore witness to the might of the Roman Church.

Luther had been sent to Erfurt to learn Law, and the Faculty of Philosophy gave the preliminary training re-

[1] Nicholas, born at Lyre, a village in Normandy, was one of the earliest students of the Hebrew Scriptures; he explained the accepted fourfold sense of Scripture in the following distich:

"*Litera* gesta docet, quid credas *Allegoria*,
Moralis quid agas, quo tendas *Anagogia*."

Luther used his commentaries when he became Professor of Theology at Wittenberg, and acknowledged the debt; but it is too much to say:

"Si Lyra non lyrasset,
Lutherus non saltasset."

quired. The young student worked hard at the prescribed tasks. The Scholastic Philosophy, he said, left him little time for classical studies, and he attended none of the Humanist lectures. He found time, however, to read a good many Latin authors privately, and also to learn something of Greek. Virgil and Plautus were his favourite authors; Cicero also charmed him; he read Livy, Terence, and Horace. He seems also to have read a volume of selections from Propertius, Persius, Lucretius, Tibullus, Silvius Italicus, Statius, and Claudian. But he was never a member of the Humanist circle; he was too much in earnest about religious questions, and of too practical a turn of mind.

The scanty accounts of Luther's student days show that he was a hardworking, bright, sociable youth, and musical to the core. His companions called him "the Philosopher," "the Musician," and spoke of his lute-playing, of his singing, and of his ready power in debate. He took his various degrees in unusually short time. He was Bachelor in 1502, and Master in 1505. His father, proud of his son's success, had sent him the costly present of a *Corpus Juris.* He may have begun to attend the lectures in the Faculty of Law, when he suddenly plunged into the Erfurt Convent of the Augustinian Eremites.

The action was so sudden and unexpected, that contemporaries felt bound to give all manner of explanations, and these have been woven together into accounts which are legendary.[1] Luther himself has told us that he entered the monastery because he *doubted of himself*; that in his

[1] There is one persistent contemporary suggestion, that Luther was finally driven to take the step by the sudden death of a companion, for which a good deal may be said. Oergel has shown, from minute researches in the university archives, that a special friend of Luther's, Hieronymus Pontz of Windsheim, who was working along with him for his Magister's degree, died suddenly of pleurisy before the end of the examination; that a few weeks after Luther had taken his degree, another promising student whom he knew died of the plague; that the plague broke out again in Erfurt three months afterwards; and that Luther entered the convent a few days after this second appearance of the plague.—Cf. Georg Oergel, *Vom jungen Luther* (Erfurt, 1899), pp. 35–41.

case the proverb was true, "Doubt makes a monk." He also said that his resolve was a sudden one, because he knew that his decision would grieve his father and his mother.

What was the doubting? We are tempted in these days to think of intellectual difficulties, and Luther's doubting is frequently attributed to the self-questioning which his contact with Humanism at Erfurt had engendered. But this idea, if not foreign to the age, was strange to Luther. His was a simple pious nature, practical rather than speculative, sensitive and imaginative. He could play with abstract questions; but it was pictures that compelled him to action. He has left on record a series of pictures which were making deeper and more permanent impression on him as the years passed; they go far to reveal the history of his struggles, and to tell us what the doubts were which drove him into the convent. The picture on the window in Mansfeld church of Jesus sitting on a rainbow, with frowning countenance and drawn sword in His hand, coming to judge the wicked; the altar-piece at Magdeburg representing a great ship sailing heavenwards, no one within the ship but priests or monks, and in the sea laymen drowning, or saved by ropes thrown to them by the priests and monks who were safe on board; the living picture of the prince of Anhalt, who to save his soul had become a friar, and carried the begging sack on his bent shoulders through the streets of Magdeburg; the history of St. Elizabeth blazoned on the windows of the church at Eisenach; the young Carthusian at Eisenach, who the boy thought was the holiest man he had ever talked to, and who had so mortified his body that he had come to look like a very old man; the terrible deathbed scene of the Erfurt ecclesiastical dignitary, a man who held twenty-two benefices, and whom Luther had often seen riding in state in the great processions, who was known to be an evil-liver, and who when he came to die filled the room with his frantic cries. Luther doubted whether he could ever do what he believed had to be done by him to save his soul if he remained in the world. That was what compelled him to become a monk, and bury himself in the convent. The lurid fires of Hell and the pale shades of Purgatory, which are the permanent background to Dante's Paradise, were present to Luther's mind from childhood. Could he escape the one and gain entrance to the other if he remained in the world? He doubted it, and entered the convent.

§ 3. *Luther in the Erfurt Convent.*

It was a convent of the Augustinian Eremites, perhaps the most highly esteemed of monastic orders by the common people of Germany during the earlier decades of the sixteenth century. They represented the very best type of that superstitious mediæval revival which has been already described.[1] It is a mistake to suppose that because they bore the name of Augustine, the evangelical theology of the great Western Father was known to them. Their leading theologians belonged to another and very different school. The two teachers of theology in the Erfurt convent, when Luther entered in 1505, were John Genser of Paltz, and John Nathin of Neuenkirchen. The former was widely known from his writings in favour of the strictest form of papal absolutism, of the doctrine of *Attrition*, and of the efficacy of papal *Indulgences*. It is not probable that Luther was one of his pupils; for he retired broken in health and burdened with old age in 1507.[2] The latter, though unknown beyond the walls of the convent, was an able and severe master. He was an ardent admirer of Gabriel Biel, of Peter d'Ailly, and of William of Occam their common master. He thought little of any inde-

[1] Cf. above, pp. 127 ff.

[2] In my chapter on Luther in the *Cambridge Modern History*, ii. p. 114, where notes were not permitted, I have said with too much abruptness that John of Paltz was "the teacher of Luther himself." Luther was certainly taught the theology of John of Paltz, and the latter was residing in the monastery during two years of Luther's stay there; but it is more probable that Luther's actual instructor was Nathin.

pendent study of the Holy Scriptures. "Brother Martin," he once said to Luther, "let the Bible alone; read the old teachers; they give you the whole marrow of the Bible; reading the Bible simply breeds unrest."[1] Afterwards he commanded Luther on his canonical obedience to refrain from Bible study.[2] It was he who made Luther read and re-read the writings of Biel, d'Ailly, and Occam, until he had committed to memory long passages; and who taught the Reformer to consider Occam "his dear Master." Nathin was a determined opponent of the Reformation until his death in 1529; but Luther always spoke of him with respect, and said that he was "a Christian man in spite of his monk's cowl."

Luther had not come to the convent to study theology; he had entered it to save his soul. These studies were part of the convent discipline; to engage in them, part of his vow of obedience. He worked hard at them, and pleased his superiors greatly; worked because he was a submissive monk. They left a deeper impress on him than most of his biographers have cared to acknowledge. He had more of the Schoolman in him and less of the Humanist than any other of the men who stood in the first line of leaders in the Reformation movement. Some of his later doctrines, and especially his theory of the Sacrament of the Supper, came to him from these convent studies in d'Ailly and Occam. But in his one great quest—how to save his soul, how to win the sense of God's pardon—they were more a hindrance than a help. His teachers might be Augustinian Eremites, but they had not the faintest knowledge of Augustinian experimental theology. They belonged to the most pelagianising school of mediæval Scholastic; and their last word always was that man must work out his own salvation. Luther tried to work it out

[1] In the *Tischreden* (Preger, Leipzig, 1888), i. 27, the saying is attributed to Bartholomæus Usingen, who is erroneously called Luther's teacher in the Erfurt convent. Usingen did not enter the convent before 1512. He was a professor in the University of Erfurt, not in the convent.

[2] N. Selneccer, *Historia . . . D. M. Lutheri*: "Jussus est omissis Sacris Bibliis ex obedientia legere scholastica et sophistica scripta."

in the most approved later mediæval fashion, by the strictest asceticism. He fasted and scourged himself; he practised all the ordinary forms of maceration, and invented new ones; but all to no purpose. For when an awakened soul, as he said long afterwards, seeks to find rest in work-righteousness, it stands on a foundation of loose sand which it feels running and travelling beneath it; and it must go from one good work to another and to another, and so on without end. Luther was undergoing all unconsciously the experience of Augustine, and what tortured and terrified the great African was torturing him. He had learned that man's goodness is not to be measured by his neighbour's but by God's, and that man's sin is not to be weighed against the sins of his neighbours, but against the righteousness of God. His theological studies told him that God's pardon could be had through the Sacrament of Penance, and that the first part of that sacrament was sorrow for sin. But then came a difficulty. The older, and surely the better theology, explained that this godly sorrow (*contritio*) must be based on love to God. Had he this love? God always appeared to him as an implacable Judge, inexorably threatening punishment for the breaking of a law which it seemed impossible to keep. He had to confess to himself that he sometimes almost hated this arbitrary Will which the nominalist Schoolmen called God. The more modern theology, that taught by the chief convent theologian, John of Paltz, asserted that the sorrow might be based on meaner motives (*attritio*), and that this attrition was changed into contrition in the Sacrament of Penance itself. So Luther wearied his superiors by his continual use of this sacrament. The slightest breach of the most trifling conventual regulation was looked on as a sin, and had to be confessed at once and absolution for it received, until the perplexed lad was ordered to cease confession until he had committed some sin worth confessing. His brethren believed him to be a miracle of piety. They boasted about him in their monkish fashion, and in all the monasteries around, and as far away as Grimma, the monks and nuns talked about the young saint in the Erfurt convent. Meanwhile the "young saint" himself lived a life of mental anguish, whispering to himself that he was "gallows-ripe." Writing in 1518, years after the conflict was over, Luther tells us that no pen could describe the mental anguish he endured.[1] Gleams of comfort came to him, but they were transient. The Master of the Novices gave him salutary advice; an aged brother gave him momentary comfort. John Staupitz, the Vicar-General of the Congregation, during his visits to the convent was attracted by the traces of hidden conflicts and sincere endeavour of the young monk, with his high cheek-bones, emaciated frame, gleaming eyes, and looks of settled despair. He tried to find out his difficulties. He revoked Nathin's order that Luther should not read the Scriptures. He encouraged him to read the Bible; he gave him a *Glossa Ordinaria* or conventual ecclesiastical commentary, where passages were explained by quotations from eminent Church Fathers, and difficulties were got over by much pious allegorising; above all, he urged him to become a good *localis* and *textualis* in the Bible, *i.e.* one who, when he met with difficulties, did not content himself with commentaries, but made collections of parallel passages for himself, and found explanations of one in the others. Still this brought at first little help. At last Staupitz saw the young man's real difficulty, and gave him real and lasting assistance. He showed Luther that he had been rightly enough contrasting man's sin and God's holiness, and measuring the depth of the one by the height of the other; that he had been following the truest instincts of the deepest piety when he had set over-against each other the righteousness of God and the sin and helplessness of man; but that he had gone wrong when he kept these two

[1] Modern Romanists describe all this as the self-torturing of an hysterical youth. They are surely oblivious to the fact that the only great German mediæval Mystic who has been canonised by the Romish Church, Henry Suso, went through a similar experience; and that these very experiences were in both cases looked on by contemporaries as the fruits of a more than ordinary piety.

thoughts in a *permanent* opposition. He then explained that, according to God's promise, the righteousness of God might become man's own possession in and through Christ Jesus. God had promised that man could have fellowship with Him; all fellowship is founded on personal trust; and trust, the personal trust of the believing man on a personal God who has promised, gives man that fellowship with God through which all things that belong to God can become his. Without this personal trust or faith, all divine things, the Incarnation and Passion of the Saviour, the Word and the Sacraments, however true as matters of fact, are outside man and cannot be truly possessed. But when man trusts God and His promises, and when the fellowship, which trust or faith always creates, is once established, then they can be truly possessed by the man who trusts. The just live by their faith. These thoughts, acted upon, helped Luther gradually to win his way to peace, and he told Staupitz long afterwards that it was he who had made him see the rays of light which dispelled the darkness of his soul.[1] In the end, the vision of the true relation of the believing man to God came to him suddenly with all the force of a personal revelation, and the storm-tossed soul was at rest. The sudden enlightenment, the personal revelation which was to change his whole life, came to him when he was reading the *Epistle to the Romans* in his cell. It came to Paul when he was riding on the road to Damascus; to Augustine as he was lying under a fig-tree in the Milan garden; to Francis as he paced anxiously the flag-stones of the Portiuncula chapel on the plain beneath Assisi; to Suso as he sat at table in the morning. It spoke through different words:—to Paul, "Why persecutest thou Me?";[2] to Augustine, "Put ye on the Lord Jesus Christ, and make not provision for the flesh";[3] to Francis, "Get you no gold, nor silver, nor brass in your purses, no wallet for your journey, neither two coats, nor shoes, nor staff";[4] to Suso, "My son, if

[1] *Resolutiones*, Preface.
[2] Acts viii. 4.
[3] Rom. xiii. 14.
[4] Matt. x. 9.

thou wilt hear My words."[1] But though the words were different, the personal revelation, which mastered the men, was the same: That trust in the All-merciful God, who has revealed Himself in Jesus Christ, creates companionship with God, and that all other things are nothing in comparison with this fellowship. It was this contact with the Unseen which fitted Luther for his task as the leader of men in an age which was longing for a revival of moral living inspired by a fresh religious impulse.[2]

It is not certain how long Luther's protracted struggle lasted. There are indications that it went on for two years, and that he did not attain to inward peace until shortly before he was sent to Wittenberg in 1508. The intensity and sincerity of the conflict marked him for life. The conviction that he, weak and sinful as he was, nevertheless lived in personal fellowship with the God whose love he was experiencing, became the one fundamental fact of life on which he, a human personality, could take his stand as on a foundation of rock; and standing on it, feeling his own strength, he could also be a source of strength to others Everything else, however venerable and sacred it might once have seemed, might prove untrustworthy without hereafter disturbing Luther's religious life, provided only this one thing remained to him. For the moment, however, nothing seemed questionable. The inward change

[1] Prov. ii. 1.

[2] "If we review all the men and women of the West since Augustine's time, whom, for the disposition which possessed them, history has designated as eminent Christians, we have always the same type; we find marked conviction of sin, complete renunciation of their own strength, and trust in grace, in the personal God who is apprehended as the *Merciful One* in the humility of Christ. The variations of this frame of mind are innumerable —but the fundamental type is the same. This frame of mind is taught in sermons and in instruction by truly pious Romanists and by Evangelicals; in it youthful Christians are trained, and dogmatics are constructed in harmony with it. It has always produced so powerful an effect, even where it is only preached as the experience of others, that he who has come in contact with it can never forget it; it accompanies him as a pillar of cloud by day and of fire by night; he who imagines that he has long shaken it off, sees it rising up suddenly before him again."—Harnack's *History of Dogma*. v. 74 (Eng. trans., London, 1898).

altered nothing external. He still believed that the Church was the "Pope's House"; he accepted all its usages and institutions—its Masses and its relics, its indulgences and its pilgrimages, its hierarchy and its monastic life. He was still a monk and believed in his vocation.

Luther's theological studies were continued. He devoted himself especially to Bernard, in whose sermons on the *Song of Solomon* he found the same thoughts of the relation of the believing soul to God which had given him comfort. He began to show himself a good man of business with an eye to the heart of things. Staupitz and his chiefs entrusted him with some delicate commissions on behalf of the Order, and made quiet preparations for his advancement. In 1508 he, with a few other monks, was sent from Erfurt to the smaller convent at Wittenberg, to assist the small University there.

§ 4. *Luther's early Life in Wittenberg.*

About the beginning of the century, Frederick the Wise, Elector of Saxony and head of the Ernestine branch of his family, had resolved to establish a University for his dominions. Frederick had maintained close relations with the Augustinian Eremites ever since he had made acquaintance with them when a schoolboy at Grimma, and the Vicar-General, John Staupitz, along with Dr. Pollich of Mellerstadt, were his chief advisers. It might almost be said that the new University was, from the beginning, an educational establishment belonging to the Order of monks which Luther had joined. Staupitz himself was one of the professors, and Dean of the Faculty of Theology; another Augustinian Eremite was Dean of the Faculty of Arts; the Patron Saints of the Order, the Blessed Virgin and St. Augustine, were the Patron Saints of the University; St. Paul was the Patron Saint of the Faculty of Theology, and on the day of his conversion there was a special celebration of the Mass with a sermon, at which the Rector (Dr. Pollich) and the whole teaching staff were present.

The University was poorly endowed. Electoral Saxony was not a rich principality; some mining industry did exist in the south end, and Zwickau was the centre of a great weaving trade; but the great proportion of the inhabitants, whether of villages or towns, subsisted on agriculture of a poor kind. There was not much money at the Electoral court. A sum got from the sale of Indulgences some years before, which Frederick had not allowed to leave the country, served to make a beginning. The prebends attached to the Church of All Saints (the Castle Church) supplied the salaries of some professors; the others were Augustinian Eremites, who gave their services gratuitously.

The town of Wittenberg was more like a large village than the capital of a principality. In 1513 it only contained 3000 inhabitants and 356 rateable houses. The houses were for the most part mean wooden dwellings, roughly plastered with clay. The town lay in the very centre of Germany, but it was far from any of the great trade routes; the inhabitants had a good deal of Wendish blood in their veins, and were inclined to be sluggish and intemperate. The environs were not picturesque, and the surrounding country had a poor soil. Altogether it was scarcely the place for a University. Imperial privileges were obtained from the Emperor Maximilian, and the University was opened on the 18th of October 1502.

One or two eminent teachers had been induced to come to the new University. Staupitz collected promising young monks from many convents of his Order and enrolled them as students, and the University entered 416 names on its books during its first year. This success seems to have been somewhat artificial, for the numbers gradually declined to 56 in the summer session of 1505. Staupitz, however, encouraged Frederick to persevere.

It was in the interests of the young University that Luther and a band of brother monks were sent from Erfurt to the Wittenberg convent. There he was set to teach the Dialectic and Physics of Aristotle,—a hateful task,—but whether to the monks in the convent or in the University it is impossible to say. All the while Staupitz urged him to study theology in order to teach it. It was then that Luther began his systematic study of Augustine. He also began to preach. His first sermons were delivered in an old chapel, 30 feet long and 20 feet wide, built of wood plastered over with clay. He preached to the monks. Dr. Pollich, the Rector, went sometimes to hear him, and spoke to the Elector of the young monk with piercing eyes and strange fancies in his head.

His work was interrupted by a command to go to Rome on business of his Order (autumn 1511). His selection was a great honour, and Luther felt it to be so; but it may be questioned whether he did not think more of the fact that he would visit the Holy City as a devout pilgrim, and be able to avail himself of the spiritual privileges which he believed were to be found there. When he got to the end of his journey and first caught a glimpse of the city, he raised his hands in an ecstasy, exclaiming, "I greet thee, thou Holy Rome, thrice holy from the blood of the martyrs."

When his official work was done he set about seeing the Holy City with the devotion of a pilgrim. He visited all the famous shrines, especially those to which Indulgences were attached. He listened reverently to all the accounts given of the relics which were exhibited to the pilgrims, and believed in all the tales told him. He thought that if his parents had been dead he could have assured them against Purgatory by saying Masses in certain chapels. Only once, it is said, his soul showed revolt. He was slowly climbing on his knees the *Scala Santa* (really a mediæval staircase), said to have been the stone steps leading up to Pilate's house in Jerusalem, once trodden by the feet of our Lord; when half-way up the thought came into his mind, *The just shall live by his faith*; he stood upright and walked slowly down. He saw, as thousands of pious German pilgrims had done before his time, the moral corruptions which disgraced the Holy City—infidel priests who scoffed at the sacred mysteries they performed, and princes of the Church who lived in open sin. He saw and loathed the moral degradation, and the scenes imprinted themselves on his memory; but his home and cloister training enabled him, for the time being, in spite of the loathing, to revel in the memorials of the old heroic martyrs, and to look on their relics as storehouses of divine grace. In later days it was the memories of the vices of the Roman Court that helped him to harden his heart against the sentiment which surrounded the Holy City.

When Luther returned to Wittenberg in the early summer of 1512, his Vicar-General sent him to Erfurt to complete his training for the doctorate in theology. He graduated as Doctor of the Holy Scripture, took the Wittenberg Doctor's oath to defend the evangelical truth vigorously (*viriliter*), was made a member of the Wittenberg Senate, and three weeks later suceeeded Staupitz as Professor of Theology.

Luther was still a genuine monk, with no doubt of his vocation. He became sub-prior of the Wittenberg convent in 1512, and was made the District Vicar over the eleven convents in Meissen and Thuringia in 1515. But that side of his life may be passed over. It is his theological work as professor in Wittenberg University that is important for his career as a reformer.

§ 5. *Luther's early Lectures in Theology.*

From the beginning his lectures on theology differed from those ordinarily given, but not because he had any theological opinions at variance with those of his old teachers at Erfurt. No one attributed any sort of heretical views to the young Wittenberg professor. His mind was intensely practical, and he believed that theology might be made useful to guide men to find the grace of God and to tell them how, having acquired through trust a sense of fellowship with God, they could persevere in a life of joyous obedience to God and His commandments. The Scholastic theologians of Erfurt and elsewhere did not look on theology as a practical discipline of this kind. Luther thought that theology ought to discuss such matters, and he knew that his main interest in theology lay on this practical side. Besides, as he has told us, he regarded himself as specially set apart to lecture on the Holy Scriptures. So, like John Colet, he began by expounding the Epistles of St. Paul and the Psalms.

Luther never knew much Hebrew, and he used the Vulgate in his prelections. He had a huge widely printed volume on his desk, and wrote out the heads of his lectures between the printed lines. Some of the pages still survive in the Wolfenbüttel Library, and can be studied.[1]

He made some use of the commentaries of Nicholas de Lyra, but got most assistance from passages in Augustine, Bernard, and Gerson,[2] which dealt with practical religion.[3]

[1] The Wolfenbüttel Library contains the Psalter (Vulgate) used by Luther in lecturing on the Psalms. The book was printed at Wittenberg in 1513 by John Gronenberg, and contains Luther's notes written on the margin and between the printed lines.

[2] Luther's indebtedness to Gerson (Jean Charlier, born in 1363 at Gerson, a hamlet near Rethel in the Ardennes, believed by some to be the author of the *De Imitatione Christi*) has not been sufficiently noticed. It may be partially estimated by Luther's own statement that most experimental divines, including Augustine, when dealing with the struggle of the awakened soul, lay most stress on that part of the conflict which comes from temptations of the flesh ; Gerson confines himself to those which are purely spiritual. Luther, during his soul-anguish in the convent, was a young monk who had lived a humanly stainless life, *sans peur et sans reproche* ; Augustine, a middle-aged professor of rhetoric, had been living for years in a state of sinful concubinage.

[3] It is commonly said that Luther made use of the *mystical* passages found in these and other authors ; but *mystical* is a very ambiguous word. It is continually used to express personal or individual piety in general ; or this personal religion as opposed to that religious life which is consciously lived within the fellowship of men called the Church, provided with the external means of grace. These are, however, very loose uses of the word. The fundamental problem, even in Christian Mysticism, appears to me to be how to bridge the gulf between the creature and the Creator, while the problem in Reformation theology is how to span the chasm between the sinful man and the righteous God. Hence in mysticism the *tendency* is always to regard sin as imperfection, while in the Reformation theology sin is always the power of evil and invariably includes the thought of guilt. Luther was no mystic in the sense of desiring to be lost *in* God : he wished to be saved *through* Christ.

His lectures were experimental. He started with the fact of man's sin, the possibility of reaching a sense of pardon and of fellowship with God through trust in His promises. From the beginning we find in the germ what grew to be the main thoughts in the later Lutheran theology. Men are redeemed apart from any merits of their own; God's grace is really His mercy revealed in the mission and work of Christ; it has to do with the forgiveness of sins, and is the fulfilment of His promises; man's faith is trust in the historical work of Christ and in the verity of God. These thoughts were for the most part all expressed in the formal language of the Scholastic Theology of the day. They grew in clearness, and took shape in a series of propositions which formed the common basis of his teaching: man wins pardon through the free grace of God: when man lays hold on God's promise of pardon he becomes a new creature; this sense of pardon is the beginning of a new life of sanctification; the life of faith is Christianity on its inward side; the contrast between the law and the gospel is something fundamental: there is a real distinction between the outward and visible Church and the ideal Church, which latter is to be described by its spiritual and moral relations to God after the manner of Augustine. All these thoughts simply pushed aside the ordinary theology as taught in the schools without staying to criticise it.

In the years 1515 and 1516, which bear traces of a more thoroughgoing study of Augustine and of the German mediæval Mystics, Luther began to find that he could not express the thoughts he desired to convey in the ordinary language of Scholastic Theology, and that its phrases suggested ideas other than those he wished to set forth. He tried to find another set of expressions. It is characteristic of Luther's conservatism, that in theological phraseology, as afterwards in ecclesiastical institutions and ceremonies, he preferred to retain what had been in use provided only he could put his own evangelical meaning into it in a not too arbitrary way.[1] Having found that the Scholastic phraseology did not always suit his purpose, he turned to the popular mystical authors, and discovered there a rich store of phrases in which he could express his ideas of the imperfection of man towards what is good. Along with this change in language, and related to it, we find evidence that Luther was beginning to think less highly of the monastic life with its *external* renunciations. The thought of predestination, meaning by that not an abstract metaphysical category, but the conception that the whole believer's life, and what it involved, depended in the last resort on God and not on man, came more and more into the foreground. Still there does not seem any disposition to criticise or to repudiate the current theology of the day.

The earliest traces of *conscious* opposition appeared about the middle of 1516, and characteristically on the practical and not on the speculative side of theology. They began in a sermon on Indulgences, preached in July 1516. Once begun, the breach widened until Luther could contrast "our theology"[2] (the theology taught by Luther and his colleagues at Wittenberg) with what was taught elsewhere, and notably at Erfurt. The former represented Augustine and the Holy Scriptures, and the latter was founded on Aristotle. In September 1517 he raised the standard of theological revolt, and wrote directly against the "Scholastic Theology"; he declared that it was Pelagian at heart, and buried out of sight the Augustinian doctrines of grace; he lamented the fact that it neglected to teach the supreme value of faith and of inward righteousness; that it en-

[1] Of course, Luther's intense individuality appeared in his language from the first. Take as an example a note on Ps. lxxxiv. 4: "As the meadow is to the cow, the house to the man, the nest to the bird, the rock to the chamois, and the stream to the fish, so is the Holy Scripture to the believing soul."

[2] The expression is interesting, because it shows that Luther's influence had made at least two of his colleagues change their views. Nicholas Amsdorf and Andrew Bodenstein of Carlstadt had come to Wittenberg to teach Scholastic Theology, and Amsdorf had made a great name for himself as an exponent of the older type of that theology.

couraged men to seek escape from what was due for sin by means of Indulgences, instead of exhorting them to practise the inward repentance which belongs to every genuine Christian life.

It was at this interesting stage of his own religious development that Luther felt himself forced to oppose publicly the sale of Indulgences in Germany.

By the year 1517, Luther had become a power in Wittenberg both as a preacher and as a teacher. He had become the preacher in the town church, from whose pulpit he delivered many sermons every week, taking infinite pains to make himself understood by the "raw Saxons." He became a great preacher, and, like all great preachers, he denounced prevalent sins, and bewailed the low standard of morals set before the people by the higher ecclesiastical authorities; he said that religion was not an easy thing; that it did not consist in the decent performance of external ceremonies; that the sense of sin, the experience of the grace of God, and the fear of God and the overcoming of that fear through the love of God, were all continuous experiences.

His exegetical lectures seemed like a rediscovery of the Holy Scriptures. Grave burghers of Wittenberg matriculated as students in order to hear them. The fame of the lecturer spread, and students from all parts of Germany crowded to the small remote University, until the Elector became proud of his seat of learning and of the man who had made it prosper.

Such a man could not keep silent when he saw what he believed to be a grave source of moral evil approaching the people whose souls God had given him in charge; and this is how Luther came to be a Reformer.

Up to this time he had been an obedient monk, doing diligently the work given him, highly esteemed by his superiors, fulfilling the expectations of his Vicar-General, and recognised by all as a quiet and eminently pious man. He had a strong, simple character, with nothing of the quixotic about him. Of course he saw the degradation of much of the religious life of the times, and had attended at least one meeting where those present discussed plans of reformation. He had then (at Leitzkau in 1512) declared that every true reformation must begin with individual men, that it must reveal itself in a regenerate heart aflame with faith kindled by the preaching of a pure gospel.

§ 6. *The Indulgence-seller.*

What drew Luther from his retirement was an Indulgence proclaimed by Pope Leo X., farmed by Albert of Brandenburg, the Archbishop of Mainz, and preached by John Tetzel, a Dominican monk, who had been commissioned by Albert to sell for him the *Papal Letters*, as the Indulgence tickets were called. It had been announced that the money raised by the sales would be used to build the Basilica of St. Peter to be a tomb worthy of the great Apostle, who rested, it was said, in a Roman grave.

The Indulgence-seller had usually a magnificent reception when he entered a German town. Frederick Mecum (Myconius), who was an eye-witness, thus describes the entrance of Tetzel into the town of Annaberg in Ducal Saxony:

> "When the Commissary or Indulgence-seller approached the town, the Bull (proclaiming the Indulgence) was carried before him on a cloth of velvet and gold, and all the priests and monks, the town council, the schoolmasters and their scholars, and all the men and women went out to meet him with banners and candles and songs, forming a great procession; then all the bells ringing and all the organs playing, they accompanied him to the principal church; a red cross was set up in the midst of the church, and the Pope's banner was displayed; in short, one might think they were receiving God Himself."

The Commissary then preached a sermon extolling the Indulgence, declaring that "the gate of heaven was open," and that the sales would begin.

Many German princes had no great love for the Indulgence-sellers, and Frederick, the Elector of Saxony, had prohibited Tetzel from entering his territories. But the lands of Ernestine (Electoral) and Albertine (Ducal) Saxony were so mixed up that it was easy for the Commissary to command the whole population of Electoral Saxony without actually crossing the frontier. The "Red Cross" had been set up in Zerbst in Ducal Saxony a few miles to the west, and at Jüterbogk in the territory of Magdeburg a few miles to the east of Wittenberg, and people had gone from the town to buy the Indulgence. Luther believed that the sales were injurious to the moral and religious life of his townsmen; the reports of the sermons and addresses of the Indulgence-seller which reached him appeared to contain what he believed to be both lies and blasphemies. He secured a copy of the letter of recommendation given by the Archbishop to his Commissary, and his indignation grew stronger. Still it was only after much hesitation, after many of his friends had urged him to interfere, and in deep distress of mind, that he resolved to protest. When he had determined to do something he went about the matter with a mixture of caution and courage which were characteristic of the man.

The Church of All Saints (the Castle Church) in Wittenberg had always been intimately connected with the University; its prebendaries were professors; its doors were used as a board on which to publish important academic documents; and notices of public academic "disputations," common enough at the time, had frequently appeared there. The day of the year which drew the largest concourse of townsmen and strangers to the church was All Saints' Day, the first of November. It was the anniversary of the consecration of the building, and was commemorated by a prolonged series of services. The Elector Frederick was a great collector of relics, and had stored his collection in the church.[1] He had also procured an

[1] An illustrated catalogue of Frederick's collection of relics was prepared by Lucas Cranach, and published under the title, *Wittenberger Heiligthumsbuch vom Jahre 1509.* It has been reprinted by G. Hirth of Munich in his *Liebhaber-Bibliothek alter Illustratoren in Facsimile-Reproduktion*, No. vi.

Indulgence to benefit all who came to attend the anniversary services and look at the relics.

On All Saints' Day, Luther nailed his Ninety-five Theses to the door of the church. It was a strictly academic proceeding. The Professor of Theology in Wittenberg, wishing to elucidate the truth, offered to discuss, either by speech or by writing, the matter of Indulgences.[1] He put forth ninety-five propositions or heads of discussion which he proposed to maintain. Academic etiquette was strictly preserved; the subject, judged by the numberless books which had been written on it, and the variety of opinions expressed, was eminently suitable for debate; the Theses were offered as subjects of debate; and the author, according to the usage of the time in such cases, was not supposed to be definitely committed to the opinions expressed.

The Theses, however, differed from most programmes of academic discussions in this, that everyone wanted to read them. A duplicate was made in German. Copies of the Latin original and the translation were sent to the University printing-house, and the presses could not throw them off fast enough to meet the demand which came from all parts of Germany.

[1] "Amore et studio elucidandæ veritatis hæc subscripta disputabuntur Wittenbergæ, præsidente R. P. Martino Luther, artium et sacræ theologiæ magistro eiusdemque ibidem lectore ordinario. Quare petit, ut qui non possunt verbis præsentes nobiscum disceptare, agant id literis absentes. In nomine Domini nostri Hiesu Christi. Amen."

CHAPTER II.

FROM THE BEGINNING OF THE INDULGENCE CONTROVERSY TO THE DIET OF WORMS.[1]

§ 1. *The Theory and Practice of Indulgences in the Sixteenth Century.*

THE practice of *Indulgences* pervaded the whole penitential system of the later mediæval Church, and had done so from the beginning of the thirteenth century. Its beginnings go back a thousand years before Luther's time.

In the ancient Church, lapse into serious sin involved separation from the Christian fellowship, and readmission to communion was only to be had by public confession made in presence of the whole congregation, and by the manifestation of a true repentance in performing certain *satisfactions*,[2]

[1] SOURCES: Thomas Aquinas, *Summa Theologiæ, Supplementum Tertiæ Partis*, Quæstiones xxv.–xxvii.; Alexander of Hales, *Summa Theologiæ*, iv.; Bonaventura, *Opera Omnia; In Librum Quartum Sententiarum*, dist. xx.; vol. v. 264 ff. (Moguntiæ, 1609); Denzinger, *Enchiridion Symbolorum et Definitionum, quæ de rebus fidei et morum a conciliis œcumenicis et summis pontificibus emanarunt*, 9th ed. (Würzburg, 1900), p. 175; Köhler, *Documenta zum Ablassstreit von 1517* (Tübingen, 1902).

LATER BOOKS: F. Beringer (Soc. Jes.), *Der Ablass, sein Wesen und Gebrauch*, 12th ed. (Paderborn, 1898); Bouvier, *Treatise on Indulgences* (London, 1848); Lea, *A History of Auricular Confession and Indulgence in the Latin Church*, 3 vols. (Philadelphia, 1896); Brieger, *Das Wesen des Ablasses am Ausgange des Mittelalters* (Leipzig, 1897); Harnack, *History of Dogma*, vi. pp. 243–270; Götz, "Studien zur Geschichte des Busssacraments" in *Zeitschrift für Kirchengeschichte*, xv. 321 ff., xvi. 541 ff.; Schneider, *Der Ablass* (1881); *Cambridge Modern History*, II. iv.

[2] The use of the word *satisfaction* to denote an outward sign of sorrow for sin which was supposed to be well-pleasing to God and to afford reasonable ground for the congregation restoring a lapsed member, is very old—much older than the use of the word to denote the work of Christ. It is found as early as the time of Tertullian and Cyprian.

such as the manumission of slaves, prolonged fasting, extensive almsgiving, etc. These *satisfactions* were the open signs of heartfelt sorrow, and were regarded as at once well-pleasing to God and evidence to the Christian community that the penitent had true repentance, and might be received back again into their midst. The confession was made to the whole congregation; the amount of *satisfaction* deemed necessary was estimated by the congregation, and readmission was also dependent on the will of the whole congregation. It often happened that these *satisfactions* were mitigated or exchanged for others. The penitent might fall sick, and the fasting which had been prescribed could not be insisted upon without danger of death; in such a case the external sign of sorrow which had been demanded might be exchanged for another. Or it might happen that the community became convinced of the sincerity of the repentance without insisting that the whole of the prescribed *satisfaction* need be performed.[1] These exchanges and mitigations of *satisfactions* were the small beginnings of the later system of Indulgences.

In course of time the public confession of sins made to the whole congregation was exchanged for a private confession made to the priest, and instead of the public *satisfaction* imposed by the whole congregation, it was left to the priest to enjoin a *satisfaction* or external sign of

[1] Tertullian was no believer in any indulgence shown to penitent sinners, and his account of the way in which penitents appeared before the congregation to ask for a remission or mitigation of the ecclesiastical sentence pronounced against them is doubtless a caricature, but it may be taken as a not unfair description of what must have frequently taken place: "You introduce into the Church the penitent adulterer for the purpose of melting the brotherhood by his supplications. You lead him into the midst, clad in sackcloth, covered with ashes, a compound of disgrace and horror. He prostrates himself before the widows, before the elders, suing for the tears of all; he seizes the edges of their garments, he clasps their knees, he kisses the prints of their feet. Meanwhile you harangue the people and excite their pity for the sad lot of the penitent. Good pastor, blessed father that you are, you describe the coming back of your goat in recounting the parable of the lost sheep. And in case your ewe lamb may take another leap out of the fold . . . you fill all the rest of the flock with apprehension at the very moment of granting indulgence."—(*De Pudicitia*, 13.)

sorrow which he believed was appropriate to the sin committed and confessed. The substitution of a private confession to the priest for a public confession made to the whole congregation, enlarged the circle of sins confessed. The *secret* sins of the heart whose presence could be elicited by the questions of the confessor were added to the open sins seen of men. The circle of *satisfactions* was also widened in a corresponding fashion.

When the imposition of *satisfactions* was left in the hands of the priest, it was felt necessary to provide some check against the arbitrariness which could not fail to result. So books were published containing lists of sins with the corresponding appropriate *satisfactions* which ought to be demanded from the penitents. If it be remembered that some of the sins mentioned were very heinous (murders, incests, outrages of all kinds), it is not surprising that the appropriate *satisfactions* or *penances*, as they came to be called, were very severe in some cases, and extended over a course of years. From the seventh century there arose a practice of commuting *satisfactions* or penances. A penance of several years' practice of fasting might be commuted into saying so many prayers or psalms, into giving a definite amount of alms, or even into a money fine—and in this last case the analogy of the *Wehrgeld* of the Germanic tribal codes was frequently followed.[1] These customary commutations were frequently inserted in the *Penitentiaries* or books of discipline. This new custom commonly took the form that the penitent, who visited a certain church on a prescribed day and gave a contribution to its funds, had the penance, which had been imposed upon him by the priest in the ordinary course of discipline, shortened by one-seventh, one-third, one-half, as the case might be. This was in every case the commutation or relaxation of the penance or outward sign of sorrow which

[1] In one book of discipline a man who has committed certain sins is ordered either to go on pilgrimage for ten years, or to live on bread and water for two years, or to pay 12s. a year. Detailed information may be found in Schmitz, *Die Bussbücher und die Bussdisziplin der Kirche*.

had been imposed according to the regulations of the Church, laid down in the *Penitentiaries* (*relaxatio de injuncta pœnitentia*). This was the real origin of Indulgences, and these earliest examples were invariably a relaxation of ecclesiastical penalties which had been imposed according to the regular custom in cases of discipline. It will be seen that Luther expressly excluded this kind of Indulgence from his attack. He declared that what the Church had a right to impose, it had a right to relax. It was at first believed that this right to relax or commute imposed penances was in the hands of the priests who had charge of the discipline of the members of the Church; but the abuses of the system by the priests ended by placing the power to grant Indulgences in the hands of the bishops, and they used the money procured in building many of the great mediæval cathedrals. Episcopal abuse of Indulgences led to their being reserved for the Popes.

Three conceptions, all of which belong to the beginning of the thirteenth century, combined to effect a great change on this old and simple idea of Indulgences. These were—(1) the formulation of the thought of a *treasury of merits* (*thesaurus meritorum*); (2) the change of the *institution* into the *Sacrament* of Penance; and (3) the distinction between *attrition* and *contrition* in the thought of the kind of sorrow God demands from a real penitent.

The conception of a storehouse of merits (*thesaurus meritorum* or *indulgentiarum*) was first formulated by Alexander of Hales[1] in the thirteenth century, and his ideas were accepted, enlarged, and made more precise by succeeding theologians.[2] Starting with the existing practice in the Church that some penances (such as pilgrimages) might be vicariously performed, and bringing together the several thoughts that the faithful are members of one body, that the good deeds of each of the members are the common property of all, and therefore that the more

[1] *Summa*, iv. 23.

[2] Thomas Aquinas, *Summa Theologiæ*, iii., *Supplementum*, Quæs. xxv. 1.

sinful can benefit by the good deeds of their more saintly brethren, and that the sacrifice of Christ was sufficient to wipe out the sins of all, theologians gradually formulated the doctrine that there was a common storehouse which contained the good deeds of living men and women, of the saints in heaven and the inexhaustible merits of Christ, and that all these merits accumulated there had been placed under the charge of the Pope, and could be dispensed by him to the faithful. The doctrine was not very precisely defined by the beginning of the sixteenth century, but it was generally believed in, taught, and accepted. It went to increase the vague sense of supernatural, spiritual powers attached to the person of the Bishop of Rome. It had one important consequence on the doctrine of Indulgences. They might be the payment out of this treasury of an absolute equivalent for the *satisfaction* due by the penitent for his sins; they were no longer merely the substitution of one form of penance for another, or the relaxation of a penance enjoined.

The *institution* of Penance contained within it the four practices of *Sorrow* for the sins committed (*contritio*); the *Confession* of these sins to the priest; *Satisfaction*, or the due manifestation of sorrow in the ways prescribed by the Church through the command of the confessor; and the *Pardon* (*absolutio*) pronounced by the priest in God's name. The pardon followed the *satisfaction*. But when the *institution* became the *Sacrament of Penance*, the order was changed: absolution followed confession and came before satisfaction, which it had formerly followed. Satisfaction lost its old meaning. It was no longer the outward sign of sorrow and the necessary precedent of pardon or absolution. According to the new theory, the absolution which immediately followed confession had the effect of removing the whole guilt of the sins confessed, and with the guilt the whole of the eternal punishment due. This cancelling of guilt and of eternal punishment did not however, forthwith open the gates of heaven to the pardoned sinner. It was felt that the justice of God could not permit the baptized sinner to escape from all punishment whatever. Hence it was said that although eternal punishment had disappeared with the absolution, there remained temporal punishment due for the sins, and that heaven could not be entered until this temporal punishment had been endured.[1] Temporal punishments might be of two kinds—those endured in this life, or those suffered in a place of punishment after death. The penance imposed by the priest, the satisfaction, now became the temporal punishment due for sins committed. If the priest had imposed the due amount, and if the penitent was able to perform all that had been imposed, the sins were expiated. But if the priest had imposed less than the justice of God actually demanded, then these temporal pains had to be completed in Purgatory. This gave rise to great uncertainty; for who could feel assured that the priest had calculated rightly, and had imposed satisfactions or temporal penalties which were of the precise amount demanded by the justice of God? Hence the pains of Purgatory threatened every man. It was here that the new idea of Indulgences came in to aid the faithful by securing him against the pains of Purgatory, which were not included in the absolution obtained in the *Sacrament of Penance*. Indulgences in the sense of relaxations of imposed penances went into the background, and the really valuable Indulgence was one which, because of the merits transferred from the storehouse of merits, was an equivalent in God's sight for the temporal punishments due for sins. Thus, in the opinion of Alexander of Hales, of Bonaventura,[2] and, above all, of Thomas Aquinas, the real

[1] "Du sprichst 'So ich am letsten in todes not,
Ain yeder priester mich zu absolviren not':
Von Schuld ist war, noch nitt von pein, so du bist tod,
Ja für ain stund in fegfeür dort.
Gabst du des Kaysers güte."
—(Wackernagel, *Das deutsche Kirchenlied*, etc. ii. 1068.)

[2] Bonaventura, *In Librum Quartum Sententiarum*, Dist. xx. Quæst. 5. Alexander of Hales, *Summa*, iv. Quæst. 59; Thomas Aquinas, *Summa*, iii., *Suppl.* Quæst. i. 2.

value of Indulgences was that they procured the remission of penalties due after absolution, whether these penalties were penances imposed by the priest or not; and when the uncertainty of the imposed penalties is remembered, the most valuable of all Indulgences were those which had regard to the unimposed penalties; the priest might make a mistake, but God did not blunder.

While Indulgences were always connected with satisfactions, and changed with the changes in the meaning of the latter term, they were not the less influenced by a distinction which came to be drawn between *attrition* and *contrition*, and by the application of the distinction to the theory of the Sacrament of Penance. During the earlier Middle Ages and down to the thirteenth century, it was always held that *contrition* (sorrow prompted by love) was the one thing taken into account by God in pardoning the sinner. The theologians of the thirteenth century, however, began to draw a distinction between this godly sorrow and a certain amount of sorrow which might arise from a variety of causes of a less worthy nature, and especially from servile fear. This was called *attrition*; and it was held that this *attrition*, though of itself too imperfect to win the pardon of God, might become perfected through the confession heard by the priest, and in the sacramental absolution pronounced by him. Very naturally, though perhaps illogically, it was believed that an imperfect sorrow, though sufficient to procure absolution, and, therefore, the blotting out of eternal punishment, merited more temporal punishment than if it had been sorrow of a godly sort. But it was these temporal penalties (including the pains of Purgatory) that Indulgences provided for. Hence, Indulgences appealed more strongly to the indifferent Christian, who knew that he had sinned, and at the same time felt that his sorrow was not the effect of his love to God. He knew that his sins deserved *some* punishment. His conscience, however weak, told him that he could not sin with perfect impunity, and that something more was needed than his perfunctory confession to a priest. He felt that he must do *something*—fast, or go on a pilgrimage, or purchase an Indulgence. It was at this point that the Church intervened to show him how his poor performance could be transformed by the power of the Church and its treasury of merits into something so great that the penalties of Purgatory could be actually evaded. His cheap sorrow, his careless confession, need not trouble him. Hence, for the ordinary indifferent Christian, *Attrition*, *Confession*, and *Indulgence* became the three heads of the scheme of the Church for his salvation. The one thing that satisfied his conscience was the burdensome thing he had to do, and that was to procure an Indulgence—a matter made increasingly easy for him as time went on.

It must not be supposed that this doctrine of *Attrition*, and its evident effect in deadening the conscience and in lowering the standard of morality, had the undivided support of the theologians of the later Middle Ages, but it was the doctrine taught by most of the Scotist theologians, who took the lead in theological thinking during these times. It was set forth in its most extravagant form by such a representative man as John of Paltz in Erfurt; it was preached by the pardon-sellers; it was eagerly welcomed by *indifferent* Christians, who desired to escape the penalties of sin without abandoning its enjoyments; it exalted the power of the priesthood; and it was specially valuable in securing good sales of Indulgences, and therefore in increasing the papal revenues. It lay at the basis of the whole theory and practice of Indulgences, which confronted Luther when he issued his *Theses*.

History shows us that gross abuses had always gathered round the practice of Indulgences, even in their earlier and simpler forms. The priests had abused the system, and the power of issuing Indulgences had been taken from them and confined to the bishops. The bishops, in turn, had abused the privilege, and the Popes had gradually assumed that the power to grant an Indulgence belonged to the Bishop of Rome exclusively, or to those to whom he might delegate it; and this assumption seemed both reasonable and salutary. The power was at first sparingly used. It is true that Pope Urban II., in 1095, promised to the Crusaders an Indulgence such as had never before been heard of—a complete remission of all imposed canonical penances; but it was not until the thirteenth and fourteen centuries that Indulgences, now doubly dangerous to the moral life from the new theories which had arisen, were lavished even more unsparingly than in the days when any bishop had power to grant them. From the beginning of the fourteenth century they were given to raise recruits for papal wars. They were lavished on the religious Orders, either for the benefit of the members or for the purpose of attracting strangers and their gifts to their churches. They were bestowed on cathedrals and other churches, or on individual altars in churches, and had the effect of endowments. They were joined to special collections of relics, to be earned by the faithful who visited the shrines. They were given to hospitals, and for the upkeep of bridges and of roads. Wherever they are met with in the later Middle Ages, and it would be difficult to say where they are not to be found, they are seen to be associated with sordid money-getting, and, as Luther remarked in an early sermon on the subject, they were a very grievous instrument placed in the hand of avarice.

The practice of granting Indulgences was universally prevalent and was universally accepted; but it was not easy to give an explanation of the system, in the sense of showing that it was an essential element in Christian discipline. No mediæval theologian attempted to do any such thing. Bonaventura and Thomas Aquinas, the two great Schoolmen who did more than any others to provide a theological basis for the system, tell us quite frankly that it is their business to accept the fact that Indulgences do exist as part of the penitentiary discipline of the Church, and, accepting it, they thought themselves bound to construct a reasonable theory.[1] The practice altered, and new theories were needed to explain the variations. It is needless to say that these explanations did not always agree; and that there were very great differences of opinion about what an Indulgence really effected for the man who bought it.

Of all these disputed questions the most important was: Did an Indulgence give remission for the guilt of sin, or only for certain penalties which followed the sinful deed? This is a question about which modern Romanists are extremely sensitive.

The universal answer given by all defenders of Indulgences who have written on the subject since the Council of Trent, is that guilt (*culpa*) and eternal punishment (*pœnæ eternæ*) are dealt with in the Sacrament of Penance, and that Indulgences relate only to temporal punishments, including under that designation the pains of Purgatory. This modern opinion is confirmed by the most eminent authorities of the mediæval Church. It has been accepted in the description of the theory of Indulgences given above, since it has been said that the principal use of Indulgences was to secure against Purgatory. But these statements do not exhaust the question. Mediæval theology did not create Indulgences, it only followed and tried to justify the practices of the Pope and of the Roman Curia,—a rather difficult task. The question still remains whether some of the Papal Bulls promulgating Indulgences did not promise the removal of guilt as well as security against temporal punishments. If these be examined, spurious Bulls being set aside, it will be found that many of them make no mention of the need of previous confession and of priestly absolution; that one or two expressly make mention of a remission of guilt as well as of penalty; and that many (especially those which pro-

[1] Thomas Aquinas, *Summa Theologiæ*, iii., *Supplem.* Quæstio xxv. 1: "Ecclesia universalis non potest errare . . . ecclesia universalis indulgentias approbat et facit. Ergo indulgentiæ aliquid valent . . . quia impium esset dicere quod Ecclesia aliquid vanè faceret."

claim a Jubilee Indulgence) use language which inevitably led intelligent laymen like Dante to believe that the Popes did proclaim the remission of guilt as well as of penalty. Of course, it may be said that in those days the distinction between guilt (*culpa*) and penalty (*pœna*) had not been very exactly defined, and that the phrase *remission of sins* was used to denote both remission of guilt and remission of penalty; still it is difficult to withstand the conclusion that, even in theory, Indulgences had been declared to be efficacious for the removal of the guilt of sin in the presence of God.

These questions of the theological meaning of an Indulgence, though necessary to understand the whole situation, had after all little to do with Luther's action. He approached the whole matter from the side of the practical effect of the proclamation of an Indulgence on the minds of common men who knew nothing of refined theological distinctions; and the evidence that the common people did generally believe that an Indulgence did remove the guilt of sin is overwhelming. Contemporary chroniclers are to be found who declare that Indulgences given to Crusaders remit the guilt as well as the punishment; contemporary preachers assert that plenary Indulgences remit guilt, and justify their opinion by declaring that such Indulgences were supposed to contain within them the Sacrament of Penance. The popular guide-books written for pilgrims to Rome and Compostella spread the popular idea that Indulgences acquired by such pilgrimages do remit guilt as well as penalty. The popular belief was so thoroughly acknowledged, that even Councils had to throw the blame for it on the pardon-sellers, or, like the Council of Constance, impeached the Pope and compelled him to confess that he had granted Indulgences for the remission of guilt as well as of penalty. This widespread popular belief of itself justified Luther in calling attention to this side of the matter.

Moreover, it is well to see what the theory of the most respected theologians actually meant when looked at practically. Since the formulation of the Sacrament of Penance, the theory had been that all guilt of sin and all eternal punishment were remitted in the priestly absolution which followed the confession of the penitent. The Sacrament of Penance had abolished guilt and Hell. But there remained the actual sins to be punished, because the justice of God demanded it, and this was done in the temporal pains of Purgatory. The "common man," if he thought at all about it, may be excused if he considered that guilt and Hell, taken away by the one hand, were restored by the other. There remained for him the sense that God's justice demanded *some* punishment for the sins he had committed; and if this was not guilt according to theological definition, it was probably all that he could attain to. He was taught and believed that punishment awaited him for these actual sins of his; and a punishment which might last thousands of years in Purgatory was not very different from an eternal punishment in his eyes. The Indulgence came to him filled as he was with these vague thoughts, and offered him a sure way of easing his conscience and avoiding the punishment he knew he deserved. He had only to pay the price of a *Papal Ticket*, perform the canonical good deed required, whatever it might be, and he was assured that his punishment was remitted, and God's justice satisfied. This may not involve the thought of the remission of guilt in the theological sense of the word, but it certainly misled the moral instincts of the "common man" about as much as if it did. It is not surprising that the common people made the theological mistake, if mistake it was, and saw in every plenary Indulgence the promise of the remission of guilt as well as of penalty,[1] for with them remission of guilt and quieting of conscience were one and the same thing. It was this practical moral effect of Indulgences, and not the theological explanation of the theory, which stirred Luther to make his protest.

[1] Cf. the hymn, "Der guldin Ablass," of the fifteenth century, in Wackernagel, ii. 283–284.

§ 2. *Luther's Theses.*[1]

Luther's *Theses* are singularly unlike what might have been expected from a Professor of Theology. They lack theological definition, and contain many repetitions which might have been easily avoided. They are simply ninety-five sturdy strokes struck at a great ecclesiastical abuse which was searing the consciences of many. They look like the utterances of a man who was in close touch with the people; who had been greatly shocked at reports brought to him of what the pardon-sellers had said; who had read a good many of the theological explanations of the practice of Indulgence, and had noted down a few things which he desired to contradict. They read as if they were meant for laymen, and were addressed to their common sense of spiritual things. They are plain and easily understood, and keep within the field of simple religion and plain moral truths.

The *Theses* appealed irresistibly to all those who had been brought up in the simple evangelical faith which distinguished the quiet home life of so many German families, and who had not forsaken it. They also appealed to all who had begun to adopt that secular or non-ecclesiastical piety which, we have seen, had been spreading quietly but rapidly throughout Germany at the close of the Middle Ages. These two forces, both religious, gathered round Luther. The effect of the *Theses* was almost imme-

[1] SOURCES: Köhler, *Luthers 95 Theses samt seinen Resolutionen sowie den Gegenschriften von Wimpina-Tetzel, Eck, und Prierias und den Antworten Luthers darauf* (Leipzig, 1903); Emil Reich, *Select Documents illustrating Mediæval and Modern History* (London, 1905).

LATER BOOKS: J. E. Kapp, *Sammlung einiger zum päpstlichen Ablass, überhaupt . . . aber zu der . . . zwischen Martin Luther und Johann Tetzel hiervongeführten Streitigkeit gehörigen Schriften, mit Einleitungen und Anmerkungen versehen* (Leipzig, 1721), and *Kleine Nachlese einiger . . . zur Erläuterung der Reformationsgeschichte nützlicher Urkunden* (Four parts, Leipzig, 1727–1733); Bratke, *Luthers 95 Theses und ihre dogmenhistorischen Voraussetzungen* (Göttingen, 1884); Dieckhoff, *Der Ablassstreit dogmengeschichtlich dargestellt* (Gotha, 1886); Gröne, *Tetzel und Luther* (Soest, 1860).

diate: the desire to purchase Indulgences cooled, and the sales almost stopped.

The Ninety-five *Theses* made six different assertions about Indulgences and their efficacy:

i. An Indulgence is and can only be the remission of a merely ecclesiastical penalty; the Church can remit what the Church has imposed; it cannot remit what God has imposed.

ii. An Indulgence can never remove guilt; the Pope himself cannot do such a thing; God has kept that in His own hand.

iii. It cannot remit the divine punishment for sin; that also is in the hands of God alone.

iv. It can have no efficacy for souls in Purgatory; penalties imposed by the Church can only refer to the living; death dissolves them; what the Pope can do for souls in Purgatory is by prayer, not by jurisdiction or the power of the keys.

v. The Christian who has true repentance has already received pardon from God altogether apart from an Indulgence, and does not need one; Christ demands this true repentance from every one.

vi. The Treasury of Merits has never been properly defined, it is hard to say what it is, and it is not properly understood by the people; it cannot be the merits of Christ and of His saints, because these act of themselves and quite apart from the intervention of the Pope; it can mean nothing more than that the Pope, having the power of the keys, can remit ecclesiastical penalties imposed by the Church; the true Treasure-house of merits is the Holy Gospel of the grace and glory of God.

The Archbishop of Mainz, finding that the publication of the *Theses* interfered with the sale of the Indulgences, sent a copy to Rome. Pope Leo, thinking that the whole thing was a monkish quarrel, contented himself with asking the General of the Augustinian Eremites to keep his monks quiet. Tetzel, in conjunction with a friend, Conrad Wimpina, published a set of counter-theses. John Mayr of Eck, professor at Ingolstadt, by far the ablest opponent Luther ever had, wrote an answer to the *Theses* which he entitled *Obelisks*;[1] and Luther replied in a tract with the title *Asterisks*. At Rome, Silvester Mazzolini (1460– ?) of Prierio, a Dominican monk, papal censor for the Roman Province and an Inquisitor, was profoundly dissatisfied with the *Ninety-five Theses*, and proceeded to criticise them severely in a *Dialogue about the Power of the Pope; against the Presumptuous Conclusions of Martin Luther*. The book reached Germany by the middle of January 1518. The Augustinian Eremites held their usual annual chapter at Heidelberg in April 1518, and Luther heard his *Theses* temperately discussed by his brother monks. He found the opposition to his views much stronger than he had expected; but the discussion was fair and honest, and Luther enjoyed it after the ominous silence kept by most of his friends, who had thought his action rash. When he returned from Heidelberg he began a general answer to his opponents. The book, *Resolutiones*, was probably the most carefully written of all Luther's writings. He thought long over it, weighed every statement carefully, and rewrote portions several times. The preface, addressed to his Vicar-General, Staupitz, contains some interesting autobiographical material; the book itself was addressed to the Pope; it was a detailed defence of his *Theses*.[2]

The *Ninety-five Theses* had a circulation which was, for the time, unprecedented. They were known throughout Germany in a little over a fortnight; they were read over Western Europe within four weeks "as if they had been circulated by angelic messengers," says Myconius enthusiastically. Luther was staggered at the way they were

[1] The *Obelisks* of Eck were printed and circulated privately long before they were published; a copy was in Luther's hand on March 4th, 1518; it was answered by him on March 24th, and was published in the August following.

[2] Köhler has collected together the *Ninety-five Theses*, the *Resolutiones*, and the attacks on the *Theses* by Wimpina-Tetzel, Eck, and Prierias, and published them in one small book (Leipzig, 1903). It is a handbook of reference, and the text of the documents has been carefully examined.

received; he said that he had not meant to determine, but to debate. The controversy they awakened increased their popularity. In the *Theses*, and especially in the *Resolutiones*, Luther had practically discarded all the practices which the Pope and the Roman Curia had introduced in the matter of Indulgences from the beginning of the thirteenth century, and all the ingenious explanations Scholastic theologians had brought forward to justify these practices. The readiest way to refute him was to assert the power of the Roman Bishop; and this was the line taken by his critics. Their arguments amount to this: the power to issue an Indulgence is simply a particular instance of the power of papal jurisdiction, and Indulgences are simply what the Pope proclaims them to be. Therefore, to attack Indulgences is to attack the power of the Pope, and that cannot be tolerated. The Roman Church is virtually the Universal Church, and the Pope is practically the Roman Church. Hence, as the representative of the Roman Church, which in turn represents the Church Universal, the Pope, when he acts officially, cannot err. Official decisions are given in actions as well as in words, custom has the force of law. Therefore, whoever objects to such a long-established system as Indulgences is a heretic, and does not deserve to be heard.[1]

But the argument which appealed most powerfully to the Roman Curia was the fact that the sales of the *Papal Tickets* had been declining since the publication of the *Theses*. Indulgences were the source of an enormous revenue, and anything which checked their sale would cause financial embarrassment. Pope Leo X. in his "enjoyment of the Papacy" lived lavishly. He had a huge income, much greater than that of any European monarch, but he lived beyond it. His income amounted to between four and five hundred thousand ducats; but he had spent seven hundred thousand on his war about the Duchy of Urbino; the magnificent reception of his brother Julian

[1] The arguments were all founded on Thomas Aquinas, *Summa*, iii., *Supplementum*, Quæstio xxv. 1.

and his bride in Rome (1514) had cost him fifty thousand ducats; and he had spent over three hundred thousand on the marriage of his nephew Lorenzo (1518). Voices had been heard in Rome as well as in Germany protesting against this extravagance. The Pope was in desperate need of money. It is scarcely to be wondered that Luther was summoned to Rome (summons dated July 1518, and received by Luther on August 7th) to answer for his attack on the Indulgence system. To have obeyed would have meant death.

The peremptory summons could be construed as an affront to the University of Wittenberg, on whose boards the *Ninety five Theses* had been posted. Luther wrote to his friend Spalatin (George Burkhardt of Spalt, 1484–1545), who was chaplain and private secretary to the Elector Frederick, suggesting that the prince ought to defend the rights of his University. Spalatin wrote at once to the Elector and also to the Emperor Maximilian, and the result was that the summons to Rome was cancelled, and it was arranged that the matter was to be left in the hands of the Papal Legate in Germany, Thomas de Vio, Cardinal Cajetan[1] (1470–1553), and Luther was ordered to present himself before that official at Augsburg. The interview (October 1518) was not very satisfactory. The cardinal demanded that Luther should recant his heresies without any argument. When pressed to say what the heresies were, he named the statement in the 58th Thesis that the merits of Christ work effectually without the intervention of the Pope, and that in the *Resolutiones* which said that the sacraments are not efficacious apart from faith in the recipient. There was some discussion notwithstanding the Legate's declaration; but in the end Luther was ordered to recant or

[1] Thomas de Vio was born at Gæta, a town situated on a promontory about fifty miles north of Naples, and was called Cajetanus from his birthplace. His baptismal name was James, and he took that of Thomas in honour of Thomas Aquinas. He had entered the Dominican Order at the age of sixteen; he was a learned man, a Scholastic of the older Thomist type, and not without evangelical sympathies; but he had the Dominican idea that ecclesiastical discipline must be maintained at all costs.

depart. He wrote out an appeal from the Pope ill-informed to the Pope well-informed, also an appeal to a General Council, and returned to Wittenberg.

When Luther had posted his *Theses* on the doors of the Church of All Saints, he had been a solitary monk with nothing but his manhood to back him; but nine months had made a wonderful difference in the situation. He now knew that he was a representative man, with supporters to be numbered by the thousand. His colleagues at Wittenberg were with him; his students demonstratively loyal (they had been burning the Wimpina-Tetzel counter-theses); his theology was spreading among all the cloisters of his Order in Germany, and even in the Netherlands; and the rapid circulation of his *Theses* had shown him that he had the ear of Germany. His first task, on his return to Wittenberg, was to prepare for the press an account of his interview with Cardinal Cajetan at Augsburg, and this was published under the title, *Acta Augustana*.

Luther was at pains to take the people of Germany into his confidence; he published an account of every important interview he had; the people were able to follow him step by step, and he was never so far in advance that they were unable to see his footprints. The immediate effect of the *Acta Augustana* was an immense amount of public sympathy for Luther. The people, even the Humanists who had cared little for the controversy, saw that an eminently pious man, an esteemed teacher who was making his obscure University famous, who had done nothing but propose a discussion on the notoriously intricate question of Indulgences, was peremptorily ordered to recant and remain silent. They could only infer that the Italians treated the Germans contemptuously, and wished simply to drain the country of money to be spent in the luxuries of the papal court. The Elector Frederick shared the common opinion, and was, besides, keenly alive to anything which touched his University and its prosperity. There is no evidence to show that he had much sympathy with Luther's views. But the University of Wittenberg, the seat of learning he had founded, so long languishing with a very precarious life and now flourishing, was the apple of his eye; and he resolved to defend it, and to protect the teacher who had won renown for it.

The political situation in Germany was too delicate, and the personal political influence of Frederick too great, for the Pope to act rashly in any matter in which that prince took a deep interest. The country was on the eve of an election of a King of the Romans; Maximilian was old, and an imperial election might occur at any time; and Frederick was one of the most important factors in either case. So the Pope resolved to act cautiously. The condemnation of Luther by the Cardinal-Legate was held over, and a special papal delegate was sent down to Germany to make inquiries. Every care was taken to select a man who would be likely to be acceptable to the Elector. Charles von Miltitz, a Saxon nobleman belonging to the Meisen district, a canon of Mainz, Trier, and Meissen, a papal chamberlain, an acquaint- of Spalatin's, the Elector's own agent at the Court of Rome, was sent to Germany. He took with him the "Golden Rose" as a token of the Pope's personal admiration for the Elector. He was furnished with numerous letters from His Holiness to the Elector, to some of the Saxon councillors, to the magistrates of Wittenberg, in all of which Luther figured as a child of the Devil. The phrase was probably forgotten when Leo wrote to Luther some time afterwards and called him his dear son.

When Miltitz got among German speaking people he found that the state of matters was undreamt of at the papal court. He was a German, and knew the Germans. He could see, what the Cardinal-Legate had never perceived, that he had to deal not with the stubbornness of a recalcitrant monk, but with the slow movement of a nation. When he visited his friends and relations in Augsburg and Nürnberg, he found that three out of five were on Luther's side. He came to the wise resolution that he would see both Luther and Tetzel privately before producing his credentials. Tetzel he could not see. The unhappy man wrote to Miltitz that he dared not stir from his convent, so greatly was he in danger from the violence of the people. Miltitz met Luther in the house of Spalatin; he at once disowned the speeches of the pardon-sellers; he let it be seen that he did not think much of the Cardinal-Legate's methods of action; he so prevailed on Luther that the latter promised to write a submissive letter to the Pope, to advise people to reverence the Roman See, to say that Indulgences were useful in the remission of canonical penances. Luther did all this; and if the Roman Curia had supported Miltitz there is no saying how far the reconciliation would have gone. But the Roman Curia did not support the papal chamberlain, and Miltitz had also to reckon with John Eck, who was burning to extinguish Luther in a public discussion.

The months between his interview at Augsburg (October 1518) and the Disputation with John Eck at Leipzig (June 1519) had been spent by Luther in hard and disquieting studies. His opponents had confronted him with the Pope's absolute supremacy in all ecclesiastical matters. This was one of Luther's oldest inherited beliefs. The Church had been for him "the Pope's House," in which the Pope was the house-father, to whom all obedience was due. It was hard for him to think otherwise. He had been re-examining his convictions about justifying faith and attempting to trace clearly their consequences, and whether they did lead to his declarations about the efficacy of Indulgences. He could come to no other conclusion. It became necessary to investigate the evidence for the papal claim to absolute authority. He began to study the Decretals, and found, to his amazement and indignation, that they were full of frauds; and that the papal supremacy had been forced on Germany on the strength of a collection of Decretals many of which were plainly forgeries. It is difficult to say whether the discovery brought more joy or more grief to Luther. Under the combined influences of historical study, of the opinions of the early Church Fathers, and of the Holy Scriptures, one of his oldest landmarks was crumbling to pieces. His mind was in a whirl of doubt. He was half-exultant and half-terrified at the result of his studies; and his correspondence reveals how his mood of mind changed from week to week. It was while he was thus "on the swither," tremulously on the balance, that John Eck challenged him to dispute at Leipzig on the primacy and supremacy of the Roman Pontiff. The discussion might clear the air, might make himself see where he stood. He accepted the challenge almost feverishly.

§ 3. *The Leipzig Disputation.*[1]

Leipzig was an enemies' country, and his Wittenberg friends would not allow Luther to go there unaccompanied. The young Duke Barnim, who was Rector of the University of Wittenberg, accompanied Carlstadt and Luther, to give them the protection of his presence. Melanchthon, who had been a member of the teaching staff of Wittenberg since August 1518, Justus Jonas, and Nicholas Amsdorf went along with them. Two hundred Wittenberg students in helmets and halberts formed a guard, and walked beside the two country carts which carried their professors. An eye-witness of the scenes at Leipzig has left us sketches of what he saw:

"In the inns where the Wittenberg students lodged, the landlord kept a man standing with a halbert near the table to keep the peace while the Leipzig and the Wittenberg students disputed with each other. I have seen the same myself in the house of Herbipolis, a bookseller, where I went to dine . . . for there was at table a Master Baumgarten . . . who was so hot against the Wittenbergers that the host had to restrain him with a halbert to make him keep the peace so long as the Wittenbergers were in the house and sat and ate at the table with him."

[1] Seidemann, *Die Leipziger Disputation im Jahre 1519* (Dresden, 1843).

The University buildings at Leipzig did not contain any hall large enough for the audience, and Duke George lent the use of his great banqueting-room for the occasion. The discussions were preceded by a service in the church.

"When we got to the church . . . they sang a Mass with twelve voices which had never been heard before. After Mass we went to the Castle, where we found a great guard of burghers in their armour with their best weapons and their banners; they were ordered to be there twice a day, from seven to nine in the morning and from two to five in the afternoon, to keep the peace while the Disputation lasted." [1]

First, there was a Disputation between Carlstadt and Eck, and then, on the fourth of July, Eck and Luther faced each other—both sons of peasants, met to protect the old or cleave a way for the new.

It was the first time that Luther had ever met a controversialist of European fame. John Eck came to Leipzig fresh from his triumphs at the great debates in Vienna and Bologna, and was and felt himself to be the hero of the occasion.

"He had a huge square body, a full strong voice coming from his chest, fit for a tragic actor or a town crier, more harsh than distinct; his mouth, eyes, and whole aspect gave one the idea of a butcher or a soldier rather than of a theologian. He gave one the idea of a man striving to overcome his opponent rather than of one striving to win a victory for the truth. There was as much sophistry as good reasoning in his arguments; he was continually misquoting his opponents' words or trying to give them a meaning they were not intended to convey."

"Martin," says the same eye-witness,

"is of middle height; his body is slender, emaciated by study and by cares; one can count almost all the bones; he stands in the prime of his age; his voice sounds clear and distinct . . . however hard his opponent pressed him he maintained his calmness and his good nature, though in debate he sometimes used bitter words. . . . He carried a

[1] *Zeitschrift für die historische Theologie* for 1872, p. 534.

bunch of flowers in his hand, and when the discussion became hot he looked at it and smelt it."[1]

Eck's intention was to force his opponent to make some declaration which would justify him in charging Luther with being a partisan of the mediæval heretics, and especially of the Hussites. He continually led the debate away to the Waldensians, the followers of Wiclif, and the Bohemians. The audience swayed with a wave of excitement when Luther was gradually forced to admit that there might be some truth in some of the Hussite opinions:

"One thing I must tell which I myself heard in the Disputation, and which took place in the presence of Duke George, who came often to the Disputation and listened most attentively; once Dr. Martin spoke these words to Dr. Eck when hard pressed about John Huss: 'Dear Doctor, the Hussite opinions are not all wrong.' Thereupon said Duke George, so loudly that the whole audience heard, 'God help us, the pestilence!' (Das walt, die Sucht), and he wagged his head and placed his arms akimbo. That I myself heard and saw, for I sat almost between his feet and those of Duke Barnim of Pomerania, who was then the Rector of Wittenberg."[2]

So far as the dialectic battle was concerned, Eck had been victorious. He had done what he had meant to do. He had made Luther declare himself. All that was now needed was a Papal Bull against Luther, and the world would be rid of another pestilent heretic. He had done what the more politic Miltitz had wished to avoid. He had concentrated the attention of Germany on Luther, and had made him the central figure round which all the smouldering discontent could gather. As for Luther, he returned to Wittenberg full of melancholy forebodings. They did not prevent him preparing and publishing for the German people an account of the Disputation, which

[1] Petri Mosellani, "Epistola de Disput. Lips." in Löscher's *Reformations Acta et Documenta* (Leipzig, 1720–1729), i. pp. 242 ff.

[2] *Zeitschrift für die historische Theologie* for 1872, p. 535. The diarist is M. Sebastian Froscher.

was eagerly read. His arguments had been historical rather than theological. He tried to show that the acknowledgment of the supremacy of the Bishop of Rome was barely four hundred years old in Western Europe, and that it did not exist in the East. The Greek Church, he said, was part of the Church of Christ, and it would have nothing to do with the Pope; the great Councils of the Early Christian centuries knew nothing about papal supremacy. Athanasius, Basil, the Gregories, Cyprian himself, had all taken Luther's own position, and were heretics, according to Eck. Luther's speeches at Leipzig laid the foundation of that modern historical criticism of institutions which has gone so far in our own days.

In some respects the Leipzig Disputation was the most important point in the career of Luther. It made him see for the first time what lay in his opposition to Indulgences. It made the people see it also. His attack was no criticism, as he had at first thought, of a mere excrescence on the mediæval ecclesiastical system. He had struck at its centre; at its ideas of a priestly mediation which denied the right of every believer to immediate entrance into the very presence of God. It was after the Disputation at Leipzig that the younger German Humanists rallied round Luther to a man; that the burghers saw that religion and opposition to priestly tyranny were not opposite things; and that there was room for an honest attempt to create a Germany for the Germans independent of Rome. Luther found himself a new man after Leipzig, with a new freedom and wider sympathies. His depression fled. Sermons, pamphlets, letters from his tireless pen flooded the land, and were read eagerly by all classes of the population.

§ 4. *The Three Treatises.*[1]

Three of these writings stand forth so pre-eminently that they deserve special notice: *The Liberty of a Christian Man*, *To the Christian Nobility of the German Nation*, and

[1] Wace and Buchheim, *Luther's Primary Works* (London, 1896).

On the Babylonian Captivity of the Church. These three books are commonly called in Germany the *Three Great Reformation Treatises*, and the title befits them well. They were all written during the year 1520, after three years spent in controversy, at a time when Luther felt that he had completely broken from Rome, and when he knew that he had nothing to expect from Rome but a sentence of excommunication. His teaching may have varied in details afterwards, but in all essential positions it remained what is to be found in these books.

The tract on *The Liberty of a Christian Man*, "a very small book so far as the paper is concerned," said Luther, "but one containing the whole sum of the Christian life," had a somewhat pathetic history. Miltitz, hoping against hope that the Pope would not push things to extremities, had asked Luther to write out a short summary of his inmost beliefs and send it to His Holiness. Luther consented, and this little volume was the result. It has for preface Luther's letter to Pope Leo X., which concludes thus: "I, in my poverty, have no other present to make you, nor do you need to be enriched by anything but a spiritual gift." It was probably the last of the three published (Oct. 1520), but it contains the principles which underlie the other two.

The booklet is a brief statement, free from all theological subtleties, of the priesthood of all believers which is a consequence of the fact of justification by faith alone. Its note of warning to Rome, and its educational value for pious people in the sixteenth century, consisted in its showing that the man who fears God and trusts in Him need not fear the priests nor the Church. The first part proves that every spiritual possession which a man has or can have must be traced back to his faith; if he has faith, he has all; if he has not faith, he has nothing. It is the possession of faith which gives liberty to a Christian man; God is with him, who can be against him?

"Here you will ask, 'If all who are in the Church are priests, by what character are those whom we now call priests to be distinguished from the laity?' I reply, By the use of those words *priests, clergy, spiritual person, ecclesiastic*, an injustice has been done, since they have been transferred from the remaining body of Christians to those few who are now, by a hurtful custom, called ecclesiastics. For the Holy Scripture makes no distinction between them, except that those who are now boastfully called Popes, Bishops, and Lords, it calls ministers, servants, and stewards, who are to serve the rest in the ministry of the Word, for teaching the faith of Christ and the liberty of believers. For though it is true that we are all equally priests, yet cannot we, nor ought we if we could, all to minister and teach publicly."

The second part shows that everything that a Christian man does must come from his faith. It may be necessary to use all the ceremonies of divine service which past generations have found useful to promote the religious life; perhaps to fast and practise mortifications of the flesh; but if such things are to be really profitable, they must be kept in their proper place. They are good deeds not in the sense of making a man good, but as the signs of his faith; they are to be practised with joy because they are done for the sake of the God who has united Himself with man through Jesus Christ.

Nothing that Luther has written more clearly manifests that combination of revolutionary daring and wise conservatism which was characteristic of the man. There is no attempt to sweep away any ecclesiastical machinery, provided only it be kept in its proper place as a means to an end. But religious ceremonies are not an end in themselves; and if through human corruption and neglect of the plain precepts of God's word they hinder instead of help the true growth of the soul, they ought to be swept away; and the fact that the soul of man needs absolutely nothing in the last resort but the word of God dwelling in him, gives men courage and calmness in demanding their reformation.

Luther applied those principles to the reformation of the Church in his book on the *Babylonian Captivity of the Church* (Sept.–Oct. 1520). He subjected the elaborate sacramental system of the Church to a searching criticism, and concluded that there are only two, or perhaps three, scriptural sacraments—the Eucharist, Baptism, and Penance. He denounced the doctrine of Transubstantiation as a "monstrous phantom" which the Church of the first twelve centuries knew nothing about, and said that any endeavour to define the precise manner of Christ's Presence in the sacrament is simply indecent curiosity. Perhaps the most important practical portion of the book deals with the topic of Christian marriage. In no sphere of human life has the Roman Church done more harm by interfering with simple scriptural directions:

> "What shall we say of those impious human laws by which this divinely appointed manner of life has been entangled and tossed up and down? Good God! it is horrible to look upon the temerity of the tyrants of Rome, who thus, according to their caprices, at one time annul marriages and at another time enforce them. Is the human race given over to their caprice for nothing but to be mocked and abused in every way, that these men may do what they please with it for the sake of their own fatal gains? . . . And what do they sell? The shame of men and women, a merchandise worthy of these traffickers, who surpass all that is most sordid and most disgusting in their avarice and impiety."

Luther points out that there is a clear scriptural law on the degrees within which marriage is unlawful, and says that no human regulations ought to forbid marriages outside these degrees or permit them within. He also comes to the conclusion that divorce *a mensa et thoro* is clearly permitted in Scripture; though he says that personally he hates divorce, and "prefers bigamy to it."

The appeal *To the Christian Nobility of the German Nation* made the greatest immediate impression. It was written in haste, but must have been long thought over. Luther began the introduction on June 23rd (1520); the book was ready by the middle of August; and by the 18th, four thousand copies were in circulation throughout Germany, and the presses could not print fast enough for the demand. It was a call to all Germany to unite against Rome.

It was nobly comprehensive: it grasped the whole situation, and summed up with vigour and clearness all the German grievances which had hitherto been stated separately and weakly; it brought forward every partial proposal of reform, however incomplete, and quickened it by setting it in its proper place in one combined scheme. All the parts were welded together by a simple and courageous faith, and made living by the moral earnestness which pervaded the whole.

Luther struck directly at the imaginary mysterious semi-supernatural power supposed to belong to the Church and the priesthood which had held Europe in awed submission for so many centuries. Reform had been impossible, the appeal said, because the walls behind which Rome lay entrenched had been left standing—walls of straw and paper, but in appearance formidable. These sham fortifications are: the *Spiritual Power* which is believed to be superior to the temporal power of kings and princes, the conception that *no one can interpret Scripture but the Pope*, the idea that *no one can summon a General Council but the Bishop of Rome.* These are the threefold lines of fortification behind which the Roman Curia has entrenched itself, and the German people has long believed that they are impregnable. Luther sets to work to demolish them.

The Romanists assert that the Pope, bishops, priests, and monks belong to and constitute the *spiritual estate*, while princes, lords, artisans, and peasants are the *temporal estate*, which is subject to the spiritual. But this *spiritual estate* is a mere delusion. The real *spiritual estate* is the whole body of believers in Jesus Christ, and they are spiritual because Jesus has made all His followers priests to God and to His Christ. A cobbler belongs to the *spiritual estate* as truly as a bishop. The clergy are distinguished from the laity not by an indelible character imposed upon them in a divine mystery called ordination, but because they have been set apart to do a particular kind of work in the commonwealth. If a Pope, bishop, priest, or monk neglects to do the work he is there to do, he deserves to be punished as much as a careless mason or tailor, and is as accountable to the civil authorities. The *spiritual priesthood of all believers*, the gift of the faith which justifies, has shattered the first and most formidable of these papal fortifications.

It is foolish to say that the *Pope alone can interpret Scripture*. If that were true, where is the need of Holy Scriptures at all?

> "Let us burn them, and content ourselves with the unlearned gentlemen at Rome, in whom the Holy Ghost alone dwells, who, however, can dwell in pious souls only. If I had not read it, I could never have believed that the devil should have put forth such follies at Rome and find a following."

The Holy Scripture is open to all, and can be interpreted by all true believers who have the mind of Christ and approach the word of God humbly seeking enlightenment.

The third wall falls with the other two. It is nonsense to say that *the Pope alone can call a Council.* We are plainly taught in Scripture that if our brother offends we are to tell it to the Church; and if the Pope offends, and he often does, we can only obey Scripture by calling a Council. Every individual Christian has a right to do his best to have it summoned; the temporal powers are there to enforce his wishes; Emperors called General Councils in the earlier ages of the Church.

The straw and paper walls having been thus cleared away, Luther proceeds to state his indictment. There is in Rome one who calls himself the Vicar of Christ, and who lives in a state of singular resemblance to our Lord and to St. Peter, His apostle. For this man wears a triple crown (a single one does not content him), and keeps up such a state that he needs a larger personal revenue than the Emperor. He has surrounding him a number of men, called cardinals, whose only apparent use is that they serve to draw to themselves the revenues of the richest convents, endowments, and benefices in Europe, and spend the money thus obtained in keeping up the state of a great monarch in Rome. When it is impossible to seize the whole revenue of an ecclesiastical benefice, the Curia joins some ten or twenty together, and mulcts each in a good round sum for the benefit of the cardinal. Thus the priory of Würzburg gives one thousand gulden yearly, and Bamberg, Mainz, and Trier pay their quotas. The papal court is enormous,—three thousand papal secretaries, and hangers-on innumerable; and all are waiting for German benefices, whose duties they never fulfil, as wolves wait for a flock of sheep. Germany pays more to the Curia than it gives to its own Emperor. Then look at the way Rome robs the whole German land. Long ago the Emperor permitted the Pope to take the half of the first year's income from every benefice—the *Annates*—to provide for a war against the Turks. The money was never spent for the purpose destined; yet it has been regularly paid for a hundred years, and the Pope demands it as a regular and legitimate tax, and uses it to pay posts and offices at Rome.

"Whenever there is any pretence of fighting the Turk, they send out commissions for collecting money, and often proclaim Indulgences under the same pretext. . . . They think that we, Germans, will always remain such great fools, and that we will go on giving money to satisfy their unspeakable greed, though we see plainly that neither *Annates* nor *Indulgence-money* nor anything — not one farthing—goes against the Turks, but all goes into their bottomless sack, . . . and all this is done in the name of Christ and of St. Peter."

The chicanery used to get possession of German benefices for officials of the Curia, the exactions on the bestowal of the *pallium*, the trafficking in exemptions and permissions to evade laws ecclesiastical and moral, are all trenchantly described. The most shameless are those connected with marriage. The Curial Court is described as a place

"where vows are annulled; where a monk gets leave to quit his cloister; where priests can enter the married life for money; where bastards can become legitimate, and dishonour and shame may arrive at high honours, and all evil repute and disgrace is knighted and ennobled; where a marriage is suffered that is in a forbidden degree, or has some other defect. . . . There is a buying and selling, a changing, blustering, and bargaining, cheating and lying, robbing and stealing, debauchery and villainy, and all kinds of contempt of God, that Antichrist himself could not reign worse."

The plan of reform sketched includes — the complete abolition of the power of the Pope over the State; the creation of a national German Church, with an ecclesiastical Council of its own to be the final court of appeal for Germany, and to represent the German Church as the Diet did the German State; some internal religious reforms, such as the limitation of the number of pilgrimages, which were destroying morality and creating a distaste for honest work; reductions in the mendicant orders and in the number of vagrants who thronged the roads, and were a scandal in the towns.

"It is of much more importance to consider what is necessary for the salvation of the common people than what St. Francis, or St. Dominic, or St. Augustine, or any other man laid down, especially as things have not turned out as they expected."

He proposes the inspection of all convents and nunneries, and permission given to those who are dissatisfied with their monastic lives to return to the world; the limitation of ecclesiastical holy days, which are too often nothing but scenes of drunkenness, gluttony, and debauchery; a married priesthood, and an end put to the degrading concubinage of the German priests.

"We see how the priesthood is fallen, and how many a poor priest is encumbered with a woman and children, and burdened in his conscience, and no one does anything to help him, though he might very well be helped. . . . I will not conceal my honest counsel, nor withhold comfort from that unhappy crowd who now live in trouble with wife and children, and remain in shame with a heavy conscience hearing their wife called a priest's harlot, and their children bastards. . . . I say that these two (who are minded in their hearts to live together in conjugal fidelity) are surely married before God."

The appeal concludes with some solemn words addressed to the luxury and licensed immorality of the German towns.

None of Luther's writings produced such an instantaneous effect as this. It was not the first programme urging common action in the interests of a united Germany, but it was the most complete, and was recognised to be so by all who were working for a Germany for the Germans.

The three "Reformation treatises" were the statement of Luther's case laid before the people of the Fatherland, and were a very effectual antidote to the Papal Bull excommunicating him, which was ready for publication in Germany.

§ 5. *The Papal Bull.*

The Bull, *Exurge Domine*, was scarcely worthy of the occasion. The Pope seems to have left its construction in the hands of Prierias, Cajetan, and Eck, and the contents seem to show that Eck had the largest share in framing it. Much of it reads like an echo of Eck's statements at Leipzig a year before. It began pathetically: "Arise, O Lord, plead Thine own cause; remember how the foolish man reproacheth Thee daily; the foxes are wasting Thy vineyard, which Thou hast given to Thy Vicar Peter; the boar out of the wood doth waste it, and the wild beast of the field doth devour it." St. Peter is invoked, and the Pope's distress at the news of Luther's misdeeds is described at length. The most disturbing thing is that the errors of the Greeks and of the Bohemians were being revived, and that in Germany, which had hitherto been so faithful to the Holy See. Then came forty-one propositions, said to be Luther's, which are condemned as "heretical or scandalous, or false or offensive to pious ears, or seducing to simple minds, and standing in the way of the Catholic faith."[1] All faithful people were ordered to burn Luther's books wherever they could find them. Luther himself had refused to come to Rome and submit to instruction; he had even appealed to a General Council, contrary to the decrees of Julius II. and Pius II.; he was therefore inhibited from preaching; he and all who followed him were ordered to make public recantation within sixty days; if they did not, they were to be treated as heretics, were to be seized and imprisoned by the magistrates, and all towns or districts which sheltered them were to be placed under an interdict.

Among the forty-one propositions condemned was one —that the burning of heretics was a sin against the Spirit of Christ—to which the Pope seemed to attach special significance, so often did he repeat it in letters to the Elector Frederick and other authorities in Germany. The others may be arranged in four classes—against Luther's opinions about Indulgences; his statements about Purgatory his declarations that the efficacy of the sacraments depended upon the spiritual condition of those who received them; that penance was an outward sign of sorrow, and that good works (ecclesiastical and moral) were to be regarded as the signs of faith rather than as making men actually righteous; his denial of the later *curial* assertions of the nature of the papal monarchy over the Church. Luther's opinions on all these points could be supported by abundant testimony from the earlier ages of the Church, and most of his criticisms were directed against theories which had not been introduced before the middle of the thirteenth century. The Bull made no attempt to argue about the truth of the positions taken in its sentences. There was nothing done to show that Luther's opinions were wrong. The one dominant note running all through the papal deliverance was the simple assertion of the Pope's right to order any discussion to cease at his command.

This did not help to commend the Bull to the people of Germany, and was specially unsuited to an age of restless

[1] Denzinger, *Enchiridion*, etc. p. 175.

mental activity. The method adopted for publishing it in Germany was still less calculated to win respect for its decisions. The publication was entrusted to John Eck of Ingolstadt, who was universally recognised as Luther's personal enemy; and the hitherto unheard of liberty was granted to him to insert at his pleasure the names of a certain number of persons, and to summon them to appear before the Roman Curia. He showed how unfit he was for this responsible task by inserting the names of men who had criticised or satirised him—Adelmann, Pirkheimer, Carlstadt, and three others.[1]

Eck discovered that it was an easier matter to get permission from the Roman Curia to frame a Bull against the man who had stopped the sale of Indulgences, and was drying up a great source of revenue, than to publish the Bull in Germany. It was thought at Rome that no man had more influence among the bishops and Universities, but the Curia soon learnt that it had made a mistake. The Universities stood upon their privileges, and would have nothing to do with John Eck. The bishops made all manner of technical objections. Many persons affected to believe that the Bull was not authentic; and Luther himself did not disdain to take this line in his tract, *Against the Execrable Bull of Antichrist.* Eck, who had come down to Germany inflated with vanity, found himself mocked and scorned. Pirkheimer dubbed him *gehobelter Eck*, Eck "polished off," and the epithet stuck Nor was the publication any easier when the pretence of unauthenticity could be maintained no longer. The University of Wittenberg refused to publish the Bull,

[1] In a pamphlet written by Eck in 1519, he had asserted that all the theologians in Germany were opposed to Luther save a few unlearned canons. This called forth, towards the end of the year, *The Answer of an Unlearned Canon*, which was generally ascribed to Bernard Adelmann, a canon of Augsburg, but which was really written by Oecolampadius. Pirkheimer had written a caustic attack on Eck in a satire, in which German coarseness was clothed in elegant latinity, entitled *Eccius Dedolatus* (*The Corner planed off*, Eck being the German for "corner"), published in *Lateinische Litteraturdenkmäler des 15 und 16 Jahrhundertes* (Berlin, 1891). Carlstadt had opposed Eck at Leipzig.

on the ground that the Pope would not have permitted its issue had he known the true state of matters, and they blamed Eck for misinforming His Holiness: the Council of Electoral Saxony agreed with the Senate; and their action was generally commended. Spalatin said that he had seen at least thirty letters from great princes and learned men of all districts in Germany, from Pomerania to Switzerland, and from the Breisgau to Bohemia, encouraging Luther to stand firm. Eck implored the bishops of the dioceses surrounding Wittenberg—Merseburg, Meissen, and Brandenburg—to publish the Bull. They were either unwilling or powerless.

Luther had been expecting a Bull against him ever since the Leipzig Disputation. His correspondence reveals that he met it undismayed. What harm could a papal Bull do to a man whose faith had given him fellowship with God? What truth could there be in a Bull which clearly contradicted the Holy Scriptures? St. Paul has warned us against believing an angel from heaven if he uttered words different from the Scriptures, which are our strength and our consolation; why should we pin our faith to a Pope or a Council? The Bull had done one thing for him, it had made him an excommunicated man, and therefore had freed him from his monastic vows. He could leave the convent when he liked, only he did not choose to do so. When he heard that his writings had been burnt as heretical by order of the Papal Legates, he resolved to retaliate. It was no sudden decision. Eleven months previously he had assured Spalatin (January 1520) that if Rome condemned and burnt his writings he would condemn and burn the papal Decretal Laws. On December 10th (1520) he posted a notice inviting the Wittenberg students to witness the burning of the papal Constitutions and the books of Scholastic Theology at nine o'clock in the morning.[1] A multitude of students,

[1] A copy of Luther's notice has been preserved in the MS. "Annals" of Peter Schumann in the *Zwickau Ratsschulbibliothek* at Zwickau. It has been printed in Kolde's *Analecta Lutherana* (Gotha, 1883), p. 26: "Quis-

burghers, and professors met in the open space outside the Elster Gate between the walls and the river Elbe. A great bonfire had been built. An oak tree planted long ago still marks the spot. One of the professors kindled the pile; Luther laid the books of the Decretals on the glowing mass, and they caught the flames; then amid solemn silence he placed a copy of the Bull on the fire, saying in Latin: *As thou hast wasted with anxiety the Holy One of God, so may the eternal flames waste thee* (*Quia tu conturbasti Sanctum Domini, ideoque te conturbet ignis eternus*). He waited till the paper was consumed, and then with his friends and fellow-professors he went back to the town. Some hundreds of students remained standing round the fire. For a while they were sobered by the solemnity of the occasion and sang the *Te Deum.* Then a spirit of mischief seized them, and they began singing funeral dirges in honour of the burnt Decretals. They got a peasant's cart, fixed in it a pole on which they hung a six-foot-long banner emblazoned with the Bull, piled the small cart with the books of Eck Emser, and other Romish controversialists, hauled it along the streets and out through the Elster Gate, and, throwing books and Bull on the glowing embers of the bonfire, they burnt them. Sobered again, they sang the *Te Deum* and finally dispersed.

It is scarcely possible for us in the twentieth century to imagine the thrill that went through Germany, and indeed through all Europe, when the news sped that a poor monk had burnt the Pope's Bull. Papal Bulls had been burnt before Luther's days, but the burners had been for the most part powerful monarchs. This time it was done by a monk, with nothing but his courageous faith to back him. It meant that the individual soul had discovered its

quis veritatis Evangelicæ studio teneatur. Adesto sub horam nonam, modo ad templum S. Crucis extra mœnia oppidi, ubi pro veteri et apostolico ritu impii pontificiarum constitutionum et scholasticæ theologiæ libri cremabuntur quandoquidem eo processit audatia inimicorum Evangelii, ut pios ac evangelicos Luteri exusserit. Age pia et studiosa juventus ad hoc pium ac religiosum spectaculum constituito. Fortassis enim nunc tempus est quo revelari Antichristum opportuit."

true value. If eras can be dated, modern history began on December 10th, 1520.

§ 6. *Luther the Representative of Germany.*

Hitherto we have followed Luther's personal career exclusively. It may be well to turn aside for a little to see how the sympathy of many classes of the people was gathering round him.

The representatives of foreign States who were present at the Diet of Worms, of England, Spain, and Venice, all wrote home to their respective governments about the extraordinary popularity which Luther enjoyed among almost every class of his fellow-countrymen; and, as we shall see, the despatches of Aleander, the papal nuncio at the Diet, are full of statements and complaints which confirm these reports. This popularity had been growing since 1517, and there are traces that many thoughtful men had been attracted to Luther some years earlier. The accounts of Luther's interview with Cardinal Cajetan at Augsburg, and his attitude at the Leipzig Disputation, had given a great impulse to the veneration with which people regarded him; but the veneration itself had been quietly growing, apart from any striking incidents in his career. The evidence for what follows has been collected chiefly from such private correspondence as has descended to us; and most stress has been laid on letters which were not addressed to Luther, and which were never meant to be seen by him. Men wrote to each other about him, and described the impression he was making on themselves and on the immediate circle of their acquaintances. We learn from such letters not merely the fact of the esteem, but what were the characteristics in the man which called it forth.[1]

A large part of the evidence comes from the correspondence of educated men, who, if they were not all

[1] Fr. v. Bezold has some excellent pages on this subject in his *Geschichte der deutschen Reformation* (Berlin, 1890), pp. 278 ff. I have used the material he has collected, and added to it from my own reading.

Humanists strictly so called, belonged to that increasing class on whom the New Learning had made a great impression, and had produced the characteristic habit of mind which belonged to its possessors. The attitude and work of Erasmus had prepared them to appreciate Luther. The monkish opponents of the great Humanist had been thoroughly in the right when they feared the effects of his revolutionary ways of thinking, however they might be accompanied with appeals against all revolutionary action. He had exhibited his idea of what a life of personal religion ought to be in his *Enchiridion*; he had exposed the mingled Judaism and paganism of a great part of the popular religion; he had poured scorn on the trifling subtleties of scholastic theology, and had asked men to return to a simple "Christian Philosophy"; above all, he had insisted that Christianity could only renew its youth by going back to the study of the Holy Scriptures, and especially of the New Testament; and he had aided his contemporaries to make this return by his edition of the New Testament, and by his efforts to bring within their reach the writings of the earlier Church Fathers. His Humanist followers in Germany believed that they saw in Luther a man who was doing what their leader urged all men to do. They saw in Luther an Erasmus, who was going to the root of things. He was rejecting with increasing determination the bewildering sophistries of Scholasticism, and, what was more, he was showing how many of these had arisen by exalting the authority of the pagan Aristotle over that of St. Paul and St. Augustine. He had painfully studied these Schoolmen, and could speak with an authority on this matter; for he was a learned theologian. The reports of his lectures, which were spreading throughout Germany, informed them that he based his teaching on a simple exposition of the Holy Scriptures in the Vulgate version, which was sanctioned by the mediæval Church. He had revolted, and was increasingly in revolt, against those abuses in the ordinary religious life which were encouraged from sordid motives by the Roman Curia,—abuses which

Erasmus had pierced through and through with the light darts of his sarcasm; and Luther knew, as Erasmus did not, what he was speaking about, for he had surrendered himself to that popular religion, and had sought in it desperately for a means of reconciliation with God without succeeding in his quest. They saw him insisting, with a strenuousness no Humanist had exhibited, on the Humanist demand that every man had a right to stand true to his own personal conscientious convictions. If some of them, like Erasmus, in spite of their scorn of monkery, still believed that the highest type of the religious life was a sincere self-sacrificing Franciscan monk, they saw their ideal in the Augustinian Eremite, whose life had never been stained by any monkish scandal, and who had been proclaimed by his brother monks to be a model of personal holiness. They were sure that when he pled heroically for the freedom of the religious life, his courage, which they could not emulate, rested on a depth and strength of personal piety which they sadly confessed they themselves did not possess. If they complained at times that Luther spoke too strongly against the Pope, they admitted that he was going to the root of things in his attack. All clear-sighted men perceived that the *one* obstacle to reform was the theory of the papal monarchy, which had been laboriously constructed by Italian canonists after the failure of Conciliar reform,—a theory which defied the old mediæval ecclesiastical tradition, and contradicted the solemn decisions of the great German Councils of Constance and Basel. Luther's attacks on the Papacy were not stronger than those of Gerson and d'Ailly, and his language was not more unmeasured than that of their common master, William of Occam. There was nothing in these early days to prevent men who were genuinely attached to the mediæval Church, its older theology and its ancient rites, from rallying round Luther. When the marches began to be redd, and the beginnings of a Protestant Church confronted the mediæval, the situation was changed. Many who had enthusiastically supported Luther left him.

Conrad Mutianus, canon of Gotha, and the veteran leader of the Erfurt circle of Humanists, wrote admiringly of the originality of Luther's sermons as early as 1515. He applauded the stand he took at Leipzig, and spoke of him as *Martinum, Deo devotissimum doctorem.* His followers were no longer contented with a study of the classical authors. Eobanus Hessus, crowned "poet-king" of Germany, abandoned his *Horace* for the *Enchiridion* of Erasmus and the Holy Scriptures. Justus Jonas (Jodocus Koch of Nordlingen) forsook classical Greek to busy himself with the Epistles to the Corinthians. The wicked satirist, Curicius Cordus, betook himself to the New Testament. They did this out of admiration for Erasmus, "their father in Christ." But when Luther appeared, when they read his pamphlets circulating through Germany, when they followed, step by step, his career, they came under the influence of a new spell. The *Erasmici*, to use the phrases of the times, diminished, and the *Martiniani* increased in numbers. One of the old Erfurt circle, Johannes Crotus Rubeanus, was in Rome. His letters, passed round among his friends, made no small impression upon them. He told them that he was living in the centre of the plague-spot of Europe. He reviled the Curia as devoid of all moral conscience. "The Pope and his carrion-crows" were sitting content, gorged on the miseries of the Church. When Crotus received from Germany copies of Luther's writings, he distributed them secretly to his Italian friends, and collected their opinions to transmit to Germany. They were all sympathetically impressed with what Luther said, but they pitied him as a man travelling along a very dangerous road; no real reform was possible without the destruction of the whole curial system, and that was too powerful for any man to combat. Yet Luther was a hero; he was the *Pater Patriæ* of Germany; his countrymen ought to erect a golden statue in his honour; they wished him God-speed. When Crotus returned to Germany and got more in touch with Luther's work, he felt more drawn to the Reformer, and wrote enthusiastically to his friends that Luther was the personal revelation of Christ in modern times. So we find these Humanists declaring that Luther was the St. Paul of the age, the modern Hercules, the Achilles of the sixteenth century.

No Humanist circle gave Luther more enthusiastic support than that of Nürnberg. The soil had been prepared by a few ardent admirers of Staupitz, at the head of whom was Wenceslas Link, prior of the Augustinian-Eremites in Nürnberg, and a celebrated preacher. They had learned from Staupitz that blending of the theology of Augustine with the later German mysticism which was characteristic of the man, and it prepared them to appreciate the deeper experimental teaching of Luther. Among these Nürnberg Humanists was Christopher Scheurl, a jurist, personally acquainted with Luther and with Eck. The shortlived friendship between the two antagonists had been brought about by Scheurl, whose correspondence with Luther began in 1516. Scheurl was convinced that Luther's cause was the "cause of God." He told Eck this. He wrote to him (February 18th, 1519) that all the most spiritually minded clergymen that he knew were devoted to Luther; that "they flew to him in dense troops, like starlings"; that their deepest sympathies were with him; and that they confessed that their holiest desires were prompted by his writings. Albert Dürer expressed his admiration by painting Luther as St. John, the beloved disciple of the Lord. Caspar Nützel, one of the most dignified officials of the town, thought it an honour to translate Luther's *Ninety-five Theses* into German. Lazarus Sprengel delighted to tell his friends how Luther's tracts and sermons were bringing back to a living Christianity numbers of his acquaintances who had been perplexed and driven from the faith by the trivialities common in ordinary sermons. Similar enthusiasm showed itself in Augsburg and other towns. After the Leipzig Disputation, the great printer of Basel, Frobenius, became an ardent admirer of Luther; reprinted most of his writings, and despatched them to Switzerland, France, the Netherlands, Italy,

England, and Spain. He delighted to tell of the favourable reception they met with in these foreign countries,—how they had been welcomed by Lefèvre in France, and how the Swiss Cardinal von Sitten had said that Luther deserved all honour, for he spoke the truth, which no special pleading of an Eck could overthrow. The distinguished jurist Ulrich Zasius of Freiburg said that Luther was an "angel incarnate," and while he deprecated his strong language against the Pope, he called him the "Phœnix among Christian theologians," the "flower of the Christian world," and the "instrument of God." Zasius was a man whose whole religious sympathies belonged to the mediæval conception of the Church, yet he spoke of Luther in this way.

It is perhaps difficult for us now to comprehend the state of mind which longed for the new and yet clung to the old, which made the two Nürnberg families, the Ebners and the Nützlers, season the ceremonies at their family gathering to celebrate their daughters taking the veil with speeches in praise of Luther and of his writings. Yet this was the dominant note in the vast majority of the supporters of Luther in these earlier years.

Men who had no great admiration for Luther personally had no wish to see him crushed by the Roman Curia by mere weight of authority. Even Duke George of Saxony, who had called Luther a pestilent fellow at the Leipzig Disputation, had been stirred into momentary admiration by the *Address to the Christian Nobility of the German Nation*, and had no great desire to publish the Bull within his dominions; and his private secretary and chaplain, Jerome Emser, although a personal enemy who never lost an opportunity of controverting Luther, nevertheless hoped that he might be the instrument of effecting a reformation in the Church. Jacob Wimpheling of Strassburg, a thoroughgoing mediævalist who had manifested no sympathy for Reuchlin, and his friend Christopher of Utenheim, Bishop of Basel, hoped that the movement begun by Luther might lead to that reformation of the Church on mediæval lines which they both earnestly desired.

Perhaps no one represented better the attitude of the large majority of Luther's supporters, in the years between 1517 and 1521, than did the Prince, who is rightly called Luther's protector, Frederick the Elector of Saxony. It is a great though common mistake to suppose that Frederick shared those opinions of Luther which afterwards grew to be the Lutheran theology. His brother John, and in a still higher degree his nephew John Frederick, were devoted Lutherans in the theological sense; but there is no evidence to show that Frederick ever was.

Frederick never had any intimate personal relations with Luther. At Spalatin's request, he had paid the expenses of Luther's *promotion* to the degree of Doctor of the Holy Scriptures; he had, of course, acquiesced in his appointment to succeed Spalatin as Professor of Theology; and he must have appreciated keenly the way in which Luther's work had gradually raised the small and declining University to the position it held in 1517. A few letters were exchanged between Luther and Frederick, but there is no evidence that they ever met in conversation; nor is there any that Frederick had ever heard Luther preach. When he lay dying he asked Luther to come and see him; but the Reformer was far distant, trying to dissuade the peasants from rising in rebellion, and when he reached the palace his old protector had breathed his last.

The Elector was a pious man according to mediæval standards. He had received his earliest lasting religious impressions from intercourse with Augustinian Eremite monks when he was a boy at school at Grimma, and he maintained the closest relations with the Order all his life. He valued highly all the external aids to a religious life which the mediæval Church had provided. He believed in the virtue of pilgrimages and relics. He had made a pilgrimage to the Holy Land, and had brought back a great many relics, which he had placed in the Church of All Saints in Wittenberg, and he had agents at Venice and other Mediterranean ports commissioned to secure other relics for his collection. He continued to purchase them as late as the year 1523. He believed in Indulgences of the older type,—Indulgences which remitted in whole or in part ecclesiastically imposed *satisfactions*,—and he had procured two for use in Saxony. One served as an endowment for the upkeep of his bridge at Torgau, and he had once commissioned Tetzel to preach its virtues; the other was to benefit pilgrims who visited and venerated his collection of relics on All Saints' Day. But it is clear that he disliked Indulgences of the kind Luther had challenged, and had small belief in the good faith of the Roman Curia. He had prevented money collected for one plenary Indulgence leaving the country, and he had forbidden Tetzel to preach the last Indulgence within his territories. His sympathies were all with Luther on this question. He was an esteemed patron of the pious society called *St. Ursula's Schifflein*. He went to Mass regularly, and his attendances became frequent when he was in a state of hesitation or perplexity. When he was at Köln (November 1520), besieged by the papal nuncios to induce him to permit the publication of the Bull against Luther within his lands, Spalatin noted that he went to Mass three times in one day. His reverence for the Holy Scriptures must have created a bond of sympathy between Luther and himself. He talked with his private secretary about the incomparable majesty and power of the word of God, and contrasted its sublimities with the sophistries and trivialities of the theology of the day. He maintained firmly the traditional policy of his House to make the decisions of the Councils of Constance and of Basel effective within Electoral Saxony, in spite of protests from the Curia and the higher ecclesiastics, and was accustomed to consider himself responsible for the ecclesiastical as well as for the civil good government of his lands. Aleander had considered it a master-stroke of policy to procure the burning of Luther's books at Köln while the Elector was in the city. Frederick only regarded the deed as a petty insult to himself. He was a staunch upholder of the rights and liberties of the German nation, and remembered that by an old concordat, which every Emperor had sworn to maintain, every German had the right to appeal to a General Council, and could not be condemned without a fair trial; and this Bull had made Luther's appeal to a Council one of the reasons for his condemnation. So, in spite of the "golden rose" and other blandishments, in spite of threats that he might be included in the excommunication of his subject and that the privileges of his University might be taken away, he stood firm, and would not withdraw his protection from Luther. He was a pious German prince of the old-fashioned type, with no great love for Italians, and was not going to be browbeaten by papal nuncios. His attitude towards Luther represents very fairly that of the great mass of the German people on the eve of the Diet of Worms.

CHAPTER III.

THE DIET OF WORMS.[1]

§ 1. *The Roman Nuncio Aleander.*

ROME had done its utmost to get rid of Luther by ecclesiastical measures, and had failed. If he was to be overthrown, if the new religious movement and the national uprising which enclosed it were to be stifled, this could only be done by the aid of the supreme secular authority. The Curia turned to the Emperor.

Maximilian had died suddenly on the 12th of January 1519. After some months of intriguing, the papal di-

[1] SOURCES: *Deutsche Reichstagsakten unter Kaiser Karl V.*, 3 vols. have been published (Gotha, 1893–1901); Balan, *Monumenta Reformationis Lutheranæ ex tabulis S. Sedis secretis 1521–1525* (Ratisbon, 1883–1884); Læmmer, *Monumenta Vaticana historiam ecclesiasticam sæculi 16 illustrantia* (Freiburg, 1861); *Meletematum Romanorum Mantissa* (Regensburg, 1875); Brieger, *Aleander und Luther 1521: Die vervollständigten Aleander-Depeschen nebst Untersuchungen über den Wormser Reichstag* (Gotha, 1894); *Calendar of Spanish State Papers* (London, 1886); *Calendar of Venetian State Papers*, vols. iii.–vi. (London, 1864–1884); *Letters and Papers, Foreign and Domestic, of the reign of Henry VIII.*, vols. iii.–xix. (London, 1860–1903); V. E. Loescher, *Vollständige Reformations-Acta und Documenta*, 3 vols. (Leipzig, 1713–1722); Spalatin, *Annales Reformationis* (Leipzig, 1768); *Chronikon*, 2nd vol. of Mencke's *Scriptores rerum Germanicarum præcipue Saxonicarum*, 3 vols. (Leipzig, 1728–1730); *Historischer Nachlass und Briefe* (Jena, 1851); also the sources mentioned under the first chapter of this part.

LATER BOOKS: Hausrath, *Aleander und Luther auf dem Reichstage zu Worms* (Berlin, 1897); Kolde, *Luther und der Reichstag zu Worms 1521* (Halle, 1883); Friedrich, *Der Reichstag zu Worms 1521* (Munich, 1871); Ranke, *Deutsche Geschichte im Zeitalter der Reformation* (Leipzig, 1881; Eng. trans., London, 1905); Armstrong, *The Emperor Charles V.* (London, 1902); v. Bezold, *Geschichte der deutschen Reformation* (Berlin, 1890); Creighton, *A History of the Papacy*, vol. vi. (London, 1897); Gebhardt, *Die Gravamina der deutschen Nation* (Breslau, 1895).

plomacy being very tortuous, his grandson Charles, the young King of Spain, was unanimously chosen to be his successor (June 28th, 1519). Troubles in Spain prevented him leaving that country at once to take possession of his new dignities. He was crowned at Aachen on the 23rd of October 1520, and opened his first German Diet on January 22nd, 1521, at Worms.

The Pope had selected two envoys to wait on the young Emperor, the Protonotary Marino Caraccioli (1469–1530), who was charged with the ordinary diplomatic business, and Jerome Aleander, the Director of the Vatican Library, who was appointed to secure the outlawry of Luther.

The Roman Curia had in Aleander one of the most clear-sighted, courageous, and indefatigable of diplomatists. He was an Italian, born of a burgher family in the little Venetian town of Motta (1480–1542), educated at Padua and Venice; he had begun life as a Humanist, had lectured on Greek with distinction in Paris, and had been personally acquainted with many of the German Humanists, who could not forgive the "traitor" who had deserted their ranks to serve an obscurantist party. His graphic letters, full of minute details, throb with the hopes and fears of the papal diplomacy. The reader has his fingers on the pulse of those momentous months. The Legate was in a land where "every stone and every tree cried out, 'Luther.'" Landlords refused him lodging. He had to shiver during these winter months in an attic without a stove. The stench and dirt of the house were worse than the cold. When he appeared on the streets he saw scowling faces, hands suddenly carried to the hilts of swords, heard curses shrieked after him. He was struck on the breast by a Lutheran doorkeeper when he tried to get audience of the Elector of Saxony, and no one in the crowd interfered to protect him. He saw caricatures of himself hanging head downwards from a gibbet. He received the old deadly German feud-letters from Ulrich von Hutten, safe in the neighbouring castle of Ebernberg, about a day's ride distant.[1] The imperial Councillors to whom he complained had neither the men nor the means to protect him. When he tried to publish answers to the attacks on the Papacy which the Lutheran presses poured forth, he could scarcely find a printer; and when he did, syndicates bought up his pamphlets and destroyed them. As the weeks passed he came to understand that there was only one man on whom he could rely—the young Emperor, believed by all but himself to be a puppet in the hands of his Councillors, whom Pope Leo had called a "good child," but whom Aleander from his first interview at Antwerp had felt to be endowed with "a prudence far beyond his years," and to "have much more at the back of his head than he carried on his face." He also came to believe that the one man to be feared was the old Elector of Saxony, "that basilisk," that "German fox," that "marmot with the eyes of a dog, who glanced obliquely at his questioners."

Aleander was a pure worldling, a man of indifferent morals, showing traces of cold-blooded cruelty (as when he slew five peasants for the loss of one of his dogs, or tried to get Erasmus poisoned). He believed that every man had his price, and that low and selfish motives were alone to be reckoned with. But he did the work of the Curia at Worms with a thoroughness which merited the rewards he obtained afterwards.[2] He had spies everywhere—in the households of the Emperor and of the leading princes, and among the population of Worms. He had no hesitation in lying when he thought it useful for the "faith," as he frankly relates.[3] The Curia had laid a difficult task upon him. He was to see that Luther was put under the ban of the Empire at once and unheard. The Bull had condemned him; the secular power had nothing to do but execute the sentence. Aleander had little difficulty in persuading the Emperor to this course within his hereditary

[1] Kalkoff, *Die Depeschen*, etc. pp. 46, 50, 58, 69, etc.

[2] He became Archbishop of Brindisi and Oria, and then a Cardinal.

[3] Brieger, *Aleander und Luther 1521: Die vervollständigten Aleander-Depeschen*, p. 53 (Gotha, 1884); *non superstitiose verax*, Erasmus said.

dominions. An edict was issued ordering Luther's books to be burnt, and the Legate had the satisfaction of presiding at several literary *auto-da-fés* in Antwerp and elsewhere. He was also successful with some of the ecclesiastical princes of Germany.[1] But it was impossible to get this done at Worms. Failing this, it was Aleander's business to see that Luther's case was kept separate from the question of German national grievances against the Papacy, and that, if it proved to be impossible to prevent Luther appearing before the Diet, he was to be summoned there simply for the purpose of making public recantation. With the assistance of the Emperor he was largely successful.[2]

§ 2. *The Emperor Charles V.*

Aleander was not the real antagonist of Luther at Worms; he was not worthy of the name. The German Diet was the scene of a fight of faiths; and the man of faith on the mediæval side was the young Emperor. He represented the believing past as Luther represented the believing future.[3] "What my forefathers established at

[1] Kalkoff, *Die Depeschen des Nuntius Aleander*, etc. pp. 19, 20, 23, 24, 265, 266.

[2] Brieger, *Aleander und Luther 1521: Die vervollständigten Aleander-Depeschen* (Gotha, 1884), *Quellen und Forschungen zur Geschichte der Reformation*, i.; Friedensburg, *Eine ungedrückte Depesche Aleanders von seiner ersten Nuntiatur bei Karl V.*, in *Quellen und Forschungen aus italienischen Archiven*, i. (1897); Kalkoff, *Die Depeschen des Nuntius Aleander vom Wormser Reichstage 1521* (Halle, 1897, 2nd ed.); Kolde, *Luther und der Reichstag zu Worms 1521* (Halle, 1883); Hausrath, *Aleander und Luther auf dem Reichstage zu Worms* (Berlin, 1897); Gebhardt, *Die Gravamina der deutschen Nation* (Breslau, 1895, 2nd ed.).

[3] "Reserved as Charles was, the shock struck out the most outspoken confession of his faith that he ever uttered. Nowhere else is it possible to approach so closely to the workings of his spiritual nature, save in the confidential letters to his brother in the last troubled hours of rule, when he repeated that it was not in his conscience to rend the seamless mantle of the Church."—Armstrong, *The Emperor Charles V.*, i. 71 (London, 1902). But we have another glimpse in the conversation with his sister Maria, in which he confesses that he had come to think better of the Lutherans, for he had learned to know that they taught nothing outside the Apostles' Creed. Cf. Kawerau, *Johann Agricola von Eisleben*, p. 100 (Berlin, 1881).

Constance and other Councils," he said, "it is my privilege to uphold. A single monk, led astray by private judgment, has set himself against the faith held by all Christians for a thousand years and more, and impudently concludes that all Christians up till now have erred. I have therefore resolved to stake upon this cause all my dominions, my friends, my body and my blood, my life and soul."[1] The crisis had not come suddenly on him. As early as May 12th, 1520, Juan Manuel, his ambassador at Rome, had written to him asking him to pay some attention to "a certain Martin Luther, who belongs to the following of the Elector of Saxony," and whose preaching was causing some discontent at the Roman Curia. Manuel thought that Luther might prove useful in a diplomatic dispute with the Curia.[2] Charles had had time to think over the matter in his serious, reserved way; and this was the decision he had come to. The declaration was all the more memorable when it is remembered that Charles owed his election to that rising feeling of nationality which supported Luther,[3] and that he had to make sure of German assistance in his coming struggle with Francis I. A certain grim reality lurked in the words, that he was ready to stake his dominions on the cause he adopted. There is much to be said for the opinion that "the Lutheran question made a man of the boy-ruler."[4]

On the other hand, it is well to remember that the young Emperor did not take the side of the Pope nor commit himself to the Curial ideas of the absolute character of papal supremacy. He laid stress on the unity of the Catholic (mediæval) Church, on the continuity of its rites, and on the need of maintaining its authority; but the seat of that authority was for him a General Council. The declaration in no way conflicts with the changes in imperial

[1] *Deutsche Reichstagsakten*, etc. ii. 595.

[2] *Calendar of State Papers, Spanish, 1509–1525*, p. 305 (London, 1866).

[3] For an account of the indirect causes which led to the election of Charles, cf. v. Bezold, *Geschichte der deutschen Reformation*, pp. 193 ff. (Berlin, 1890).

[4] Armstrong, *The Emperor Charles V.*, p. 73 (London, 1902).

policy which may be traced during the opening weeks of the Diet, nor with that future action which led to the Sack of Rome and to the Augsburg Interim (1548). It is possible that the young ruler had read and admired Luther's earlier writings, and that he had counted on him as an aid in bringing the Church to a better condition. It is more than probable that he already believed that it was his duty to free the Church from the abuses which abounded;[1] but Luther's fierce attack on the Pope disgusted him, and a reformation which came from the people threatened secular as well as ecclesiastical authority. He had made up his mind that Luther must be condemned, and told the German princes that he would not change one iota of his determination. But this did not prevent him making use of Luther to further his diplomatic dealings with the Pope and wring concessions from the Curia. For one thing, the Pope had been interfering with the Inquisition in Spain,

[1] Charles v. had for his confessor Jean Glapion, who figured largely in the preliminary scenes before Luther arrived at Worms. He had a remarkable conversation with Dr. Brück, the Elector of Saxony's Chancellor, in which he professed to speak for the Emperor as well as for himself. Luther's earlier writings had given him great pleasure; he believed him to be a "plant of renown," able to produce splendid fruit for the Church. But the book on the *Babylonian Captivity* had shocked him; he did not believe it to be Luther's; it was not in his usual style; if Luther had written it, it must have been because he was momentarily indignant at the papal Bull, and as it was anonymous, it could easily be repudiated; or if not repudiated, it might be explained, and its sentences shown to be capable of a Catholic interpretation. If this were done, and if Luther withdrew his violent writings against the Pope, there was no reason why an amicable arrangement should not be come to. The Papal Bull could easily be got over, it could be withdrawn on the ground that Luther had never had a fair trial. It was a mistake to suppose that the Emperor was not keenly alive to the need for a reformation of the Church; there were limits to his devotion to the Pope; the Emperor believed that he would deserve the wrath of God if he did not try to amend the deplorable condition of the Church of Christ. Such was Glapion's statement. It is a question how far he was sincere, and how far he could speak for the Emperor. He was a friend and admirer of Erasmus; but the Dutchman had said that no man could conceal his own views so skilfully. The Elector heard that after this conversation Glapion had got from Aleander 400 copies of the Bull against Luther, and had distributed them among Franciscan monks. This made him doubt his sincerity, and he refused to grant him an audience. Cf. *Reichstagsakten*, ii. 477 ff.

trying to mitigate its severity; and Charles, like his maternal grandfather, Ferdinand of Aragon, believed that the Holy Office was a help in curbing the freedom-loving people of Spain, and had no wish to see his instrument of punishment made less effectual. For another, it was evident that Francis I. was about to invade Italy, and Charles wished the Pope to take his side. If the Pope gave way to him on both of these points, he was ready to carry out his wishes about Luther as far as that was possible.[1]

§ 3. *In the City of Worms.*

The city of Worms was crowded with men of diverse opinions and of many different nationalities. The first Diet of the youthful Emperor (Charles was barely one and twenty), from whom men of all parties expected so much, had attracted much larger numbers than usually attended these assemblies. Weighty matters affecting all Germany were down on the *agenda*. There was the old constitutional

[1] A study of dates throws light on these bargainings. In Oct. 1520, Charles issued an edict ordering the burning of Luther's books within his hereditary dominions. In the following weeks Aleander was pressing Charles to make the edict universal; this was declared to be impossible, and (Nov. 28th) Charles wrote to the Elector of Saxony ordering him to produce Luther at Worms, and to hinder him from writing anything more against the Pope; as it were in answer (Dec. 12th), the Pope intimated to Charles that he had withdrawn his briefs about the Inquisition in Spain. The Emperor reached Worms about the middle of December. On Jan. 3rd (1521) the Pope simplified matters for the Emperor by issuing a new Bull, *Decet Romanum*, containing the names of Luther and Hutten; the Diet opened Jan. 28th; Aleander made his three hours' speech against Luther on Feb. 13; Feb. 19th, the Estates resolved that Luther should appear before them, and not for the simple purpose of recantation—he was to be heard, and to receive a safe conduct; March 6th, the imperial invitation and safe conduct, beginning with the words, *nobilis, devote, nobis dilecte*; Aleander protested vehemently against this address; the Emperor drafted a universal mandate ordering the burning of Luther's books; this probably was not published; it was withdrawn in favour of a mandate ordering all Luther's books to be delivered up to the magistrates; this was published in Worms on March 27th, and caused rioting; April 17th and 18th, Luther appeared before the Diet; May 8th, Charles received the Pope's pledge to take his side against Francis; Diet agreed to the ban against Luther on May 25th; Charles dated the ban May 8th.

question of monarchy or oligarchy bequeathed from the Diets of Maximilian; curiosity to see whether the new ruler would place before the Estates a truly imperial policy, or whether, like his predecessors, he would subordinate national to dynastic considerations; the deputies from the cities were eager to get some sure provisions made for ending the private wars which disturbed trade; all classes were anxious to provide for an effective central government when the Emperor was absent from Germany; local statesmen felt the need of putting an end to the constant disputes between the ecclesiastical and secular powers within Germany; but the hardest problem of all, and the one which every man was thinking, talking, disputing about, was: "To take notice of the books and descriptions made by Friar Martin Luther against the Court of Rome."[1] Other exciting questions were stirring the crowds met at Worms besides those mentioned on the *agenda* of the Diet. Men were talking about the need of making an end of the papal exactions which were draining Germany of money, and the air was full of rumours of what Sickingen and the knights might attempt, and whether there was going to be another peasant revolt. These questions were instinctively felt to hang together, and each had an importance because of the way in which it was connected with the religious and social problems of the day. For the people of Germany and for the foreign representatives who were gathered together at Worms, it is unquestionable that the Lutheran movement, and how it was to be dealt with, was the supreme problem of the moment. All these various things combined to bring together at Worms a larger concourse of people than had been collected in any German town since the meeting of the General Council at Constance in 1414.

Worms was one of the oldest towns in Germany. Its people were turbulent, asserting their rights as the inhabitants of a free imperial city, and in constant feud with

[1] *Calendar of State Papers, Henry VIII. Letters and Papers, Foreign and Domestic* (London, 1867), III. i. p. 445.

their bishop. They had endured many an interdict, were fiercely anti-clerical, and were to a man on Luther's side. The crowded streets were thronged with princes, their councillors and their retinues; with high ecclesiastical dignitaries and their attendant clergy; with nobles and their "riders"; with landsknechts, artisans, and peasants. Spanish, French, and Italian merchants, on their way homewards from the Frankfurt fair, could be seen discussing the last phase of the Lutheran question, and Spanish nobles and Spanish merchants more than once came to blows in the narrow thoroughfares. The foreign merchants, especially the Spaniards, all appeared to take the Lutheran side; not because they took much interest in doctrines, but because they felt bound to stand up for the man who had dared to say that no one should be burned for his opinions. These Spanish merchants made themselves very prominent. They joined in syndicates with the more fervent German partisans of Luther to buy up and destroy papal pamphlets; they bought Luther's writings to carry home. Aleander curses these *marrani*,[1] as he calls them, and relates that they are getting Luther's works translated into Spanish. It is probable that many of them had Moorish blood in them, and knew the horrors of the Inquisition. Aleander's spies told him that caricatures of himself and other prominent papalists were hawked about, and that pictures of Luther with the Dove hovering over his head, Luther with his head crowned with a halo of rays, Luther and Hutten,[2] the one with a Bible and the other with a sword, were eagerly bought in the streets. These pictures were actually sold in the courts and rooms of the episcopal palace where the Emperor was lodged. On the steps of the churches, at the doors of public buildings, colporteurs offered to eager

[1] Kalkoff, *Die Depeschen*, etc. p. 106.

[2] This was probably the frontispiece of a small book containing four of Hutten's tracts, and entitled *Gespräch Büchlin: Herr Ulrichs von Hutten. Feber das Erst: Feber das ander: Vadiscus, oder die Römische Dreifaltigkeit: Die Anschawenden*; with the motto, *Odivi ecclesiam malignantium.* It is figured in v. Bezold's *Geschichte der deutschen Reformation*, p. 307 (Berlin, 1890).

buyers the tracts of Luther against the Pope, and the satires of Ulrich von Hutten in Latin and in German. On the streets and in open spaces like the Market, crowds of keen disputants argued about the teaching of Luther, and praised him in the most exaggerated ways.

Inside the Electoral College opinion was divided. The Archbishop of Köln, the Elector of Brandenburg, and his brother the Archbishop of Mainz, were for Luther's condemnation, while the Elector of Saxony had great influence over the Archbishop of Trier and the Count Palatine of the Rhine. The latter, says Aleander, scarcely opened his mouth during the year, but now "roared like ten bulls" on Luther's behalf. Aleander had his first opportunity of addressing the Diet on February 13th. He spoke for three hours, and made a strong impression. He dwelt on Luther's doctrinal errors, which he said were those of the Waldenses, of Wiclif, and of the Hussites. He said that Luther denied the Presence of Christ in the Holy Supper, and that he was a second Arius.[1] During the days that followed the members of the Diet came to a common understanding. They presented a memorial in German (February 19th) to the Emperor, in which they reminded him that no imperial edict could be published against Luther without their consent, and that to do so before Luther had a hearing would lead to bloodshed; they proposed that Luther should be invited to come to Worms under a safe conduct, and in the presence of the Diet be asked whether he was the author of the books that were attributed to him, and whether he could clear himself of the accusation of denying fundamental articles of the faith; that he should also be heard upon the papal claims, and the Diet would judge upon them; and, finally, they prayed the Emperor to deliver Germany from the papal tyranny.[2] The Emperor agreed that Luther should be summoned under a safe conduct and interrogated about his books, and whether he had denied any fundamental doctrines. But he utterly refused to permit any discussion on the authority of the

[1] *Reichstagsakten*, ii. pp. 495 ff. [2] *Ibid.* 515 ff.

Pope, and declared that he would himself communicate with His Holiness about the complaints of Germany.[1]

The documents in the *Reichstagsakten* reveal not only that there was a decided difference of opinion between the Emperor and the majority of the Estates about the way in which Luther ought to be treated, but that the policy of the Emperor and his advisers had changed between November 1520 and February 1521. Aleander had found no difficulty in persuading Charles and his Flemish councillors that, so far as the Emperor's hereditary dominions were concerned, the only thing that the civil power had to do was to issue an edict homologating the Papal Bull banning Luther and his adherents, and ordering his books to be burnt. This had been done in the Netherlands. They had made difficulties, however, about such summary action within the German Empire. Aleander was told that the Emperor could do nothing until after the coronation at Aachen (October 1520);[2] and in November, much to the nuncio's disgust, the Emperor had written to the Elector of Saxony (November 28th, 1520) from Oppenheim asking him to bring Luther with him to the Diet.[3] At that time Luther had no great wish to go to the Diet, unless it was clearly understood that he was summoned not for the purpose of merely making a recantation, but in order that he might defend his views with full liberty of speech. He was not going to recant, and he could say so as easily and clearly at Wittenberg as at Worms. The situation had changed at Worms. The Emperor had come over to the nuncio's side completely. He now saw no need for Luther's appearance. The Diet had nothing to do but to place Luther under the ban of the Empire, because he had been declared to be a heretic by the Roman Pontiff. Aleander claimed all the credit for this change; but it is more than

[1] *Reichstagsakten*, ii. pp. 518 ff.

[2] Brieger, *Aleander und Luther 1521: Die vervollständigten Aleander-Depeschen nebst Untersuchungen über den Wormser Reichstag* (Gotha, 1884), p. 19.

[3] *Deutsche Reichstagsakten unter Kaiser Carl V.* (Gotha, 1896), ii. 466; Brieger, *Aleander*, etc. pp. 19, 20.

probable that the explanation lies in the shifting imperial and papal policy. In the end of 1520 the policy of the Roman Curia was strongly anti-imperialist. The Emperor's ambassador at Rome, Don Manuel, had been warning his master of the papal intrigues against him, and suggesting that Charles might show some favour to a "certain Martin Luther"; and this advice might easily have inspired the letter of the 28th of November. At all events the papal policy had been changing, and showing signs of becoming less hostile to the Emperor. However the matter be accounted for, Aleander found that after the Emperor's presence within Worms it was much more easy for him to press the papal view about Luther upon Charles and his advisers.[1]

On the other hand, the Germans in the Diet held stoutly to the opinion that no countryman of theirs should be placed under the ban of the Empire without being heard in his defence, and that they and not the Bishop of Rome were to be the judges in the matter.

The two months before Luther's appearance saw open opposition between the Emperor and the Diet, and abundant secret intrigue—an edict proposed against Luther,[2] which the Diet refused to accept;[3] an edict proposed to order the burning of Luther's books, which the Diet also objected to;[4] this edict revised and limited to the seizure of Luther's writings, which was also found fault with by the Diet; and, finally, the Emperor issuing this revised edict on his own authority and without the consent of the Diet.[5]

[1] Cf. p. 267, note.

[2] The draft was dated February 15th, and will be found in the *Reichstagsakten*, ii. 507 ff.

[3] The answer of the Diet was dated February 19th, and is to be found in the *Reichstagsakten*, ii. 514 ff., and discussions thereanent, pp. 517, 518 f.

[4] The second draft edict proposed to summon Luther to make recantation only, and at the same time ordered his books to be burnt, which was equivalent to a condemnation, *Reichstagsakten*, ii. 520.

[5] The revised draft edict in its final form was dated March 10th, four days after the citation and safe conduct, and it is probable that it was finally issued by the Emperor for the purpose of frightening Luther, and preventing him obeying the citation and trusting to the safe conduct, *Reichstagsakten*, ii. 529 ff. and notes.

The command to appear before the Diet on April 16th, 1521, and the imperial safe conduct were entrusted to the imperial herald, Caspar Strum, who delivered them at Wittenberg on the 26th of March.[1] Luther calmly finished some literary work, and left for the Diet on April 2nd. He believed that he was going to his death. "My dear brother," he said to Melanchthon at parting, "if I do not come back, if my enemies put me to death, you will go on teaching and standing fast in the truth; if you live, my death will matter little." The journey seemed to the indignant Papists like a royal progress; crowds came to bless the man who had stood up for Germany against the Pope, and who was going to his death for his courage; they pressed into the inns where he rested, and often found him solacing himself with music. His lute was always comforting to him in times of excitement. Justus Jonas, the famous German Humanist, who had turned theologian much to Erasmus' disgust, joined him at Erfurt. The nearer he came to Worms, the sharper became the disputes there. Friends and foes feared that his presence would prove oil thrown on the flames. The Emperor began to wish he had not sent the summons. Messengers were despatched secretly to Sickingen, and a pension promised to Hutten to see whether they could not prevent Luther's appearance.[2] Might he not take refuge in the Ebernberg, scarcely a day's journey from Worms? Was it not possible to arrange matters in a private conference with Glapion, the Emperor's confessor? Bucer was sent to persuade him. The herald significantly called his attention to the imperial edict ordering magistrates to seize his writings. But nothing daunted Luther. He would not go to the Ebernberg; he could see Glapion at Worms, if the confessor wished an inter-

[1] Luther received three safe conducts, one from the Emperor in the citation, one from the Elector of Saxony, and one from Duke George of Saxony. *Reichstagsakten*, ii. 526 ff.

[2] Cf. Aleander's letter of April 5th, 1521. Brieger, *Aleander und Luther*, etc. pp. 119 ff.

view; what he had to say would be said publicly at Worms.

Luther had reached Oppenheim, a town on the Rhine about fifteen miles north from Worms, and about twenty east from the Ebernberg, on April 14th. There he for the last time rejected the insidious temptations of his enemies and the distracted counsels of his friends, that he should turn aside and seek shelter with Francis von Sickingen. There he penned his famous letter to Spalatin, that he would come to Worms if there were as many devils as tiles on the house roofs to prevent him, and at the same time asked where he was to lodge.[1]

The question was important. The Romanists had wished that Luther should be placed under the Emperor's charge as a prisoner of State, or else lodged in the Convent of the Augustinian Eremites, where he could be under ecclesiastical surveillance. But the Saxon nobles and their Elector had resolved to trust no one with the custody of their countryman. The Elector Frederick and part of his suite had found accommodation at an inn called *The Swan*, and the rest of his following were in the House of the Knights of St. John. Both houses were full; but it was arranged that Luther was to share the room of two Saxon gentlemen, v. Hirschfeld and v. Schott, in the latter building.[2] Next morning, Justus Jonas, who had reached Worms before Luther, after consultation with Luther's friends, left the town early on Tuesday morning (April 16th) to meet the Reformer, and tell him the arrangements made. With him went the two gentlemen with whom Luther was to lodge.[3] A large number of Saxon noblemen with their attendants accompanied them. When it was known that they had set out to meet Luther, a great crowd of people (nearly two thousand, says Secretary Vogler), some on horseback and some on foot, followed to welcome Luther, and did meet him about two and a half miles from the town.[4]

[1] Spalatin's *Annales Reformationis* (Cyprian's edition), p. 38.
[2] *Reichstagsakten*, ii. 850. [3] *Ibid.* p. 850. [4] *Ibid.* p. 853, note.

§ 4. *Luther in Worms.*

A little before eleven o'clock the watcher on the tower by the Mainz Gate blew his horn to announce that the procession was in sight, and soon afterwards Luther entered the town. The people of Worms were at their *Morgenimbiss* or *Frühmahl*, but all rushed to the windows or out into the streets to see the arrival.[1] Caspar Sturm, the herald, rode first, accompanied by his attendant, the square yellow banner, emblazoned with the black two-headed eagle, attached to his bridle arm. Then came the cart,—a genuine Saxon *Rollwegelin*,—Luther and three companions sitting in the straw which half filled it. The waggon had been provided by the good town of Wittenberg, which had also hired Christian Goldschmidt and his three horses at three gulden a day.[2] Luther's companions were his *socius itinerarius*, Brother Petzensteiner of Nürnberg;[3] his colleague Nicholas Amsdorf; and a student of Wittenberg, a young Pomeranian noble, Peter Swaven, who had been one of the Wittenberg students who had accompanied Luther with halbert and helmet to the Leipzig Disputation (July 1519). Justus Jonas rode immediately behind the waggon, and then followed the crowd of nobles and people who had gone out to meet the Reformer.

Aleander in his attic room heard the shouts and the trampling in the streets, and sent out one of his people to find out the cause, guessing that it was occasioned by Luther's arrival. The messenger reported that the procession had made its way through dense crowds of people, and that the waggon had stopped at the door of the House of the Knights of St. John. He also informed the nuncio that Luther had got out, saying, as he looked round with his piercing eyes, *Deus erit pro me*, and that a priest had

[1] *Reichstagsakten*, ii. 863.

[2] Lingke, *Luther's Reisegeschichte*, pp. 83 f.

[3] Every monk when on a journey had to be accompanied by a brother of the Order. Petzensteiner left his convent and married (July 1522), Kolde, *Analecta Lutherana*, p. 38. For the entry into Worms, cf. *Reichstagsakten*, ii. 850, 859; Balan, *Monumenta*, etc. p. 170.

stepped forward, received him in his arms, then touched or kissed his robe thrice with as much reverence as if he were handling the relics of a saint. "They will say next," says Aleander in his wrath, "that the scoundrel works miracles."[1]

After travel-stains were removed, Luther dined with ten or twelve friends. The early afternoon brought crowds of visitors, some of whom had come great distances to see him. Then came long discussions about how he was to act on the morrow before the Diet. The Saxon councillors v. Feilitzsch and v. Thun were in the same house with him: the Saxon Chancellor, v. Brück, and Luther's friend Spalatin, were at *The Swan*, a few doors away. Jerome Schurf, the Professor of Law in Wittenberg, had been summoned to Worms by the Elector to act as Luther's legal adviser, and had reached the town some days before the Reformer.

How much Luther knew of the secret intrigues that had been going on at Worms about his affairs it is impossible to say. He probably was aware that the Estates had demanded that he should have a hearing, and should be confronted by impartial theologians, and that the complaints of the German nation against Rome should be taken up at the same time; also that the Emperor had refused to allow any theological discussion, or that the grievances against Rome should be part of the proceedings. All that was public property. The imperial summons and safe conduct had not treated him as a condemned heretic.[2] He had been addressed in it as *Ehrsamer*, *lieber*, *andächtiger*—terms which would not have been used to a heretic, and which were ostentatiously omitted from the safe conduct sent him by Duke George of Saxony.[3] He knew also that the Emperor had nevertheless published an edict ordering the civil authorities to seize his

[1] Brieger, *Aleander*, etc. p. 143; *Zeitschrift f. Kirchengeschichte*, iv. 326.

[2] *Reichstagsakten*, ii. 569; Förstemann, *Urkundenbuch*, 68 f., *Tischreden*, iv. 349; Brieger, *Aleander*, etc. p. 146.

[3] *Reichstagsakten*, ii. 514, 519 f., 526.

books, and to prevent more from being printed, published, or sold, and that such an edict threw doubts upon the value of the safe conduct.[1] But he probably did not know that this edict was a third draft issued by the Emperor without consulting the Diet. Nor is it likely that he knew how Aleander had been working day and night to prevent his appearance at the Diet from being more than a mere formality, nor how far the nuncio had prevailed with the Emperor and with his councillors. His friends could tell him all this—though even they were not aware until next morning how resolved the Emperor was that Luther should not be permitted to make a speech.[2] They knew enough, however, to be able to impress on Luther that he must restrain himself, and act in such a way as to force the hands of his opponents, and gain permission to speak at length in a second audience. The Estates wished to hear him if the Emperor and his entourage had resolved to prevent him from speaking. These consultations probably settled the tactics which Luther followed on his first appearance before the Diet.[3]

Next morning (Wednesday, April 17th), Ulrich von Pappenheim, the marshal of ceremonies, came to Luther's room before ten o'clock, and, greeting him "courteously and with all respect," informed him that he was to appear before the Emperor and the Diet that day at four o'clock, when he would be informed why he had been summoned.[4] Immediately after the marshal had left, there came an urgent message from a Saxon noble, Hans von Minkwitz, who was dying in his lodgings, that Luther would come to hear his confession and administer the sacrament to him. Luther instantly went to soothe and comfort the dying man, notwithstanding his own troubles.[5] We have no

[1] *Reichstagsakten*, ii. 573.

[2] *Ibid.* p. 891, where it is said that the imperial entourage and the dependants of the Curia hated a public appearance of Luther worse than foreigners dislike "Einbecker beer."

[3] Cf. Luther's letters to Cranach (April 21st, 1521), and to the Elector Frederick, De Wette, *Dr. Martin Luthers Briefe*, etc. i. 588, 599.

[4] *Reichstagsakten*, ii. 545.

[5] *Ibid.* p. 859.

information how the hours between twelve and four were spent. It is almost certain that there must have been another consultation. Spalatin and Brück had discovered that the conduct of the audience was not to be in the hands of Glapion, the confessor of the Emperor, as they had up to that time supposed, but in those of John Eck, the Orator or Official of the Archbishop of Trier.[1] This looked badly for Luther. Eck had been officiously busy in burning Luther's books at Trier; he lodged in the same house and in the room next to the papal nuncio.[2] Aleander, indeed, boasts that Eck was entirely devoted to him, and that he had been able to draft the question which Eck put to Luther during the first audience.[3]

§ 5. *Luther's first Appearance before the Diet of Worms.*[4]

A little before four o'clock, the marshal and Caspar Sturm, the herald, came to Luther's lodging to escort him to the audience hall. They led the Reformer into the street to conduct him to the Bishop's Palace, where the Emperor was living along with his younger brother Ferdinand, afterwards King of the Romans and Emperor, and where the Diet met.[5] The streets were thronged; faces looked down from every window; men and women had crowded the roofs to catch a glimpse of Luther as he passed. It was difficult to force a way through the crowd, and, besides, Sturm, who was responsible for Luther's safety, feared that some Spaniard might deal the

[1] The terms *Orator* and *Official* have a great many meanings in Mediæval ecclesiastical Latin. They probably mean here the president of the Archbishop's Ecclesiastical Court. John Eck was a Doctor of Canon Law. Archbishop Parker signed himself the *Orator* of Cecil (*Calendar of State Papers, Elizabeth, Foreign Series, 1559–1560*, p. 84).

[2] Brieger, *Aleander*, etc. p. 145.

[3] *Ibid.* p. 145.

[4] This paragraph and the succeeding one are founded on the following sources: The official report written by John Eck of Trier; the *Acta Wormaciæ*, a narrative in the handwriting of Spalatin; and the statements of fourteen persons, Germans, Italians, and a Spaniard, all present in the Diet on the 17th and 18th of April 1521.

[5] *Reichstagsakten*, ii. 574.

Reformer a blow with a dagger in the crowd. So the three turned into the court of the Swan Hotel; from it they got into the garden of the House of the Knights of St. John; and, as most of the courts and gardens of the houses communicated with each other, they were able to get into the court of the Bishop's Palace without again appearing on the street.[1]

The court of the Palace was full of people eager to see Luther, most of them evidently friendly. It was here that old General Frundsberg, the most illustrious soldier in Germany, who was to be the conqueror in the famous fight at Pavia, clapped Luther kindly on the shoulder, and said words which have been variously reported. "My poor monk! my little monk! thou art on thy way to make a stand as I and many of my knights have never done in our toughest battles. If thou art sure of the justice of thy cause, then forward in the name of God, and be of good courage: God will not forsake thee." From out the crowd, "here and there and from every corner, came voices saying, 'Play the man! Fear not death; it can but slay the body: there is a life beyond.'"[2] They went up the stair and entered the audience hall, which was crammed. While the marshal and the herald forced a way for Luther, he passed an old acquaintance, the deputy from Augsburg. "Ah, Doctor Peutinger," said Luther, "are you here too?"[3] Then he was led to where he was to stand before the Emperor; and these two lifelong opponents saw each other for the first time. "The fool entered smiling," says Aleander (perhaps the lingering of the smile with which he had just greeted Dr. Peutinger): "he looked slowly round, and his face sobered." "When he faced the Emperor," Aleander goes on to say, "he could not hold his head still, but moved it up and down and from side to side."[4] All eyes were fixed on Luther, and many an account was written describing his appearance. "A man of middle height," says an unsigned Spanish paper pre-

[1] *Reichstagsakten*, ii. 547.
[2] *Ibid.* p. 549.
[3] *Ibid.* p. 862.
[4] Brieger, *Aleander*, etc. p. 147.

served in the British Museum, "with a strong face, a sturdy build of body, with eyes that scintillated and were never still. He was clad in the robe of the Augustinian Order, but with a belt of hide, with a large tonsure, newly shaven, and a coronal of short thick hair."[1] All noticed his gleaming eyes; and it was remarked that when his glance fell on an Italian, the man moved uneasily in his seat, as if "the evil eye was upon him." Meanwhile, in the seconds before the silence was broken, Luther was making *his* observations. He noticed the swarthy Jewish-looking face of Aleander, with its gleam of hateful triumph. "So the Jews must have looked at Christ," he thought.[2] He saw the young Emperor, and near him the papal nuncios and the great ecclesiastics of the Empire. A wave of pity passed through him as he looked. "He seemed to me," he said, "like some poor lamb among swine and hounds."[3] There was a table or bench with some books upon it. When Luther's glance fell on them, he saw that they were his own writings, and could not help wondering how they had got there.[4] He did not know that Aleander had been collecting them for some weeks, and that, at command of the Emperor, he had handed them over to John Eck, the Official of Trier, for the purposes of the audience.[5] Jerome Schurf made his way to Luther's side, and stood ready to assist in legal difficulties.

The past and the future faced each other—the young Emperor in his rich robes of State, with his pale, vacant-looking face, but "carrying more at the back of his head than his countenance showed," the descendant of long lines of kings, determined to maintain the beliefs, rites, and rules of that Mediæval Church which his ancestors had upheld; and the monk, with his wan face seamed with the traces of spiritual conflict and victory, in the poor dress of his

[1] *Reichstagsakten*, ii. 632.
[2] De Wette, *Dr. Martin Luthers Briefe*, etc. i. 589.
[3] *Luther's Works* (Erlangen edition), xxiv. 322.
[4] *Ibid.* lxiv. 369.
[5] Brieger, *Aleander*, etc. p. 146.

Order, a peasant's son, resolute to cleave a way for the new faith of evangelical freedom, the spiritual birthright of all men.

The strained silence [1] was broken by the Official of Trier, a man of lofty presence, saying, in a clear, ringing voice so that all could hear distinctly, first in Latin and then in German:

"'Martin Luther, His Imperial Majesty, Sacred and Victorious (*sacra et invicta*), on the advice of all the Estates of the Holy Roman Empire, has ordered you to be summoned here to the throne of His Majesty, in order that you may recant and recall, according to the force, form, and meaning of the citation-mandate decreed against you by His Majesty and communicated legally to you, the books, both in Latin and in German, published by you and spread abroad, along with their contents: Wherefore I, in the name of His Imperial Majesty and of the Princes of the Empire, ask you: First, Do you confess that these books exhibited in your presence (I show him a bundle of books written in Latin and in German) and now named one by one, which have been circulated with your name on the title-page, are yours, and do you acknowledge them to be yours? Secondly, Do you wish to retract and recall them and their contents, or do you mean to adhere to them and to reassert them?'" [2]

The books were not named; so Jerome Schurf called out, "Let the titles be read." [3] Then the notary, Maximilian Siebenberger (called Transilvanus),[4] stepped forward and, taking up the books one by one, read their titles and briefly described their contents.[5] Then Luther, having briefly and precisely repeated the two questions put to him, said:

[1] *Reichstagsakten*, ii. 633. [2] *Ibid.* p. 588.
[3] *Ibid.* p. 547. [4] *Ibid.* p. 633.
[5] The names of the books collected and placed on the table have been curiously preserved on a scrap of paper stored in the archives of the Vatican Library; they were all editions published by Frobenius of Basel (*Reichstagsakten*, ii. 548 and note). It may be sufficient to say that among them (twenty-five or so) were the appeal *To the Christian Nobility of the German Nation*, the tract *On the Liberty of a Christian Man*, *The Babylonian Captivity of the Church of Christ*, *Against the Execrable Bull of Antichrist*, some commentaries, and some tracts on religious subjects "not contentious," says the official record.

"'To which I answer as shortly and correctly as I am able. I cannot deny that the books named are mine, and I will never deny any of them:[1] they are all my offspring; and I have written some others which have not been named.[2] But as to what follows, whether I shall reaffirm in the same terms all, or shall retract what I may have uttered beyond the authority of Scripture,—because the matter involves a question of faith and of the salvation of souls, and because it concerns the Word of God, which is the greatest thing in heaven and on earth, and which we all must reverence,—it would be dangerous and rash in me to make any unpremeditated declaration, because in unpremeditated speech I might say something less than the fact and something more than the truth; besides, I remember the saying of Christ when He declared, "Whosoever shall deny Me before men, him will I also deny before My Father which is in heaven, and before His angels." For these reasons I beg, with all respect, that your Imperial Majesty give me time to deliberate, that I may answer the question without injury to the Word of God and without peril to my own soul.'"[3]

Luther made his answer in a low voice—so low that the deputies from Strassburg, who were sitting not far from him, said that they could not hear him distinctly.[4] Many present inferred from the low voice that Luther's spirit was broken, and that he was beginning to be afraid. But from what followed it is evident that Luther's whole procedure on this first appearance before the Diet was intended to defeat the intrigues of Aleander, which had for

[1] This was probably an answer to the suggestion made by Glapion to Chancellor Brück, that if Luther would only deny the authorship of the *Babylonian Captivity of the Church of Christ*, which had been published anonymously, matters might be arranged.

[2] The sentence, "And I have written some others which have not been named," was an aside spoken in a lower tone, but distinctly (*Reichstagsakten*, ii. 589, 860).

[3] *Reichstagsakten*, ii. 548. In Eck's official report Luther's answer is given very briefly; instead of Luther's words the Official says: "As to the other part of the question, whether he wished to retract their contents and to sing another tune (*palinodiam canere*), he began to invent a chain of idle reasons (*causas nectere*) and to seek means of escape (*diffugias quærere*)" (*Reichstagsakten*, ii. 589).

[4] *Reichstagsakten*, ii. 851, 863: "Wir habent den Luther nit wol horen reden, dann er mit niederer stim geredet" (Kolde, *Analecta*, p. 30 n.).

their aim to prevent the Reformer addressing the Diet in a long speech; and in this he succeeded, as Brück and Spalatin hoped he would.

The Estates then proceeded to deliberate on Luther's request. Aleander says that the Emperor called his councillors about him; that the Electors talked with each other; and that the separate Estates deliberated separately.[1] We are informed by the report of the Venetian ambassadors that there was some difficulty among some of them in acceding to Luther's request. But at length the Official of Trier again addressed Luther:

"'Martin, you were able to know from the imperial mandate why you were summoned here, and therefore you do not really require any time for further deliberation, nor is there any reason why it should be granted. Yet His Imperial Majesty, moved by his natural clemency, grants you one day for deliberation, and you will appear here to-morrow at the same hour,—but on the understanding that you do not give your answer in writing, but by word of mouth.'"[2]

The sitting, which, so far as Luther was concerned, had occupied about an hour, was then declared to be ended, and he was conducted back to his room by the herald. There he sat down and wrote to his friend Cuspinian in Vienna "from the midst of the tumult":

"This hour I have been before the Emperor and his brother, and have been asked whether I would recant my books. I have said that the books were really mine, and

[1] Brieger, *Aleander*, etc. p. 146.

[2] *Reichstagsakten*, ii. 549. Aleander, writing to Rome, says that the Official went on to say in the name of the Emperor that Luther ought to bear it in mind that he had written many things against the Pope and the Apostolic Chair, and had scattered recklessly many heretical statements which had caused great scandal, and which, if not speedily ended, would kindle such a great conflagration as neither Luther's recantation nor the imperial power could extinguish; and that he exhorted Luther to be mindful of this (Brieger, *Aleander*, p. 147). In Eck's official report these remarks are given as the opinions of those princes who did not wish that Luther's request should be granted; but they must have been included in his speech, for Peutinger confirms the nuncio's report (*Reichstagsakten*, ii. 589 f., 860).

have asked for some delay about recantation. They have given me no longer space and time than till to-morrow for deliberation. Christ helping me, I do not mean to recant one jot or tittle."[1]

§ 6. *Luther's Second Appearance before the Diet.*

The next day, Thursday, April 18th, did not afford much time for deliberation. Luther was besieged by visitors. Familiar friends came to see him in the morning; German nobles thronged his hostel at midday; Bucer rode over from the Ebernberg in the afternoon with congratulations on the way that the first audience had been got through, and bringing letters from Ulrich von Hutten. His friends were almost astonished at his cheerfulness. "He greeted me and others," said Dr. Peutinger, who was an early caller, "quite cheerfully—'Dear Doctor,' he said, 'how is your wife and child?' I have never found or seen him other than the right good fellow he is."[2] George Vogler and others had "much pious conversation" with him, and wrote, praising his thorough heroism.[3] The German nobles greeted Luther with a bluff heartiness—"Herr Doctor, How are you? People say you are to be burnt; that will never do; that would ruin everything."[4]

The marshal and the herald came for Luther a little after four o'clock, and led him by the same private devious ways to the Bishop's Palace. The crowds on the streets were even larger than on the day before. It was said that more than five thousand people, Germans and foreigners, were crushed together in the street before the Palace. The throng was so dense that some of the delegates, like Oelhafen from Nürnberg, could not get through it.[5] It was six o'clock before the Emperor, accompanied

[1] De Wette, *Dr. Martin Luthers Briefe*, i. 587.

[2] *Reichstagsakten*, ii. 862. [3] *Ibid.* p. 853.

[4] *Reichstagsakten*, ii. 549 n.; *Luther's Works* (Erlangen edition), lxiv. 369.

[5] "I was on my way to the audience to hear (Luther's) speech, but the throng was so dense that I could not get through" (Sixtus Oelhafen to Hector Pömer, *Reichstagsakten*, ii. 854).

by the Electors and princes, entered the hall. Luther and the herald had been kept waiting in the court of the Palace for more than an hour and a half, bruised by the dense moving crowd. In the hall the throng was so great that the princes had some difficulty in getting to their seats, and found themselves uncomfortably crowded when they reached them.[1] Two notable men were absent. The papal nuncios refused to be present when a heretic was permitted to speak. Such proceedings were the merest tomfoolery (*ribaldaria*), Aleander said. When Luther reached the door, he had still to wait; the princes were occupied in reaching their places, and it was not etiquette for him to appear until they were seated.[2] The day was darkening, and the gloomy hall flamed with torches.[3] Observers remarked Luther's wonderfully cheerful countenance as he made his way to his place.[4]

The Emperor had intrusted the procedure to Aleander, to his confessor Glapion, and to John Eck, who had conducted the audience on the previous day.[5] The Official was again to have the conduct of matters in his hands. As soon as Luther was in his place, Eck "rushed into words" (*prorupit in verba*).[6] He began by recapitulating what had taken place at the first audience; and in saying that Luther had asked time for consideration, he insinuated that every Christian ought to be ready at all times to give a reason for the faith that is in him, much more a learned theologian like Luther. He declared that it was now time for Luther to answer plainly whether he adhered to the contents of the books he had acknowledged to be his, or whether he was prepared to recant them. He spoke first in Latin and then in German, and it was noticed that his speech in Latin was very bitter.[7]

Then Luther delivered his famous speech before the Diet. He had freed himself from the web of intrigue that

[1] *Reichstagsakten*, ii. 864.
[2] Walch, xv. 2301.
[3] *Ibid.* p. 2233.
[4] *Reichstagsakten*, ii. 853.
[5] Brieger, *Aleander*, etc. p. 172.
[6] *Reichstagsakten*, ii. 549
[7] *Ibid.* p. 550.

Aleander had been at such pains to weave round him to compel him to silence, and stood forth a free German to plead his cause before the most illustrious audience the Fatherland could offer to any of its sons.

Before him was the Emperor and his brother Ferdinand, Archduke of Austria, destined to be King of the Romans and Emperor in days to come, and beside them, seated, all the Electors and the great Princes of the Empire, lay and ecclesiastical, among them four Cardinals. All round him standing, for there was no space for seats, the Counts, Free Nobles and Knights of the Empire, and the delegates of the great cities, were closely packed together.[1] Ambassadors and the political agents of almost all the countries in Europe were there to swell the crowd—ready to report the issue of this momentous day. For all believed that whatever weighty business for Germany was discussed at this Diet, the question raised by Luther was one of European importance, and affected the countries which they represented. The rumour had gone about, founded mainly on the serene appearance of Luther, that the monk was about to recant;[2] and most of the political agents earnestly hoped it might be true. That and that only would end, they believed, the symptoms of disquiet which the governments of every land were anxiously watching.

The diligence of Wrede has collected and printed in the *Reichstagsakten*[3] several papers, all of which profess to give Luther's speech; but they are mere summaries, some longer and some shorter, and give no indication of the power which thrilled the audience. Its effect must be sought for in the descriptions of the hearers.

The specimens of his books which had been collected by Aleander were so representative that Luther could speak of all his writings. He divided them into three classes. He had written books for edification which he could truly say had been approved by all men, friends and foes alike,

[1] Myconius, *Historia Reformationis* (Leipzig, 1718), p. 39.

[2] *Reichstagsakten*, ii. 578.

[3] *Ibid.* pp. 550 ff., 557 ff., 591 ff. etc.

and it was scarcely to be expected that he, the author, should be the only man to recant the contents of such writings as even the Papal Bull had commended. In a second class of writings he had attacked the papal tyranny which all Germany was groaning under; to recant the contents of these books would be to make stronger and less endurable the monstrous evil he had protested against; he therefore refused to recall such writings; no loyal German could do so. He had also written against individual persons who had supported the Papacy; it was possible that he had written too strongly in some places and against some men; he was only a man and not God, and was liable to make mistakes; he remembered how Christ, who could not err, had acted when He was accused, and imitating Him, he was quite ready, if shown to be wrong, by evangelical or prophetic witnesses, to renounce his errors, and if he were convinced, he assured the Emperor and princes assembled that he would be the first to throw his books into the fire. He dwelt upon the power of the word of God which must prevail over everything, and showed that many calamities in times past had fallen upon nations who had neglected its teachings and warnings. He concluded as follows:

"I do not say that there is any need for my teaching or warning the many princes before me, but the duty I owe to *my* Germany will not allow me to recant. With these words I commend myself to your most serene Majesty and to your principalities, and humbly beg that you will not permit my accusers to triumph over me causelessly. I have spoken (*Dixi*)."

Luther had spoken in Latin; he was asked to repeat what he had said in German. The Hall had been packed the torches gave forth warmth as well as light. Luther steamed with perspiration, and looked wan and overpowered; the heat was intense. Friends thought that the further effort would be too much for his strength. The Saxon councillor, Frederick von Thun, regardless of etiquette, called out loudly, "If you cannot do it you have done enough, Herr Doctor."[1] But Luther went on and finished his address in German. His last words were, "Here I stand (*Hie bin Ich*)."

Aleander, the papal nuncio, who was not present, relates that while Luther was speaking of the books in which he had attacked the Papacy, and was proceeding "with great venom" to denounce the Pope,[2] the Emperor ordered him to pass from that subject and to proceed with his other matters. The Emperor had certainly told the Estates that he would not allow the question of Luther's orthodoxy and complaints against the Holy See to be discussed together; and that lends some support to Aleander's statement.[3] But when it is seen that not one of the dozen deputies present who write accounts of the scene mentions the interruption; when it is not found in the official report; when it is remembered that Charles could not understand either German or Latin, the story of the interruption is a very unlikely one. Aleander was not remarkable for his veracity —"a man, to say the least, not bigotedly truthful (*non superstitiose verax*)," says Erasmus;[4] and the nuncio on one occasion boasted to his masters in Rome that he could lie well when occasion required it.[5]

Several letters descriptive of the scene, written by men who were present in the Diet, reveal the intense interest taken by the great majority of the audience in the appearance and speech of Luther. His looks, his language, the attitude in which he stood, are all described. When artists portray the scene, either on canvas or in bronze, Luther is invariably represented standing upright, his shoulders squared, and his head thrown back. That was not how he stood before Charles and the Diet. He was a monk,

[1] *Luther's Works* (Erlangen edition), lxiv. 370.

[2] Brieger, *Aleander*, etc. p. 152.

[3] *Reichstagsakten*, ii. 530.

[4] *Desiderii Erasmi Roterodami Opera Omnia* (Leyden, 1703), iii. 1095: "Jam audio multis persuasum, ex meis scriptis exstitisse totam hanc Ecclesiæ procellam: cujus verissimi rumoris præcipuus auctor fuit Hieronymus Aleander, homo, ut nihil aliud dicam, non superstitiose verax."

[5] Brieger, *Aleander*, etc. p. 41.

trained in the conventional habits of monkish humility. He stood with a stoop of the head and shoulders, with the knees slightly bent, and without gestures. The only trace of bodily emotion was betrayed by bending and straightening his knees.[1] He addressed the Emperor and the Estates with all respect,—"Most serene Lord and Emperor, most illustrious Princes, most clement Lords,"—and apologised for any lack of etiquette on the ground that he was convent-bred and knew nothing of the ways of Courts; but it was noticed by more than one observer that he did not address the spiritual princes present.[2] Many a witness describes the charm of his cheerful, modest, but undaunted bearing.[3] The Saxon official account says, "Luther spoke simply, quietly, modestly, yet not without Christian courage and fidelity—in such a way, too, that his enemies would have doubtless preferred a more abject spirit and speech"; and it goes on to relate that his adversaries had confidently counted on a recantation, and that they were correspondingly disappointed.[4] Many expected that, as he had never before been in such presence, the strange audience would have disconcerted him; but, to their wonder and delight, he spoke "confidently, reasonably, and prudently, as if he were in his own lecture-room."[5] Luther himself was surprised that the unaccustomed surroundings affected him so little. "When it came to my turn," he says, "I just went on."[6] The beauty of his diction pleased his audience —"many fair and happy words," say Dr. Peutinger and others.[7]

When Luther had finished, the Official, mindful that it was his duty to extract from Luther a distinct recantation, addressed him in a threatening manner (*increpabundo similis*), and told him that his answer had not been to the point. The question was that Luther, in some of his books, denied decisions of Councils: Would he reaffirm or recant what he had said about these decisions? the Emperor

[1] *Reichstagsakten*, ii. 860 n. [2] *Ibid.* p. 860. [3] *Ibid.* p. 853.
[4] *Ibid.* pp. 550, 551. [5] Myconius, *Historia Reformationis*, p. 39.
[6] Walch, xv. 233. [7] *Reichstagsakten*, ii. 861.

demanded a plain (*non cornutum*) answer. "If His Imperial Majesty desires a plain answer," said Luther, "I will give it to him, *neque cornutum neque dentatum*, and it is this: It is impossible for me to recant unless I am proved to be in the wrong by the testimony of Scripture or by evident reasoning; I cannot trust either the decisions of Councils or of Popes, for it is plain that they have not only erred, but have contradicted each other. My conscience is thirled to the word of God, and it is neither safe nor honest to act against one's conscience. God help me! Amen!"[1]

When he had finished, the Emperor and the princes consulted together; then at a sign from Charles,[2] the Official addressed Luther at some length. He told him that in his speech he had abused the clemency of the Emperor, and had added to his evil deeds by attacking the Pope and Papists (*papistæ*) before the Diet. He briefly recapitulated Luther's speech, and said that he had not sufficiently distinguished between his books and his opinions; there might be room for discussion had Luther brought forward anything new, but his errors were old—the errors of the Poor Men of Lyons, of Wiclif, of John and Jerome Huss (the learned Official gave Huss a brother unknown to history),[3] which were decided upon at the Council of Constance, where the whole German nation had been gathered together; he again asked him to retract such opinions. To this Luther replied as before, that General Councils had erred, and that his conscience did not allow him to retract. By this time the torches had burnt to their sockets, and the hall was growing dark.[4] Wearied with the crowd and the heat, numbers were preparing to leave. The Official, making a last effort, called out loudly, "Martin, let your conscience alone; recant your errors and you will be safe and sound; you can never show that a Council has erred." Luther declared that Councils had erred, and that he could prove it.[5] Upon this the Emperor

[1] *Reichstagsakten*, ii. 555. [2] *Ibid.* p. 591. [3] *Ibid.* p. 861 n.

[4] Cochlæus, *Commentarius*, etc. p. 34.

[5] *Reichstagsakten*, ii. 556–558, 581, 582, 591–594.

made a sign to end the matter.[1] The last words Luther was heard to say were, "God come to my help" (*Got kum mir zu hilf*).[2]

It is evident from almost all the reports that from the time that Luther had finished his great speech there was a good deal of confusion, and probably of conversation, among the audience. All that the greater portion of those present heard was an altercation between Luther and the Official, due, most of the Germans thought, to the overbearing conduct of Eck, and which the Italians and Spaniards attributed to the pertinacity of Luther.[3] "Luther asserted that Councils had erred several times, and had given decisions against the law of God. The Official said No, Luther said Yes, and that he could prove it. So the matter came to an end for that time."[4] But all understood that there was a good deal said about the Council of Constance.

The Emperor left his throne to go to his private rooms; the Electors and the princes sought their hotels. A number of Spaniards, perceiving that Luther turned to leave the tribunal, broke out into hootings, and followed "the man of God with prolonged howlings."[5] Then the Germans, nobles and delegates from the towns, ringed him

[1] Aleander wrote that the Emperor said that he did not wish to hear more: *et allora fù detto per Cesar, che bastava et che non voleva più udir, ex quo questui negava li Concilii* (Brieger, *Aleander*, etc. p. 153).

[2] *Reichstagsakten*, ii. 862 (Dr. Peutinger to the Council of Augsburg). The famous ending: *Hie stehe ich, ich kann nicht anders thun, Gott helfe mir, Amen,* which gives such a dramatic finish to the whole scene, is not to be found in the very earliest records. It first appeared in an account published in Wittenberg without date, but which is probably very early, and also in the 1546 edition of *Luther's Works.* Various versions are given of the last words Luther uttered—*Gott helf mir, Amen,* in the *Acta Wormaciæ* (*Reichstagsakten*, ii. 557), which are believed to have been corrected by Luther himself; *So helf mir Gott, denn kein widerspruch kan ich nicht thun, Amen,* is given by Spalatin in his *Annales* (p. 41). Every description of the scene coming from contemporary sources shows that there was a great deal of confusion; it is most likely that in the excitement men carried away only a general impression and not an exact recollection of the last words of Luther. If it were not for Dr. Peutinger's very definite statement written almost immediately after the event, there seems to be no reason why the dramatic ending should not have been the real one.

[3] *Reichstagsakten*, ii. 636. [4] *Ibid.* p. 862 [5] *Ibid.* p. 558.

round to protect him, and as they passed from the hall they all at once, and Luther in the midst of them, thrust forward arms and raised hands high above their heads, in the way that a German knight was accustomed to do when he had unhorsed his antagonist in the tourney, or that a German landsknecht did when he had struck a victorious blow. The Spaniards rushed to the door shouting after Luther, "To the fire with him, to the fire!"[1] The crowd on the street thought that Luther was being sent to prison, and thought of a rescue.[2] Luther calmed them by saying that the company were escorting him home. Thus, with hands held high in stern challenge to Holy Roman Empire and mediæval Church, they accompanied Luther to his lodging

Friends had got there before him—Spalatin, ever faithful; Oelhafen, who had not been able to reach his place in the Diet because of the throng. Luther, with beaming face, stretched out both his hands, exclaiming, "I am through, I am through!"[3] In a few minutes Spalatin was called away. He soon returned. The old Elector had summoned him only to say, "How well, father, Dr. Luther spoke this day before the Emperor and the Estates; but he is too bold for me." The sturdy old German prince wrote to his brother John, "From what I have heard this day, I will never believe that Luther is a heretic"; and a few days later, "At this Diet, not only Annas and Caiaphas, but also Pilate and Herod, have conspired against Luther." Frederick of Saxony was no Lutheran, like his brother John and his nephew John Frederick; and he was the better able to express what most German princes were thinking about Luther and his appearance before the

[1] *Reichstagsakten*, ii. 636. Aleander says that Luther alone raised his hand and made this gesture; he was not present; the Spaniard who recounts the incident as given above was a spectator of the scene.

[2] *Luther's Works* (Erlangen edition), lxiv. 370; Wrampelmeyer, *Tagebuch über Dr. Martin Luther, geführt von Dr. Conrad Cordatus*, p. 477; *et descendi de pretorio conductus, do sprangen Gesellen herfur, die sagten, "Wie, furt yhr yhn gefangen? Das must nicht sein."*

[3] *Reichstagsakten*, ii. 853.

Diet. Even Duke George was stirred to a momentary admiration; and Duke Eric of Brunswick, who had taken the papal side, could not sit down to supper without sending Luther a can of Einbecker beer from his own table.[1] As for the commonalty, there was a wild uproar in the streets of Worms that night—men cursing the Spaniards and Italians, and praising Luther, who had compelled the Emperor and the prelates to hear what he had to say, and who had voiced the complaints of the Fatherland against the Roman Curia at the risk of his life. The voice of the people found utterance in a placard, which next morning was seen posted up on the street corners of the town, "Woe to the land whose king is a child." It was the beginning of the disillusion of Germany. The people had believed that they were securing a German Emperor when, in a fit of enthusiasm, they had called upon the Electors to choose the grandson of Maximilian. They were beginning to find that they had selected a Spaniard.

§ 7. *The Conferences.*

Next day (April 19th) the Emperor proposed that Luther should be placed under the ban of the Empire. The Estates were not satisfied, and insisted that something should be done to effect a compromise. Luther had not been treated as they had proposed in their memorandum of the 19th February. He had been peremptorily ordered to retract. The Emperor had permitted Aleander to regulate the order of procedure on the day previous (April 18th), and the result had not been satisfactory. Even the Elector of Brandenburg and his brother, the hesitating Archbishop of Mainz, did not wish matters to remain as they were. They knew the feelings of the German people, if they were ignorant of the Emperor's diplomatic dealings with the Pope. The Emperor gave way, but told them that he would let them hear his own view of the matter. He produced a sheet of paper, and read a short statement prepared by

[1] Selnecker, *Historia . . . D. M. Lutheri* (1575), p. 108.

himself in the French tongue—the language with which Charles was most familiar. It was the memorable declaration of his own religious position, which has been referred to already.[1] Aleander reports that several of the princes became pale as death when they heard it.[2] In later discussions the Emperor asserted with warmth that he would never change one iota of his declaration.

Nevertheless, the Diet appointed a Commission (April 22nd) to confer with Luther, and at its head was placed the Archbishop of Trier, who was perhaps the only one among the higher ecclesiastics of Germany whom Luther thoroughly trusted. They had several meetings with the Reformer, the first being on the 24th of April. All the members of the Commission were sincerely anxious to arrange a compromise; but after the Emperor's declaration that was impossible, as Luther himself clearly saw. No set of resolutions, however skilfully framed, could reconcile the Emperor's belief that a General Council was infallible and Luther's phrase, "a conscience bound to the Holy Scriptures." No proposals to leave the final decision to the Emperor and the Pope, to the Emperor alone, to the Emperor and the Estates, to a future General Council (all of which were made), could patch up a compromise between two such contradictory standpoints. Compromise must fail in a fight of faiths, and that was the nature of the opposition between Charles v. and Luther throughout their lives. What divided them was no subordinate question about doctrine or ritual; it was fundamental, amounting to an entirely different conception of the whole round of religion. The moral authority of the individual conscience confronted the legal authority of an ecclesiastical assembly. In after days the monk regretted that he had not spoken out more boldly before the Diet. Shortly before his death,

[1] Cf. p. 264–5. The complete text of the Emperor's declaration is to be found in the *Reichstagsakten*, ii. 594; Förstemann, *Neues Urkundenbuch zur Geschichte der evangelischen Kirchen-Reformation* (Hamburg, 1842), i. 75; Armstrong, *The Emperor Charles V.*, i. 70 (London, 1902).

[2] Brieger, *Aleander und Luther 1521*, p. 154 (Gotha, 1884): *Dove molti rimasero più pallidi che se fossero stati morti.*

the Emperor expressed his regret that he had not burned the obstinate heretic. When the Commission had failed, Luther asked leave to reveal his whole innermost thoughts to the Archbishop of Trier, under the seal of confession, and the two had a memorable private interview. Aleander fiercely attacked the Archbishop for refusing to disclose what passed between them; but the prelate was a German bishop with a conscience, and not an unscrupulous dependant on a shameless Curia. No one knew what Luther's confession was. The Commission had to report that its efforts had proved useless. Luther was ordered to leave Worms and return to Wittenberg, without preaching on the journey; his safe conduct was to expire in twenty-one days after the 26th of April. At their expiry he was liable to be seized and put to death as a pestilent heretic. There remained only to draft and publish the edict containing the ban. The days passed, and it did not appear.

Suddenly the startling news reached Worms that Luther had disappeared, no one knew where. Aleander, as usual, had the most exact information, and gives the fullest account of the rumours which were flying about. Cochlæus, who was at Frankfurt, sent him a man who had been at Eisenach, had seen Luther's uncle, and had been told by him about the capture. Five horsemen had dashed at the travelling waggon, had seized Luther, and had ridden off with him. Who the captors were or by whose authority they had acted, no one could tell. "Some blame me," says Aleander, "others the Archbishop of Mainz: would God it were true!" Some thought that Sickingen had carried him off to protect him; others, the Elector of Saxony; others, the Count of Mansfeld. One persistent rumour declared that a personal enemy of the Elector of Saxony, one Hans Beheim, had been the captor; and the Emperor rather believed it. On May 14th a letter reached Worms saying that Luther's body had been found in a silver-mine pierced with a dagger. The news flew over Germany and beyond it that Luther had been done to death by emissaries of the Roman Curia; and so persistent was the belief, that

Aleander prepared to justify the deed by alleging that the Reformer had broken the imperial safe conduct by preaching at Eisenach and by addressing a concourse of people at Frankfurt.[1] Albert Dürer, in Ghent, noted down in his private diary that Luther, "the God-inspired man," had been slain by the Pope and his priests as our Lord had been put to death by the priests in Jerusalem. "O God, if Luther is dead, who else can expound the Holy Gospel to us!"[2] Friends wrote distracted letters to Wittenberg imploring Luther to tell them whether he was alive or imprisoned.[3] The news created the greatest consternation and indignation in Worms. The Emperor's decision had been little liked even by the princes most incensed against Luther. Aleander could not get even the Archbishop of Mainz to promise that he would publish it. When the Commission of the Diet had failed to effect a compromise, the doors of the Rathhaus and of other public buildings in Worms had been placarded with an intimation that four hundred knights had sworn that they would not leave Luther unavenged, and the ominous words *Bundschuh, Bundschuh, Bundschuh* had appeared on it. The Emperor had treated the matter lightly; but the German Romanist princes had been greatly alarmed.[4] They knew, if he did not, that the union of peasants with the lower nobility had been a possible source of danger to Germany for nearly a century; they remembered that it was this combination which had made the great Bohemian rising successful. Months after the Diet had risen, Romanist partisans in Germany sent anxious communications to the Pope about

[1] Brieger, *Luther und Aleander 1521* (Gotha, 1884), pp. 208 ff.; Kalkoff, *Die Depeschen des Nuntius Aleander vom Wormser Reichstage 1521* (Halle, 1897), pp. 235 ff.

[2] Leitschuh, *Albrecht Dürer's Tagebuch der Reise in die Niederlande* (Leipzig, 1884), pp. 82–84.

[3] Kolde, *Analecta Lutherana* (Gotha, 1883), pp. 31, 32: "Quare, mi doctissime Luthere, si me amas, si reliquos, qui adhuc mecum curam tui habent, Evangeliique Dei, per te tanto labore, tanta cura, tot sudoribus, tot periculis prædicati fac sciamus, an vivas, an captus sis."

[4] Brieger, *Luther und Aleander 1521* (Gotha, 1884), p 158; Kalkoff, *Die Depeschen des Nuntius Aleander* (Halle, 1897), p. 182.

the dangers of a combination of the lesser nobility with the peasants.[1] The condition of Worms had been bad enough before, and when the news of Luther's murder reached the town the excitement passed all bounds. The whole of the Imperial Court was in an uproar. When Aleander was in the royal apartments the highest nobles in Germany pressed round him, telling him that he would be murdered even if he were "clinging to the Emperor's bosom." Men crowded his room to give him information of conspiracies to slay both himself and the senior Legate Caraccioli.[2] The excitement abated somewhat, but the wiser German princes recognised the abiding gravity of the situation, and how little the Emperor's decision had done to end the Lutheran movement. The true story of Luther's disappearance was not known until long afterwards. After the failure of the conferences, the Elector of Saxony summoned two of his councillors and his chaplain and private secretary, Spalatin, and asked them to see that Luther was safely hidden until the immediate danger was past. They were to do what they pleased and inform him of nothing. Many weeks passed before the Elector and his brother John knew that Luther was safe, living in their own castle on the Wartburg. This was his "Patmos," where he doffed his monkish robes, let the hair grow over his tonsure, was clad as a knight, and went by the name of Junker Georg. His disappearance did not mean that he ceased to be a great leader of men; but it dates the beginning of the national opposition to Rome.

§ 8. *The Ban.*

After long delay, the imperial mandate against Luther was prepared. It was presented (May 25th) to an informal meeting of some members of the Diet after the Elector of Saxony and many of Luther's staunchest supporters had

[1] Cf. Letter of Cochlæus to the Pope (June 19th) in Brieger's *Zeitschrift für Kirchengeschichte*, xviii. p. 118.

[2] Brieger, *Luther und Aleander 1521* (Gotha, 1884), p. 211.

left Worms.[1] Aleander, who had a large share in drafting it, brought two copies, one in Latin and the other in German, and presented them to Charles on a Sunday (May 26th) after service. The Emperor signed them before leaving the church. "Are you contented now?" said Charles, with a smile to the Legate; and Aleander overflowed with thanks. Few State documents, won by so much struggling and scheming, have proved so futile. The uproar in Germany at the report of Luther's death had warned the German princes to be chary of putting the edict into execution.

The imperial edict against Luther threatened all his sympathisers with extermination. It practically proclaimed an Albigensian war in Germany. Charles had handed it to Aleander with a smile. Aleander despatched the document to Rome with an exultation which could only find due expression in a quotation from Ovid's *Art of Love.* Pope Leo celebrated the arrival of the news by comedies and musical entertainments. But calm observers, foreigners in Germany, saw little cause for congratulation and less for mirth. Henry VIII. wrote to the Archbishop of Mainz congratulating him on the overthrow of the "rebel against Christ"; but Wolsey's agent at the Diet informed his master that he believed there were one hundred thousand Germans who were still ready to lay down their lives in Luther's defence.[2] Velasco, who had struck down the Spanish rebels in the battle of Villalar, wrote to the Emperor that the victory was God's gratitude for his dealings with the heretic monk; but Alfonso de Valdès, the Emperor's secretary, said in a letter to a Spanish correspondent:

"Here you have, as some imagine, the end of this tragedy; but I am persuaded it is not the end, but the

[1] The important clauses in the Edict of Worms are printed in Emil Reich's *Select Documents illustrating Mediæval and Modern History* (London, 1905), p. 209.

[2] *Letters and Papers, Foreign and Domestic, of the Reign of Henry VIII.*, III. i. p. cccxxxviii. Letter from Tunstal to Wolsey of date January 21st, 1521.

beginning of it. For I see that the minds of the Germans are greatly exasperated against the Roman See, and they do not seem to attach great importance to the Emperor's edicts; for since their publication, Luther's books are sold with impunity at every step and corner of the streets and market-places. From this you will easily guess what will happen when the Emperor leaves. This evil might have been cured with the greatest advantage to the Christian commonwealth, had not the Pope refused a General Council, had he preferred the public weal to his own private interests. But while he insists that Luther shall be condemned and burnt, I see the whole Christian commonwealth hurried to destruction unless God Himself help us."

Valdès, like Gattinara and other councillors of Charles, was a follower of Erasmus. He lays the blame of all on the Pope. But what a disillusion this Diet of Worms ought to have been to the Erasmians! The Humanist young sovereigns and the Humanist Pope, from whom so much had been expected, congratulating each other on Luther's condemnation to the stake!

The foreboding of Alfonso de Valdès was amply justified. Luther's books became more popular than ever, and the imperial edict did nothing to prevent their sale either within Germany or beyond it. Aleander was soon to learn this. He had retired to the Netherlands, and busied himself with *auto-da-fés* of the prohibited writings; but he had to confess that they were powerless to prevent the spread of Luther's opinions, and he declared that the only remedy would be if the Emperor seized and burnt half a dozen Lutherans, and confiscated all their property.[1] The edict had been published or repeated in lands outside Germany and in the family possessions of the House of Hapsburg. Henry VIII. ordered Luther's books to be burnt in England;[2] the Estates of Scotland prohibited their introduction into the realm under the severest penalties in 1525.[3] But such

[1] Brieger, *Aleander und Luther 1521* (Gotha, 1884), p. 263; cf. pp. 249 ff.

[2] *Letters and Papers, Foreign and Domestic, of the Reign of Henry VIII.* iii. 449, 485.

[3] *Act. Parl. Scot.* ii. 295.

edicts were easily evaded, and the prohibited writings found their way into Spain, Italy, France, Flanders, and elsewhere, concealed in bales of merchandise. In Germany there was no need for concealment; the imperial edict was not merely disregarded, but was openly scouted. The great Strassburg publisher, Gruniger, apologised to his customers, not for publishing Luther's books, but for sending forth a book against him; and Cochlæus declared that printers gladly accepted any MS. against the Papacy, printed it *gratis*, and spent pains in issuing it with taste, while every defender of the established order had to pay heavily to get his book printed, and sometimes could not secure a printer at any cost.

§ 9. *Popular Literature*

The Reformation movement may almost be said to have created the German book trade. The earliest German printed books or rather booklets were few in number, and of no great importance—little books of private devotion, of popular medicine, herbals, almanacs, travels, or public proclamations. Up to 1518 they barely exceeded fifty a year. But in the years 1518–1523 they increased enormously, and four-fifths of the increase were controversial writings prompted by the national antagonism to the Roman Curia. This increase was at first due to Luther alone;[1] but from 1521 onwards he had disciples, fellow-

[1] v. Ranke in his *Deutsche Geschichte im Zeitalter der Reformation* (2nd ed., Leipzig, 1882), ii. 56, and Dr. Burkhardt, archivist at Weimar, in the *Zeitschrift für die historische Theologie* (Gotha) for 1862, p. 456—both founding on the confessedly imperfect information to be found in Panzer's *Annalen der älteren deutschen Litteratur* (1788–1802)—have made the following calculations:—the number of printed books issued in the German language, and within Germany, from 1480–1500, did not exceed forty a year; the years 1500–1512 show about the same average; in the year 1513 the number of books and booklets issued from German presses in the German language was 35; in 1514 it was 47; in 1515, 46; in 1516, 55; in 1517, 37; then Luther's printed appeals to the German people began to appear in the shape of sermons, tracts, controversial writings, etc., and the German publications of the year 1518 rose to 71, of which no less than 20

workers, opponents, all using in a popular way the German language, the effective literary power of which had been discovered by the Reformer.[1] These writers spread the new ideas among the people, high and low, throughout Germany.[2]

There are few traces of combined action in the anti-Romanist writings in the earlier stages of the controversy; it needed literary opposition to give them a semblance of unity. Each writer looks at the general question from his own individual point of view. Luther is the hero with nearly all, and is spoken about in almost extravagant terms. He is the prophet of Germany, the Elias that was to come, the Angel of the Revelation "flying through the mid-heaven with the everlasting Gospel in his hands," the national champion who was brought to Worms to be silenced, and yet was heard by Emperor, princes, and papal nuncios. Some of the authors were still inclined to make Erasmus their leader, and declared that they were fighting under the banner of that "Knight of Christ"; others looked on Erasmus and Luther as fellow-workers, and one homely pamphlet compares Erasmus to the miller who grinds the flour, and Luther to the baker who bakes it into bread to feed the people. Perhaps the most striking feature of

were from Luther's pen; in 1519 the total number was 111, of which 50 were Luther's; in 1520 the total was 208, of which 133 were Luther's; in 1521 (when Luther was in the Wartburg), Luther published 20 separate booklets; in 1522, 130; and in 1523 the total number was 498, of which 180 were Luther's; cf. Weller, *Repertorium Typographicum* (Nördlingen, 1864–1874), for further information. From Luther's Letter to the Nürnberg Council (Enders, v. 244), it may be inferred that the first edition of each of his writings was usually sold out in seven or eight weeks.

[1] It was Luther's appeal to the *Christian Nobility of the German Nation* which taught Ulrich von Hutten the powers of the German language; Strauss, *Ulrich von Hutten, His Life and Times* (London, 1874), p. 241.

[2] A number of the more important of these controversial writings have been reprinted under the title *Flugschriften aus der Reformationszeit* in the very useful series *Neudrucke deutscher Litteraturwerke*, in the course of publication by Niemeyer of Halle; cf. also Kuczynski, *Thesaurus libellorum historiam Reformatorum illustrantium* (Leipzig, 1870); O. Schade, *Satiren und Pasquillen aus der Reformationszeit*, 3 vols. (Hanover, 1856–1858).

the times was the appearance of numberless anonymous pamphlets, purporting to be written by the unlearned for the unlearned. They are mostly in the form of dialogues, and the scene of the conversations recorded was often the village alehouse, where burghers, peasants, weavers, tailors, and shoemakers attack and vanquish in argument priests, monks, and even bishops. One striking feature of this new popular literature is the glorification of the German peasant. He is always represented as an upright, simple-minded, reflective, and intelligent person, skilled in Bible lore, and even in Church history, and knowing as much of Christian doctrine "as three priests and more." He may be compared with the idealised peasant of the pre-revolution literature in France, although he lacks the refinement, and knows nothing of high-flown moral sentiment; but he is much liker the Jak Upland or Piers Plowman of the days of the English Lollards. Jak Upland and Hans Mattock (*Karsthans*), both hate the clergy and abominate the monks and the begging friars, but the German exhibits much more ferocity than the Englishman. The Lollard describes the fat friar of the earlier English days with his swollen dewlap wagging under his chin "like a great goose-egg," and contrasts him with the pale, poverty-stricken peasant and his wife, going shoeless to work over ice-bound roads, their steps marked with the blood which oozed from the cut feet; the German pamphleteer pours out an endless variety of savage nicknames —cheese-hunters, sausage-villains, begging-sacks, sourmilk crocks, the devil's fat pigs, etc. etc. It is interesting to note that most of this coarse controversial literature, which appeared between 1518 and 1523, came from those regions in South Germany where the social revolution had found an almost permanent establishment from the year 1503. It was the sign that the old spirit of communist and religious enthusiasm, which had shown itself spasmodically since the movement under Hans Böhm, had never been extinguished, and it was a symptom that a peasants' war might not be far off. Very little was needed to kindle afresh the smouldering hatred of the peasant against the priests. When German patriots declaimed against the exactions of the Roman Curia, the peasant thought of the great and lesser tithes, of the marriage, baptismal, and burial fees demanded from him by his own parish priest. When Reformers and popular preachers denounced the scandals and corruptions in the Church, the peasant applied them to some drunken, evil-living, careless priest whom he knew. It should be remembered that the character *Karsthans* was invented in 1520, not by a Lutheran sympathiser, but by Thomas Murner, one of Luther's most determined opponents,[1] when he was still engaged in writing against the clerical disorders of the times. This virulent attack on priests and monks had other sources than the sympathy for Luther.[2] It was the awakening of old memories, prompted partly by an underground ceaseless Hussite propaganda, and partly, no doubt, by the new ideas so universally prevalent.

Some of this coarse popular literature had a more direct connection with the Lutheran movement. A booklet which appeared in 1521, entitled *The New and the Old God,* and which had an immense circulation, may be taken as an example. Like many of its kind, it had an illustrated title-page, which was a graphic summary of its contents. There appeared as the representatives of the New God, the Pope, some Church Fathers, and beneath them, Cajetan, Silvester Prierias, Eck, and Faber; over-against them were the Old God as the Trinity, the four Evangelists, St. Paul with a sword, and behind him Luther. It attacked the ceremonies, the elaborate services, the obscure doctrines which had been thrust on the Church by bloody persecutions, and had

[1] Murner was in England in 1523 hoping for an audience from Henry VIII., in whose defence he had written against Luther. "The king desires out of pity that he should return to Germany, for he was one of the chief stays against the faction of Luther, and ordered Wolsey to pay him £100." Cf. Letter of Sir Thomas More to Wolsey: *Letters and Papers, Foreign and Domestic, Henry VIII.*, III. ii. 3270.

[2] Compare chapter on Social Conditions, pp. 96 ff.

changed Christianity into Judaism, and contrasted them with the unchanging Word of the Old God, with its simple story of salvation and its simple doctrines of faith, hope, and love. To the same class belong the writings of the voluminous controversialist, John Eberlin of Günzburg, whom his opponents accused of seducing whole provinces, so effective were his appeals to the "common" man. He began by a pamphlet addressed to the young Emperor, and published, either immediately before or during the earlier sitting of the Diet of Worms in 1521, a daring appeal, in which Luther and Ulrich von Hutten are called the messengers of God to their generation. It was the first of a series of fifteen, all of which were in circulation before the beginning of November of the same year.[1] They were called the "Confederates" (*Bundsgenossen*). The contents of these and other pamphlets by Eberlin may be guessed from their titles—*Of the forty days' fast before Easter and others which pitifully oppress Christian folk. An exhortation to all Christians that they take pity on Nuns. How very dangerous it is that priests have not wives* (the frontispiece represents the marriage of a priest by a bishop, in the background the marriage of two monks, and two musicians on a raised seat). *Why there is no money in the country. Against the false clergy, bare-footed monks, and Franciscans*, etc., etc. He exposes as trenchantly as Luther did the systematic robbery of Germany to benefit the Roman Curia—300,000 gulden sent out of the country every year, and a million more given to the begging friars. He wrote fiercely against the monks who take to this life, because they were too lazy to work like honest people, and called them all sorts of nicknames—*cloister swine, the Devil's landsknechts*, etc., twenty-four thousand of them sponge on Germany and four hundred thousand on the rest of Europe. He tells of a parish priest who thought that he must really begin to read the Scriptures: his

[1] Eberlin's most important pamphlets have been edited by Enders and published in Niemeyer's *Flugschriften aus der Reformationszeit*, and form Nos. xi. xv. and xviii. of the series (Halle, 1896, 1900, 1902).

parishioners are reading it, the mothers to the children and the house-fathers to the household; they trouble him with questions taken from it, and he is often at his wit's end to answer; he asked a friend where he ought to begin, and was told that there was a good deal about priests and their duties in the Epistles to Timothy and Titus; he read, and was horrified to find that bishops and priests ought to be "husbands of one wife," etc. Eberlin had been a Franciscan monk, and was true to the revolutionary traditions of his Order. He preached a social as well as an evangelical reformation. The Franciscan Order sent forth a good many Reformers: men like Stephen Kampen, who had come to adopt views like those of Eberlin without any teaching but the leadings of his heart; or John Brissmann, a learned student of the Scholastic Theology, who like Luther had found that it did not satisfy the yearnings of his soul; or like Frederick Mecum (Myconius), whose whole spiritual development was very similar to that of Luther. Pamphlets like those of Eberlin, and preaching like that of Kampen, had doubtless some influence in causing popular risings against the priests that were not uncommon throughout Germany in 1521, after the Diet of Worms had ended its sittings—the Erfurt tumult, which lasted during the months of April, May, June, and July, may be instanced as an example.

§ 10. *The Spread of Luther's Teaching.*

It may be said that the very year in which the imperial edict against Luther was published (1521) gave evidence that a silent movement towards the adoption of the principles for which Luther was testifying had begun among monks of almost all the different Orders. The Augustinian Eremites, Luther's own Order, had been largely influenced by him. Whole communities, with the prior at their head, had declared for the Reformation both in Germany and in the Low Countries. No other monastic Order was so decidedly upon the side of the

Reformer, but monks of all kinds joined in preaching and teaching the new doctrines. Martin Bucer had been a Dominican, Otto Braunfells a Carthusian, Ambrose Blauer a Benedictine. The case of Oecolampadius (John Hussgen (?) Hausschein) was peculiar. He had been a distinguished Humanist, had come under serious religious impressions, and had entered the Order of St. Bridget; but he was not long there when he joined the ranks of the Reformers, and was sheltered by Franz von Sickingen in his castle at Ebernberg.[1] Urban Rhegius, John Eck's most trusted and most talented student at Ingolstadt, had become a Carmelite, and had quitted his monastery to preach the doctrines of Luther. John Bugenhagen belonged to the Order of the Præmonstratenses. He was a learned theologian. Luther's struggle against Indulgences had displeased him. He got hold of *The Babylonian Captivity of the Christian Church*, and studied it for the purpose of refuting it. The study so changed him that he felt that "the whole world may be wrong, but Luther is right"; he won over his prior and most of his companions, and became the Reformer of Pomerania.

Secular priests all over Germany declared for the new evangelical doctrines. The Bishop of Samlund in East Prussia boldly avowed himself to be on Luther's side, and was careful to have the Lutheran doctrines preached throughout his diocese; and other bishops showed themselves favourable to the new evangelical faith. Many of the most influential parish priests did the like, and their congregations followed them. Sometimes the superior clergy forbade the use of the church, and the people followed their pastor while he preached to them in the fields. Sometimes (as in the case of Hermann Tast) the priest preached under the lime trees in the churchyard, and

[1] Oecolampadius is thought by Böcking to have been the author of the celebrated pamphlet, *Neukarsthans* (Summer, 1521), often attributed to Hutten. Sickingen is one of the speakers; the author shows an acquaintance with Scripture and with theology which Hutten could scarcely command; and the idea of ecclesiastical polity sketched seems to be taken from Marsilius of Padua.

his parishioners came armed to protect him. If priests were lacking to preach the Lutheran doctrines, laymen came forward. If they could not preach, they could sing hymns. Witness the poor weaver of Magdeburg, who took his stand near the statue of Kaiser Otto in the market-place, and sang two of Luther's hymns, "Aus tiefer Not schrei Ich zu dir," and "Es woll' uns Gott gnädig sein," while the people crowded round him on the morning of May 6th, 1524. The Bürgermeister coming from early Mass heard him, and ordered him to be imprisoned, but the crowd rescued him. Such was the beginning of the Reformation in Magdeburg.[1] When men dared not, women took their place. Argula Grunbach, a student of the Scriptures and of Luther's writings, challenged the University of Ingolstadt, under the eyes of the great Dr. Eck himself, to a public disputation upon the truth of Luther's position.

Artists lent their aid to spread the new ideas, and many cartoons made the doctrines and the aims of the Reformers plain to the common people. These pictures were sometimes used to illustrate the title-pages of the controversial literature, and were sometimes published as separate broadsides. In one, Christ is portrayed standing at the *door* of a house, which represents His Church. He invites the people to enter by the door; and Popes, cardinals, and monks are shown climbing the walls to get entrance in a clandestine fashion.[2] In another, entitled the *Triumph of Truth*, the common folk of a German town are represented singing songs of welcome to honour an approaching procession. Moses, the patriarchs, the prophets, and the apostles, carry on their shoulders the Ark of the Holy Scriptures. Hutten comes riding on his warhorse, and to

[1] Hülsse, *Die Einführung der Reformation in der Stadt Magdeburg* (Magdeburg, 1883), p. 46.

[2] The woodcut was first used to illustrate Hans Sachs' poem, "Der gut Hirt und der böss Hirt, Johannis am Zehenden Capitel"; and is given in a facsimile reproduction of several of Hans Sachs' poems, sacred and secular, entitled *Hans Sachs im Gewande seiner Zeit*, Gotha, 1821. The poems were originally issued as large broad-sheets illustrated with a single woodcut, and were meant to be fixed on the walls of rooms.

the tail of the horse is attached a chain which encloses a crowd of ecclesiastics—an archbishop with his mitre fallen off, the Pope with his tiara in the act of tumbling and his pontifical staff broken; after them, cardinals, then monks figured with the heads of cats, pigs, calves, etc. Then comes a triumphal car drawn by the four living creatures, who represent the four evangelists, on one of which rides an angel. Carlstadt stands upright in the front of the car; Luther strides alongside. In the car, Jesus sits saying, *I am the Way, and the Truth, and the Life.* Holy martyrs follow, singing songs of praise. German burghers are spreading their garments on the road, and boys and girls are strewing the path with flowers.[1] Perhaps the most important work of this kind was the *Passional Christi et Antichristi.*[2] Luther planned the book, Luke Cranach designed the pictures, and Melanchthon furnished the texts from Scripture and the quotations from Canon Law. It is a series of pairs of engravings representing the lives of our Lord and of the Pope, so arranged that wherever the book opened two contrasting pictures could be seen at the same time. The contrasts were such as these:—Jesus washing the disciples' feet; the Pope holding out his toe to be kissed: Jesus healing the wounded and the sick; the Pope presiding at a tournament: Jesus bending under His Cross; the Pope carried in state on men's shoulders: Jesus driving the money-changers out of the Temple; the Pope and his servants turning a church into a market for Indulgences, and sitting surrounded with strong boxes and piles of coin. It was a "good book for the laity," Luther said.

One of the signs of the times was the enthusiasm displayed in the imperial cities for the cause of Luther. The way had been prepared. Burgher songs had for long described the ecclesiastical abuses, and had borne witness

[1] Many of these Reformation cartoons are to be found in G. Hirth, *Kulturgeschichtliches Bilderbuch aus drei Jahrhunderten*, i. ii. (Munich, 1896), and one or two in the illustrations in von Bezold, *Geschichte der deutschen Reformation* (Berlin, 1890).

[2] The *Passional Christi et Antichristi* has been reproduced in facsimile by W. Scherer (Berlin, 1885).

to the widespread hatred of the clergy shared in by the townsfolk. Wolfgang Capito and Frederick Mecum (Myconius), both sons of burghers, inform us that their fathers taught them when they were boys that Indulgences were nothing but a speculation on the part of cunning priests to get their hands into the pockets of simple-minded laity. Keen observers of the trend of public feeling like Wimpheling and Pirkheimer had noticed with some alarm the gradual spread of the Hussite propaganda in the towns, and had made the fact one of their reasons for desiring and insisting on a reformation of the Church. The growing sympathy for the Hussite opinions in the cities is abundantly apparent. Some leading Reformers, Capito for instance, told their contemporaries that they had frequently listened to Hussite discourses when they were boys; and the libraries of burghers not infrequently contained Hussite pamphlets. Men in the towns had been reading, thinking, and speaking in private to their familiar friends about the disorders in the life and doctrine of the Church of their days, and were eager to welcome the first symptoms of a genuine attempt at reform.

The number of editions of the German Vulgate, rude as many of these versions were, shows what a Bible-reading people the German burghers had become, enables us to wonder less at the way in which the controversial writers assume that the laity knew as much of the Scriptures as the clergy, and lends credibility to contemporary assertions that women and artisans knew their Bibles better than learned men at the Universities.

These things make us understand how the townsmen were prepared to welcome Luther's simple scriptural teaching, how his writings found such a sale all over Germany, how they could say that he taught what all men had been thinking, and said out boldly what all men had been whispering in private. They explain how the burghers of Strassburg nailed Luther's Ninety-five Theses to the doors of every church and parsonage in the city in 1518; how the citizens of Constance drove away with threats the imperial messenger who came to publish the Edict of Worms in their town; how the people of Basel applauded their pastor when he carried a copy of the Scriptures instead of the Host in the procession on Corpus Christi Day; how the higher clergy of Strassburg could not expel the nephew and successor of the famed Geiler of Keysersberg although he was accused of being a follower of Luther; and how his friend Matthew Zell, when he was prohibited from preaching in the pulpit from which Geiler had thundered, was able to get carpenters to erect another in a corner of the great cathedral, from which he spoke to the people who crowded to hear him. When the clergy persuaded the authorities in many towns (Goslar, Danzig, Worms, etc.) to close the churches against the evangelical preachers, the townspeople listened to their sermons in the open air; but generally from the first the civic authorities sided with the people in welcoming a powerful evangelical preacher. Matthew Zell and, after him, Martin Bucer became the Reformers of Strassburg: Kettenbach and Eberlin, of Ulm; Oecolampadius and Urbanus Rhegius, of Augsburg; Andrew Osiander, of Nürnberg; John Brenz, of Hall, in Swabia; Theobald Pellicanus (Pellicanus, *i.e.* of Villigheim), of Nördlingen; Matthew Alber, of Reutlingen; John Lachmann, of Heilbron; John Wanner, of Constance; and so on. The gilds of *Mastersingers* welcomed the Reformation. The greatest of the civic poets, Hans Sachs of Nürnberg, was a diligent collector and reader of Luther's books. He published in 1523 his famous poem, "The Wittenberg Nightingale" (*Die Wittembergisch Nachtigall, Die man jetz höret überall*). The nightingale was Luther, and its song told that the moonlight with its pale deceptive gleams and its deep shadows was passing away, and the glorious sun was rising. The author praises the utter simplicity of Luther's scriptural teaching, and contrasts it with the quirks and subtleties of Romish doctrine. Even a peasant, he says, can understand and know that Luther's teaching is good and sound. In a later short poem he contrasts evangelical and Romish preaching. The original edition was illustrated by a woodcut showing two preachers addressing their respective audiences. The one is saying, *Thus saith the Lord*; and the other, *Thus saith the Pope.*

§ 11. *Andrew Bodenstein of Carlstadt.*[1]

Every great movement for reform bears within it the seeds of revolution, of the "tumult," as Erasmus called it, and Luther's was no exception to the general rule. Every Reformer who would carry through his reforming ideas successfully has to struggle against men and circumstances making for the "tumult," almost as strenuously as against the abuses he seeks to overcome. We have already seen how these germs of revolution abounded in Germany, and how the revolutionists naturally allied themselves with the Reformer, and the cause he sought to promote.

While Luther was hidden away in the Wartburg, the revolution seized on Wittenberg. At first his absence did not seem to make any difference. The number of students had increased until it was over a thousand, and the town itself surprised eye-witnesses who were acquainted with other University towns in Germany. The students went about unarmed; they mostly carried Bibles under their arms; they saluted each other as "brothers at one in Christ." No rift had yet appeared among the band of leaders, although his disappointment in not obtaining the Provostship of All Saints had begun to isolate Andrew Bodenstein of Carlstadt. Unanimity did not mean dulness; Wittenberg was seething with intellectual life. Since its foundation the University had been distinguished for weekly Public Disputations in which students and professors took part. In the earlier years of its existence the theses discussed had been suggested by the Scholastic Theology and Philosophy in vogue; but since 1518 the new questions which were stirring Germany had been the subjects of debate, and this had given a life and eagerness to the

[1] H. Barge. *Andreas Bodenstein von Karlstadt*, 2 vols. (Leipzig, 1905).

University exercises. When Justus Jonas came to Wittenberg from Erfurt, he wrote enthusiastically to a friend about the "unbelievable wealth of spiritual interests in the little town of Wittenberg." None of the professors took a keener interest in these Public Discussions than Andrew Bodenstein of Carlstadt. He had been a very successful teacher; had come under Luther's magnetic influence; and had accepted the main ideas of the new doctrines. He had not the full-blooded humanity of Luther, nor his sympathetic tact, nor his practical insight into how things would work. He lacked altogether Luther's solid basis of conservative feeling, which made him know by instinct that new ideas and new things could only flourish and grow if they were securely rooted in what was old. It was enough for Carlstadt that his own ideas, however hastily evolved, were clear, and his aims beneficent, to make him eager to see them at once reduced to practice. He had the temperament of a revolutionary rather than that of a Reformer.

He was strongly impressed with the fundamental contradictions which he believed to exist between the new evangelical doctrines preached by Luther and the theories and practices of the mediæval religious life and worship. This led him to attack earnestly and bitterly monastic vows, celibacy, a distinctive dress for the clergy, the idea of a propitiatory sacrifice in the Mass, and the presence and use of images and pictures in the churches. He introduced all these questions of practical interest into the University weekly Public Discussions; he published theses upon them; he printed two books—one on monastic vows and the other on the Mass—which had an extensive circulation both in German and in Latin (four editions were speedily exhausted). The prevailing idea in all these publications, perhaps implied rather than expressed, was that the new evangelical liberty could only be exercised when everything which suggested the ceremonies and usages of the mediæval religious life was swept away. His strongest denunciations were reserved for the practice of celibacy; he dwelt on the divine institution of marriage, its moral and spiritual necessity, and taught that the compulsory marriage of the clergy was better than the enforced celibacy of the mediæval Church. Zwilling, a young Augustinian Eremite, whose preaching gifts had been praised by Luther, went even further than Carlstadt in his fiery denunciation of the Mass as an idolatrous practice.

The movement to put these exhortations in practice began first among the clergy. Two priests in parishes near Wittenberg married; several monks left their cloisters and donned lay garments; Melanchthon and several of his students, in semi-public fashion, communicated in both kinds in the parish church on Michaelmas Day (Sept. 29th), 1521, and his example seems to have been followed by other companies.

Zwilling's fiery denunciations of the idolatry of the Mass stirred the commonalty of the town. On Christmas Eve (Dec. 24–25), 1521, a turbulent crowd invaded the parish church and the Church of All Saints. In the former they broke the lamps, threatened the priests, and in mockery of the worship of praise they sang folk-songs, one of which began: "There was a maid who lost a shoe"—so the indignant clergy complained to the Elector.[1]

Next day, Christmas, Carlstadt, who was archdeacon, conducted the service in All Saints' Church. He had doffed his clerical robes, and wore the ordinary dress of a layman. He preached and then dispensed the Lord's Supper in an "evangelical fashion." He read the usual service, but omitted everything which taught a propitiatory sacrifice; he did not elevate the Host; and he placed the Bread in the hands of every communicant, and gave the Cup into their hands. On the following Sundays and festival days the Sacrament of the Supper was dispensed in the same manner, and we are told that "hic pæne urbs et cuncta civitas communicavit sub utraque specie."

[1] Cf. Barge, *Andreas Bodenstein von Karlstadt*, i. 357; the letter is printed in ii. 558-559.

During the closing days of the year 1521, so full of excitement for the people of Wittenberg, three men, known in history as the *Zwickau Prophets,* came to the town (Dec. 27th). Zwickau, lying about sixty-four miles south of Wittenberg, was the centre of the weaving trade of Saxony, and contained a large artisan population. We have seen that movements of a religious-communistic kind had from time to time appeared among the German artisans and peasants since 1476. Nicolaus Storch, a weaver in Zwickau, proclaimed that he had visions of the Angel Gabriel, who had revealed to him: "Thou shalt sit with me on my throne." He began to preach. Thomas Münzer, who had been appointed by the magistrates tc be town preacher in St. Mary's, the principal church in Zwickau, praised his discourses, declaring that Storch expounded the Scriptures better than any priest. Some writers have traced the origin of this Zwickau movement to Hussite teachings. Münzer allied himself with the extreme Hussites *after* the movement had begun, and paid a visit to Bohemia, taking with him some of his intimates, but our sources of information, which are scanty, do not warrant any decided opinion about the origin of the outbreak in Zwickau. After some time Storch and others were forced to leave the town. Three of them went to Wittenberg—Storch himself, the seer of heavenly visions, another weaver, and Marcus Thomä Stubner, who had once been a pupil of Melanchthon, and was therefore able to introduce his companions to the Wittenberg circle of Reformers. Their arrival and addresses increased the excitement both in the town and in the University. Melanchthon welcomed his old pupil, and was impressed by the presence of a certain spiritual power in Stubner and in his companions. Some of their doctrines, however, especially their rejection of infant baptism, repelled him, and he gradually withdrew from their companionship.

Carlstadt took advantage of the strong excitement in Wittenberg to press on the townspeople and on the magistrates his scheme of reformation; and on Jan. 24th, 1522 the authorities of the town of Wittenberg published their famous ordinance.

This document, the first of numerous civic and territorial attempts to express the new evangelical ideas in legislation, deserves careful study.[1] It concerns itself almost exclusively with the reform of social life and of public worship. It enjoins the institution of a common chest to be under the charge of two of the magistrates, two of the townsmen, and a public notary. Into this the revenues from ecclesiastical foundations were to be placed, the annual revenues of the guilds of workmen, and other specified monies. Definite salaries were to be paid to the priests, and support for the poor and for the monks was to be taken from this common fund. Begging, whether by ordinary beggars, monks, or poor students, was strictly prohibited. If the common chest was not able to afford sufficient for the support of the helpless and orphans, the townsfolk had to provide what was needed. No houses of ill-fame were allowed within the town. Churches were places for preaching; the town contained enough for the population; and the building of small chapels was prohibited. The service of the Mass was shortened, and made to express the evangelical meaning of the sacrament, and the elements were to be placed in the hands of the communicants. All this was made law within the town of Wittenberg; and the reformation was to be enforced. Not content with these regulations, Carlstadt engaged in a crusade against the use of pictures and images in the churches (the regulations had permitted three altars in every church and one picture for each altar). Everything which recalled the older religious usages was to be done away with, and flesh was to be eaten on fast days.

This excitement bred fanaticism. Voices were raised

[1] The ordinance is printed in Richter's *Die evangelischen Kirchenordnungen des sechszehnten Jahrhunderts* (Weimar, 1846), ii. 484, and, with a more correct text, in Sehling's *Die evangelischen Kirchenordnungen des 16ten Jahrhunderts* (Leipzig), 1902, I. i. 697.

declaring that, as all true Christians were taught by the Spirit of God, there was no need either for civil rulers or for carnal learning. It is believed by many that Carlstadt shared these fancies, and it has been said that in his desire to "simplify" himself, he dressed as a peasant and worked as a labourer (he had married) on his father-in-law's farm It is more probable that he found himself unable to rule the storm his hasty measures had raised, and that he saw many things proposed with which he had no sympathy.

§ 12. *Luther back in Wittenberg.*

Melanchthon felt himself helpless in presence of the "tumult," declared that no one save Luther himself could quell the excitement, and eagerly pressed his return. The revolutionary movement was extending beyond Wittenberg, in other towns in Electoral Saxony such as Grimma and Altenberg. Duke George of Saxony, the strenuous defender of the old faith, had been watching the proceedings from the beginning. As early as Nov. 21st, 1521, he had written to John Duke of Saxony, the brother of the Elector, warning him that, against ecclesiastical usage, the Sacrament of the Supper was being dispensed in both kinds in Wittenberg; he had informed him (Dec. 26th) that priests were threatened while saying the Mass; he had brought the "tumultuous deeds" in Electoral Saxony before the *Reichsregiment* in January, with the result that imperial mandates were sent to the Elector Frederick and to the Bishops of Meissen, Merseburg, and Naumburg, requiring them to take measures to end the disturbances. The Elector was seriously disquieted. His anxieties were increased by a letter from Duke George (Feb. 2nd, 1522), declaring that Carlstadt and Zwilling were the instigators of all the riotous proceedings. He had commissioned one of his councillors, Hugold of Einsiedel, to try to put matters right; but the result had been small. It was probably in these circumstances that he wrote his *Instruction* to Oswald, a burgher of Eisenach, with the intention that the contents should be communicated to Luther in the Wartburg. The *Instruction* may have been the reason why Luther suddenly left the asylum where he had remained since his appearance at Worms by the command and under the protection of his prince.[1]

If this *Instruction* did finally determine him, it was only one of many things urging Luther to leave his solitude. He cared little for the influence of the Zwickau Prophets,[2] estimating them at their true value, but the weakness of Melanchthon, the destructive and dangerous impetuosity of Carlstadt, the spread of the tumult beyond Wittenberg, the determination of Duke George to make use of these outbursts to destroy the whole movement for reformation, and the interference of the *Reichsregiment* with its mandates, made him feel that the decisive moment had come when he must be again among his own people.

He started on his lonely journey, most of it through an enemy's country, going by Erfurt, Jena, Borna, and Leipzig. He was dressed as "Junker Georg," with beard on his chin and sword by his side. At Erfurt he had a good-humoured discussion with a priest in the inn; and Kessler, the Swiss student, tells how he met a stranger sitting in the parlour of the "Bear" at Jena with his hand on the hilt of his sword, and reading a small Hebrew Psalter. He got to Wittenberg on Friday, March 7th; spent that afternoon and the next day in discussing the situation with his friends Amsdorf, Melanchthon, and Jerome Schurf.[3]

On Sunday he appeared in the pulpit, and for eight successive days he preached to the people, and the plague was stayed. Many things in the movement set agoing by Carlstadt met with his approval. He had come to believe in the marriage of the clergy; he disapproved strongly of

[1] This *Instruction* will be found in Enders, *Dr. Martin Luthers Briefwechsel*, iii. 292–295. Its effect on Luther's return to Wittenberg is discussed at length by von Bezold (*Zeitschrift für Kirchengeschichte*, xx. 186 ff.), Kawerau (*Luther's Rückkehr*, etc., Halle, 1902), and by Barge (*Andreas Bodenstein von Karlstadt*, Leipzig, 1905, p. 432 ff.).

[2] See his letters to Spalatin in Enders, *Dr. Martin Luthers Briefwechsel*, iii. 271, 286.

[3] Johann Kessler, *Sabbata* (edited by Egli and Schoch, St. Gall, 1902).

private Masses; he had grave doubts on the subject of monastic vows; but he disapproved of the violence, of the importance attached to outward details, and of the use of force to advance the Reformation movement:

"The Word created heaven and earth and all things; the same Word will also create now, and not we poor sinners. *Summa summarum*, I will preach it, I will talk about it, I will write about it, but I will not use force or compulsion with anyone; for faith must be of freewill and unconstrained, and must be accepted without compulsion. To marry, to do away with images, to become monks or nuns, or for monks and nuns to leave their convents, to eat meat on Friday or not to eat it, and other like things—all these are open questions, and should not be forbidden by any man. If I employ force, what do I gain? Changes in demeanour, outward shows, grimaces, shams, hypocrisies. But what becomes of the sincerity of the heart, of faith, of Christian love? All is wanting where these are lacking; and for the rest I would not give the stalk of a pear. What we want is the heart, and to win that we must preach the gospel. Then the word will drop into one heart to-day, and to-morrow into another, and so will work that each will forsake the Mass."

He made no personal references; he blamed no individuals; and in the end he was master of the situation.

When he had won back Wittenberg he made a tour of those places in Electoral Saxony where the Wittenberg example had been followed. He went to Zwickau, to Altenberg, and to Grimma—preaching to thousands of people, calming them, and bringing them back to a conservative reformation.

CHAPTER IV.

FROM THE DIET OF WORMS TO THE CLOSE OF THE PEASANTS' WAR.

§ 1. *The continued spread of Lutheran Teaching.*

THE imperial edict issued against Luther at the Diet of Worms could scarcely have been stronger than it was,[1] and yet, like many another edict of Emperor and Diet, it was wholly ineffective. It could only be enforced by the individual Estates, who for the most part showed great reluctance to put it into operation. It was published in the territories of Archduke Ferdinand of Austria, of the Elector of Brandenburg, of Duke George of Saxony, and of the Dukes of Bavaria; but none of these princes, except the Archduke and Duke George, seemed to care much for the old religion. In most of the ecclesiastical States the authorities were afraid of riots following the publication,

[1] The edict said: "In the first place, we command that all, particularly all princes, estates, and subjects, shall not, after the expiry of the above twenty days, which terminate on the 14th of the present month of May, offer to Luther either shelter, food, or drink, or help him in any way with words or deeds, secretly or openly. On the contrary, wherever you get possession of him, you shall at once put him in prison and send him to me, or, at anyrate, inform me thereof without any delay. For that holy work you shall be recompensed for your trouble and expenses. Likewise you ought, in virtue of the holy constitution and ban of our Empire, to deal in the following way with all the partisans, abettors, and patrons of Luther. You shall put them down, and confiscate their estates to your own profit, unless the said persons can prove that they have mended their ways and asked for papal absolution. Furthermore, we command, under the aforesaid penalties, that nobody shall buy, sell, read, keep, copy, or print any of the writings of Martin Luther which have been condemned by our holy father the Pope, whether in Latin or in German, nor any other of his wicked writings."

and did nothing. Thus, in Bremen, we are told that as late as December 1522 the people had never seen the edict. The cities treated it as carelessly. The authorities in Nürnberg, Ulm, Augsburg, and Strassburg posted it up publicly as an official document, and took no further trouble. In Strassburg the printers went on issuing Luther's books and tracts as fast as their printing-presses could produce them; and at Constance the populace drove the imperial commissioners from the town when they came to publish the edict.

The action of the newly constituted *Reichsregiment* was as indecisive. When the disturbances broke out at Wittenberg, under Carlstadt and the Zwickau Prophets, Duke George, by playing on the fears of a spread of Hussitism, could get mandates issued to the Elector of Saxony and neighbouring bishops to inquire into and crush the disorders; but after Luther's return and the restoration of tranquillity his pleadings were ineffectual. It was in vain that he insisted that Luther's presence in Wittenberg was an insult to the Empire. He was told that the *Reichsregiment* was able to judge for itself what were insults, and that when they saw them they would punish. Archduke Ferdinand, the President, doubtless sympathised with Duke George, but he was powerless; the Elector of Saxony had the greatest influence, and it was always exerted on the side of Luther.

In January 1522 a new Pope had been chosen, who took the title of Adrian VI. His election was a triumph for the party that confessed the urgent need of reforms, and thought that they ought to be effected by the hierarchy and from within the Church. Adrian was a pious man according to his lights, one who felt deeply the corruption which was degrading the Church. He believed that the revolt of Luther was a punishment sent by God for the sins of the generation. He had been the tutor of Charles V., and ascended the papal throne with the determination to reform corruptions, and to begin his reforms by attacking the source of all—the Roman Curia. But he was a Dominican monk, and had all the Dominican ideas about the need of maintaining mediæval theology intact, and about the strict maintenance of ecclesiastical discipline He was as ignorant as his predecessor of the state of matters in Germany, and regarded Luther as another Mahomet, who was seducing men from the higher Christian life by pandering to their fleshly appetites.

The *Reichsregiment* met with the Diet at Nürnberg in 1522–1523, and to this Diet the Pope sent, as nuncio, Francesco Chieregati, Bishop of Terramo, in the kingdom of Naples. The nuncio was given lengthy instructions, which set forth the Pope's opinion of the corruptions in the Church and his intention to cure them, but which demanded the delivery of Luther into the hands of the Roman Curia, and the punishment of priests, monks, and nuns who had broken their vows of celibacy.[1] Chieregati was no sooner in Germany than he understood that it would be impossible for him to get the Pope's demand carried out, and he informed his master of the state of matters. When he met the Diet and presented the papal requests, he was practically answered that Germany had grievances against Rome, and that they would need to be set right ere the Curia could expect to get its behests fulfilled. They intimated that since the Pope had admitted the corruptions in the Church, it was scarcely to be expected that they should blame Luther for having pointed them out. They presented the nuncio with a list of one hundred German grievances against the Roman Curia;[2] and suggested that the most convenient way of settling them would be for the Pope to make over immediately, for the public use of Germany, the German *annates*,[3] and that a German Council should be held on German soil, and within one of the larger German cities.

[1] The Pope's instructions to his nuncio will be found in Wrede, *Deutsche Reichstagsakten unter Kaiser Karl V.*, iii. 393 ff.

[2] Compare Gebhardt, *Die Gravamina der Deutschen Nation*, 2nd ed., Breslau, 1895.

[3] The *annates* were the first year's stipend of an ecclesiastical benefice, usually reckoned at a fixed rate.

The practical result of this fencing at the Diet of 1522, repeated in 1523, was that the progress of the Lutheran movement was not checked. How deeply the people of Germany had drunk in the teaching of Luther may be learnt from the letters of the nuncio to the Curia, and from those of the Archduke Ferdinand to the Emperor. Both use the same expression, that "among a thousand men scarcely one could be found untainted by Lutheran teaching."

Adrian VI. died suddenly after a few months' reign, and the next Pope, Clement VII., a Medici and completely under the influence of the French king, belonged to the old unreforming party, whose only desire was to maintain all the corrupting privileges of the Roman Curia. He selected and sent to Germany, as his nuncio, Lorenzo Campeggio, one of the ablest of Italian diplomatists, to negotiate with the *Reichsregiment* and the Diet which met at Speyer in 1524.

Campeggio, like his predecessor, found that the German Nation was determinedly hostile to Rome. When he made his official entry into Augsburg, and raised his hands to give the usual benediction to the crowds of people, they received the blessing with open derision. He was so impressed with their attitude, that when he reached Nürnberg he doffed his official robes and entered the town as quietly as possible; indeed, he received a message from the authorities asking him "to avoid making the sign of the cross, or using the benediction, seeing how matters then stood." The presence of the Legate seemed to increase the anti-papal zeal of the people. The Pope was openly spoken of as Antichrist. Planitz, the energetic commissary of the Elector of Saxony, reckoned that nearly four thousand people in the city partook of the Sacrament of the Supper in both kinds, and informs us that among them were members of the *Reichsregiment*, and Isabella, Queen of Sweden, the sister of the Emperor.

Yet the experienced Italian diplomatist thought that he could discern signs more favourable to his master than the previous Diet had exhibited. The *Reichsregiment*, which had hitherto shielded the Lutheran movement, had lost the confidence of many classes of people, and was tottering to its fall. It had showed itself unable to enforce the Lands-Peace. It was the princes who had defeated the rising of the Free Nobles under Franz von Sickingen; it was the Swabian League, an association always devoted to the House of Austria, that had crushed the Franconian robber nobles; and both princes and League were irritated at the attempts of the *Reichsregiment*, which had endeavoured to rob them of the fruits of their successes. The cities had been made to bear all the taxation needed to support the central government, and the system of monopolies arising from combinations among the great commercial houses had been threatened. The cities and the capitalists had made a secret agreement with the Emperor, and von Hannart had been sent by the Emperor from Spain to the Diet of 1524 to work along with the towns for the overthrow of the central government. The Diet itself had passed a vote of no confidence in the government. In these troubled waters a crafty fisher might win some success.

His success was more apparent than real. The Diet of 1524 did not absolutely refuse to enforce the Edict of Worms against Luther and his followers; they promised to execute it "as well as they were able, and as far as was possible," and the cities had made it plain that the enforcement was impossible. They renewed their demand for a General Council to meet in a suitable German town to settle the affairs of the Church in Germany, and again declared that meanwhile nothing should be preached contrary to the Word of God and the Holy Gospel. They went further, and practically resolved that a National Council, to deliberate on the condition of the Church in Germany, should meet at Speyer in November and make an interim settlement of its ecclesiastical affairs, to last until the meeting of a General Council. It is true that, owing to the exertions of the nuncio and of von Hannart, the phrase National Synod was omitted, and the meeting was to be one of the Estates of Germany at which the councillors and learned divines of the various princes were to formulate all the disputed points, and to consider anew the grievances of the German nation against the Papacy; but neither the nuncio nor von Hannart deceived themselves as to the real meaning of the resolution. "It will be a National Council for Germany," said Hannart in his report. Nothing could be more alarming to the Pope. There was always a possibility of managing a General Council; but a German National Synod, including a large number of lay representatives, meeting in a German town, foreshadowed an independent National German Church which would insist on separation from the Roman See. The Pope wrote to Henry VIII. of England asking him to harass the German merchants; he induced the Emperor to forbid the proposed meeting of the German States; and, what was more important, he instructed his nuncio to take steps secretly to form a league of German princes who were still favourable to maintaining the mediæval Church with its doctrines, ceremonies, and usages. This inaugurated the religious divisions of Germany.

§ 2. *The beginnings of Division in Germany.*

The Diet of Speyer (1524) may perhaps be taken as the beginning of the separation of Germany into two opposite camps of Protestant and Roman Catholic, although the real parting of the ways actually occurred after the Peasants' War. The overthrow, or at least discrediting of the *Reichsregiment*, placed the management of everything, including the settlement of the religious question, in the hands of the princes, none of whom, with the exception of the Elector of Saxony, cared much for the idea of nationality; while some of them, however anxious they were, or once had been, for ecclesiastical reforms, were genuinely afraid of the "tumult" which they believed might lurk behind any conspicuous changes in religious usages. Duke George of Saxony, who was keenly alive to the corruptions in the Church, dreaded above all things the beginnings of a Hussite movement in Germany. He knew that an assiduous, penetrating, secret Hussite, or rather Taborite propaganda had been going on in Germany for long. As early as the Leipzig Disputation (1519), when John Eck had skilfully forced Luther into the avowal that he approved of some things in the Hussite revolt, Duke George was seen to put his arms akimbo, to wag his long beard, and was heard to ejaculate, "God help us! The plague!" A fear of Hussite revolution displays itself in his correspondence, and very notably in his letters to Duke John of Saxony and to the Elector about the disturbances in Wittenberg. It was a triumph for the Roman Curia when its partisans, from Eck onwards, were able to fix the stigma of Hussitism on the Lutheran movement; and the career of the Zwickau Prophets, notwithstanding their suppression by Luther, was, to many, an indication of what might lie behind the new preaching. When the Peasants' War came in 1525, many of the earlier sympathisers with Luther saw in it an indication of the dangers into which they fancied that Luther was leading Germany. It is also to be noticed that many of the Humanists now began to desert the Lutheran cause; his Augustinian theology made them think that he was bent on creating a new Scholastic which seemed to them almost as bad as the old, which they had been delighted to see him attack.

The Roman Curia was quick to take advantage of all these alarms. Its efforts were so successful, that it was soon able to create a Roman Catholic Party among the South German princes, and to secure its steadfastness by promising a few concessions, and by permitting the authorities to retain for the secular uses of their States about one-fifth of the ecclesiastical revenues in each State. The leading States in this Roman Catholic federation were Austria and Bavaria, and so long as Duke George lived, Ducal Saxony in middle Germany. This naturally called forth a distinctly Lutheran party, no longer national, which included the Elector of Saxony, the Landgrave of Hesse, the Margraf of Brandenburg, his brother Albert, and many others. Albert was at the head of the Teutonic Order in East Prussia. He secularised his semi-ecclesiastical principality, became the first Duke of Prussia, and his State from the beginning adopted the evangelical faith.

It was not until the Peasants' War was over that this division was clearly manifested. The Reformation had spread in simple natural fashion, without any attempt at concerted action, or any design to impose a new and uniform order of public worship, or to make changes in ecclesiastical government. Luther himself was not without hopes that the great ecclesiastical principalities might become secular lordships, that the bishops would assume the lead in ecclesiastical reform, and that there would be a great National Church in Germany, with little external change—enough only to permit the evangelical preaching and teaching. It is true that the Emperor had shown clearly his position by sending martyrs to the stake in the Netherlands, and that symptoms of division had begun to manifest themselves during 1524, as we have seen. Still these things did not prevent such an experienced statesman as the Elector of Saxony from confidently expecting a peaceful and, so far as Germany was concerned, a unanimous and hearty solution of the religious difficulties. The storm burst suddenly which was to shatter these optimistic expectations, and to change fundamentally the whole course of the Lutheran Reformation. This was the Peasants' War.

§ 3. *The Peasants' War.*[1]

From one point of view this insurrection was simply the last, the most extensive, and the most disastrous of

[1] Sources: Baumann, *Quellen zur Geschichte des Bauernkrieges in Ober-Schwaben* (Stuttgart, 1877); *Die Zwölf Artikel der oberschwäbischen Bauern* (Kempten, 1896); *Akten zur Geschichte des Bauernkrieges aus Ober-Schwaben* (Freiburg, 1881); Beger, *Zur Geschichte des Bauernkrieges nach Urkunden zu Karlsruhe* (in *Forschungen zur deutschen Geschichte*, vols. xxi.-xxii., Göttingen, 1862); Ryhiner, *Chronik des Bauernkrieges* (*Basler Chroniken*, vi., 1902); Waldau, *Materialien zur Geschichte des Bauern-*

those revolts which, we have already seen, had been almost chronic in Germany during the later decades of the fifteenth and in the beginning of the sixteenth century. All the social and economic causes which produced them[1] were increasingly active in 1524–1525. It is easy to show, as many Lutheran Church historians have done with elaborate care, that the Reformation under Luther had nothing in common with the sudden and unexpected revolt, —as easy as to prove that there was little in common between the "Spiritual Poverty" of Francis of Assisi and the vulgar communism of the *Brethren and Sisters of the Free Spirit*, between the doctrines of Wiclif and the gigantic labour strike headed by Wat Tyler and Priest Ball, between the teaching of Huss and the extreme Taborite fanatics. But the fact remains that the voice of Luther awoke echoes whereof he never dreamt, and that its effects cannot be measured by some changes in doctrine, or by a reformation in ecclesiastical organisation. The times of the Reformation were ripe for revolution, and the words of the bold preacher, coming when all men were restless and most men were oppressed, appealing especially to those who felt the burden heavy and the yoke galling, were followed by far-resounding reverberations. Besides, Luther's message was democratic. It destroyed the aristocracy of the saints, it levelled the barriers between the layman and the priest, it taught the equality of all men before God, and the right of every man of faith to stand in God's presence whatever be his rank and condition of life. He had not confined himself to preaching a new theology. His message was eminently practical. In his *Appeal to*

krieges (Chemnitz, 1791–1794); Vogt, *Die Korrespondenz des Schwäbischen Bundes-Hauptmanns, 1524–1527* (Augsburg, 1879–1883).

LATER BOOKS: Zimmermann, *Allgemeine Geschichte des grossen Bauernkrieges*, 3 vols. (Stuttgart, 1856); E. Belfort Bax, *The Peasants' War in Germany* (London, 1899); Kautsky, *Communism in Central Europe in the time of the Reformation* (London, 1897); Stern, *Die Socialisten der Reformationszeit* (Berlin, 1883). The literature on the Peasants' War is very extensive.

[1] Compare above, p. 106.

the Nobility of the German Nation, Luther had voiced all the grievances of Germany, had touched upon almost all the open sores of the time, and had foretold disasters not very far off.

Nor must it be forgotten that no great leader ever flung about wild words in such a reckless way. Luther had the gift of strong smiting phrases, of words which seemed to cleave to the very heart of things, of images which lit up a subject with the vividness of a flash of lightning. He launched tracts and pamphlets from the press about almost everything,—written for the most part on the spur of the moment, and when the fire burned. His words fell into souls full of the fermenting passions of the times. They drank in with eagerness the thoughts that all men were equal before God, and that there are divine commands about the brotherhood of mankind of more importance than all human legislation. They refused to believe that such golden ideas belonged to the realm of spiritual life alone, or that the only prescriptions which denied the rights of the common man were the decrees of the Roman Curia. The successful revolts of the Swiss peasants, the wonderful victories of Zisca, the people's leader, in the near Bohemian lands, were illustrations, they thought, of how Luther's sledge-hammer words could be translated into corresponding deeds.

Other teachings besides Luther's were listened to. Many of the Humanists, professed disciples of Plato, expounded to friends or in their class-rooms the communistic dreams of the *Republic,* and published *Utopias* like the brilliant sketch of the ideal commonwealth which came from the pen of Thomas More. These speculations "of the Chair" were listened to by the "wandering students," and were retailed, with forcible illustrations, in a way undreamt of by their scholarly authors, to audiences of artisans and peasants who were more than ready to give them unexpected applications.[1]

[1] Lindsay, *Luther and the German Reformation* (Edinburgh, 1900), 169 ff.; Stern, *Die Socialisten der Reformationszeit*, Berlin, 1883.

The influence of popular astrology must not be forgotten; for the astrologists were powerful among all classes of society, in the palaces of the princes, in the houses of the burghers, and at the peasant market gatherings and church ales. In these days they were busy pointing out heavenly portents, and foretelling calamities and popular risings.[1]

The missionaries of the movement belonged to all sorts and conditions of men—poor priests sympathising with the grievances of their parishioners; wandering monks who had deserted their convents, especially those belonging to the Franciscan Order; poor students on their way from University to University; artisans, travelling in German fashion from one centre of their trade to another. They found their audiences on the village greens under the lime trees, or in the public-houses in the lower parts of the towns. They talked the rude language of the people, and garnished their discourse with many a scriptural quotation. They read to excited audiences small pamphlets and broadsides, printed in thick letters on coarse paper, which discussed the burning questions of the day.

The revolt began unexpectedly, and without any preconcerted preparation or formulation of demands, in June 1524, when a thousand peasants belonging to the estate of Count Sigismund of Lupfen rose in rebellion against their lord at Stühlingen, a few miles to the north-west of Schaffhausen, and put themselves under the leadership of Hans Müller, an old landsknecht. Müller led his peasants, one of them carrying a flag blazoned with the imperial colours of red, black, and yellow, to the little town of Waldshut, about half-way between Schaffhausen and Basel. The people of the town fraternised with the peasants, and the formidable "Evangelical Brotherhood" was either formed then or the roots of it were planted. The news spread fast, east and west. The peasants of the districts round about the Lake of Constance—in the Allgau, the

[1] Friedrich, *Astrologie und Reformation, oder die Astrologen als Prediger der Reformation und Urheber des Bauernkrieges*, München, 1864

Klettgau, the Hegau, and Villingen—rose in rebellion. The revolt spread northwards into Lower Swabia, and the peasants of Leiphen, led by Jacob Wehe, were joined by some of the troops of Truchsess, the general of the Swabian League. The peasants of Salzburg, Styria, and the Tyrol rose. These three eastern risings had most staying power in them. The Salzburg peasants besieged the Cardinal Archbishop in his castle; they were not reduced till the spring of 1526, and only after having extorted concessions from their over-lords. The Tyrolese peasants, under their wise leader, Michael Gaismeyer, shut up Archduke Ferdinand in Innsbruck, and in the end gained substantial concessions. The rising in Styria was a very strong one; it lasted till 1526, and was eventually put down by bringing Bohemian troops into the country. From Swabia the flames of insurrection spread into Franconia, where a portion of the insurgents were led by an escaped criminal. the notorious Jäklein Rohrbach. It was this band which perpetrated the wanton massacre of Weinsberg, the one outstanding atrocity of the insurrection. The band and the deed were repudiated by the rest of the insurgents. Thomas Münzer, who, banished from Zwickau and then from Alstedt, had settled in Mühlhausen, his heart aflame with the wrongs of the commonalty, preached insurrection to the peasants in Thüringen. He issued fiery proclamations:

"Arise! Fight the battle of the Lord! On! On! On! The wicked tremble when they hear of you. On! On! On! Be pitiless although Esau gives you fair words (Gen. xxxiii.). Heed not the groans of the godless; they will beg, weep, and entreat you for pity like children. Show them no mercy, as God commanded to Moses (Deut. vii.), and as He has revealed the same to us. Rouse up the towns and the villages; above all, rouse the miners. . . . On! On! On! while the fire is burning let not the blood cool on your swords! Smite pinke-pank on the anvil of Nimrod! Overturn their towers to the foundation; while one of them lives you will not be free from the fear of man. While they reign over you it is of no use to speak of the fear of God. On! while it is day! God is with you."

The words were meant to rouse the miners of Mansfeld. They failed in their original intention, but they sent bands of armed insurgents through Thüringen and the Harz, and within fourteen days about forty convents and monasteries were destroyed, and the inmates (many of them poor women with no homes to return to) were sent adrift.

The revolt spread like a conflagration, one province catching fire from another, until in the early spring months of 1525 almost all Germany was in uproar. The only districts which escaped were Bavaria in the south, Hesse, and the north and north-east provinces. The insurgents were not peasants only. The poorer population of many of the towns fraternised with the insurgents, and compelled the civic authorities to admit them within their walls.

§ 4. *The Twelve Articles*

Statements of grievances were published which, naturally, bore a strong resemblance to those issued in the earlier social uprisings. The countrymen complained of the continuous appropriation of the woodlands by the proprietors, and that they were not allowed to fish in the streams or to kill game in their fields. They denounced the proprietors' practice of compelling his peasants to do all manner of unstipulated service for him without payment —to repair his roads, to assist at his hunts, to draw his fish-ponds. They said that their crops were ruined by game which they were not allowed to kill, and by hunters in pursuit of game; that the landlord led his streams across their meadow land, and deprived them of water for irrigation. They protested against arbitrary punishments, unknown to the old consuetudinary village law-courts (*Haingerichte*).

They formulated their demands for justice in various series of articles, all of which had common features, but contained some striking differences. Some dwelt more on the grievances of the peasants, others voiced the demands of the working classes of the towns, others again contained traces of the political aspirations of the more educated leaders of the movement. Almost all protest that they ask for nothing contrary to the requirements of just authority, whether civil or ecclesiastical, nor to the gospel of Christ. The peasants declared that each village community should be at liberty to choose its own pastor, and to dismiss him if he proved to be unsatisfactory; that while they were willing to pay the great tithes (*i.e.* a tenth of the produce of the crops), the lesser tithes (*i.e.* a tenth of the eggs, lambs, foals, etc.) should no longer be exacted; that these great tithes should be reserved to pay the village priest's stipend, and that what remained over should go to support the poor; that, since God had made all men free, serfdom should be abolished; and that, while they were willing to obey lawful authority, peasants ought not to be called on to submit to the arbitrary commands of their landlords. They insisted that they had a right to fish in the streams (not in fish-ponds), to kill game and wild birds, for these were public property. They demanded that the woodlands, meadows, and ploughlands which had once belonged to the village community, but which had been appropriated by the landlords, should be restored. They insisted that arbitrary services of every kind should be abolished, and that whatever services, beyond the old feudal dues, were demanded, should be paid for in wages. They called for the abolition of the usage whereby the landlord was permitted, in the name of death-duty, to seize on the most valuable chattel of the deceased tenant; and for the creation of impartial courts of justice in the country districts. They concluded by asking that all their demands should be tested by the word of God, and that if any of them should be found to be opposed to its teaching, it should be rejected.[1]

The townspeople asked that all class privileges should be abolished in civic and ecclesiastical appointments; that

[1] Cf. "The Twelve Peasant Articles" in Emil Reich, *Select Documents illustrating Mediæval and Modern History*, p. 212

the administration of justice in the town's courts should be improved; that the local taxation should be readjusted; that all the inhabitants should be permitted to vote for the election of the councillors; and that better provision should be made for the care of the poor. Some of the more ambitious manifestoes contained demands for a thorough reconstruction of the entire administration of the Empire, on a scheme which involved the overthrow of all feudal courts of justice, and contemplated a series of imperial judicatories, rising from revived Communal Courts to a central Imperial Court of Appeal for the whole Empire. Some manifestoes demanded a unification of the coinage, weights, and measures throughout the Empire; a confiscation of ecclesiastical endowments for the purpose of lessening taxation, and for the redemption of feudal dues; a uniform rate of taxes and customs duties; restraint to be placed on the operations of the great capitalists; the regulation of commerce and trade by law; and the admission of representatives from all classes in the community into the public administration. In every case the Emperor was regarded as the Lord Paramount. There were also declarations of the sovereignty of the people, made in such a way as to suggest that the writings of Marsilius of Padua had been studied by some of the leaders among the insurgents. The most famous of all these declarations was the Twelve Articles. The document was adopted by delegates from several of the insurrectionary bands, which met at Memmingen in Upper Swabia, to unite upon a common basis of action. If not actually drafted by Schappeler, a friend of Zwingli, the articles were probably inspired by him. These Twelve Articles gave something like unity to the movement; although it must be remembered that documents bearing the title do not always agree. The main thought with the peasant was to secure a fair share of the land, security of tenure, and diminution of feudal servitudes; and the idea of the artisan was to obtain full civic privileges and an adequate representation of his class on the city council.

§ 5. *The Suppression of the Revolt.*

During the earlier months of 1525 the rising carried everything before it. Many of the smaller towns made common cause with the peasants; indeed, it was feared that all the towns of Swabia might unite in supporting the movement. Prominent nobles were forced to join the "Evangelical Brotherhood" which had been formally constituted at Memmingen (March 7th). Princes, like the Cardinal Elector of Mainz and the Bishop of Würzburg, had to come to terms with the insurgents. Germany had been denuded of soldiers, drafted to take part in the Italian wars of Charles v. The ruling powers engaged the insurgents in negotiations simply for the purpose of gaining time, as was afterwards seen. But the rising had no solidity in it, nor did it produce, save in the Tyrol, any leader capable of effectually controlling his followers and of giving practical result to their efforts. The insurgents became demoralised after their first successes, and the whole movement had begun to show signs of dissolution before the princes had recovered from their terror. Philip of Hesse aided the Elector of Saxony (John, for Frederick had died during the insurrection) to crush Münzer at Frankenhausen (May 15th, 1525), the town of Mühlhausen was taken, and deprived of its privileges as an imperial city, and the revolt was crushed in North Germany.

George Truchsess, the general of the Swabian League, his army strengthened by mercenaries returning to Germany after the battle of Pavia, mastered the bands in Swabia and in Franconia. The Elsass revolt was suppressed with great ferocity by Duke Anthony of Lorraine. None of the German princes showed any consideration or mercy to their revolting subjects save the old Elector Frederick and Philip of Hesse. The former, on his deathbed, besought his brother to deal leniently with the misguided people; Philip's peasantry had fewer matters to complain of than had those of any other province, the Landgrave discussed their grievances with them, and made concessions which effectually prevented any revolt. Everywhere else, save in the Tyrol, the revolt was crushed with merciless severity, and between 100,000 and 150,000 of the insurgents perished on the field or elsewhere. The insurrection maintained itself in the Tyrol, in Salzburg, and in Styria until the spring of 1526; in all other districts of Germany the insurgents were crushed before the close of 1525. No attempt was made to cure the ills which led to the rising. The oppression of the peasantry was intensified. The last vestiges of local self-government were destroyed, and the unfortunate people were doomed for generations to exist in the lowest degradation. The year 1525 was one of the saddest in the annals of the German Fatherland.

The Peasants' War had a profound, lasting, and disastrous effect on the Reformation movement in Germany. It affected Luther personally, and that in a way which could not fail to react upon the cause which he conspicuously led. It checked the spread of the Reformation throughout the whole of Germany. It threw the guidance of the movement into the hands of the evangelical princes, and destroyed the hope that it might give birth to a reformed National German Church.

§ 6. *Luther and the Peasants' War.*

The effect of the rising upon Luther's own character and future conduct was too important for us to entirely pass over his personal relations to the peasants and their revolt. He was a peasant's son. "My father, my grandfather, my forebears, were all genuine peasants," he was accustomed to say. He had seen and pitied the oppression of the peasant class, and had denounced it in his own trenchant fashion. He had reproved the greed of the landlords, when he said that if the peasant's land produced as many coins as ears of corn, the profit would go to the landlord only. He had publicly expressed his approval of many of the proposals in the Twelve Articles long before they had been formulated and adopted at Memmingen in March 1525, and had advocated a return to the old communal laws or usages of Germany. He formally declared his agreement with the substance of the Twelve Articles after they had become the "charter" of the revolt. But Luther, rightly or wrongly, held that no real good could come from armed insurrection. He believed with all the tenacity of his nature, that while there might be two roads to reform, the way of peace, and the way of war, the pathway of peace was the only one which would lead to lasting benefit. After the storm burst he risked his life over and over again in visits he paid to the disaffected districts, to warn the people of the dangers they were running. After Münzer's attempt to rouse the miners of Mansfeld, and carry fire and sword into the district where his parents were living, Luther made one last attempt to bring the misguided people to a more reasonable course. He made a preaching tour through the disaffected districts. He went west from Eisleben to Stolberg (April 21st, 1525); thence to Nordhausen, where Münzer's sympathisers rang the bells to drown his voice; south to Erfurt (April 28th); north again to the fertile valley of the Golden Aue and to Wallhausen (May 1st); south again to Weimar (May 3rd), where news reached him that his Elector was dying, and that he had expressed the wish to see him,—a message which reached him too late. It was on this journey, or shortly after his return to Wittenberg (May 6th), that Luther wrote his vehement tract, *Against the murdering, thieving hordes of Peasants.* He wrote it while his mind was full of Münzer's calls to slaughter, when the danger was at its height, with all the sights and sounds of destruction and turmoil in eye and ear, while it still hung in the balance whether the insurgent bands might not carry all before them. In this terrible pamphlet Luther hounded on the princes to crush the rising. It is this pamphlet, all extenuating circumstances being taken into account, which must ever remain an ineffaceable stain on his noble life and career.[1]

As for himself, the Peasants' War imprinted in him a deep distrust of all who had any connection with the rising. He had not forgotten Carlstadt's action at Wittenberg in 1521–1522, and when Carlstadt was found attempting to preach the insurrection in Franconia and Swabia, Luther never forgave him. His deep-rooted and unquenchable suspicion of Zwingli may be traced back to his discovery that friends of the Zurich Reformer had been at Memmingen, had aided the revolutionary delegates to draft the Twelve Articles, and had induced them to shelter themselves under the shield of a religious Reformation. What is perhaps more important, the Peasants' War gave to Luther a deep and abiding distrust of the "common man" which was altogether lacking in the earlier stages of his career, which made him prevent every effort to give anything like a democratic ecclesiastical organisation to the Evangelical Church, and which led him to bind his Reformation in the chains of secular control to the extent of regarding the secular authority as possessing a quasi-episcopal function.[2] It is probably true that he saved the Reformation in Germany by cutting it loose from the revolutionary movement; but the wrench left marks on his own character as well as on that of the movement he headed. Luther's enemies were quick to make capital out of his relations with the peasants, and Emser compared him to Pilate, who washed his hands after betraying Jesus to the Jews.

[1] After speaking about the duties of the authorities, he proceeds: "In the case of an insurgent, every man is both judge and executioner. Therefore, whoever can should knock down, strangle, and stab such publicly or privately, and think nothing so venomous, pernicious, and devilish as an insurgent. . . . Such wonderful times are these, that a prince can merit heaven better with bloodshed than another with prayer."

[2] Luther dissuaded the Landgrave of Hesse from permanently adopting the democratic ecclesiastical constitution drafted by Francis Lambert for the Church of Hesse in 1526. The rejected constitution has been printed by Richter in his *Die evangelischen Kirchenordnungen des sechszehnten Jahrhunderts* (Weimar, 1846), i. 56.

§ 7. *Germany divided into two separate Camps.*

The insurrection, altogether apart from its personal effects on Luther, had a profound influence on the whole of the German Reformation. Some princes who had hitherto favoured the Romanist side were confirmed in their opposition; others who had hesitated, definitely abandoned the cause of Reform. For both, it seemed that a social revolution of a desperate kind lay behind the Protestant Reformation. Many an innocent preacher of the new faith perished in the disturbances—sought out and slain by the princes as an instigator of the rebellion. Duke Anthony of Lorraine, for example, in his suppression of the revolt in Elsass, made no concealment of his belief that evangelical preachers were the cause of the rising, and butchered them without mercy when he could discover them. The Curia found that the Peasants' War was an admirable text to preach from when they insisted that Luther was another Huss, and that the movement which he led was a revival of the ecclesiastical and social communism of the extreme Hussites (Taborites); that all who attacked the Church of Rome were engaged in attempting to destroy the bases of society. It was after the Peasants' War that the Roman Catholic League of princes grew strong in numbers and in cohesion.

The result of the war also showed that the one strong political element in Germany was the princedom. The *Reichsregiment*, which still preserved a precarious existence, had shown that it had no power to cope with the disturbances, and its attempts at mediation had been treated with contempt. From this year, 1525, the political destiny of the land was distinctly seen to be definitely shaping for territorial centralisation round the greater princes and nobles. It was inevitable that the conservative religious Reformation should follow the lines of political growth, with the result that there could not be a National Evangelical Church of Germany. It could only find outcome in territorial Churches under the rule and protection of those princes who from motives of religion and conscience had adopted the principles which Luther preached.

The more radical religious movement broke up into fragments, and reappeared in the guise of the maligned and persecuted Anabaptists,—a name which embraced a very wide variety of religious opinions,—some of whom appropriated to themselves the aspirations of the social revolution which had been crushed by the princes. The conservative and Lutheran Reformation found its main elements of strength in the middle classes of Germany; while the Anabaptists had their largest following among the artisans and working men of the towns.

The terrors of the time separated Germany into two hostile camps—the one accepting and the other rejecting the ecclesiastical Reformation, which ceased to be a national movement in any real sense of the word.

CHAPTER V.

FROM THE DIET OF SPEYER, 1526, TO THE RELIGIOUS PEACE OF AUGSBURG, 1555.

§ 1. *The Diet of Speyer, 1526.*[1]

WHEN Germany emerged from the social revolution in the end of 1525, it soon became apparent that the religious question remained unsettled, and was dividing the country into two parties whose differences had become visibly accentuated, and that both held as strongly as ever to their distinctive principles. Perhaps one of the reasons for the increased strain was the conduct of many of the Romanist princes in suppressing the rebellion. The victories of the Swabian League in South Germany were everywhere followed by religious persecution. Men were condemned to confiscation of goods or to death, not for rebellion, for they had never taken part in the rising, but for their confessed attachment to Lutheran teaching. The Lutheran preachers were special objects of attack. Aichili, who acted as a provost-marshal to the Swabian League, made himself conspicuous by plundering, mulcting, and

[1] SOURCES (besides those given in earlier chapters): Ney, "Analecten zur Geschichte des Reichstags zu Speier im Jahr 1526" (*Zeitschrift für Kirchengeschichte*, viii. ix. xii.); Friedensburg, *Beiträge zum Briefwechsel zwischen Hertzog Georg von Sachsen und Landgraf Philip von Hessen* (*Neuer Archiv für Sächs. Gesch.* vi.); Balan, *Clementis VII. Epistolæ* (vol. i. of *Monumenta Sæculi XVI. Historiam illustrantia*, Innsbruck, 1885); Casanova, *Lettere di Carlo V. and Clemente VII. 1527–1533* (Florence, 1893); Lanz, *Correspondenz des Kaisers Karl V.* (Leipzig, 1845); Bradford, *Correspondence of Charles V.* (London, 1850).

LATER BOOKS: Schomburgk, *Die Pack'schen Handel* (Maurenbrecher's *Hist. Taschenbuch*, Leipzig, 1882); Stoy, *Erste Bündnisbestrebungen evangelischen Stände* (Jena, 1888); *Cambridge Modern History*, ii. vi.

putting them to death. It is said that he hung forty Lutheran pastors on the trees by the roadside in one small district. The Roman Catholic princes had banded themselves together for mutual defence as early as July 1525. The more influential members of this league were Duke George of Saxony, the Electors of Brandenburg and Mainz, and Duke Henry of Brunswick-Wolfenbüttel. Duke Henry was selected to inform the Emperor of what they had done, and to secure his sympathy and support. He told Charles v. that the league had been formed "against the Lutherans in case they should attempt by force or cunning to gain them over to their unbelief."

On the other hand, the Protestant princes had a mutual understanding—it does not seem to have been a definite league—to defend one another against any attack upon their faith. The leaders were John of Saxony, Philip of Hesse, Dukes Otto, Ernest, and Francis of Brunswick-Lüneberg, and the Counts of Mansfeld. Philip of Hesse was the soul of the union. They could count on the support of many of the imperial cities, some of them, such as Nürnberg, being in districts where the country lying around was ruled by Romanist princes.

The Diet, which met at Augsburg in 1525, was very thinly attended, and both parties waited for the Diet which was to be held at Speyer in the following year.

There never had been any doubt about the position and opinions of the Emperor on the religious question. He had stated them emphatically at the Diet of Worms. He had been educated in the beliefs of mediæval Catholicism; he valued the ceremonies and usages of the mediæval worship; he understood no other ecclesiastical polity; he believed that the Bishop of Rome was the head of the Church on earth; he had consistently persecuted Protestants in his hereditary dominions from the beginning; he desired the execution of the Edict of Worms against Luther. If he had remained in Germany, all his personal and official influence would have been thrown into the scale against the evangelical faith. Troubles in Spain, and the prosecution of the war against Francis of France had prevented his presence in Germany after his first brief visit. He had now conquered and taken Francis prisoner at the battle of Pavia. The terms of the Treaty of Madrid bound Francis to assist Charles in suppressing Lutheranism and other pernicious sects in Germany, and when it was signed the Emperor seemed free to crush the German Protestants. But his very success was against him; papal diplomacy wove another web around him; he was still unable to visit the Fatherland, and the religious question had to be discussed at Speyer in his absence.

When the Diet met, the national hostility to Rome showed no signs of abatement. The subject of German grievances against the Curia was again revived, and it was alleged that the chief causes of the Peasants' War were the merciless exactions of clerical landholders. Perhaps this opinion was justified by the fact that the condition of the peasantry on the lands of monasteries and of bishops was notoriously worse than that of those under secular proprietors; and that, while the clerical landholders had done little to subdue the rebels, they had been merciless after the insurgents had been subdued. There was truth enough in the charge to make it a sufficient answer to the accusation that the social revolution had been the outcome of Luther's teaching.

Ferdinand of Austria presided in his brother's absence, and, acting on the Emperor's instructions, he demanded the enforcement of the Edict of Worms and a decree of the Diet to forbid all innovations in worship and in doctrine. He promised that if these imperial demands were granted, the Emperor would induce the Pope to call a General Council for the definite settlement of the religious difficulties. But the Diet was not inclined to adopt the suggestions. The Emperor was at war with the Pope. Many of the clerical members felt themselves to be in a delicate position, and did not attend. The Lutheran sympathisers were in a majority, and the delegates from the cities insisted that it was impossible to enforce the Edict of Worms. The Committee of Princes[1] proposed to settle the religious question by a compromise which was almost wholly favourable to the Reformation. They suggested that the marriage of priests, giving the cup to the laity, the use of German as well as Latin in the baptismal and communion services, should be recognised; that all private Masses should be abolished; that the number of ecclesiastical holy days should be largely reduced; and that in the exposition of Holy Writ the rule ought to be that scripture should be interpreted by scripture. After a good deal of fencing, the Diet finally resolved on a deliverance which provided that the word of God should be preached without disturbance, that indemnity should be granted for past offences against the Edict of Worms, and that, until the meeting of a General Council to be held in a German city each State should so live as it hoped to answer for its conduct to God and to the Emperor.

The decision was a triumph for the territorial system as well as for the Reformation, and foreshadowed the permanent religious peace of Augsburg (1555). It is difficult to see how either Charles or Ferdinand could have accepted it. Their acquiescence was probably due to the fact that the Emperor was then at war with the Pope (the sack of Rome under the Constable Bourbon took place on May 6th, 1527), and that the threat of a German ecclesiastical revolt was a good weapon to use against His Holiness. Ferdinand was negotiating for election to the crowns of Hungary and Bohemia, and dared not offend his German subjects. Both brothers looked on any concessions to the German Lutherans as temporary compromises to be withdrawn as soon as they were able to enforce their own views.

The Protestant States and cities at once interpreted this decision of the Diet to mean that they had the legal right to organise territorial Churches and to introduce such

[1] The Diet was accustomed to appoint a Committee of Princes to put in shape their more important ordinances. The ordinance was called a "recess."

changes into public worship as would bring it into harmony with their evangelical beliefs.[1] The latent evangelical feeling at once manifested itself. Almost all North Germany, except Brandenburg, Ducal Saxony, and Brunswick-Wolfenbüttel, became Lutheran within three years. Still it has to be noticed that the legal recognition was accorded to the secular authorities, and that a ruling prince, who had no very settled religious convictions, might change the religion of his principality from political or selfish motives. It became evident in 1529 that political feeling or fear of the Emperor was much stronger than resolutions to support the evangelical Reformation.

Soon after the Diet, Philip of Hesse committed a political blunder which, in the opinion of many of his evangelical friends, involved disloyalty to the Fatherland, made them chary of associating themselves with him, and greatly weakened the Protestant party. For most of these North German princes, in spite of their clinging to the disruptive territorial principle, had a rugged conscientious patriotism which made them feel that no good German should seek the aid of France or make alliance with a Czech. Many of the Roman Catholic princes, irritated at the spread and organisation of Lutheranism which followed the decision of the Diet of 1526, had been persecuting by confiscation of goods and by death their Lutheran subjects. The Landgrave had married the daughter of Duke George of Saxony, and he knew that his father-in-law was continually uttering threats against the Elector of Saxony. Brooding over these things, Philip became gradually convinced that the Romanist princes were planning a deadly assault on the Lutherans, and that first the Elector and then he himself would be attacked and their territories partitioned among the conquerors. He had no proof, but his suspicions were strong. Chance brought him in contact with Otto von Pack, the steward of the Chancery of Ducal Saxony, who, on being questioned, admitted that the sus-

[1] A description of the changes in organisation and worship introduced after the decision of the Diet of 1526 is reserved for a separate chapter.

picions of Philip were correct, and promised to procure a copy of the treaty. Pack was a scoundrel. No such treaty existed. He forged a document which he declared to be a copy of a genuine treaty, and got 4000 gulden for his pains. Philip took the forgery to the Elector of Saxony and to Luther, both of whom had no doubt of its genuine character. They both, however, refused to agree to Philip's plan of seeking assistance outside the Empire. The Landgrave believed the situation too dangerous to be faced passively. He tried to secure the assistance of Francis of France and of Zapolya, the determined opponent of the House of Austria in Hungary. It was not until he had fully committed himself that the discovery was made that the document he had trusted in was nothing but a forgery. His hasty action in appealing to France and Hungary to interfere in the domestic concerns of the Empire was resented by his co-religionists. When the Diet met at Speyer, the Lutherans were divided and discredited. On the other hand, the Pope and the Emperor were no longer at war, and the clerical members flocked to the Diet in large numbers.

At this memorable Diet of Speyer (1529), a compact Roman Catholic majority faced a weak Lutheran minority. The Emperor, through his commissioners, declared at the outset that he abolished, "by his imperial and absolute authority (*Machtvollkommenheit*)," the clause in the ordinance of 1526 on which the Lutherans had relied when they founded their territorial Churches; it had been the cause, he said, "of much ill counsel and misunderstanding." The majority of the Diet upheld the Emperor's decision, and the practical effect of the ordinance which was voted was to rescind that of 1526. It declared that the German States which had accepted the Edict of Worms should continue to do so; which meant that there was to be no toleration for Lutherans in Romanist districts. It said that in districts which had departed from the Edict no further innovations were to be made, save that no one was to be prevented from hearing Mass; that sects which denied the sacrament of the true Body and Blood of Christ (Zwinglians) should no more be tolerated than Anabaptists. What was most important, it declared that no ecclesiastical body should be deprived of its authority or revenues. It was this last clause which destroyed all possibility of creating Lutheran Churches; for it meant that the mediæval ecclesiastical rule was everywhere to be restored, and with it the right of bishops to deal with all preachers within their dioceses.

§ 2. *The Protest.*[1]

It was this ordinance which called forth the celebrated PROTEST, from which comes the name *Protestant.* The Protest was read in the Diet on the day (April 19th, 1529) when all concessions to the Lutherans had been refused. Ferdinand and the other imperial commissioners would not permit its publication in the "recess," and the protesters had a legal instrument drafted and published, in which they embodied the Protest, with all the necessary documents annexed. The legal position taken was that the unanimous decision of one Diet (1526) could not be rescinded by a majority in a second Diet (1529). The Protesters declared that they meant to abide by the "recess" of 1526; that the "recess" of 1529 was not to be held binding on them, because they were not consenting parties. When forced to make their choice between obedience to God and obedience to the Emperor, they were compelled to choose the former; and they appealed, from the wrongs done to them at the Diet, to the Emperor, to the next free General Council of Holy Christendom, or to an ecclesiastical congress of the German nation. The document was signed by the Elector John of Saxony, Margrave George of Brandenburg, Dukes Ernest and Francis of Brunswick-Lüneburg, Landgrave Philip of Hesse, and Prince Wolfgang of Anhalt. The fourteen cities which adhered were Strassburg, Nürnberg, Ulm, Constance, Lindau, Mem-

[1] Ney, *Geschichte des Reichstages zu Speier in 1529* (Hamburg, 1880); Tittmann, *Die Protestation zu Speyer* (Leipzig, 1829).

mingen, Kempten, Nördlingen, Heilbronn, Reutlingen, Isny, St. Gallen, Weissenburg, and Windsheim. Many of these cities were Zwinglian rather than Lutheran; but all united in face of the common danger.

The Protest at Speyer embodied the principle, not a new one, that a minority of German States, when they felt themselves oppressed by a majority, could entrench themselves behind the laws of the Empire; and the idea is seen at work onward to the Diet of 1555, when it was definitely recognised. Such a minority, to maintain a successful defence, had to be united and able to protect itself by force if necessary. This was at once felt; and three days after the Protest had been read in the Diet (April, 22nd), Electoral Saxony, Hesse, and the cities of Strassburg, Ulm, and Nürnberg had concluded a "secret and particular treaty." They pledged themselves to mutual defence if attacked on account of God's word, whether the onslaught came from the Swabian League, from the *Reichsregiment*, or from the Emperor himself. Soon after the Diet, proposals were brought forward to make the compact effective and extensive,—one drafted by representatives of the cities and the other by the Elector of Saxony,—which provided very thoroughly for mutual support; but neither took into account the differences which lay behind the Protest. These divergences were strong enough to wreck the union.

The differences which separated the German Protestants were not wholly theological, although their doctrinal disputes were most in evidence.

§ 3. *Luther and Zwingli.*

A movement for reformation, which owed little or nothing to Wittenberg, had been making rapid progress in Switzerland, and two of the strongest cantons, Zurich and Bern, had revolted from the Roman Church. Its leader, Huldreich Zwingli, was utterly unlike Luther in temperament, training, and environment.

He had never gone through the terrible spiritual conflicts which had marked Luther for life, and had made him the man that he was. No deep sense of personal sin had ever haunted him, to make his early manhood a burden to him. Long after he had become known as a Reformer, he was able to combine a strong sense of moral responsibility with some laxity in private life. Unlike both Luther and Calvin, he was not the type of man to be leader in a deeply spiritual revival.

He had been subjected to the influences of Humanism from his childhood. His uncle, Bartholomew Zwingli, parish priest at Wildhaus, and the dean of Wesen, under whose charge the boy was placed, had a strong sympathy for the New Learning, and the boy imbibed it. His young intellect was fed on Homer and Pindar and Cicero; and all his life he esteemed the great pagans of antiquity as highly as he did any Christian saint. If it can be said that he bent before the dominating influence of any one man, it was Erasmus and not Luther who compelled him to admiration. He had for a teacher Thomas Wyttenbach, who was half Reformer and half disciple of Erasmus; and learned from him to study the Scriptures and the writings of such earlier Church Fathers as Origen, Jerome, and Chrysostom. Like many another Humanist north of the Alps, the mystical Christian Platonism of Pico della Mirandola had some influence on him. He had never studied the Scholastic Theology, and knew nothing of the spell it cast over men who had been trained in it. Of all the Reformers, Luther was the least removed from the mediæval way of looking at religion, and Zwingli had wandered farthest from it.

His earliest ecclesiastical surroundings were also different from Luther's. He had never been taught in childhood to consider the Church to be the Pope's House, in which the Bishop of Rome was entitled to the reverence and obedience due to the house-father. In his land the people had been long accustomed to manage their own ecclesiastical affairs. The greater portion of Switzerland had known but little either of the benefits or disadvantages of mediæval episcopal rule. Church property paid its share of the communal taxes, and even the monasteries and convents were liable to civil inspection. If a stray tourist at the present day wanders into the church which is called the Cathedral in that survival of ancient mediæval republics, San Marino, he will find that the seats of the "consuls" of the little republic occupy the place where he expects to find the bishop's chair. The civil power asserted its supremacy over the ecclesiastical in most things in these small mediæval republics. The Popes needed San Marino to be a thorn in the side of the Malatesta of Rimini, they hired most of their soldiers from the Swiss cantons, and therefore tolerated many things which they would not have permitted elsewhere.

The social environment of the Swiss Reformer was very different from that of Luther. He was a free Swiss who had listened in childhood to tales of the heroic fights of Morgarten, Sempach, Morat, and Nancy, and had imbibed the hereditary hatred of the House of Hapsburg. He had no fear of the "common man," Luther's bugbear after the Peasants' War. Orderly democratic life was the air he breathed, and what reverence Luther had for the Emperor "who protected poor people against the Turk," and for the lords of the soil, Zwingli paid to the civic fathers elected by a popular vote. When the German Reformer thought of Zwingli he was always muttering what Archbishop Parker said of John Knox—"God keep us from such visitations as Knockes hath attempted in Scotland; the people to be orderers of things!"[1]

Owing doubtless to this republican training, Zwingli had none of that aloofness from political affairs which was a marked characteristic of Luther. He believed that his mission had as much to do with politics as with religion, and that religious reformation was to be worked out by political forces, whether in the more limited sphere of

[1] *Calendar of State Papers, Foreign Series, of the reign of Elizabeth, 1559–1560*, p. 84.

Switzerland or in larger Germany. He had never taken a step forward until he had carried along with him the civic authorities of Zurich. His advance had always been calculated. Luther's *Theses* (November 1517) had been the volcanic outburst of a conscience troubled by the sight of a great religious scandal, and their author had no intention of doing more than protesting against the one great evil; he had no idea at the time where his protest was leading him. Zwingli's *Theses* (January 1523) were the carefully drafted programme of a Reformation which he meant to accomplish by degrees, and through the assistance of the Council of Zurich. His mind was full of political combinations for the purpose of carrying out his plans of reformation. As early as 1524 he was in correspondence with Pirkheimer about the possibility of a league between Nürnberg and Zurich—two powerful Protestant towns. This league did not take shape. But in 1527 a religious and political league (*das christliche Bürgerrecht*) was concluded between Zurich and Constance, an imperial German town; St. Gallen joined in 1528; Biel, Mühlhausen, and Basel in 1529; even Strassburg, afraid of the growing power of the House of Hapsburg, was included in 1530. The feverish political activity of Zwingli commended him to Philip of Hesse almost as strongly as it made him disliked, and even feared, by Ferdinand of Austria. The Elector of Saxony and Luther dreaded his influence over "the young man of Hesse."

Melanchthon was the first to insist on the evil influences of Zwingli's activity for the peace of the Empire. He persuaded himself that had the Lutherans stood alone at Speyer, the Romanists would have been prepared to make concessions which would have made the Protest needless. He returned to Wittenberg full of misgivings. The Protest might lead to a defiance of the Emperor, and to a subversion of the Empire. Was it right for subjects to defend themselves by war against the civil power which was ordained of God? "My conscience," he wrote, "is disquieted because of this thing; I am half dead with thinking about it."

He found Luther only too sympathetic; resolute to maintain that if the prince commanded anything which was contrary to the word of God, it was the duty of the subject to offer what passive resistance he was able, but that it was never right to oppose him actively by force of arms. Still less was it the duty of a Christian man to ally himself for such resistance with those who did not hold "the whole truth of God." Luther would therefore have nothing to do with an alliance offensive and defensive against the Emperor with cities who shared in what he believed to be the errors of Zwingli.

This meant a great deal more than a break with the Swiss. The south German towns of Strassburg, Memmingen, Constance, Lindau, and others were more Zwinglian than Lutheran. It was not only that they were inclined to the more radical theology of the Swiss Reformer; they found that his method of organising a reformed Church, drafted for the needs of Zurich, suited their municipal institutions better than the territorial organisations being adopted by the Lutheran Churches of North Germany. To Luther, whose views of the place of the "common man" in the Church had been changed by the Peasants' War, this was of itself a danger which threatened the welfare of the infant Churches. It made ecclesiastical government too democratic; and it did this in the very centres where the democracy was most dangerous. He could not forget that the mob of these German towns had taken part in the recently suppressed social revolution, that their working-class population was still the recruiting ground of the Anabaptist sectaries, and that at Memmingen itself Zwinglian partisans had helped to organise the revolution, and to link it on to the religious awakening. Besides, the attraction which drew these German cities to the Swiss might lead to larger political consequences which seemed to threaten what unity remained to the German Empire. It might result in the detachment of towns from the German Fatherland, and in the formation of new cantons cut adrift from Germany to increase the strength of the Swiss Confederation

§ 4. *The Marburg Colloquy.*[1]

All these thoughts were in the minds of Luther and of his fellow theologians, and had their weight with the Elector of Saxony, when their refusal to join rendered the proposed defensive league impossible. No one was more disappointed than the Landgrave of Hesse, the ablest political leader whom the German Reformation produced. He knew more about Zwingli than his fellow princes in North Germany; he had a keen interest in theological questions; he sympathised to some extent with the special opinions of Zwingli; and he had not the dread of democracy which possessed Luther and his Elector. He believed, rightly as events showed, that differences or suspected differences in theology were the strongest causes of separation; he was correct in supposing that the Lutheran divines through ignorance magnified those points of difference; and he hoped that if the Lutherans and the Swiss could be brought together, they would learn to know each other better. So he tried to arrange for a religious conference in his castle at Marburg. He had many a difficulty to overcome so far as the Lutherans were concerned. Neither Luther nor Melanchthon desired to meet Zwingli. Melanchthon thought that if a conference was to be held, it would be much better to meet Oecolampadius and perhaps some learned Romanists. Zwingli, on the other hand, was eager to meet Luther. He responded at once.

[1] SOURCES: Schirrmacher, *Briefe und Acten zu der Geschichte des Religionsgespräches zu Marburg, 1529, und des Reichstages zu Augsburg, 1530* (Gotha, 1876); Bucer, *Historische Nachricht von dem Gespräch zu Marburg* (Simler, *Sammlung*, II. ii. 471 ff.); Rudolphi Collini, "Summa Colloquii Marpurgensis," printed in Hospinian, *Historia sacramentaria*, ii. 123*b*–126*b*, and in *Zwinglii Opera*, iv. 175–180 (Zurich, 1841); Brieger in *Zeitschrift für Kirchengeschichte*, i. 628 ff.

LATER BOOKS: Ebrard, *Das Dogma vom heiligen Abendmahl und seine Geschichte*, vol. ii. (Frankfurt a. M. 1846; the author has classified the accounts of the persons present at the conference, and given a combined description of the discussion, pp. 308 n. and 314 ff.); Erichson, *Das Marburger Religionsgespräch* (Strassburg, 1880); Bess, *Luther in Marburg, 1529* (*Preuss. Jahrbücher*, civ. 418–431, Berlin, 1901).

He came, without waiting for leave to be given by the Zurich Council, across a country full of enemies. The conference met from October 30th to November 5th, 1529. Luther was accompanied by Melanchthon, Justus Jonas, and Cruciger, Frederick Mecum from Gotha, Osiander from Nürnberg, Brenz from Hall, Stephan Agricola from Augsburg, and others. With Zwingli came Oecolampadius, Bucer, and Hedio from Strassburg, Rudolph Collin (who has left the fullest account of the discussion), two councillors from Basel and from Zurich, and Jacob Sturm from Strassburg. After a preliminary conference between Zwingli and Melanchthon on the one hand, and Luther and Oecolampadius on the other, the real discussion took place in the great hall of the Castle. The tourist is still shown the exact spot where the table which separated the disputants was placed.

This *Marburg Colloquy*, as the conference was called, had important results for good, although it was unsuccessful in fulfilling the expectations of the Landgrave. It showed a real and substantial harmony between the two sets of theologians on all points save one. Fifteen theological articles (*The Marburg Articles*) stated the chief heads of the Christian faith, and fourteen were signed by Luther and by Zwingli. The one subject on which they could not come to an agreement was the relation of the Body of Christ to the elements Bread and Wine in the Sacrament of the Supper. It was scarcely to be expected that there could be harmony on a doctrinal matter on which there had been such a long and embittered controversy.

Both theologians found in the mediæval doctrine of the Sacrament of the Supper what they believed to be an overwhelming error destructive to the spiritual life. It presupposed that a priest, in virtue of mysterious powers conferred in ordination, could give or withhold from the Christian people the benefits conveyed in the Sacrament. It asserted that the priest could change the elements Bread and Wine into the very Body and Blood of Christ, and that unless this change was made there was no presence of Christ in the sacrament, and no possibility of sacramental grace for the communicant. Luther attacked the problem as a mediæval Christian, content, if he was able to purge the ordinance of this one fault, to leave all else as he found it. Zwingli came as a Humanist, whose fundamental rule was to get beyond the mediæval theology altogether, and attempt to discover how the earlier Church Fathers could aid him to solve the problem. This difference in mental attitude led them to approach the subject from separate sides; and the mediæval way of looking at the whole subject rendered difference of approach very easy. The mediæval Church had divided the Sacrament of the Lord's Supper into two distinct parts—the Mass and the Eucharist.[1] The Mass was inseparably connected with the thought of the great Sacrifice of Christ upon the Cross, and the Eucharist with the thought of the believer's communion with the Risen Living Christ. Zwingli attacked the Romanist doctrine of the Mass, and Luther sought to give an evangelical meaning to the mediæval conception of the Eucharist. Hence the two Protestant antagonists were never exactly facing each other.

Luther's convent studies in D'Ailly, Biel, and their common master, William of Occam, enabled him to show that there might be the presence of the Glorified Body of Christ, extended in space, in the elements Bread and Wine in a natural way, and without any priestly miracle: and that satisfied him; it enabled him to deny the priestly miracle and keep true in the most literal way to the words of the institution, "This is My Body."

Zwingli, on the other hand, insisted that the primary reference in the Lord's Supper was to the death of Christ, and that it was above all things a commemorative rite. He transformed the mediæval Mass into an evangelical sacrament, by placing the idea of commemoration where the mediæval theologian had put that of repetition, and held that the means of appropriation was faith and not

[1] In the *Canons and Decrees of the Council of Trent* the Sacrifice of the Mass is defined in the 22nd Session, and the Eucharist in the 13th Session.

eating with the mouth. This he held to be a return to the belief of the early centuries, before the conception of the sacrament had been corrupted by pagan ideas.

Like Luther, he served himself heir to the work of earlier theologians; but he did not go to Occam, Biel, or D'Ailly, as the German Reformer had done. Erasmus, who had no liking for the priestly miracle in the Mass, and cared little for a rigid literal interpretation of the words of the institution, had declared that the Sacrament of the Supper was the symbol of commemoration, of a covenant with God, and of the fellowship of all believers in Christ, and this commended itself to Zwingli's conception of the social character of Christianity; but he was too much a Christian theologian to be contented with such a vague idea of the rite. Many theologians of the later Middle Ages, when speculation was more free than it could be after the stricter definitions of the Council of Trent, had tried to purify and spiritualise the beliefs of the Church about the meaning of the central Christian rite. Foremost among them was John Wessel (*c.* 1420–1489), with his long and elaborate treatise, *De Sacramento Eucharistiæ.* He had taught that the Lord's Supper is the rite in which the death of Christ is presented to and appropriated by the believer; that it is above all things a commemoration of that death and a communion or participation in the benefits which followed; that communion with the spiritual presence of Jesus is of far more importance than any corporeal contact with the Body of Christ; and that this communion is shared in through faith. These thoughts had been taken over by Christopher Honius, a divine of the Netherlands, who had enforced them by insisting that our Lord's discourse in the 6th chapter of St. John's Gospel had reproved any materialistic conception of the Lord's Supper; and that *therefore* the words of the institution must not be taken in their rigid literal meaning. He had been the first to suggest that the word *is* in "This is My Body" must mean *signifies.* Wessel and Honius were the predecessors of Zwingli, and he wove their thoughts into his doctrine of the Lord's Supper. It should be remembered that Luther had also been acquainted with the labours of Wessel and of Honius, and that so far from attracting they had repelled him, simply because he thought they failed to give the respect due to the literal meaning of the words of the institution.

It must not be forgotten that Luther knew Zwingli only as in some way connected with Andrew Bodenstein of Carlstadt. Carlstadt had professed to accept the theory of Honius about the nature of the relation of the Presence of Christ to the elements of Bread and Wine—saying that the latter were *signs*, and nothing more, of the former. A controversy soon raged in Wittenberg to the scandal of German Protestantism. Luther insisted more and more on the necessity of the Presence in the elements of the Body of Christ " corporeally extended in space "; while Carlstadt denied that Presence in any sense whatsoever. Luther insisted with all the strength of language at his command that the literal sense of the words of the institution must be preserved, and that the words "This is My Body" must refer to the Bread and to the Wine; while Carlstadt thought it was more likely that while using the words our Lord pointed to His own Body, or if not, that religious conviction compelled another interpretation than the one on which Luther insisted.

The dust of all this controversy was in the eyes of the theologians when they met at Marburg, and prevented them carefully examining each other's doctrinal position. In all essential matters Luther and Zwingli were not so far apart as each supposed the other to be. Their respective theories, put very shortly, may be thus summed up.

Zwingli, looking mainly at the mediæval doctrine of the Mass, taught: (1) The Lord's Supper is not a *repetition* of the sacrifice of Christ on the Cross, but a *commemoration* of that sacrifice once offered up; and the elements are not a newly offered Christ, but the *signs* of the Body and Blood of the Christ who was once for all offered on Calvary. (2) That forgiveness for sin is not won by *partaking* in a newly offered Christ, but by *believing* in a Christ once offered up. (3) That the benefits of the work of Christ are always appropriated by faith, and that the atonement is so appropriated in the sacrament, whereby Christ becomes our food; but the food, being neither carnal nor corporeal, is not appropriated by the mouth, but by faith indwelling in the soul. Therefore there is a Real Presence of Christ in the sacrament, but it is a spiritual Presence, not a corporeal one. A real and living faith always involves the union of the believer with Christ, and therefore the Real Presence of Christ; and the Presence of Christ, which is in every act of faith, is in the sacrament to the faithful partaker. (4) That while the Lord's Supper primarily refers to the sacrifice of Christ, and while the elements, Bread and Wine, are the symbols of the crucified Body of Christ, the partaking of the elements is also a symbol and pledge of an ever-renewed living union with the Risen Christ. (5) That as our Lord Himself has specially warned His followers against thinking of feeding on Him in any corporeal or carnal manner (John vi.), the words of the institution cannot be taken in a strictly literal fashion, and the phrase "This is My Body" means "This signifies My Body." The fourth position had been rather implicitly held than explicitly stated.

Luther, looking mainly at the mediæval doctrine of the Eucharist, taught: (1) That the primary use of the sacrament was to bring believing communicants into direct touch with the Living Risen Christ. (2) That to this end there must be in the Bread and Wine the local Presence of the Glorified Body of Christ, which he always conceived as "body extended in space"; the communicants, coming into touch with this Body of Christ, have communion with Him, such as His disciples had on earth and as His saints now have in heaven. (3) That this local Presence of Christ does not presuppose any special priestly miracle, for, in virtue of its *ubiquity*, the Glorified Body of Christ is *everywhere* naturally, and therefore is in the Bread and in the Wine; this natural Presence becomes a sacramental

Presence because of the promise of God attached to the reverent and believing partaking of the sacrament. (4) That communion with the Living Risen Christ implies the appropriation of the Death of Christ, and of the Atonement won by this death; but this last thought of Luther's, which is Zwingli's first thought, lies implicitly in his teaching without being dwelt upon.

The two theories, so far as doctrinal teaching goes, are supplementary to each other rather than antagonists. Each has a weak point. Luther's depends on a questionable mediæval idea of *ubiquity*, and Zwingli's on a somewhat shallow exegesis. It was unfortunate, but only natural, that when the two theological leaders were brought together at Marburg, instead of seeking the mutual points of agreement, each should attack the weak point in the other's theory. Luther began by chalking the words *Hoc est Corpus Meum* on the table before him, and by saying, "I take these words literally; if anyone does not, I shall not argue but contradict"; and Zwingli spent all his argumentative powers in disputing the doctrine of *ubiquity*. The long debate went circling round these two points and could never be got away from them. Zwingli maintained that the Body of Christ was at the Right Hand of God, and could not be present, extended in space, in the elements, which were signs representing what was absent. Luther argued that the Body of Christ was in the elements, as, to use his own illustration, the sword is present in the sheath. As a soldier could present his sheathed sword and say, truly and literally, *This is my sword*, although nothing but the sheath was visible; so, although nothing could be seen or felt but Bread and Wine, these elements in the Holy Supper could be literally and truly called the Body and Blood of Christ.

The substantial harmony revealed in the fourteen articles which they all could sign showed that the Germans and the Swiss had one faith. But Luther insisted that their difference on the Sacrament of the Supper prevented them becoming one visible brotherhood, and the immediate purpose of the Landgrave of Hesse was not fulfilled.

Undaunted by his defeat, Philip next attempted a less comprehensive union. If Luther and Zwingli could not be included within the one brotherhood, might not the German cities of the south and the Lutheran princes be brought together? Another conference was arranged at Schwabach (October 1529), when a series of theological articles were to be presented for agreement. Luther prepared seventeen articles to be set before the conference. They were based on the Marburg Articles; but as Luther had stated his own doctrine of the Holy Supper in its most uncompromising form, it is not to be wondered at that the delegates from the southern cities hesitated to sign. They said that the confession (for the articles took that form) was not in conformity with the doctrines preached among them, and that they would need to consult their fellow-citizens before committing them to it. Thus Philip's attempts to unite the Protestants of Germany failed a second time, and a divided Protestantism awaited the coming of the Emperor, who had resolved to solve the religious difficulty in person.

§ 5. *The Emperor in Germany.*

Charles v. was at the zenith of his power. The sickly looking youth of Worms had become a grave man of thirty, whose nine years of unbroken success had made him the most commanding figure in Europe. He had quelled the turbulent Spaniards; he had crushed his brilliant rival of France at the battle of Pavia; he had humbled the Pope, and had taught His Holiness in the Sack of Rome the danger of defying the Head of the Holy Roman Empire; and he had compelled the reluctant Pontiff to invest him with the imperial crown. He had added to and consolidated the family possessions of the House of Hapsburg, and but lately his brother Ferdinand had won, in name at least, the crowns of Bohemia and Hungary. He was now determined to visit Germany, and by his personal presence and influence to end the religious difficulty which was distracting that portion of his vast dominions. He also meant to secure the succession to the Empire for his brother Ferdinand, by procuring his election as King of the Romans.

Charles came from Italy over the Brenner Pass in the spring time, and was magnificently received by the Tyrolese, eager to do all honour to the grandson of their beloved Kaiser Max. His letters to his brother, written on the stages of the journey, reveal as fully as that reserved soul could unbosom itself, his plans for the pacification of Germany. He meant to use every persuasion possible, to make what compromises his conscience permitted (for Catholicism was a faith with Charles), to effect a peaceful settlement. But if these failed, he was determined to crush the Reformation by force. He never seems to have doubted that he would succeed. Never a thought crossed his mind that he was about to encounter a great spiritual force whose depth and intensity he was unable to measure, and which was slowly creating a new world unknown to himself and to his contemporaries. While at Innsbruck he invited the Elector of Saxony to visit him, and was somewhat disappointed that the Lutheran prince did not accept; but this foretaste of trouble did not give him any uneasiness.

The summons to the Diet, commanding the Electors, princes, and all the Estates of the Empire to meet at Augsburg on the 8th of April 1530, had been issued when Charles was at Bologna. No threats marred the invitation. The Emperor announced that he meant to leave all past errors to the judgment of the Saviour; that he wished to give a charitable hearing to every man's opinions, thoughts, and ideas; and that his only desire was to secure that all might live under the one Christ, in one Commonwealth, one Church, and one Unity.[1] He left Innsbruck on the 6th of June, and, travelling slowly, reached the bridge on

[1] Schirrmacher, *Briefe und Acten zu der Geschichte des Religionsgespräches zu Marburg und des Reichstages zu Augsburg, 1530*, pp. 33, 34.

the Lech, a little distance from Augsburg, on the evening of the 15th. There he found the great princes of the Empire, who had been waiting his arrival from two o'clock in the afternoon. They alighted to do him reverence, and he graciously dismounted also, and greeted them with all courtesy. Charles had brought the papal nuncio, Cardinal Campeggio, in his train. Most of the Electors knelt to receive the cardinal's blessing; but John of Saxony stood bolt upright, and refused the proffered benediction.

The procession—one of the most gorgeous Germany had ever seen—was marshalled for the ceremonial entry into the town. The retinues of the Electors were all in their appropriate colours and arms—Saxony, by ancient prescriptive right, leading the van. Then came the Emperor alone, a baldachino carried over his head. He had wished the nuncio and his brother to ride beside him under the canopy; but the Germans would not suffer it; no Pope's representative was to be permitted to ride shoulder to shoulder with the head of the German Empire entering the most important of his imperial cities.[1]

Augsburg was then at the height of its prosperity. It was the great trading centre between Italy and the Levant and the towns of Northern Europe. It was the home of the Welsers and of the Fuggers, the great capitalists of the later mediæval Europe. It boasted that its citizens were the equals of princes, and that its daughters, in that age of deeply rooted class distinctions, had married into princely houses. To this day the name of one of its streets —Philippine Welser Strasse—commemorates the wedding of an heiress of the Welsers with an archduke of Austria; and the wall decorations of the old houses attest the ancient magnificence of the city.[2]

At the gates of the town, the clergy, singing *Advenisti*

[1] There are several contemporary accounts of this meeting at the bridge of the Lech, and of the procession; for one, see Schirrmacher, *Briefe und Acten*, etc. pp. 54–57.

[2] It was a somewhat doubtful honour for a city to be chosen as the meeting place of a Diet. The burghers of Augsburg hired 2000 landsknechts to protect them during the session (Schirrmacher, *Briefe und Acten*, p. 52).

desiderabilis, met the procession. All, Emperor, clergy, princes, and their retinues, entered the cathedral. The *Te Deum* was sung, and the Emperor received the benediction. Then the procession was re-formed, and accompanied Charles to his lodgings in the Bishop's Palace.

There the Emperor made his first attempt on his Lutheran subjects. He invited the Elector of Saxony, George of Brandenburg, Philip of Hesse, and Francis of Lüneburg to accompany him to his private apartments. He told them that he had been informed that they had brought their Lutheran preachers with them to Augsburg, and that he would expect them to keep them silent during the sittings of the Diet. They refused. Then Charles asked them to prohibit controversial sermons. This request was also refused. In the end Charles reminded them that his demand was strictly within the decision of 1526; that the Emperor was lord over the imperial cities; and he promised them that he would appoint the preachers himself, and that there would be no sermons—only the reading of Scripture without comment. This was agreed to. He next asked them to join him in the Corpus Christi procession on the following day. They refused—Philip of Hesse with arguments listened to by Ferdinand with indignation, and by Charles with indifference, probably because he did not understand German. The Emperor insisted. Then old George of Brandenburg stood forth, and told His Majesty that he could not, and would not obey. It was a short, rugged speech, though eminently respectful, and ended with these words, which flew over Germany, kindling hearts as fire lights flax: "Before I would deny my God and His Evangel, I would rather kneel down here before your Majesty and have my head struck off,"—and the old man hit the side of his neck with the edge of his hand. Charles did not need to know German to understand. "Not head off, dear prince, not head off," he said kindly in his Flemish-German (*Nit Kop ab, löver Först, nit Kop ab*). Charles walked in procession through the streets of Augsburg on a blazing hot day, stooping under a heavy purple mantle, with a superfluous candle sputtering in his hand; but the evangelical princes remained in their lodgings.[1]

§ 6. *The Diet of Augsburg 1530.*[2]

The Diet was formally opened on June 20th (1530), and in the *Proposition* or Speech from the Throne it was announced that the Assembly would be invited to discuss armament against the Turk, and that His Majesty was anxious, "by fair and gentle means," to end the religious differences which were distracting Germany. The Protestants were again invited to give the Emperor in writing their opinions and difficulties. It was resolved to take the religious question first. On June 24th the Lutherans were ready with their "statement of their grievances and opinions relating to the faith." Next day (June 25th) the Diet met in the hall of the Episcopal Palace, and what is known as the *Augsburg Confession* was read by the Saxon Chancellor, Dr. Christian Bayer, in such a clear resonant voice that it was heard not only by the audience within the chamber, but also by the crowd which thronged the court outside.[3] When the reading was ended, Chancellor Brück handed the document and a duplicate in Latin to the Emperor. They were signed by the Elector of Saxony and his son John Frederick, by George, Margrave of Brandenburg, the Dukes Ernest and Francis of Lüneburg, the Landgrave of Hesse, Prince Wolfgang of Anhalt, and the delegates of the cities of Nürnberg and Reutlingen These princes knew the danger which threatened them in putting their names to the Confession. The theologians of Saxony besought their Elector to permit their names

[1] Förstemann, *Urkundenbuch*, etc. i. 268, 271; Schirrmacher, *Briefe und Acten*, etc. p. 59 and note.

[2] Sources: Schirrmacher, *Briefe und Acten*; Förstemann, *Urkundenbuch zu der Geschichte des Reichstags zu Augsburg*, 2 vols. (Halle, 1833–1835); and *Archiv für die Geschichte der kirchl. Reformation* (Halle, 1831).

Later Books: Moritz Facius, *Geschichte des Reichstags zu Augsburg* (Leipzig, 1830).

[3] Schirrmacher, *Briefe und Acten*, etc. p. 90.

to stand alone; but he answered calmly, *I, too, will confess my Christ.* He was not a brilliant man like Philip of Hesse. He was unpretentious, peace-loving, and retiring by nature—John the Steadfast, his people called him. Recent historians have dwelt on the conciliatory attitude and judicial spirit manifested by the Emperor at this Diet, and they are justified in doing so; but the mailed hand sometimes showed itself. Charles refused to invest John with his Electoral dignities in the usual feudal fashion, and his entourage whispered that if the Elector was not amenable to the Emperor's arguments, he might find the electorate taken from him and bestowed on the kindred House of Ducal Saxony, which in the person of Duke George so stoutly supported the old religion.[1] While possessing that "laudable, if crabbed constitutionalism which was the hereditary quality of the Ernestine line of Saxony,"[2] he had a genuine affection for the Emperor. Both recognised that this Diet of Augsburg had separated them irrevocably. "Uncle, Uncle," said Charles to Elector John at their parting interview, "I did not expect this from you." The Elector's eyes filled with tears; he could not speak; he turned away in silence and left the city soon afterwards.[3]

§ 7. *The Augsburg Confession.*[4]

The Augsburg Confession (*Confessio Augustana*) was what it claimed to be, a statement of "opinion and grievances," and does not pretend to be a full exposition of doctrinal tenets. The men who wrote it (Melanchthon was responsible for the phraseology) and presented it to

[1] The threat is recorded in *Archiv für Schweizerische Geschichte und Landeskunde*, i. 278.

[2] Armstrong, *The Emperor Charles V.*, i. 244.

[3] Förstemann, *Archiv*, p. 206.

[4] Schaff, The *Creeds of the Evangelical Protestant Christian Churches* (London, 1877), p. 3; cf. *History of the Creeds of Christendom* (London, 1877), pp. 220 ff.; Tschakert, *Die Augsburgische Konfession* (Leipzig, 1901).

the Diet, claimed to belong to the ancient and visible Catholic Church, and to believe in all the articles of faith set forth by the Universal Church, and particularly in the *Apostles'* and *Nicene Creeds*; but they maintained that abuses had crept in which obscured the ancient doctrines. The Confession showed why they could not remain in connection with an unreformed Church. Their position is exactly defined in the opening sentence of the second part of the Confession. "Inasmuch as the Churches among us dissent in no articles of faith from the Holy Scriptures nor the Church Catholic, and only omit a few of certain abuses, which are novel, and have crept in with time partly and in part have been introduced by violence, and contrary to the purport of the canons, we beg that your Imperial Majesty would clemently hear both what ought to be changed, and what are the reasons why people ought not to be forced against their conscience to observe these abuses."

The Confession is often represented as an attempt to minimise the differences between Lutherans and Romanists and exaggerate those between Lutherans and Zwinglians, and there are some grounds for the statement. Melanchthon had come back from the Diet of Speyer (1529) convinced that if the Lutherans had separated themselves more thoroughly from the cities of South Germany there would have been more chance of a working compromise, and it is only natural to expect that the idea should colour his sketch of the Lutheran position at Augsburg. Yet in the main the assertion is wrong. The distinctively Protestant conception of the spiritual priesthood of all believers inspires the whole document; and this can never be brought into real harmony with the Romanist position and claims. It is not difficult to state Romanist and Protestant doctrine in almost identical phrases, provided this one great dogmatic difference be for the moment set on one side. The conferences at Regensburg in 1541 (April 27–May 22) proved as much. No one will believe that Calvin would be inclined to minimise the differences between Protestants and Romanists, yet he voluntarily signed the Augsburg Confession, and did so, he says, in the sense in which the author (Melanchthon) understood it. This Augsburg Confession and Luther's Short Catechism are the symbolical books still in use in all Lutheran churches.

The *Augsburg Confession* (*Confessio Augustana*) is divided into two parts, the first expressing the views held by those who signed it, and the second stating the errors they protested against. The form and language alike show that the authors had no intention of framing an exhaustive syllabus of theological opinions or of imposing its articles as a changeless system of dogmatic truth. They simply meant to express what they united in believing. Such phrases as *our Churches teach*, *it is taught*, *such and such opinions are falsely attributed to us*, make that plain. In the first part the authors show how much they hold in common with the mediæval Church; how they abide by the teaching of St. Augustine, the great theologian of the West; how they differ from more radical Protestants like the Zwinglians, and repudiate the teachings of the Anabaptists. The Lutheran doctrine of Justification by Faith is given very clearly and briefly in a section by itself, but it is continually referred to and shown to be the basis of many portions of their common system of belief. In the second part they state what things compel them to dissent from the views and practices of the mediæval Church—the enforced celibacy of the clergy, the sacrificial character of the Mass, the necessity of auricular confession, monastic vows, and the confusion of spiritual and secular authority exhibited in the German episcopate.

The origin of the document was this. When the Emperor's proclamation summoning the Diet reached Saxony, Chancellor Gregory Brück suggested that the Saxon theologians should prepare a statement of their opinions which might be presented to the Emperor if called for.[1] This was done. The theologians went to the

[1] Förstemann, *Urkundenbuch*, i. 39: the worthy Chancellor thought that the document should be drafted "mit gründlicher bewerung derselbigen aus göttlicher schrifft."

Schwabach Articles, and Melanchthon revised them, restated them, and made them as inoffensive as he could. The document was meant to give the minimum for which the Protestants contended, and Melanchthon's conciliatory spirit shows itself throughout. It embalms at the same time some of Luther's trenchant phrases: "Christian perfection is this, to fear God sincerely; and again, to conceive great faith, and to trust assuredly that God is pacified towards us for Christ's sake; to ask, and certainly to look for, help from God in all our affairs according to our calling; and outwardly to do good works diligently, and to attend to our vocation. In these things doth true perfection and the true worship of God consist: it doth not consist in being unmarried, in going about begging, nor in wearing dirty clothes." His indifference to forms of Church government and his readiness to conserve the old appears in the sentence: "Now our meaning is not to have rule taken from the bishops; but this one thing only is requested at their hands, that they would suffer the gospel to be purely taught, and that they would relax a few observances, which cannot be observed without sin."

When the Romanist theologians presented their Confutation of this Confession to the Emperor, it was again left to Melanchthon to draft an answer—the *Apology of the Augsburg Confession.* The *Apology* is about seven times longer than the *Confession*, and is a noble and learned document. The Emperor refused to receive it, and Melanchthon spent a long time over it before it was allowed to be seen.

After taking counsel with the Romanist princes (*die Chur und Fursten so bepstisch gewesen*),[1] it was resolved to hand the Confession to a committee of Romanist theologians whom the cardinal nuncio [2] undertook to bring to-

[1] Schirrmacher, *Briefe und Acten*, etc. p. 98.

[2] Charles knew well that the nuncio would exert all his influence to prevent a settlement. In anticipation of the Diet the Emperor had privately asked Melanchthon to give him a statement of the *minimum* of concessions which would content the Lutherans. Melanchthon seems to have answered (our source of information is not very definite): the Eucharist

gether, to examine and answer it. Among them were John Eck of Ingolstadt, Faber, and Cochlæus. There was little hope of arriving at a compromise with such champions on the papal side; and Charles was soon to discover that his strongest opponents in effecting a peaceful solution were the nuncio and his committee of theologians. Five times they produced a confutation, and five times the Emperor and the Diet returned their work, asking them to redraft it in milder and in less uncompromising terms.[1] The sixth draft went far beyond the wishes of Charles, but the Emperor had to accept it and let it appear as the statement of his beliefs. It made reconciliation hopeless.

§ 8. *The Reformation to be crushed.*

The religious difficulty had not been removed by compromise. There remained force — the other alternative foreshadowed by the Emperor. The time seemed to be opportune. Protestantism was divided, and had flaunted its differences in the Emperor's presence. Philip of Hesse had signed the Augsburg Confession with hesitation, not because he did not believe its statements, but because it seemed to shut the door on a complete union among all the parties who had joined in the Protest of 1529. The four cities of Strassburg, Constance, Lindau, and Memmingen had submitted a separate Confession (the *Confessio Tetrapolitana*) to the Emperor; and the Romanist theologians had written a confutation of it also. Zwingli had sent a third.

Luther was not among the theologians present at the

in both kinds; marriage of priests permitted; the omission of the canon of the Mass; concession of the Church lands already sequestrated; and the decision of the other matters in dispute at a free General Council. Charles had sent the document to Rome; it had been debated at a conclave of cardinals, who had decided that none of the demands could be granted.

[1] One document says: "Es war aber zum ersten die *confutation* wol bey zweihundert und achtzig bletter lang gewesen, aber die key. Mäj. hat sie selbst also gereuttert und gerobt, das es nicht mehr denn zwölf bletter geblieben sind. Solchs soll Doctor Eck sehr verdrossen und wee gethan haben."—(Schirrmacher, *Briefe und Acten*, etc. p. 167.)

Diet of Augsburg. Technically he was still an outlaw, for the ban of the Diet of Worms had never been legally removed. The Elector had asked him to stay at his Castle of Coburg. There he remained, worried and anxious, chafing like a caged eagle. He feared that Melanchthon's conciliatory spirit might make him barter away some indispensable parts of evangelical truth; he feared the impetuosity of the Landgrave of Hesse and his known Zwinglian sympathies. His secretary wrote to Wittenberg that he was fretting himself ill; he was longing to get back to Wittenberg, where he could at least teach his students. It was then that Catharine got their friend Lucas Cranach to paint their little daughter Magdalena, just twelve months old, and sent it to her husband that he might have a small bit of home to cheer him. Luther hung the picture up where he could always see it from his chair, and he tells us that the sweet little face looking down upon him gave him courage during his dreary months of waiting. Posts brought him news from the Diet: that the Confession had been read to the Estates; that the Romanists were preparing a Confutation; that their reply was ready on August 3rd; that Philip of Hesse had left the Diet abruptly on the 6th, to raise troops to fight the Emperor, it was reported; that Melanchthon was being entangled in conferences, and was giving up everything. His strong ardent nature pours itself forth in his letters from Coburg (April 18th–Oct. 4th)—urging his friends to tell him how matters are going; warning Melanchthon to stand firm; taking comfort in the text, "Be ye angry, and sin not"; comparing the Diet to the rooks and the rookery in the trees below his window.[1] It was from Coburg that he wrote his charming letter to his small son.[2] It was there that he penned the letter of encouragement to the tried and loyal Chancellor Brück:

"I have lately seen two wonders: the first as I was looking out of my window and saw the stars in heaven and all that beautiful vault of God, and yet I saw no pillars on

[1] De Wette *Luther's Briefe*, etc. iv. 1–182. [2] *Ibid.* iv. 41.

which the Master-Builder had fixed this vault; yet the heavens fell not, and the great vault stood fast. Now there are some who search for the pillars, and want to touch and to grasp them; and when they cannot, they wonder and tremble as if the heaven must certainly fall, just because they cannot grasp its pillars. If they could only lay their hands on them, they think that the heaven would stand firm!

"The second wonder was: I saw great clouds rolling over us with such a ponderous weight that they seemed like a great ocean, and yet I saw no foundation on which they rested or were based, and no shore which bounded them; yet they fell not, but frowned on us and flowed on. But when they had passed by, then there shone forth both their floor and our roof, which had kept them back—a rainbow! A frail, thin floor and roof which soon melted into the clouds, and was more like a shadowy prism, such as we see through coloured glass, than a strong, firm foundation, and we might well distrust the feeble rampart which kept back that fearful weight of waters. Yet we found that this unsubstantial prism was able to bear up the weight of waters, and that it guarded us safely! But there are some who look more to the thickness and massive weight of the waters and the clouds than at this thin, light, narrow bow of promise. They would like to feel the strength of that shadowy vanishing arch, and because they cannot do this, they are always fearing that the clouds will bring back the flood."[1]

The Protestants never seemed to be in a worse plight; but, as Luther wrote, the threatened troubles passed away —for this time at least.

Campeggio was keen to crush the Reformation at once. His letters to the Curia insist that the policy of the strong arm is the only effectual way of dealing with the Lutheran princes. But Charles found that some of the South German princes who were eager that no compromise should be made with the Lutherans, were very unwilling to coerce them by force of arms. They had no wish to see the Emperor all-powerful in Germany. The Romanist Dukes of Bavaria (the Wittelsbachs) were as strongly anti-Hapsburg as Philip of

[1] De Wette, *Luther's Briefe*, etc. iv. 128.

Hesse himself; and Charles had no desire to stir the anti-Hapsburg feeling. Instead, conferences[1] were proposed to see whether some mutual understanding might not after all be reached; and the Diet was careful to introduce laymen, in the hope that they would be less uncompromising than the Romanist theologians. The meetings ended without any definite result. The Protestant princes refused to make the needful concessions, and Charles found his plans thwarted on every side. Whereupon the Romanist majority of the Diet framed a "recess," which declared that the Protestants were to be allowed to exist unmolested until April 15th, 1531; and were then to be put down by force. Meanwhile they were ordered to make no more innovations in worship or in doctrine; they were to refrain from molesting the Romanists within their territories; and they were to aid the Emperor and the Romanist princes in stamping out the partisans of Zwingli and the Anabaptists. This resolution gave rise to a second Protest, signed by the Lutheran princes and by the fourteen cities.

Nothing had stirred the wrath of Charles so much as the determined stand taken by the cities. He conceived that he, the Emperor, was the supreme Lord within an imperial city; and he employed persuasion and threats to make their delegates accept the "recess." Even Augsburg refused.

Having made their Protest, the Lutheran princes and the delegates from the protesting towns left the Diet, careless of what the Romanist majority might further do. In their absence an important ordinance was passed. The Diet decided that the Edict of Worms was to be executed; that the ecclesiastical jurisdictions were to be preserved,

[1] The whole time of the members of the Diet was not spent in theological discussions. We read of banquets, where Lutherans and Romanists sat side by side; of dances that went on far into the night; of what may be called a garden party in a "fair meadow," where a wooden house was built for the accommodation of the ladies; and of tournaments. At one of them, Ferdinand, the Emperor's brother, was thrown and his horse rolled over him; and Melanchthon wrote to Luther that six men had been killed at one of these "gentle and joyous" passages of arms.

and all Church property to be restored; and, what was most important, that the Imperial Court of Appeals for all disputed legal cases within the Empire (the *Reichskammersgericht*) should be restored. The last provision indicated a new way of fighting the extending Protestantism by harassing legal prosecutions, which, from the nature of the court, were always to be decided against the dissenters from the ecclesiastical jurisdiction of the mediæval Empire.[1] All instances of seizure of ecclesiastical benefices, all defiances of episcopal decisions, could be appealed against to this central court; and as the legal principles on which it gave its decisions and the controlling authorities which it recognised were mediæval, the Protestants could never hope for a decision in their favour. The Lutheran Church in Saxony, for example, with its pastors and schoolmasters, was supported by moneys taken from the old ecclesiastical foundations. According to this decision of the Diet, every case of such transfer of property could be appealed to this central court, which from its constitution was bound to decide against the transfer. If the Protestant princes disregarded the decisions of the central court, the Emperor was within his rights in treating them as men who had outraged the constitution of the Empire.[2]

Charles met at Augsburg the first great check in his hitherto successful career, but he was tenacious of purpose, aud never cared to hurry matters to an irrevocable conclusion. He carefully studied the problem, and three ways of dealing with the religious difficulty shaped themselves in his mind at Augsburg—by compromise, by letting the Protestants alone for a period longer or shorter, and by a General Council which would be free. It would seem

[1] The Romanist majority had resolved to fight the Protestant minority, not in the battlefield, but in the law-courts—*nicht fechten sondern rechten*, was the phrase.

[2] When the religious war did begin in 1545, Charles justified the use of force on the grounds that the Elector of Saxony and the Landgrave of Hesse had violated the constitution of the Empire, *had repudiated the decisions of the Reichskammersgericht*, and had protested against the decisions of the Diet.

that at Augsburg he first seriously resolved that the condition of Europe was such that the Pope must be *compelled* to summon a Council, and to allow it freedom of debate and action. Charles tried all three plans in Germany during the fifteen years that followed.

§ 9. *The Schmalkald League.*[1]

The Emperor published the decision of the Diet on the 19th of November, and the Protestants had to arrange some common plan of facing the situation. They met, princes and delegates of cities, in the little upland town of Schmalkalden, lying on the south-west frontier of Electoral Saxony, circled by low hills which were white with snow (December 22–31). They had to face at once harassing litigation, and, after the 15th of April, the threat that they would be stamped out by force of arms. Were they still to maintain their doctrine of passive resistance? The question was earnestly debated. Think of these earnest German princes and burghers, their lives and property at stake, debating this abstract question day after day, resolute to set their own consciences right before coming to any resolution to defend themselves! The lawyers were all on the side of active defence. The terms of the bond were drafted. The Emperor's name was carefully omitted; and the causes which compelled them to take action were rather alluded to vaguely than stated with precision. The Elector of Saxony, the Landgrave of Hesse, the Duke of Lüneburg, the Prince of Anhalt, the two Counts of Mansfeld, and the delegates from Magdeburg and Bremen signed. Pious old George of Brandenburg was not convinced that it was lawful to resist the Emperor; the deputies of Nürnberg had grave doubts also. Many others who were present felt that they must have time to make up their minds. But the league was started, and was soon to assume huge proportions.

[1] Schmidt, *Zur Geschichte des Schmalkaldischen Bundes* (*Forsch. zur Deutschen Geschichte*, xxv.); Zangemeister, *Die Schmalkaldischen Artikel von 1537* (Heidelberg, 1883); *Corpus Reformatorum*, iii. 973 ff.

The confederates had confessed the new doctrines, and had published their Confession. They now resolved that they would defend themselves if attacked by litigation or otherwise. There was no attempt to exclude the South German cities; and Charles' expectations that theological differences would prevent Protestant union within Germany were frustrated. Zwingli's heroic death at Cappel (October 11th, 1531) softened all Protestant hearts towards his followers. The South German cities followed the lead of Bucer, who was anxious for union. Many of these towns now joined the Schmalkald League. Brunswick joined. Hamburg and Rostock in the far north, Goslar and Göttingen in the centre, joined. Almost all North Germany and the more important imperial towns in the South were united in one strong confederacy by this Schmalkald League. It became one of the European Powers. Denmark wished to join. Thomas Cromwell was anxious that England should join. The league was necessarily anti-Hapsburg, and the Emperor had to reckon with it.

Its power appeared at the Diet of Nürnberg in 1532. The dreaded day (April 15th, 1531) on which the Protestants were to be reduced by fire and sword passed quietly by. Charles was surrounded with difficulties which made it impossible for him to carry out the threats he had published on November 19th, 1530. The Turks were menacing Vienna and the Duchy of Austria; the Pope was ready to take advantage of any signs of imperial weakness; France was irreconcilable; England was hostile; and the Bavarian dukes were doing what they could to lessen the Hapsburg power in Germany.

When the Diet met at Nürnberg in 1532, the Emperor knew that he was unable to coerce the Lutherans, and returned to his earlier courteous way of treating them. They were more patriotic than the German Romanists for whom he had done so much. Luther declared roundly that the Turks must be met and driven back, and that all Germans must support the Emperor in repelling the invasion. At the Diet a "recess" was proposed, in which the religious truce was indefinitely extended; the processes against the Protestants in the *Reichskammersgericht* were to be quashed, and no State was to be proceeded against in matters arising out of religious differences. The Romanist members refused to accept it; the "recess" was never published. But the Protestant States declared that they would trust in the imperial word of honour, and furnished the Emperor with troops for the defence of Vienna, and the invasion was repelled.

The history of the struggle in Germany between the Diet of 1532 and the outbreak of war in 1546 is very intricate, and cannot be told as a simple contest between Reformation and anti-Reformation.

In the sixteenth century, almost all thoughtful and earnest-minded men desired a Reformation of the Church. The Roman Curia was the only opponent to all reforms of any kind. But two different ideas of what Reformation ought to be, divided the men who longed for reforms. The one desired to see the benumbed and formalist mediæval Church filled with a new religious life, while it retained its notable characteristics of a sacerdotal ministry and a visible external unity under a uniform hierarchy culminating in the Papacy. The other wished to free the human spirit from the fetters of a merely ecclesiastical authority, and to rebuild the Church on the principle of the spiritual priesthood of all believing men and women. In the struggle in Germany the Emperor Charles may be taken as the embodiment of the first, as Luther represented the second. To the one it seemed essential to maintain the external unity and authority of the Church according to the mediæval ideal; the other could content himself with seeing the Church of the Middle Ages broken up into territorial Churches, each of which he contended was a portion of the one visible Catholic Church. Charles had no difficulty in accepting many changes in doctrine and usages, provided a genuine and lasting compromise could be arrived at which would retain all within the one ecclesiastical organisation. He consented once and again to suspend the struggle; but he would never have made himself responsible for a permanent religious settlement which recognised the Lutheran Churches He had no objection to a truce, but would never accept a lasting peace. If the Lutherans could not be brought back within the mediæval Church by compromise, then he was prepared to go to all extremes to compel them to return. Of course, he was the ruler over many lands; he was keen to extend and consolidate the family possessions of his House,—as keen as the most grasping of the petty territorial princes,—and he had to be an opportunist. But he never deviated in the main from his idea of how the religious difficulty should be solved.

But all manner of political and personal motives were at work on both sides in Germany (as elsewhere). Philip of Hesse combined a strenuous acceptance of the principles of the Lutheran Reformation with as thorough a hatred of the House of Hapsburg and of its supremacy in Germany. The Dukes of Bavaria, who were the strongest partisans of the Romanist Church in Germany, were the hereditary enemies of the House of Austria. The religious pacification of the Fatherland was made impossible to Charles, not merely by his insistence on maintaining the conceptions of the mediæval Church, but also by open and secret reluctance to see the imperial authority increased, and by jealousies aroused by the territorial aggrandisement of the House of Hapsburg. The incompatibility between the aims of the Emperor and those of his indispensable ally, the Pope, added to the difficulties of the situation.

In 1534, Philip of Hesse persuaded the Schmalkald League to espouse the cause of the banished Duke of Würtemberg. His territories had been incorporated into the family possessions of the Hapsburgs, and the people groaned under the imperial administration. The Swabian League, which had been the mainstay of the Imperialist and Romanist cause in South Germany, was persuaded to remain neutral by the Dukes of Bavaria, and Philip had little difficulty in defeating Ferdinand, and driving the Imperialists out of the Duchy. Ulrich was restored, declared in favour of the Lutheran Reformation, and Würtemberg was added to the list of Protestant States. By the terms of the Peace of Cadan (June 1534), Ferdinand publicly engaged to carry out Charles' private assurance that no Protestant was to be dragged before the *Reichskammersgericht* for anything connected with religion.[1] Another important consequence followed. The Swabian League was dissolved in 1536. This left the Schmalkald League of Protestant States and cities the only formidable confederation in Germany.

The political union among the Protestants suggested a closer approximation. The South German pastors asked to meet Luther and discuss their theological differences. They met at Wittenberg, and after prolonged discussion it was found that all were agreed save on one small point—the presence, *extended in space*, of the Body of Christ in the elements in the Holy Supper. It was agreed that this might be left an open question; and what was called the *Wittenberg Concord* was signed, which united all German Protestants (May and June 1536).[2]

Three years later (1539), Duke George of Saxony died, the most honest and disinterested of the Romanist princes. His brother Henry, who succeeded him, with the joyful consent of his subjects, pronounced for the Evangelical faith. Nothing would content him but that Luther should come to Leipzig to preside clerically on so auspicious an occasion. Luther preached in the great hall of the Castle, where twenty years earlier he had confronted Eck, and had heard Duke George declare that his opinions were pestilential.

In the same year the new Elector of Brandenburg also came over to the Evangelical side amid the rejoicings of his people; and the two great Romanist States of North

[1] Winckelmann, "Die Verträge von Kadan und Wien" (*Zeitschrift für Kirchengeschichte*, xi. 212 ff.).

[2] Cf. Kolde, *Analecta*, pp. 216 ff., 231 f., 262 f., 278 f., etc.

Germany, Electoral Brandenburg and Ducal Saxony, became Protestant.

The tide flowed so strongly that the three clerical Electors, the Archbishops of Mainz, Köln, and Trier, and some of the bishops, contemplated secularising their principalities, and becoming Protestants. This alarmed Charles thoroughly. If the proposed secularisation took place, there would be a large Protestant majority in the Electoral College, and the next Emperor would be a Protestant.

Charles had been anxiously watching the gradual decadence of the power of the Romanist princes in Germany; and reports convinced him that the advance of the Reformation among the people was still more marked. The Roman Catholic Church seemed to be in the agonies of dissolution even in places where it had hitherto been strong. Breslau, once strongly Romanist, was now almost fanatically Lutheran; in Vienna, Bishop Faber wrote, the population was entirely Lutheran, save himself and the Archduke. The Romanist Universities were almost devoid of students. In Bavaria, it was said that there were more monasteries than monks. Candidates for the priesthood had diminished in a very startling way: the nuncio Vergerio reported that he could find none in Bohemia except a few paupers who could not pay their ordination fees.

The policy of the Pope (Paul III., 1534–1549) had disgusted the German Romanist princes. He subordinated the welfare of the Church in their dominions to his anti-Hapsburg Italian schemes, and had actually allied himself with Francis of France, who was intriguing with the Turks, in order to thwart the Emperor! The action and speeches of Henry VIII. had been watched and studied by the German Romanist leaders. Could they not imitate him in Germany, and create a Nationalist Church true to mediæval doctrine, hierarchy, and ritual, and yet independent of the Pope, who cared so little for them?

All these things made Charles and Ferdinand revise

their policy. The Emperor began to consider seriously whether the way out of the religious difficulty might not be, either to grant a prolonged truce to the Lutherans (which might, though he hoped not, become permanent), or to work energetically for the creation of a German National Church, which, by means of some working compromise in doctrines and ceremonies, might be called into existence by a German National Council assembled in defiance of the Pope.

It was with these thoughts in his mind that he sent his Chancellor Held into Germany to strengthen the Romanist cause there. His agent soon abandoned the larger ideas of his master, if he ever comprehended them, and contented himself with announcing publicly that the private promise given by Charles at Nürnberg, and confirmed by Ferdinand at the Peace of Cadan, was withdrawn. The lawsuits brought against the Protestants in the *Reichskammersgericht* were not to be quashed, but were to be prosecuted to the bitter end. He also contrived at Nürnberg (June 1538) to form a league of Romanist princes, ostensibly for defence, but really to force the Protestants to submit to the decisions of the *Reichskammersgericht.* These measures did not make for peace; they almost produced a civil war, which was only avoided by the direct interposition of the Emperor.

Chancellor Held was recalled, and the Emperor sent the Archbishop of Lund to find out what terms the Protestants would accept. These proved larger than the Emperor could grant, but the result of the intercourse was that the Protestants were granted a truce which was to last for ten years.

The proposed secularisation of the ecclesiastical Electorates made Charles see that he dared not wait for the conclusion of this truce. He set himself earnestly to discover whether compromises in doctrine and ceremonies were not possible. Conferences were held between Lutheran and Romanist theologians and laymen, at Hagenau (June 1540), at Worms (November 1540), and at Regensburg

(Ratisbon, April 1541).[1] The last was the most important. The discussions showed that it was possible to state Romanist and Lutheran doctrine in ambiguous propositions which could be accepted by the theologians of both Confessions; but that there was a great gulf between them which the Evangelicals would never re-cross. The spiritual priesthood of all believers could never be reconciled with the special priesthood of the mediæval clergy. This was Charles' last attempt at a compromise which would unite of their own free will the German Lutherans with the German Romanists. He saw that the Lutherans would never return to the mediæval Church unless compelled by force, and it was impossible to use force unless the Schmalkald League was broken up altogether or seamed with divisions.

§ 10. *The Bigamy of Philip of Hesse.*[2]

The opportunity arrived. The triumphant Protestantism received its severest blow in the bigamy of Philip of Hesse, which involved the reputations of Bucer, Luther, and Melanchthon, as well as of the Landgrave.

Philip had married when barely nineteen a daughter of Duke George of Saxony. Latterly, he declared that it was impossible to maintain conjugal relations with her; that continence was impossible for him; that the condition in which he found himself harassed his whole life, and prevented him coming to the Lord's Table. In a case like his, Pope Clement VII. only a few years previously had permitted the husband to take a second wife, and why should not the Protestant divines permit him? He

[1] Spiegel, "Johannes Timannus Amsterodamus und die Colloquien zu Worms und Regensburg, 1540–1541" (*Zeitschrift für hist. Theologie*, xlii. (1872) 36 ff.); Moses, *Die Religionsverhandlungen in Hagenau und Worms, 1540-1541* (Jena, 1889).

[2] Heppe, "Urkundliche Beiträge zur Geschichte der Doppelehe des Landgrafen Philip v. Hessen" (*Zeitschrift für die historische Theologie*, xxii. (1852) 263 ff.), cf. xxxviii. 445 ff.; Schultze, *Luther und die Doppelehe des Landgrafen v. Hessen* (Paderborn (1869)).

prepared a case for himself which he submitted to the theologians, and got a reply signed by Bucer, Melanchthon, and Luther, which may be thus summarised:—

According to the original commandment of God, marriage is between one man and one woman, and the twain shall become one flesh, and this original precept has been confirmed by our Lord; but sin brought it about that first Lamech, then the heathen, and then Abraham, took more than one wife, and this was permitted by the law. We are now living under the gospel, which does not give prescribed rules for the regulation of the external life, and it has not expressly prohibited bigamy. The existing law of the land has gone back to the original requirement of God, and the plain duty of the pastorate is to insist on that original requirement of God, and to denounce bigamy in every way. Nevertheless the pastorate, in individual cases of the direst need, and to prevent worse, may sanction bigamy in a purely exceptional way; such a bigamous marriage is a true marriage (the necessity being proved) in the sight of God and of conscience; but it is not a true marriage with reference to public law or custom. Therefore such a marriage ought to be kept secret, and the dispensation which is given for it ought to be kept under the seal of confession. If it be made known, the dispensation becomes *eo ipso* invalid, and the marriage becomes mere concubinage.

Such was the strange and scandalous document to which Luther, Melanchthon, and Bucer appended their names.

Of course the thing could not be kept secret, and the moral effect of the revelation was disastrous among friends and foes. The Evangelical princes were especially aggrieved; and it was proposed that the Landgrave should be tried for bigamy and punished according to the laws of the Empire. When the matter was brought before the Emperor, he decided that no marriage had taken place, and the sole effect of the decision of the theologians was to deceive a poor maiden.[1]

[1] Luther's action is usually attributed to his desire not to offend a powerful Protestant leader. A careful study of the original documents in the case—correspondence and papers—does not confirm this view. To my mind, they show on Luther's part a somewhat sullen and crabbed con-

Philip, humiliated and sore, isolated from his friends, was an instrument ready to the Emperor's hand in his plan to weaken and, if possible, destroy the Schmalkald League. The opportunity soon arrived. The father of William Duke of Cleves Juliers and Berg had been elected by the Estates of Guelders to be their sovereign, in defiance of a treaty which had secured the succession to Charles. The father died, and the son succeeded almost immediately after the treaty had been signed. This created a powerful anti-Hapsburg State in close proximity to the Emperor's possessions in the Netherlands. William of Cleves had married his sister Sibylla to John Frederick, the Elector of Saxony, and naturally gravitated towards the Schmalkald League. In 1541 an arrangement was come to between the Emperor and Philip, according to which Philip guaranteed to prevent the Duke of Cleves from joining the League, or at least from being supported by it against the Emperor, and in return Philip was promised indemnity for all past deeds, and advancement in the Emperor's service. Young Maurice of Ducal Saxony, who had succeeded his father in the Duchy (August 18th, 1541), and had married Philip's daughter, also joined in this bargain. The Emperor had thus divided the great Protestant League; for the Elector of Saxony refused to desert his brother-in-law. In 1543 the Emperor fell upon the unbefriended Duke, totally defeated him, and took Guelders from him, while the German Protestants,

scientious fidelity to a conviction which he always maintained. With all his reverence for the word of God, he could never avoid giving a very large authority to the traditions of the Church when they did not plainly contradict a positive and direct divine commandment. The Church had been accustomed to say that it possessed a dispensing power in matrimonial cases of extreme difficulty; and, in spite of his denunciations of the dispensations granted by the Roman Curia, Luther never denied the power. On the contrary, he thought honestly that the Church did possess this power of dispensation even to the length of tampering with a fundamental law of Christian society, provided it did not contradict a *positive* scriptural commandment to the contrary. The crime of the Curia, in his eyes, was not issuing dispensations in *necessary cases*, but in giving them in cases without proved necessity, *and for money*.

hindered by Philip, saw one of their most important allies overthrown. This gave rise to recriminations, which effectually weakened the Protestant cause.

In 1544, Charles concluded a peace with France (the Peace of Crépy, November 19th), and was free to turn his attention to affairs in Germany. He forced the Pope in the same month to give way about a General Council, which was fixed to meet in March 1545. The Emperor meant this Council to be an instrument in his hands to subdue both the Protestants and the Pope. He meant it to reform the Church in the sense of freeing it from many of the corruptions which had found their way into it, and especially in diminishing the power of the Roman Curia; and in this he was supported by the Spanish bishops and by the greater part of Latin Christendom. But the Pope was the more skilful diplomatist, and out-generalled the Emperor. The Council was summoned to meet at Trent, a purely Italian town, though nominally within Germany. It was arranged that all its members must be present personally and not by deputies, which meant that the Italian bishops had a permanent majority; and the choice of Dominicans and Jesuits as the leading theologians made it plain that no doctrinal concessions would be made to the Protestants. From the first the Protestants refused to be bound in any way by its decisions, and Charles soon perceived that the instrument he had counted on had broken in his hands. If ecclesiastical unity was to be maintained in Germany, it could only be by the use of force. There is no doubt that the Emperor was loath to proceed to this last extremity; but his correspondence with his sister Mary and with his brother Ferdinand shows that he had come to regard it as a necessity by the middle of 1545.

His first endeavour was to break up the Protestant League, which was once more united. He attempted again to detach Philip of Hesse, but without success. He was able, however, to induce the Elector of Brandenburg and the Margrave of Brandenburg-Culmbach and some others to remain neutral—the Elector by promising in any event that the religious settlement which had been effected in Brandenburg (1541) should remain unaltered; and, what served him best, he persuaded young Maurice of Ducal Saxony to become his active ally.

§ 11. *Maurice of Saxony.*

Maurice of Saxony was one of the most interesting, because one of the most perplexing personalities of his time, which was rich in interesting personalities. He was a Protestant from conviction, and never wavered from his faith; yet in the conflict between the Romanist Emperor and the Protestant princes he took the Emperor's side, and contributed more than any one else to the overthrow of his fellow Protestants. His bargain with Charles was that the Electorate should be transferred from the Ernestine Saxon family to his own, the Albertine, that he should get Magdeburg and Halberstadt, and that neither he nor his people should be subject to the decrees of the Council of Trent. Then, when he had despoiled the rival family of the Electorate, he planned and carried through the successful revolt of the Protestant princes against the Emperor, and was mainly instrumental in securing the public recognition of Lutheranism in Germany and in gaining the permanent Religious Peace of 1555.[1]

§ 12. *Luther's Death.*

It was in these months, while the alarms of war were threatening Germany, that Luther passed away. He had

[1] Ranke has an interesting study of the character of Maurice in his *Deutsche Geschichte im Zeitalter der Reformation*, bk. ix. chap. vi. (vol. v. pp. 161 ff. of the 6th ed., Leipzig, 1882); but perhaps the best is given in Maurenbrecher, *Studien und Skizzen zur Geschichte der Reformationszeit* (Leipzig, 1874), pp. 135 ff. A man's deep religious convictions can tolerate strange company in most ages, and the fact that we find Romanist champions in France plunging into the deepest profligacy the one week and then undergoing the agonies of repentance the next, or that Lutheran leaders combined occasional conjugal infidelities and drinking bouts with zeal for evangelical principles, demands deeper study in psychology than can find expression, in the fashion of some modern English historians, in a few cheap sneers.

been growing weaker year by year, and had never spared himself for the cause he had at heart. One last bit of work he thought he must do. The Counts of Mansfeld had quarrelled over some trifling things in the division of their property, and had consented to accept Luther's mediation. This obliged him to journey to Eisleben in bitterly cold weather (January 1546). "I would cheerfully lay down my bones in the grave if I could only reconcile my dear Lords," he said; and that was what was required from him. He finished the arbitration to the satisfaction of both brothers, and received by way of fee endowments for village schools in the Mansfeld region. The deeds were all signed by the 17th of February (1546), and Luther's work was done at Mansfeld—and for his generation. He became alarmingly ill that night, and died on the following morning, long before dawn. "Reverend Father," said Justus Jonas, who was with him, "wilt thou stand by Christ and the doctrine thou hast preached?" The dying man roused himself to say "Yes." It was his last word. Twenty minutes later he passed away with a deep sigh.

Luther died in his sixty-third year—twenty-eight and a half years after he had, greatly daring, nailed his Theses to the door of All Saints' in Wittenberg, twenty-seven after he had discovered the meaning of his Theses during the memorable days when he faced Eck at Leipzig, and twenty-five after he had stood before the Emperor and Diet at Worms, while all Germany had hailed him as its champion against the Pope and the Spaniard. The years between 1519 and 1524 were, from an external point of view, the most glorious of Luther's life. He dominated and led his nation, and gave a unity to that distracted and divided country which it had never enjoyed until then. He spoke and felt like a prophet. "I have the gospel, not from men, but from heaven through our Lord Jesus Christ, so that I might have described myself and have glorified in being a minister and an evangelist." The position had come to him in no sudden visionary way. He had been led into it step by step, forced forward slowly by a power stronger than his own; and the knowledge had kept him humble before his God. During these years it seemed as if his dream—an expectation shared by his wise Elector, the most experienced statesman in Germany—of a Germany united under one National Church, separated from the bondage of Rome, repudiating her blasphemies, rejecting her traditions which had corrupted the religion of the ancient and purer days, and disowning her presumptuous encroachments on the domain of the civil power ordained of God, was about to come true.

Then came the disillusionment of the Peasants' War, when the dragon's teeth were sown broadcast over Germany, and produced their crop of gloomy suspicions and black fears. After the insurrection had spent itself, and in spite of the almost irretrievable damage which it, and the use made of it by papal diplomatists, did to the Reformation movement, Luther regained his serene courage, and recovered much of the ground which had been lost. But the crushing blow had left its mark upon him. He had the same trust in God, but much more distrust of man, fearing the "tumult," resolute to have nothing to do with anyone who had any connection, however slight, with those who had instigated the misguided peasants. He rallied the forces of the Reformation, and brought them back to discipline by the faith they had in himself as their leader. His personality dominated those kinglets of Germany, possessed with as strong a sense of their dignity and autocratic rights as any Tudor or Valois, and they submitted to be led by him. Electoral Saxony, Hesse, Lüneburg, Anhalt, East Prussia, and Mansfeld, and some score of imperial cities, had followed him loyally from the first; and as the years passed, Ducal Saxony and Würtemberg in the centre and south, and Brandenburg in the north, had declared themselves Protestant States. These larger principalities brought in their train all the smaller satellite States which clustered round them. It may be said that before Luther's death the much larger portion of the German Empire had been won for evangelical religion,—a territory to be roughly described as a great triangle, whose base was the shores of the Baltic Sea from the Netherlands on the west to the eastern limits of East Prussia, and whose apex was Switzerland. Part of this land was occupied by ecclesiastical principalities which had remained Roman Catholic,—the districts surrounding Köln on the west, and the territories of Paderborn, Fulda, and many others in the centre,—but, on the other hand, many stoutly Protestant cities, like Nürnberg, Constance, and Augsburg, were planted on territories which were outside these limits. The extent and power of this Protestant Germany was sufficient to resist any attempt on the part of the Emperor and the Catholic princes to overcome it by force of arms, provided only its rulers remained true to each other.

Over this wide extent of country Evangelical Churches had been established, and provisions had been made for the education of children and for the support of the poor in ordinances issued by the supreme secular authorities who ruled over its multitudinous divisions. The Mass, with its supposed substitutionary sacrifice and a mediatorial priesthood, had been abolished. The German tongue had displaced mediæval Latin in public worship, and the worshippers could take part in the services with full understanding of the solemn acts in which they were engaged. A German Bible lay on every pulpit, and the people had their copies in the pews. Translations of the Psalms and German evangelical hymns were sung, and sermons in German were preached. Pains were taken to provide an educated evangelical ministry who would preach the gospel faithfully, and conscientiously fulfil all the duties connected with the "cure of souls." The ecclesiastical property of the mediæval Church was largely used for evangelical purposes. There was no mechanical uniformity in these new arrangements. Luther refused to act the part of an ecclesiastical autocrat: he advised when called upon to give advice, he never commanded. No Wittenberg "use" was to confront the Roman "use" and be the only mode of service and ecclesiastical organisation.

The movement Luther had inaugurated had gone far beyond Germany before 1546. Every country in Europe had felt its pulsations. As early as 1519 (April), learned men in Paris had been almost feverishly studying his writings.[1] They were eagerly read in England before 1521.[2] Aleander, writing from Worms to the Curia, complains that Spanish merchants were getting translations of Luther's books made for circulation in Spain.[3] They were being studied with admiration in Italy even earlier. The Scottish Parliament was vainly endeavouring to prevent their entrance into that country by 1525.[4] The Lutheran Reformation had been legally established in Denmark, Norway, and Sweden long before Luther passed away.

Luther was the one great man of his generation, standing head and shoulders above everyone else. This does not mean that he absorbed in his individual personality everything that the age produced for the furtherance of humanity. Many impulses for good existed in that sixteenth century which Luther never recognised; for an age is always richer than any one man belonging to it. He stood outside the great artistic movement. He might have learned much from Erasmus on the one hand, and from the leaders of the Peasants' War on the other, which remained hidden from him. He is greatest in the one sphere of religion only—in the greatest of all spheres. His conduct towards Zwingli and the strong language he used in speaking of opponents make our generation discover a strain of intolerance we would fain not see in so great a man; but his contemporaries did not and could not pass the same judgment upon him. In such a divided Germany none but a man of the widest tolerance could have held together the Protestant forces as Luther did;

[1] Herminjard, *Correspondance des Reformateurs dans les pays de langue française* (Geneva and Paris, 1866–1897), i. 47, 48.

[2] *Letters and Papers, Foreign and Domestic, of the reign of Henry VIII.*, iii. 284.

[3] Kalkoff, *Die Depeschen des Nuntius Aleander* (Halle, 1897), p. 106.

[4] *Acts of the Parliament of Scotland* for 1525 and 1527.

and we can see what he was when we remember the sad effects of the petty orthodoxies of the Amsdorfs and the Osianders who came after him.

It is the fate of most authors of revolutions to be devoured by the movement which they have called into being. Luther occasioned the greatest revolution which Western Europe has ever seen, and he ruled it till his death. History shows no kinglier man than this Thuringian miner's son.

§ 13. *The Religious War.*[1]

The war began soon after Luther's death. The Emperor brought into Germany his Spanish infantry, the beginning of what was to be a curse to that country for many generations, and various manœuvrings and skirmishes took place, the most important of which was Maurice of Saxony's invasion of the Electorate. At last the Emperor met the Elector in battle at Mühlberg (April 24th, 1547), where John Frederick was completely defeated and taken prisoner. Wittenberg, stoutly defended by Sibylla, soon after surrendered. This was the end. Philip was induced to surrender on promise of favourable treatment, made by the Electors who had remained on the Emperor's side. Charles refused to be bound by the promise made in his name, and the Landgrave was also held captive. All Germany, save Constance in the south and some of the Baltic lands, lay prostrate at the Emperor's feet. It remained to be seen what use he would make of his victory.

In due time he set himself to bring about what he conceived to be a reasonable compromise which would enable all Germany to remain within one National Church. He tried at first to induce the separate parties to work

[1] Maurenbrecher, *Karl V. und die deutschen Protestanten 1545–1555* (Düsseldorf, 1865); Jahn, *Geschichte des Schmalkaldischen Krieges* (Leipzig, 1837); Le Mang, *Die Darstellung des Schmalkaldischen Krieges in den Denkwürdigkeiten Karls V.* (Jena, 1890, 1899, 1900); Brandenburg, *Moritz von Sachsen* (Leipzig, 1898).

it out among themselves; and, when this was found to be hopeless, he, like a second Justinian, resolved to construct a creed and to impose it by force upon all, especially upon the Lutherans. To begin with, he had to defy the Pope and slight the General Council for which he had been mainly responsible. He formally demanded that the Council should return to German soil (it had been transferred to Bologna), and, when this was refused, he protested against its existence and, like the German Protestants he was coercing, declared that he would not submit to its decrees. He next selected three theologians, Michael Helding, Julius von Pflug, and Agricola,—a mediævalist, an Erasmian, and a very conservative Lutheran —to construct what was called the *Augsburg Interim.*

§ 14. *The Augsburg Interim.*[1]

This document taught the dogma of Transubstantiation, the seven Sacraments, adoration of the Blessed Virgin and the Saints, retained most of the mediæval ceremonies and usages, and declared the Pope to be the Head of the Church. This was to please the Romanists. It appealed to the Lutherans by adopting the doctrine of Justification by Faith in a modified form, the marriage of priests with some reservations, the use of the Cup by the laity in the Holy Supper, and by considerably modifying the doctrine of the sacrificial character of the Mass. Of course all its propositions were ambiguous, and could be read in two ways. This was probably the intention of the framers; if so, they were highly successful.

Nothing that Charles ever undertook proved such a dismal failure as this patchwork creed made from snippets from two Confessions. However lifeless creeds may become, they all—real ones—have grown out of the living Christian

[1] Schmidt, "Agenda and Letters relating to the *Interim,*" in *Zeitschrift für historisch. Theologie,* xxxviii. (1868) pp. 431 ff., 461 ff.; Beutel, *Über den Ursprung des Augsburger Interim* (Leipzig, 1888); Meyer, *Der Augsburger Reichstag nach einem fürstlichen Tagebuch* (*Preus. Jahrb.* 1898, pp. 206–242).

experience of their framers, and have contained the very life-blood of their hearts as well as of their brains. It is a hopeless task to construct creeds as a tailor shapes and stitches coats.

Charles, however, was proud of his creed, and did his best to enforce it The Diet of 1548 showed him his difficulties. The *Interim* was accepted and proclaimed as an edict by this Diet (May 15), but only after the Emperor, very unwillingly, declared practically that it was meant for the Protestants alone. "The Emperor," said a member of the Diet, "is fighting for religion against the Pope, whom he acknowledges to be its head, and against the two parts of Christendom in Germany—the mass of the Protestants and the ecclesiastical princes." Thus from the beginning what was to be an instrument to unite German Christendom was transformed into a "strait-waistcoat for the Lutherans"; and this did not make it more palatable for them. At first the strong measures taken by the Emperor compelled its nominal acceptance by many of the Protestant princes.[1] The cities which seemed to be most refractory had their Councils purged of their democratic members, and their Lutheran preachers sent into banishment—Matthew Alber from Reutlingen, Wolfgang Musculus from Augsburg, Brenz from Hall, Osiander from Nürnberg, Schnepf from Tübingen. Bucer and Fagius had to flee from Strassburg and take refuge in England. The city of Constance was besieged and fell after a heroic defence; it was deprived of its privileges as an imperial city, and was added to the family possessions of the House of Austria. Its pastor, Blarer, was sent into banishment. Four hundred Lutheran divines were driven from their homes.

If Charles, backed by his Spanish and Italian troops, could secure a nominal submission to his *Interim*, he could not coerce the people into accepting it. The churches stood empty in Augsburg, in Ulm, and in other cities. The

[1] Maurice of Saxony was permitted to make some alterations on the *Interim* for his dominions, and his edition was called the *Leipzig Interim*.

people met it by an almost universal passive resistance—if singing doggerel verses in mockery of the *Interim* may be called passive. When the Emperor ordered Duke Christopher of Würtemberg to drive Brenz out of his refuge in his State, the Duke answered him that he could not banish his whole population. The popular feeling, as is usual in such cases, found vent in all manner of satirical songs, pamphlets, and even catechisms. As in the times before the Peasants' War, this coarse popular literature had an immense circulation. Much of it took the form of rude broadsides with a picture, generally satirical, at the top, and the song, sometimes with the music score, printed below.[1] Wandering preachers, whom no amount of police supervision could check, went inveighing against the *Interim*, distributing the rude literature through the villages and among the democracy in the towns. Soon the creed and the edict which enforced it became practically a dead letter throughout the greater part of Germany.

The presence of the Emperor's Spanish troops on the soil of the Fatherland irritated the feelings of Germans, whether Romanists or Protestants; the insolence and excesses of these soldiers stung the common people; and their employment to enforce the hated *Interim* on the Protestants was an additional insult. The citizens of one imperial city were told that if they did not accept the *Interim* they must be taught theology by Spanish troops, and of another that they would yet learn to speak the language of Spain. While the popular odium against Charles was slowly growing in intensity, he contrived to increase it by a proposal that his son Philip should have the imperial crown after his brother Ferdinand. Charles' own election had been caused by a patriotic sentiment. The people thought that a German was better than a Frenchman, and they had found out too late that they had not got a German but a Spaniard. Ferdinand had lived in Germany long enough to know its wants, and his son

[1] One of these broadsides is reproduced in von Bezold's *Geschichte der deutschen Reformation* (Berlin, 1890), p. 806.

Maximilian had shown that he possessed many qualities which appealed to the German character. The proposal to substitute Philip, however natural from Charles' point of view, and consistent with his earlier idea that the House of Hapsburg should have one head, meant to the Germans to still further "hispaniolate" Germany. This unpopularity of Charles among all ranks and classes of Germans grew rapidly between 1548 and 1552; and during the same years his foreign prestige was fast waning. He remained in Germany, with the exception of a short visit to the Netherlands; but in spite of his presence the anarchy grew worse and worse. The revolt which came might have arisen much sooner had the Protestants been able to overcome their hatred and suspicion of Maurice of Saxony, whose co-operation was almost essential. It is unnecessary to describe the intrigues which went on around the Emperor, careless though not unforewarned.

Maurice had completed his arrangements with his German allies and with France early in 1552. The Emperor had retired from Augsburg to Innsbruck. Maurice seized the Pass of Ehrenberg on the nights of May 18th, 19th, and pressed on to Innsbruck, hoping to "run the old fox to earth." Charles escaped by a few hours, and, accompanied by his brother Ferdinand, fled over the Brenner Pass amid a storm of snow and rain. It was the road by which he had entered Germany in fair spring weather when he came in 1530, in the zenith of his power, to settle, as he had confidently expected, the religious difficulties in Germany. He reached Villach in Carinthia in safety, and there waited the issue of events.

The German princes gathered in great numbers at Passau (Aug. 1552) to discuss the position and arrive at a settlement. Maurice was ostensibly the master of the situation, for his troops and those of his wild ally Albert Alcibiades of Brandenburg-Culmbach were in the town, and many a prince felt "as if they had a hare in their breast." His demands for the public good were moderate and statesmanlike. He asked for the immediate release of his father-in-law the Landgrave of Hesse; for a settlement of the religious question on a basis that would be permanent, at a meeting of German princes fairly representative of the two parties—no Council summoned and directed by the Pope would ever give fair-play to the Protestants, he said, nor could they expect to get it from the Diet where the large number of ecclesiastical members gave an undue preponderance to the Romanist side; and for a settlement of some constitutional questions. The princes present, and with them Ferdinand, King of the Romans, were inclined to accept these demands. But when they were referred to Charles at Villach, he absolutely refused to permit the religious or the constitutional question to be settled by any assembly but the Diet of the Empire. Nothing would move him from his opinion, neither the entreaties of his brother nor his own personal danger. He still counted on the divisions among the Protestants, and believed that he had only to support the "born Elector" of Saxony against the one of his own creation to deprive Maurice of his strength. It may be that Maurice had his own fears, it may be that he was glad to have the opportunity of showing that the "Spaniard" was the one enemy to a lasting peace in Germany. He contented himself with the acquiescence of John Frederick in the permanent loss of the Electorate as arranged at the Peace of Wittenberg (1547).

Charles was then free to come back to Augsburg, where he had the petty satisfaction of threatening the Lutheran preachers who had returned, and of again overthrowing the democratic government of the city. He then went to assume the command of the German army which was opposing the French. His failure to take the city of Metz was followed by his practical abandonment of the direction of the affairs of Germany, which were left in the hands of Ferdinand. The disorders of the time delayed the meeting of the Diet until 1555 (opened Feb. 5th). The Elector and the "born Elector" of Saxony were both dead—John Frederick, worn out by misfortune and imprisonment (March 3rd, 1554), and sympathised with by friends and foes alike; and Maurice, only thirty-two years of age, killed in the moment of victory at Sievershausen (July 9th, 1553).

It was in the summer of 1554 that the Emperor had handed over, in a carefully limited manner, the management of German affairs to his brother Ferdinand, the King of the Romans. The terms of devolution of authority imply that this was done by Charles to avoid the humiliation of being personally responsible for acquiescence in what was to him a hateful necessity, and the confession of failure in his management of Germany from 1530. Everyone recognised that peace was necessary at almost any price, but Ferdinand and the higher ecclesiastical princes shrunk from facing the inevitable. The King of the Romans still cherished some vague hopes of a compromise which would preserve the unity of the mediæval German Church, and the selfish policy of many of the Protestant princes encouraged him. Elector Joachim of Brandenburg wished the archbishopric of Magdeburg and the bishopric of Halberstadt for his son Sigismund, and declared that he would be content with the *Interim*! Christopher of Würtemberg cherished similar designs on ecclesiastical properties. Augustus of Saxony, Maurice's brother and successor, wished the bishopric of Meissen. All these designs could be more easily fulfilled if the external unity of the mediæval Church remained unbroken.

§ 15. *Religious Peace of Augsburg.*[1]

The Diet had been summoned for Nov. 13th (1554), but when Ferdinand reached Augsburg about the end of the year, the Estates had not gathered. He was able to open the Diet formally on Feb. 5th (1555), but none of the Electors, and only two of the great ecclesiastical princes, the Cardinal Bishop of Augsburg and the Bishop

[1] Wolf, *Der Augsburger Religionsfriede* (Stuttgart, 1890); Brandi, *Der Augsburger Religionsfriede* (Munich, 1896); Druffel, *Beiträge zur Reichs geschichte, 1553–1555* (Munich, 1896).

of Eichstadt, were present in person. While the Diet dragged on aimlessly, the Protestant princes gathered to a great Council of their own at Naumburg (March 3rd, 1555) to concert a common policy. Among those present were the Electors of Brandenburg and Saxony, the sons of John Frederick, the ill-fated "born Elector," and the Landgrave of Hesse—sixteen princes and a great number of magnates. After long debates, the assembly decided (March 13th) that they would stand by the Augsburg Confession of 1530, and that the minority would unite with the majority in carrying out one common policy. Even "fat old Interim," as Elector Joachim of Brandenburg had been nicknamed, was compelled to submit; and the Protestants stood on a firm basis with a definite programme, and pledged to support each other.

This memorable meeting at Naumburg forced the hands of the members of the Diet. Every member, save the Cardinal Bishop of Augsburg, desired a *permanent* settlement of the religious question, and their zeal appeared in the multiplicity of adjectives used to express the predominant thought—"*beständiger, beharrlicher, unbedingter, für und für ewig währender*" was the phrase. The meeting at Naumburg showed them that this could not be secured without the recognition of Lutheranism as a legal religion within the German Empire.

When the Protestant demands were formally placed before the Diet, they were found to include—security under the Public Law of the Empire for all who professed the Augsburg Confession, and for all who in future might make the same profession; liberty to hold legally all the ecclesiastical property which had been or might in the future be secularised; complete toleration for all Lutherans who were resident in Romanist States without corresponding toleration for Romanists in Lutheran States. These demands went much further than any which Luther himself had formulated, and really applied to Romanists some of the provisions of the "recess" of Speyer (1529) which, when applied to Lutherans, had called forth the Protest.

They were vehemently objected to by the Romanist members of the Diet; and, as both parties seemed unwilling to yield anything to the other, there was some danger of the religious war breaking out again. The mediation of Ferdinand for the Romanists and Frederick of Saxony for the Protestants brought a compromise after months of debate. It was agreed that the Lutheran religion should be legalised within the Empire, and that all Lutheran princes should have full security for the practice of their faith; that the mediæval episcopal jurisdiction should cease within their lands; and that they were to retain all ecclesiastical possessions which had been secularised before the passing of the Treaty of Passau (1552). Future changes of faith were to be determined by the principle *cujus regio ejus religio.* The secular territorial ruler might choose between the Romanist or the Lutheran faith, and his decision was to bind all his subjects. If a subject professed another religion from his prince, he was to be allowed to emigrate without molestation. These provisions were agreed upon by all, and embodied in the "recess." Two very important matters remained unsettled. The Romanists demanded that any ecclesiastical prince who changed his faith should thereby forfeit lands and dignities—the "ecclesiastical reservation." This was embodied in the "recess," but the Protestants declared that they would not be bound by it. On the other hand, the Protestants demanded toleration for all Lutherans living within the territories of Romanist princes. This was not embodied in the "recess," though Ferdinand promised that he would see it carried out in practice.[1] Such was the famous Peace of Augsburg. There was no reason why it should not have come years earlier and without the wild war-storm which preceded it, save the fact that, in an unfortunate fit of enthusiasm, the Germans had elected the young King of Spain to be their Emperor. They had chosen the grandson of the genial Maxmilian, believing him to be a real German, and they got a man

[1] These two unsettled questions became active in the disputes which began the Thirty Years' War

whose attitude to religion "was half-way between the genial orthodoxy of his grandfather Maxmilian and the gloomy fanaticism of his son Philip II.," and whose "mind was always travelling away from the former and towards the latter position."[1] The longer he lived the more Spanish he became, and the less capable of understanding Germany, either on its secular or religious side. His whole public life, so far as that country was concerned, was one disastrous failure. He succeeded only when he used his imperial position to increase and consolidate the territorial possessions of the House of Hapsburg; for the charge of dismembering the Empire can be brought home to Charles as effectually as to the most selfish of the princes of Germany.

The Religious Peace of Augsburg was contained in the decisions of Speyer in 1526, and it was repeated in every one of the truces which the Emperor made with his Lutheran subjects from 1530 to 1544.[2] Had any one of these been made permanent, the religious war, with its

[1] Pollard, *Cambridge Modern History*, ii. 144.

[2] The Religious Peace of Augsburg had important diplomatic consequences beyond Germany. The Lutheran form of faith was recognised to be a *religio licita* (to use the old Roman phrase) within the Holy Roman Empire, which, according to the legal ideas of the day, included all Western Christendom; and Popes could no longer excommunicate Protestants simply because they were Protestants, without striking a serious blow at the constitution of the Empire. No one perceived this sooner than the sagacious young woman who became the first Protestant Queen of England. In the earlier and unsettled years of her reign, Elizabeth made full use of the protection that a profession of the Lutheran Creed gave to shield her from excommunication. She did so when the Count de Feria, the ambassador of Philip II., threatened her with the fate of the King of Navarre (*Calendar of Letters and State Papers relating to English Affairs, preserved principally in the Archives of Simancas*, i. 61, 62); she suppressed all opinions which might be supposed to conflict with the Lutheran Creed in the Thirty-eight Articles of 1563; she kept crosses and lights on the altar of her chapel in Lutheran fashion. When the Pope first drafted a Bull to excommunicate the English Queen, and submitted it to the Emperor, he was told that it would be an act of folly to publish a document which would invalidate the Emperor's own election; and when Elizabeth was finally excommunicated in 1570, the charge against her was not being a Protestant, but sharing in "the impious mysteries of Calvin"—the Reformed or Calvinist Churches being outside the Peace of Augsburg.

outcome in wild anarchy, in embittered religious antagonisms, and its seed of internecine strife, to be reaped in the Thirty Years' War, would never have occurred. But Charles, whose mission, he fancied, was to preserve the unity "of the seamless robe of Christ," as he phrased it, could only make the attempt by drenching the fields of Germany with blood, and perpetuating and accentuating the religious antagonisms of the country which had chosen him for its Protector.

This Religious Peace of Augsburg has been claimed, and rightly, as a victory for religious liberty.

From one point of view the victory was not a great one. The only Confession tolerated was the Augsburg. The Swiss Reformation and its adherents were outside the scope of the religious peace. What grew to be the Reformed or Calvinistic Church was also outside. It was limited solely to the Lutheran, or, as it was called, the Evangelical creed. Nor was there much gain to the personal liberty of conscience. It may be said with truth that there was less freedom of conscience under the Lutheran territorial system of Churches, and also under the Roman Catholic Church reorganised under the canons and decrees of Trent, than there had been in the mediæval Church.

The victory lay in this, that the first blow had been struck to free mankind from the fetters of Romanist absolutism; that the first faltering step had been taken on the road to religious liberty; and the first is valuable not for what it is in itself, but for what it represents and for what comes after it. The Religious Peace of Augsburg did not concede much according to modern standards; but it contained the potency and promise of the future. It is always the first step which counts.

CHAPTER VI.

THE ORGANISATION OF LUTHERAN CHURCHES.[1]

Two conceptions, the second being derived from the first, lay at the basis of everything which Luther said or did about the organisation of the Christian fellowship into churches.

The primary and cardinal doctrine, which was the foundation of everything, was the spiritual priesthood of all believers. This, he believed, implied that preaching, dispensing the sacraments, ecclesiastical discipline, and so forth were not the exclusive possession of a special caste of men to whom they had been committed by God, and who therefore were mediators between God and man. These divine duties belonged to the whole community as a fellowship of believing men and women; but as a division of labour was necessary, and as each individual Christian cannot undertake such duties without disorder ensuing, the community must seek out and set apart certain of its members to perform them in its name.

[1] Sources: Richter, *Die evangelischen Kirchenordnungen des sechszehnten Jahrhunderts* (Weimar, 1846); Sehling, *Die evangelischen Kirchenordnungen des 16ten Jahrhunderts* (Leipzig, 1902); Kins, "Das Stipendiumwesen in Wittenberg und Jena . . . im 16ten Jahrhundert" (*Zeitschrift für historische Theologie*, xxxv. (1865) pp. 96 ff.); G. Schmidt, "Eine Kirchenvisitation im Jahre 1525" (*Zeitschrift für die hist. Theol.* xxxv. 291 ff.); Winter, "Die Kirchenvisitation von 1528 im Wittenberger Kreise" (*Zeitsch. für hist. Theol.* xxxiii. (1863) 295 ff.); Muther, "Drei Urkunden zur Reformationsgeschichte" (*Zeitschr. für hist. Theol.* xxx. (1860) 452 ff.); Albrecht, *Der Kleine Catechismus für die gemeine Pfarher und Prediger* (facsimile reprint of edition of 1536; Halle a. S. 1905).

Later Books: Kästner, *Die Kinderfragen: Der erste deutsche Katechismus* (Leipzig, 1902); Burkhardt, *Geschichte der deutschen Kirchen- und Schulvisitation im Zeitalter der Reformation* (Leipzig, 1879); Berlit, *Luther, Murner und das Kirchenlied des 16ten Jahrhunderts* (Leipzig, 1899).

The second conception was that secular government is an ordinance ordained of God, and that the special rule claimed by the Roman Pontiff over things secular and sacred was a usurpation of the powers committed by God to the secular authority. This Luther understood to mean that the Christian magistracy might well represent the Christian community of believers, and, in its name or associated with it, undertake the organisation and superintendence of the Church civic or territorial.

In his earlier writings, penned before the outbreak of the Peasants' War, Luther dwells most on the thought of the community of believers, their rights and powers; in the later ones, when the fear of the common man had taken possession of him, the secular authority occupies his whole field of thought. But although, before the Peasants' War, Luther does not give such a fixed place to the secular magistracy as the one source of authority or supervision over the Church, the conception was in his mind from the first.

Among the various duties which belong to the company of believers, Luther selected three as the most outstanding,—those connected with the pastorate, including preaching, dispensing the sacraments, and so forth; the service of Christian charity; and the duty of seeing that the children belonging to the community, and especially "poor, miserable, and deserted children," were properly educated and trained to become useful members of the commonwealth.

In the few instances of attempts made before the Peasants' War to formulate those conceptions into regulations for communities organised according to evangelical principles, we find the community and the magistracy combining to look after the public worship, the poor, and education. Illustrations may be seen in the Wittenberg ordinance of 1522 (Carlstadt), and the ordinances of Leisnig (1523) and Magdeburg (1524).[1] All three are examples of the

[1] Cf. for the Wittenberg ordinance, Richter, *Die evangelischen Kirchenordnungen des sechszehnten Jahrhunderts* (Weimar, 1846), ii. 484, and

local authority within a small community endeavouring, at the prompting of preachers and people, to express in definite regulations some of the demands of the new evangelical life.

Luther himself thought these earlier regulations premature, and insisted that the Wittenberg ordinance should be cancelled. He knew that changes must come; but he hoped to see them make their way gradually, almost imperceptibly, commending themselves to everyone without special enactment prescribed by external authority. He published *suggestions* for the dispensation of the Lord's Supper and of Baptism in the churches in Wittenberg as early as 1523; he collected and issued a small selection of evangelical hymns which *might* be sung in Public Worship (1524); during the same year he addressed the burgomasters and councillors of all German towns on the erection and maintenance of Christian schools; and he congratulated more than one municipality on provisions made for the care of the poor.[1] Above all, he had, while in Wartburg, completed a translation of the New Testament which, after revision by Melanchthon and other friends, was published in 1522 (Sept. 21st), and went through sixteen revised editions and more than fifty re-impressions before 1534. The translation of the Old Testament was made by a band of scholars at Wittenberg, published in instalments, and finally in complete form in 1534.

He always cherished the hope that the evangelical faith would spread quietly all over his dear Fatherland if only room were made for the preaching of the gospel.

Sehling, *Die evangelischen Kirchenordnungen des 16ten Jahrhunderts* (Leipzig, 1902), I. i. 697; for Leisnig, Richter, i. 10. An account of the Magdeburg ordinance is to be found in Funk, *Mittheilungen aus der Geschichte des evangelischen Kirchenwesens in Magdeburg* (Magdeburg, 1842), p. 210, and Richter, i. 17.

[1] Luther's early suggestions about the dispensation of the sacraments have been collected by Sehling, I. i. 2, 18. A portion of the hymn-book has been reproduced in facsimile in von Bezold's *Geschichte der deutschen Reformation*, Berlin, 1890, p. 566.

This of itself, he thought, would in due time effect a peaceful transformation of the ecclesiastical life and worship. The Diets of Nürnberg and Speyer had provided a field, always growing wider, for this quiet transformation. Luther was as indifferent to forms of Church government as John Wesley, and, like Wesley, every step he took in providing for a separate organisation was forced upon him as a practical necessity. To the very last he cherished the hope that there might be no need for any great change in the external government of the Church. The Augsburg Confession itself (1530) concludes with the words: "Our meaning is not to have rule taken from the bishops; but this one thing only is requested at their hands, that they would suffer the gospel to be purely taught, and that they would relax a few observances, which cannot be held without sin. But if they will remit none, let them look how they will give account to God for this, that by their obstinacy they afford cause of division and schism, which it were yet fit they should aid in avoiding."[1] It was not that he believed that the existence of the visible Catholic Church depended on what has been ambiguously called an apostolic succession of bishops, who, through gifts conferred in ordination, create priests, who in turn make Christians out of natural heathen by the sacraments. He did not believe that ordination needed a bishop to confer it; he made his position clear upon this point as early as 1525, and ordination was practised without bishops from that date. But he had no desire to make changes for the sake of change. The Danish Church is at once episcopal and Lutheran to this day.

It ought also to be remembered that Luther and all the Reformers believed and held firmly the doctrine of a visible Catholic Church of Christ, and that the evangelical movement which they headed was the outcome of the centuries of saintly life *within* that visible Catholic Church. They never for a moment supposed that in withdrawing themselves from the authority of the Bishop

[1] Schaff, *The Creeds of the Evangelical Protestant Churches*, p. 72.

of Rome they were separating themselves from the visible Church. Nor did they imagine that in making provision, temporary or permanent, for preaching the word, the dispensation of the sacraments, the exercise of discipline, and so forth, they were founding a new Church, or severing themselves from that visible Church within which they had been baptized. They refused to concede the term *Catholic* to their opponents, and in the various conferences which they had with them, the Roman Catholics were always *officially* designated "the adherents of the old religion," while they were termed "the associates of the Augsburg Confession."

Luther cherished the hope, as late as 1545, that there might not need to be a permanent change in the external form of the Church in Germany; and this gives all the earlier schemes for the organisation of communities professing the evangelical faith somewhat of a makeshift and temporary appearance, which they in truth possessed.

The Diet of Speyer of 1526 gave the evangelical princes and towns the right, they believed, to reorganise public worship and ecclesiastical organisation within their dominions, and this right was largely taken advantage of. Correspondents from all quarters asked Luther's advice and co-operation, and we can learn from his answers that he was anxious there should be as much local freedom as possible,—that communities should try to find out what suited them best, and that the "use" of Wittenberg should not be held to regulate the custom of all other places.

It was less difficult for the authorities in the towns to take over the charge of the ecclesiastical arrangements. They had during mediæval times some experience in the matter; and city life was so compact that it was easy to regulate the ecclesiastical portion. The prevailing type exhibited in the number of "ordinances" which have come down to us, collected by Richter and Sehling, is that a superintendent, one of the city clergy, was placed over the city churches, and that he was more or less responsible to the city fathers for the ecclesiastical life and rule within the domains of the city.

The ecclesiastical organisation of the territories of the princes was a much more difficult task. Luther proposed to the Elector of Saxony that a careful visitation of his principality should be made, district by district, in order to find out the state of matters and what required to be done.

The correspondence of Luther during the years 1525–1527 shows how urgent the need of such a visitation appeared to him. He had been through the country several times. Parish priests had laid their difficulties before him and had asked his advice. His letters describe graphically their abounding poverty, a poverty increased by the fact that the only application of the new evangelical liberty made by many of the people was to refuse to pay all clerical dues. He came to the conclusion that the "common man" respected neither priest nor preacher, that there was no ecclesiastical supervision in the country districts, and no exercise of authority to maintain even the necessary ecclesiastical buildings. He expressed the fear that if things were allowed to go on as they were doing, there would be soon neither priest's house nor schools nor scholars in many a parish. The reports of the first Saxon Visitation showed that Luther had not exaggerated matters.[1] The district about Wittenberg was in much better order than the others; but in the outlying portions a very bad state of things was disclosed. In a village near Torgau the Visitors discovered an old priest who was hardly able to repeat the Creed or the Lord's Prayer,[2] but who was

[1] Winter, "Die Kirchenvisitation von 1528 im Wittenberger Kreise" (*Zeitschrift für die historische Theologie*, xxxiii. pp. 295–322); and *Visitations Protocolle* in *Neuen Mittheilungen des thüring.-sächs. Geschichts-Verein zu Halle*, IX. ii. pp. 78 ff.

[2] The Visitation of Bishop Hooper of the diocese of Gloucester, made in 1551, disclosed a worse state of matters in England. The Visitor put these simple questions to his clergy: "How many commandments are there? Where are they to be found? Repeat them. What are the Articles of the Christian Faith (the Apostles' Creed)? Repeat them. Prove them from Scripture. Repeat the Lord's Prayer. How do you know that it is the

held in high esteem as an exorcist, and who derived a good income from the exercise of his skill in combating the evil influences of witches. Priests had to be evicted for gross immoralities. Some were tavern-keepers or practised other worldly callings. Village schools were rarely to be found. Some of the peasants complained that the Lord's Prayer was so long that they could not learn it; and in one place the Visitors found that not a single peasant knew any prayer whatsoever.

This Saxon Visitation was the model for similar ones made in almost every evangelical principality, and its reports serve to show what need there was for inquiry and reorganisation. The lands of Electoral Saxony were divided into four "circles," and a commission of theologians and lawyers was appointed to undertake the duties in each circle. The Visitation of the one "circle" of Wittenberg, with its thirty-eight parishes, may be taken as an example of how the work was done, and what kinds of alterations were suggested. The commissioners or Visitors were Martin Luther and Justus Jonas, theologians, with Hans Metzsch, Benedict Pauli, and Johann v. Taubenheim, jurists. They began in October 1528, and spent two months over their task. It was a strictly business proceeding. There is no account of either Luther or Jonas preaching while on tour. The Visitors went about their work with great energy, holding conferences with the parish priests and with the representatives of the community. They questioned the priests about the religious condition of the people—whether there was any gross and open immorality, whether the people were regular in their attendance at church and in coming to the communion. They asked the people how the priests did their work among them—in the towns their conferences were with the *Rath*, and in the country dis-

Lord's? Where is it to be found?" Three hundred and eleven clergymen were asked these questions, and only fifty answered them all; out of the fifty, nineteen are noted as having answered *mediocriter*. Eight could not answer a single one of them; and while one knew that the number of the commandments was ten, he knew nothing else [*English Historical Review* for 1904 (Jan.), pp. 98 ff.].

tricts and villages with the male heads of families. Their common work was to find out what was being done for the "cure of souls," the instruction of the youth, and the care of the poor. By "cure of souls" (*Seelsorge*) they meant preaching, dispensation of the sacraments, catechetical instruction, and the pastoral visitation of the sick. It belonged to the theologians to estimate the capacities of the pastors, and to the jurists to estimate the available income, to look into all legal difficulties that might arise, and especially to clear the entanglements caused by the supposed jurisdiction of convents over many of the parishes.

This small district was made up of three outlying portions of the three dioceses of Brandenburg, Magdeburg, and Meissen. It had not been inspected within the memory of man, and the results of episcopal negligence were manifest. At Klebitz the peasants had driven away the parish clerk and put the village herd in his house. At Bülzig there was neither parsonage nor house for parish clerk, and the priest was non-resident. So at Danna; where the priest held a benefice at Coswig, and was, besides, a chaplain at Wittenberg, while the clerk lived at Zahna. The parsonages were all in a bad state of repair, and the local authorities could not be got to do anything. Roofs were leaking, walls were crumbling, it was believed that the next winter's frost would bring some down bodily. At Pratau the priest had built all himself—parsonage, outhouses, stable, and byre. All these things were duly noted to be reported upon. As for the priests, the complaints made against them were very few indeed. In one case the people said that their priest drank, and was continually seen in the public-house. Generally, however, the complaints, when there were any, were that the priest was too old for his work, or was so utterly uneducated that he could do little more than mumble the Mass. There was scanty evidence that the people understood very clearly the evangelical theology. Partaking the Lord's Supper in both "kinds," or in one only, was the distinction recognised and appreciated between the new and the old teaching:

and when they had the choice the people universally preferred the new. In one case the parishioners complained that their priest insisted on saying the Mass in Latin and not in German. In one case only did the Visitors find any objection taken to the evangelical service. This was at Meure, where the parish clerk's wife was reported to be an enemy of the new pastor because he recited the service in German. It turned out, however, that her real objection was that the pastor had displaced her husband. At Bleddin the peasants told the Visitors that their pastor, Christopher Richter, was a learned and pious man, who preached regularly on all the Sundays and festival days, and generally four times a week in various parts of the parish. It appeared, however, that their admiration for him did not compel them to attend his ministrations with very great regularity. The energetic pastors were all young men trained at Wittenberg. The older men, peasants' sons all of them, were scarcely better educated than their parishioners, and were quite unable to preach to them. The Visitors found very few parishes indeed where three, four, five or more persons were not named to them who never attended church or came to the Lord's Table; in some parishes men came regularly to the preaching who never would come to the Sacrament. What impressed the Visitors most was the ignorance, the besotted ignorance, of the people. They questioned them directly; found out whether they knew the Apostles' Creed, the Ten Commandments, and the Lord's Prayer; and then questioned them about the meanings of the words; and the answers were disappointing.

Luther came back from the Visitation in greatly depressed spirits, and expressed his feelings in his usual energetic language. He says in his introduction to his *Small Catechism*, a work he began as soon as he returned from the Visitation:

"In setting forth this Catechism or Christian doctrine in such a simple, concise, and easy form, I have been compelled and driven by the wretched and lamentable state of affairs which I discovered lately when I acted as a Visitor. Merciful God, what misery have I seen, the common people knowing nothing at all of Christian doctrine, especially in the villages! and unfortunately many pastors are well-nigh unskilled and incapable of teaching; and although all are called Christians and partake of the Holy Sacrament, they know neither the Lord's Prayer, nor the Creed, nor the Ten Commandments, but live like poor cattle and senseless swine, though, now that the gospel is come, they have learnt well enough how they may abuse their liberty. Oh, ye bishops, how will ye ever answer for it to Christ that ye have so shamefully neglected the people, and have not attended for an instant to your office? May all evil be averted from you! (*Das euch alles unglück fliche*). Ye forbid the taking of the Sacrament in one kind, and insist on your human laws, but never inquire whether they know the Lord's Prayer, the Belief, the Ten Commandments, or any of the words of God. Oh, woe be upon you for evermore!"

The Visitors found that few books were to be seen in the parsonages. They record one notable exception, the parsonage of Schmiedeberg, where the priest had a library of twelve volumes. It could not be expected that such uneducated men could preach to much edification; and one of the recommendations of the Visitors was that copies of Luther's *Postils* or short sermons on the Lessons for the Day should be sent to all the parishes, with orders that they should be read by the pastors to their congregations.

They did not find a trace anywhere of systematic pastoral visitation or catechising.

In their practical suggestions for ending the priestly inefficiency, the Visitors made simple and homely arrangements. To take one example,—at Liessnitz, the aged pastor Conrad was quite unable from age and ignorance to perform his duties; but he was a good, inoffensive old man. It was arranged that he was to have a coadjutor, who was to be boarded by the rich man of the parish and get the fees, while the old pastor kept the parsonage and the stipend, out of which he was to pay fourteen gulden annually to his coadjutor.

The Visitors found that schools did not exist in most of the villages, and they were disappointed with the condition of the schools they found in the smaller towns. It was proposed to make the parish clerks the village schoolmasters; but they were wholly incompetent, and the Visitors saw nothing for it but to suggest that the pastors must become the village schoolmasters. The parish clerks were ordered to teach the children to repeat the *Small Catechism* by rote, and the pastors to test them at a catechising on Sunday afternoons. In the towns, where the churches usually had a *cantor* or precentor, this official was asked to train the children to sing evangelical hymns.

In their inquiries about the care of the poor, the Visitors found that there was not much need for anything to be done in the villages; but the case was different in the towns. They found that in most of them there existed old foundations meant to benefit the poor, and they discovered all manner of misuses and misappropriations of the funds. Suggestions were made for the restoration of these funds to their destined uses.

This very condensed account of what took place in the Wittenberg "circle" shows how the work of the Visitors was done; a second and a third Visitation were needed in Electoral Saxony ere things were properly arranged; but in the end good work was accomplished. The Elector refused to take any of the confiscated convent lands and possessions for civil purposes, and these, together with the Church endowments, provided stipends for the pastors, salaries for the schoolmasters, and a settled provision for the poor.

When the Visitation was completed and the reports presented, the Visitors were asked to draft and issue an *Instruction* or lengthy advice to the clergy and people of the "circle" they had inspected. This *Instruction* was not considered a regular legal document, but its contents were expected to be acted upon.

These Visitations and Instructions were the earliest attempts at the reorganisation of the evangelical Church in Electoral Saxony. The Visitors remained as a "primitive evangelical consistory" to supervise their "circles."

The Saxon Visitations became a model for most of the

North German evangelical territorial Churches, and the Instructions form the earliest collection of requirements set forth for the guidance of pastors and Christian people. The directions are very minute. The pastors are told how to preach, how to conduct pastoral visitations, what sins they must specially warn their people against, and what example they must show them. The care of schools and of the poor was not forgotten.[1]

The fact that matrimonial cases during the Middle Ages were almost invariably tried in ecclesiastical courts, made it necessary to provide some legal authority to adjudicate upon such cases when the mediæval episcopal courts had either temporarily or permanently lost their authority. This led to a provisional arrangement for the government of the Church in Electoral Saxony, which took a regular legal form. A pastor, called a superintendent, was appointed in each of the four "circles" into which the territory had been divided for the purpose of Visitation, to act along with the ordinary magistracy in all ecclesiastical matters, including the judging in matrimonial cases.[2] This Saxon arrangement also spread largely through the northern German evangelical States.

A third Visitation of Electoral Saxony was made in 1532, and led to important ecclesiastical changes which formed the basis of all that came afterwards. As a result of the reports of the Visitors, of whom Justus Jonas seems to have been the most energetic, the parishes were rearranged, the incomes of parish priests readjusted, and the whole ecclesiastical revenues of the mediæval Church within Electoral Saxony appropriated for the threefold evangelical uses of supporting the ministry, providing for schools, and caring for the poor. The doctrine, ceremonies, and worship of the evangelical Church were also settled on a definite basis.[3]

[1] Sehling, *Die evangelischen Kirchenordnungen des 16ten Jahrhunderts* (Leipzig, 1902), I. i. 142 ff.

[2] *Ibid.* I. i. 49.

[3] The rites and ceremonies of worship in the Lutheran churches are given in Daniel, *Codex Liturgicus Ecclesiæ Lutheranæ in epitomen redactus*, which forms the second volume of his *Codex Liturgicus Ecclesiæ Universæ* (Leipzig, 1848).

The Visitors pointed out that hitherto no arrangement had been made to give the whole ecclesiastical administration one central authority. The Electoral Prince had always been regarded as the supreme ruler of the Church within his dominions, but as he could not personally superintend everything, there was needed some supreme court which could act in all ecclesiastical cases as his representative or instrument. The Visitors suggested the revival of the mediæval episcopal consistorial courts modified to suit the new circumstances. Bishops in the mediæval sense of the word might be and were believed to be superfluous, but their true function, the *jus episcopale*, the right of oversight, was indispensable. According to Luther's ideas —ideas which had been gaining ground in Germany from the last quarter of the fifteenth century—this *jus episcopale* belonged to the supreme secular authority. The mediæval bishop had exercised his right of oversight through a *consistorial court* composed of theologians and canon lawyers appointed by himself. These mediæval courts, it was suggested, might be transformed into Lutheran ecclesiastical courts if the prince formed a permanent council composed of lawyers and divines to act for him and in his name in all ecclesiastical matters, including matrimonial cases. The Visitors sketched their plan; it was submitted for revision to Luther and to Chancellor Brück, and the result was the Wittenberg Ecclesiastical Consistory established in 1542.[1] That the arrangement was still somewhat provisional appears from the fact that the court had not jurisdiction over the whole of the Electoral dominions, and that other two Consistories, one at Zeitz and the other at Zwickau, were established with similar powers. But the thing to be observed is that these courts were modelled on the old mediæval consistorial episcopal courts, and that,

[1] The ordinance establishing the Wittenberg Consistory will be found in Richter, *Die evangelischen Kirchenordnungen des sechszehnten Jahrhunderts* (Weimar, 1846), i. 367; and in Sehling, *Die evangelischen Kirchenordnungen des 16ten Jahrhunderts* (Leipzig, 1902), I. i. 200. Sehling sketches the history of its institution, I. i. 55.

like them, they were composed of lawyers and of theologians. The essential difference was that these Lutheran courts were appointed by and acted in the name of the supreme secular authority. In Electoral Saxony their local bounds of jurisdiction did not correspond to those of the mediæval courts. It was impossible that they should. Electoral Saxony, the ordinance erecting the Consistory itself says, consisted of portions of "ten or twelve" mediæval dioceses. The courts had different districts assigned to them; but in all other things they reproduced the mediæval consistorial courts.

The constitutions of these courts provided for the assembling and holding of Synods to deliberate on the affairs of the Church. The General Synod consisted of the Consistory and the superintendents of the various "circles"; and particular Synods, which had to do with the Church affairs of the "circle," of the superintendent, and of all the clergy of the "circle."

Such were the beginnings of the consistorial system of Church government, which is a distinctive mark of the Lutheran Church, and which exhibits some of the individual traits of Luther's personality. We can see in it his desire to make full use of whatever portions of the mediæval Church usages could be pressed into the service of his evangelical Church; his conception that the one supreme authority on earth was that of the secular government; his suspicion of the "common" man, and his resolve to prevent the people exercising any control over the arrangements of the Church.

Gradually all the Lutheran Churches have adopted, in general outline at least, this consistorial system; but it would be a mistake to think that the Wittenberg "use" was adopted in all its details. Luther himself, as has been said, had no desire for anything like uniformity, and there was none in the beginning. All the schemes of ecclesiastical government proceed on the idea that the *jus episcopale* or right of ecclesiastical oversight belongs to the supreme territorial secular authority. All of them include within the one set of ordinances, provisions for the support of the ministry, for the maintenance of schools, and for the care of the poor—the last generally expressed by regulations about the "common chest." The great variety of forms of ecclesiastical government drafted and adopted may be studied in Richter's collection, which includes one hundred and seventy-two separate ecclesiastical constitutions, and which is confessedly very imperfect. The gradual growth of the organisation finally adopted in each city and State can be traced for a portion of Germany in Sehling's unfinished work.[1]

The number of these ecclesiastical ordinances is enormous, and the quantity is to be accounted for partly by the way in which Germany was split up into numerous small States in the sixteenth century, and also partly by the fact that Luther pled strongly for diversity.

The ordinances were promulgated in many different ways. Most frequently, perhaps, the prince published and enacted them on his own authority like any other piece of territorial legislation. Sometimes he commissioned a committee acting in his name to frame and publish. In other cases they resulted from a consultation between the prince and the magistrates of one of the towns within his dominions. Sometimes they came from the councils and the pastors of the towns to which they applied. In other instances they were issued by an evangelical bishop. And in a few cases they are simply the regulations issued by a single pastor for his own parish, which the secular authorities did not think of altering.

Although they are independent one from another, they may be grouped in families which resemble each other closely.[2]

Some of the territories reached the consistorial system

[1] The first half of the first part of Sehling's *Die evangelischen Kirchenordnungen des 16 Jahrhunderts* appeared in 1902, and the second half of the first part in 1904.

[2] Cf. article on "Kirchen-Ordnung" in the 3rd edition of Herzog's *Realencyclopädie für protestantische Theologie.*

much sooner than others. If a principality consisted in whole or in part of a secularised ecclesiastical State, the machinery of the consistorial court lay ready to the hand of the prince, and was at once adapted to the use of the evangelical Church. The system was naturally slowest to develop in the imperial cities, most of which at first preferred an organisation whose outlines were borrowed from the constitution drafted by Zwingli for Zurich.

Once only do we find an attempt to give an evangelical Church occupying a large territory a democratic constitution. It was made by Philip, Landgrave of Hesse, who was never afraid of the democracy. No German prince had so thoroughly won the confidence of his commonalty. The Peasants' War never devastated his dominions. He did not join in the virulent persecution of the Anabaptists which disgraced the Lutheran as well as the Roman Catholic States during the latter half of the sixteenth century. It was natural that Luther's earlier ideas about the rights of the Christian community (*Gemeinde*) should appeal to him. In 1526 (Oct. 6th), when the Diet of Speyer had permitted the organisation of evangelical Churches, Philip summoned a Synod at Homberg, and invited not merely pastors and ecclesiastical lawyers, but representatives from the nobles and from the towns. A scheme for ecclesiastical government, which had been drafted by Francis Lambert, formerly a Franciscan monk, was laid before the assembly and adopted. It was based on the idea that the word of God is the only supreme rule to guide and govern His Church, and that Canon Law has no place whatsoever within an evangelical Church. Scripture teaches, the document explains, that it belongs to the Christian community itself to select and dismiss pastors and to exercise discipline by means of excommunication. The latter right ought to be used in a weekly meeting (on Sundays) of the congregation and pastor. For the purposes of orderly rule the Church must have office-bearers, who ought to conform as nearly as possible to those mentioned in the New Testament Scriptures. They are bishops (pastors), elders, and deacons; and the deacons are the guardians of the poor as well as ecclesiastical officials. All these office-bearers must remember that their function is that of servants, and in no sense lordly or magisterial. They ought to be chosen by the congregation, and set apart by the laying on of hands according to apostolic practice. A bishop (pastor) must be ordained by at least three pastors, and a deacon by the pastor or by two elders. The government of the whole Church ought to be in the hands of a Synod, to consist of all the pastors and a delegate from every parish. Such in outline was the democratic ecclesiastical government proposed for the territory of Hesse and accepted by the Landgrave.[1] He was persuaded, however, by Luther's strong remonstrances to abandon it. There is no place for the democratic or representative element in the organisation of the Lutheran Churches.

[1] Richter, *Die evangelischen Kirchenordnungen*, etc. i. 56 ff.

CHAPTER VII.

THE LUTHERAN REFORMATION OUTSIDE GERMANY.[1]

THE influence of Luther went far beyond Germany. It was felt in England, France, Scotland, Holland, Poland, and Scandinavia. England went her own peculiar way; France, Holland, and Scotland, in the end, accepted the leadership of Calvin; the Lutheran Reformation, outside Germany, was really confined to Scandinavia alone.

In these Scandinavian lands the religious awakening was bound up with political and social movements more than in any other countries. The reformation in the Church was, indeed, begun by men who had studied under Luther at Wittenberg, or who had received their first promptings from his writings; but it was carried on and brought to a successful issue by statesmen who saw in it the means to deliver their land from political anarchy, caused by the overweening independence and turbulence of the great ecclesiastical lords, and who were almost compelled to look to the large possessions of the Church as a means to replenish their exhausted treasuries without ruining the overburdened taxpayers.

When Eric was crowned King of Denmark, Sweden, and Norway in 1397, the assembled nobles, representative

[1] SOURCES: Baazius, *Inventarium Eccles. Sveogothorum* (1642); Pontoppidan, *Annales ecclesiæ Danicæ*, bks. ii., iii. (Copenhagen, 1744, 1747).

LATER BOOKS: Lau, *Geschichte der Reformation in Schleswig-Holstein* (Hamburg, 1867); Willson, *History of Church and State in Norway* (London, 1903); Watson, *The Swedish Revolution under Gustavus Vasa* (Cambridge, Massachusetts, 1889); Wiedling, *Schwedische Geschichte im Zeitalter der Reformation* (Gotha, 1882); *Cambridge Modern History*, II. xvii. (Cambridge, 1903).

of the three kingdoms, agreed to the celebrated Union of Kalmar, which declared that the three lands were to be for ever united under one sovereign. The treaty was purely dynastic, its terms were vague, and it was never very effective. Without going into details, it may be said that the king lived in Denmark, and ruled in the interests of that country; that he also may be said to have ruled in Norway; but that in Sweden his authority was merely nominal, and sometimes not even that. In Denmark itself, monarchical government was difficult. The Scandinavian kingship was elective, and every election was an opportunity for reducing the privileges, authority, and wealth of the sovereign, and for increasing those of the nobles and of the great ecclesiastics, who, being privileged classes, were freed from contributing to the taxation.

In 1513, Christian II, the nephew of the Elector of Saxony, and the brother-in-law of the Emperor Charles V. (1515), came to the throne, and his accession marks the beginning of the new era which was to end with the triumph of the Reformation in all three countries. Christian was a man of great natural abilities, with a profound sense of the miserable condition of the common people within his realms, caused by the petty tyrannies of the nobles, ecclesiastical and secular. No reigning prince, save perhaps George, Duke of Saxony, could compete with him in learning; but he was cruel, partly from nature and partly from policy. He had determined to establish his rule over the three kingdoms whose nominal king he was, and to free the commonalty from their oppression by breaking the power of the nobles and of the great Churchmen. The task was one of extreme difficulty, and he was personally unsuccessful; but his efforts laid the foundation on which successors were able to build securely.

He began by conquering rebellious Sweden, and disgraced his victory by a treacherous massacre of Swedish notables at Stockholm (1520),—a deed which, in the end, led to the complete separation of Sweden from Denmark

After having thus, as he imagined, consolidated his power, he pressed forward his schemes for reform. He took pains to encourage the trade and agriculture of Denmark; he patronised learning. He wrote to his uncle (1519), Frederick, the Elector of Saxony, to send him preachers trained by Luther; and, in response to his appeal, received first Martin Reinhard, and then Andrew Bodenstein of Carlstadt. These foreigners, who could only address the people through interpreters, did not make much impression; but reformation was pushed forward by the king. He published, on his own authority, two sets of laws dealing with the nobles and the Church, and subjecting both to the sovereign. He enacted that all convents were to be under episcopal inspection. Non-resident and unlettered clergy were legally abolished. A species of kingly consistorial court was set up in Copenhagen, and declared to be the supreme ecclesiastical judicature for the country; and appeals to Rome were forbidden. It can scarcely be said that these laws were ever in operation. A revolt by the Jutlanders gave a rallying point to the disaffection caused by the proposed reforms. Christian fled from Denmark (1523), and spent the rest of his life in exile or in prison. His law-books were burnt.

The Jutlanders had called Frederick of Schleswig-Holstein, Christian's uncle, to the throne, and he was recognised King of Denmark and of Norway in 1523. He had come to the kingdom owing to the reaction against the reforms of his nephew, but in his heart he knew that they were necessary. He promised to protect the interests of the nobles, and to defend the Church against the advance of Lutheran opinions; but he soon endeavoured to find a means of evading his pledges. He found it when he pitted the nobles against the higher clergy, and announced that he had never promised to support the errors of the Church of Rome. At the National Assembly (*Herredag*) at Odense he was able to get the marriage of priests permitted, and a decree that bishops were in the future to apply to the king and not to the Pope for their Pallium. The Reformation had now native preachers to support it, especially Hans Tausen, who was called the Danish Luther, and they were encouraged by the king. At the *Herredag* at Copenhagen in 1530, twenty-one of these Lutheran preachers were summoned, at the instigation of the bishops, and formal accusations were made against them for preaching heresy. Tausen and his fellows produced a confession of faith in forty-three articles, all of which he and his companions offered to defend. A public disputation was proposed, which did not take place because the Romanist party refused to plead in the Danish language. This refusal was interpreted by the people to mean that they were afraid to discuss in a language which everyone understood. Lutheranism made rapid progress among all classes of the population.

On Frederick's death there was a disputed succession, which resulted in civil war. In the end Frederick's son ascended the throne as Christian III., King of Denmark and Norway (1536). The king, who had been present at the Diet of Worms, and who had learned there to esteem Luther highly, was a strong Lutheran, and determined to end the authority of the Romish bishops. He proposed to his council that bishops should no longer have any share in the government, and that their possessions should be forfeited to the Crown. This was approved of not merely by the council, but also at a National Asssembly which met at Copenhagen (Oct. 30th, 1536), where it was further declared that the people desired the holy gospel to be preached, and the whole episcopal authority done away with. The king asked Luther to send him some one to guide his people in their ecclesiastical matters. Bugenhagen was despatched, came to Copenhagen (1537), and took the chief ecclesiastical part in crowning the king. Seven superintendents (who afterwards took the title of bishops) were appointed and consecrated. The Reformation was carried out on conservative Lutheran lines, and the old ritual was largely preserved. Tausen's Confession was set aside in favour of the Augsburg Confession and Luther's

Small Catechism, and the Lutheran Reformation was thoroughly and legally established.

The Reformation also became an accomplished fact in Norway and Iceland, but its introduction into these lands was much more an act of kingly authority.

After the massacre of Swedish notables in Stockholm (Nov. 1520), young Gustaf Ericsson, commonly known as Gustaf Vasa, from the *vasa* or sheaf which was on his coat of arms, raised the standard of revolt against Denmark. He was gradually able to rally the whole of the people around him, and the Danes were expelled from the kingdom. In 1521, Gustaf had been declared regent of Sweden, and in 1523 he was called by the voice of the people to the throne. He found himself surrounded by almost insuperable difficulties. There had been practically no settled government in Sweden for nearly a century, and every great landholder was virtually an independent sovereign. The country had been impoverished by long wars. Two-thirds of the land was owned by the Church, and the remaining third was almost entirely in the hands of the secular nobles. Both Church and nobles claimed exemption from taxation. The trade of the country was in the hands of foreigners—of the Danes or of the Hanse Towns. Gustaf had borrowed money from the town of Lübeck for his work of liberation. The city was pressing for repayment, and its commissioners followed the embarrassed monarch wherever he went. It was hopeless to expect to raise money by further taxation of the already depressed and impoverished peasants.

In these circumstances the king turned to the Church. He compelled the bishops to give him more than one subsidy (1522, 1523); but this was inadequate for his needs. The Church property was large, and the king planned to overthrow the ecclesiastical aristocracy by the help of the Lutheran Reformation.

Lutheranism had been making progress in Sweden. Two brothers, Olaus and Laurentius Petri, sons of a blacksmith at Orebro, had been sent by their father to study in Germany. They had meant to attend the University of Leipzig; but, attracted by the growing fame of Luther, they had gone to Wittenberg, and had become enthusiastic disciples of the Reformer. On their return to Sweden (1519) they had preached Lutheran doctrine, and had made many converts—among others, Laurentius Andreæ, Archdeacon at Strengnäs. In spite of protests from the bishops, these three men were protected by the king. Olaus Petri was especially active, and made long preaching tours, declaring that he taught the pure gospel which "Ansgar, the apostle of the North, had preached seven hundred years before in Sweden."

Gustaf brought Olaus to Stockholm (1524), and made him town-clerk of the city; his brother Laurentius was appointed professor of theology at Upsala; Laurentius Andreæ was made Archdeacon of Upsala and Chancellor of Sweden. When the bishops demanded that the Reformers should be silenced, Olaus challenged them to a public disputation. The challenge was refused; but in 1524 a disputation was arranged in the king's palace in Stockholm between Olaus and Dr. Galle, who supported the old religion. The conference, which included discussion of the doctrines of Justification by Faith, Indulgences, the Mass, Purgatory, and the Temporal Power of the Pope, had the effect of strengthening the cause of the Reformation. In 1525, Olaus defied the rules of the mediæval Church by publicly marrying a wife. The same year the king called for a translation of the Scriptures into Swedish, and in 1526 Laurentius Petri published his New Testament. A translation of the whole Bible was edited by the same scholar, and published 1540–1541. These translations, especially that of the New Testament, became very popular, and the people with the Scripture in their hands were able to see whether the teaching of the preachers or of the bishops was most in accordance with the Holy Scriptures.

There is no reason to believe that the king did not take the side of the Lutheran Reformation from genuine conviction. He had made the acquaintance of the brothers Petri before he was called to be the deliverer of his country. But it is unquestionable that his financial embarrassment whetted his zeal for the reformation of the Church in Sweden. Matters were coming to a crisis, which was reached in 1527. At the Diet in that year, the Chancellor, in the name of the king, explained the need for an increased revenue, and suggested that ecclesiastical property was the only source from which it could be obtained. The bishops, Johan Brask, Bishop of Linkoeping, at their head, replied that they had the Pope's orders to defend the property of the Church. The nobles supported them. Then Gustaf presented his ultimatum. He told the Diet plainly that they must submit to the proposals of the Chancellor or accept his resignation, pay him for his property, return him the money he had spent in defence of the kingdom, and permit him to leave the country never to return. The Diet spent three days in wrangling, and then submitted to his wishes. The whole of the ecclesiastical property—episcopal, capitular, and monastic—which was not absolutely needed for the support of the Church was to be placed in the hands of the king. Preachers were meanwhile to set forth the pure gospel, until a conference held in presence of the Diet would enable that assembly to come to a decision concerning matters of religion. The Diet went on, without waiting for the conference, to pass the twenty-four regulations which made the famous Ordinances of Vesteräs, and embodied the legal Reformation. They contained provisions for secularising the ecclesiastical property in accordance with the previous decision of the Diet; declared that the king had the right of vetoing the decisions of the higher ecclesiastics; that the appointment of the parish clergy was in the hands of the bishops, but that the king could remove them for inefficiency; that the pure gospel was to be taught in every school; and that auricular confession was no longer compulsory.

While the Ordinances stripped the Swedish Church of a large amount of its property and made it subject to the king they did not destroy its episcopal organisation, nor entirely impoverish it. Most of the monasteries were deserted when their property was taken away. The king knew that the peasantry scarcely understood the Reformed doctrines, and had no wish to press them unduly on his people. For the same reason the old ceremonies and usages which did not flagrantly contradict the new doctrines were suffered to remain, and given an evangelical meaning. The first evangelical Hymn-book was published in 1530, and the Swedish "Mass" in 1531, both drafted on Lutheran models. Laurentius Andreæ was made Archbishop of Upsala (1527), and a National Synod was held under his presidency at Orebro (1528), which guided the Reformation according to strictly conservative Lutheran ideals. Thus before the death of Gustaf Vasa, Sweden had joined the circle of Lutheran Churches, and its people were slowly coming to understand the principles of the Reformation. The Reformation was a very peaceful one. No one suffered death for his religious opinions.

The fortunes of the Swedish Church were somewhat varied under the immediate successors of Gustavus. His ill-fated son showed signs of preferring Calvinism, and insisted on the suppression of some of the ecclesiastical festivals and some of the old rites which had been retained; but these attempts ended with his reign. His brother and successor, Johan III., took the opposite extreme, and coquetted long with Rome, and with proposals for reunion,—proposals which had no serious result. When Johan died in 1592, his son and successor, who had been elected King of Poland, and had become a Roman Catholic, aroused the fears of his Swedish subjects that he might go much further than his father. The people resolved to make sure of their Protestantism before their new sovereign arrived in the country. A Synod was convened at which both lay and ecclesiastical deputies were present. The members first laid down the general rule that the Holy Scriptures were their supreme doctrinal standard, and then selected the Augsburg Confession as the Confession of the Swedish

Church. Luther's Small Catechism, which had been removed from the schools by King Johan III., was restored. This meeting at Upsala settled for the future the ecclesiastical polity of Sweden. The country showed its attachment to the stricter Lutheranism by adopting the Formula of Concord in 1661

CHAPTER VIII

THE RELIGIOUS PRINCIPLES INSPIRING THE REFORMATION.[1]

§ 1. *The Reformation did not take its rise from a Criticism of Doctrines.*

THE whole of Luther's religious history, from his entrance into the convent at Erfurt to the publication of the Augsburg Confession, shows that the movement of which he was the soul and centre did not arise from any merely intellectual criticism of the doctrines of the mediæval Church, and that it resulted in a great deal more than a revision or reconstruction of a system of doctrinal conceptions.[2] There is no trace of any intellectual difficulties about doctrines or statement of doctrines in Luther's mind during the supreme crisis of his history. He was driven out of the world of human life and hope, where he was well fitted to do a man's work, by the overwhelming pressure of a great practical religious need—anxiety to save his soul. He has himself said that the proverb that doubt makes a monk was true in his case. He doubted

[1] Dorner, *History of Protestant Theology* (Edinburgh, 1871); Köstlin, *Luthers Theologie in ihrer geschichtlichen Entwickelung und in ihrem innern Zusammenhange* (Stuttgart, 1883); Theodor Harnack, *Luthers Theologie mit besonderer Beziehung auf seine Versöhnungs- und Erlösungslehre* (Erlangen, 1862–1886); A. Ritschl, *The Christian Doctrine of Justification and Reconciliation* (Edinburgh, 1872); A. Harnack, *History of Dogma*, vii. (London, 1899); Loofs, *Leitfaden zum Studium der Dogmengeschichte* (Halle, 1893); Herrmann, *Communion with God* (London, 1895); Hering, *Die Mystik Luthers in Zusammenhang seiner Theologie* (Leipzig, 1879); Denifle, *Luther und Lutherthum in der ersten Entwicklung*, vol. i. (Mainz, 1904), vol. ii. (1905); Walther, *Für Luther wider Rom* (Halle, 1906).

[2] Loofs, *Leitfaden*, etc. p. 345.

whether he could save his soul in the world, and was therefore forced to leave it and enter the convent.

He had lost whatever evangelical teaching he had learnt in childhood or in Frau Cotta's household at Eisenach. He had surrendered himself to the popular belief, fostered by the whole penitential system of the mediæval Church, that man could and must make himself fit to receive the grace of God which procures salvation. The self-torturing cry, "Oh, when wilt thou become holy and fit to obtain the grace of God?" (*O wenn will du einmal fromm werden und genug thun du einen gnädigen Gott kriegest?*), drove him into the convent. He believed, and the almost unanimous opinion of his age agreed with him, that there, if anywhere, he could find the peace he was seeking with such desperation.

Inside the convent he applied himself with all the force of a strong nature, using every means that the complicated penitential system of the Church had provided to help him, to make himself pious and fit to be the receptacle of the grace of God. He submitted to the orders of his superiors with the blind obedience which the most rigorous ecclesiastical statutes demanded; he sought the comforting consolations which confession was declared to give; he underwent every part of the complex system of expiations which the mediæval Church recommended; he made full use of the sacraments, and waited in vain for the mysterious, inexplicable experience of the grace which was said to accompany and flow from them. He persevered in spite of the feeling of continuous failure. "If a monk ever reached heaven by monkery," he has said, "I would have found my way there also; all my convent comrades will bear witness to that."[1] He gave a still stronger proof of his loyalty to the mediæval Church and its advice to men in his mood of mind; he persevered in spite of the knowledge that his comrades and his religious superiors believed him to be a young saint, while he knew that he was far other-

[1] *Luther's Works* (Erlangen edition), xxxi. 273; in *Die Kleine Antwort auf Herzog Georgen nähestes Buch.*

wise, and that he was no nearer God than he had been before he entered the monastery, or had begun his quest after the sense of pardon of sin. The contrast between what his brethren thought he must be and what his own experience told him that he was, must have added bitterness to the cup he had to drink during these terrible months in the Erfurt convent. He says himself:

"After I had made the profession, I was congratulated by the prior, the convent, and the father-confessor, because I was now an innocent child coming pure from baptism. Assuredly, I would willingly have delighted in the glorious fact that I was such a good man, who by his own deeds and without the merits of Christ's blood had made himself so fair and holy, and so easily too, and in so short a time. But although I listened readily to the sweet praise and glowing language about myself and my doings, and allowed myself to be described as a wonder-worker, who could make himself holy in such an easy way, and could swallow up death, and the devil also, yet there was no power in it all to maintain me. When even a small temptation came from sin or death I fell at once, and found that neither baptism nor monkery could assist me; I felt that I had long lost Christ and His baptism. I was the most miserable man on earth; day and night there was only wailing and despair, and no one could restrain me."[1]

He adds that all he knew of Christ at this time was that He was "a stern judge from whom I would fain have fled and yet could not escape."

During these two years of anguish, Luther believed that he was battling with himself and with his sin; he was really struggling with the religion of his times and Church. He was probing it, testing it, examining all its depths, wrestling with all its means of grace, and finding that what were meant to be sources of comfort and consolation were simply additional springs of terror. He was too clear-sighted, his spiritual senses were too acute, he was too much in deadly earnest, not to see that none of these aids were leading him to a solid ground of certainty on

[1] *Luther's Works* (Erlangen edition), xxxi. 278, 279.

which he could base his hopes for time and for eternity; and he was too honest with himself to be persuaded that he was otherwise than his despair told him.[1]

At length, guided in very faltering fashion by the Scriptures, especially by the Psalms and the Epistle to the Romans, by the Apostles' Creed, and by fellow monks, he (to use his own words) came to see that the righteousness of God (Rom. i. 17) is not the righteousness by which a righteous God punishes the unrighteous and sinners, but that by which a merciful God justifies us through faith (not *justitia, qua deus justus est et peccatores injustosque punit*, but that *qua nos deus misericors justificat per fidem*).[2] By *faith*, he says. What, then, did he mean by "faith"?

He replies:

"There are two kinds of believing: first, a believing about God which means that I believe that what is said of God is true. This faith is rather a form of knowledge than a faith. There is, secondly, a believing in God which means that I put my trust in Him, give myself up to thinking that I can have dealings with Him, and believe without any doubt that He will be and do to me according to the things said of Him. Such faith, *which throws itself upon God*, whether in life or in death, alone makes a Christian man."[3]

The faith which he prized is that religious faculty which "throws itself upon God"; and from the first Luther recognised that faith of this kind was a direct gift from God. Having it we have everything; without it we have nothing. Here we find something entirely new, or at least hitherto unexpressed, so far as mediæval theology was concerned. Mediæval theologians had recognised faith in the sense of what Luther called *frigida opinio*, and it is difficult to conceive that they did not also indirectly

[1] Harnack, *History of Dogma*, vii. 182.

[2] Loofs, *Leitfaden*, etc. p. 346.

[3] *Luther's Works* (Erlangen edition), xxii. 15. Cf. xlviii. 5: "If thou holdest faith to be simply a thought concerning God, then that thought is as little able to give eternal life as ever a monkish cowl could give it."

acknowledge that there must be something like trust or *fiducia*; but faith with them was simply one among many human efforts all equally necessary in order to see and know God. Luther recognised that there was this kind of faith, which a man begets and brings to pass in himself by assent to doctrines of some sort. But he did not think much of it. He calls it worthless because it gives us nothing.

> "They think that faith is a thing which they may have or not have at will, like any other natural human thing; so when they arrive at a conclusion and say, 'Truly the doctrine is correct, and therefore I believe it,' then they think that this is faith. Now, when they see and feel that no change has been wrought in themselves and in others, and that works do not follow, and they remain as before in the old nature, then they think that the faith is not good enough, but that there must be something more and greater."[1]

The real faith, the faith which is trust, the divine gift which impels us to throw ourselves upon God, gives us the living assurance of a living God, who has revealed Himself, made us see His loving Fatherly heart in Christ Jesus; and that is the Christian religion in its very core and centre. The sum of Christianity is—(1) God manifest in Christ, the God of grace, accessible by every Christian man and woman; and (2) unwavering trust in Him who has given Himself to us in Christ Jesus,—unwavering, because Christ with His work has undertaken our cause and made it His.

The God we have access to and Whom we can trust because we have thrown ourselves upon Him and have found that He sustains us, is no philosophical abstraction, to be described in definitions and argued about in syllogisms. He is seen and known, because we see and know Christ Jesus. "He that hath seen Me hath seen the Father." For with Luther and all the Reformers, Christ fills the whole sphere of God; and they do not recognise any theology which is not a Christology.

[1] *Luther's Works* (2nd Erlangen edition), xiii. 301.

The faith which makes us throw ourselves upon God is no mood of mere mystical abandonment .It is our very life, as Luther was never tired of saying. It is God within us, and wells forth in all kinds of activities.

"It is a living, busy, active, powerful thing, faith; it is impossible for it not to do us good continually. It never asks whether good works are to be done; it has done them before there is time to ask the question, and it is always doing them."[1]

Christianity is therefore an interwoven tissue of promises and prayers of faith. On the one side there is the Father, revealing Himself, sending down to us His promises which are yea and amen in Christ Jesus; and on the other side there are the hearts of men ascending in faith to God, receiving, accepting, and resting on the promises of God, and on God who always gives Himself in His promises.

This is what came to Luther and ended his long and terrible struggle. He is unwearied in describing it. The descriptions are very varied, so far as external form and expression go,—now texts from the Psalms, the Prophets, or the New Testament most aptly quoted; now phrases borrowed from the picturesque language of the mediæval mystics; now sentences of striking, even rugged, originality; sometimes propositions taken from the mediæval scholastic. But whatever the words, the meaning is always the same.

This conception of what is meant by Christianity is the religious soul of the Reformation. It contains within it all the distinctively religious principles which inspired it. It can scarcely be called a dogma. It is an experience, and the phrases which set it forth are the descriptions of an experience which a human soul has gone through. The thing itself is beyond exact definition—as all deep experiences are. It must be felt and gone through to be known. The Reformation started from this personal

[1] *Luther's Works* (Erlangen edition), lxiii. 125.

experience of the believing Christian, which it declared to be the one elemental fact in Christianity which could never be proved by argument and could never be dissolved away by speculation. It proclaimed the great truth, which had been universally neglected throughout the whole period of mediæval theology by everyone except the Mystics, that in order to know God man must be in living touch with God Himself. Therein lay its originality and its power. Luther rediscovered religion when he declared that the truly Christian man must cling directly and with a living faith to the God Who speaks to him in Christ, saying, "I am thy salvation." The earlier Reformers never forgot this. Luther proclaimed his discovery, he never attempted to prove it by argument; it was something self-evident—seen and known when experienced.

This is always the way with great religious pioneers and leaders. They have all had the prophetic gift of spiritual vision, and the magnetic speech to proclaim what they have seen, felt, and known. They have all had, in a far-off way, the insight and manner of Jesus.

When our Lord appeared among men claiming to be more than a wise man or a prophet, declaring that He was the Messiah, the Son of Man and the Son of God, when He announced that all men had need of Him, and that He alone could save and redeem, He set forth His claims in a manner unique among founders of religions. He made them calmly and as a matter of course. He never explained elaborately why He assumed the titles He took. He never reasoned about His position as the only Saviour. He simply announced it, letting the conviction of the truth steal almost insensibly into the minds and hearts of His followers as they saw His deeds and heard His words. He assumed that they must interpret His death in one way only. This was always His manner. It was not His way to explain mysteries our curiosity would fain penetrate. He quietly took for granted many things we would like to argue about. His sayings came from One who lived in perpetual communion with the Unseen Father, and He uttered them quietly and assuredly, confident that they carried with them their own self-evidencing power.

So it was with St. Paul. His letters and sermons are full of arguments, no doubt, full of pleadings and persuasion, but they all start from and rest upon his vision of the living, risen Saviour. His last word is always, "When it pleased God to reveal His Son in me"; that was the elemental fact which he proclaimed and which summed up everything, the personal experience from which he started on his career as an apostle. The place of Athanasius as a great religious leader has been obscured by his position as a theologian; but when we turn to his writings, where do we find less of what is commonly called dogmatic theology? There is argument, reasoning, searching for proofs and their statement; but all that belongs to the outworks in his teaching. The central citadel is a spiritual intuition—I *know* that *my* Saviour is the God Who made heaven and earth. He took his stand firmly and unflinchingly on that personal experience, and all else mattered little compared with the fundamental spiritual fact. It was not his arguments, but his unflinching faith that convinced his generation.

So it was with Augustine, Bernard,[1] Francis—so it has been with every great religious leader of the Christian people. His strength, whether of knowledge, or conviction, or sympathy,—his driving power, if the phrase may be used,—has always come from direct communion with the unseen, and rests upon the fact, felt and known by himself and communicated to others by a mysterious sympathy, that it has pleased God to reveal Christ in him in some way or other.

[1] The case of Bernard of Clairvaux is especially interesting, for we might almost call him two men in one. In his experimental moods, when he is the great revivalist preacher, exhibited in his sermons on the *Song of Songs* and elsewhere, everything that the Christian can do, say, or think, comes fom the revelation of God's grace within the individual, while in his more purely theological works he scarcely ever frees himself from the entanglements of Scholastic Theology. The doubleness in Bernard has been dwelt upon by A. Ritschl in his *Critical History of the Christian Doctrine of Justification and Reconciliation* (Edinburgh, 1872), pp. 95–101.

So it was with Luther and the Reformation in which he was the leader. Its driving power was a great religious experience, old, for it has come to the people of God in all generations, and yet new and fresh as it is the nature of all such experiences to be. He *knew* that his life was hid with Christ in God in spite of all evil, in spite of sin and sense of guilt. His old dread of God had vanished, and instead of it there had arisen in his heart a love to God in answer to the love which came from the vision of the Father revealing Himself. He had experienced this, and he had proclaimed what he had gone through; and the experience and its proclamation were the foundation on which the Reformation was built. Its beginnings were not doctrinal but experimental.

Doctrines, indeed, are never the beginnings of things; they are, at the best, storehouses of past and blessed experiences. This is true of most knowledge in all departments of research. We may recognise that there is some practical use in the rules of logic, ancient and modern, but we know that they are but the uncouth and inadequate symbols of the ways in which an indefinable mental tact, whose delicacy varies with the mind that uses it, perceives divergences and affinities, and weaves its web of knowledge in ways that are past finding out. We know that logical argument is a good shield but a bad sword, and that while syllogisms may silence, they seldom convince; that persuasion arises from a subtle sympathy of soul with soul, which is as indefinable as the personalities which exhale it. There is always at the basis of knowledge of men and things this delicate contact of personality with personality, whether we think of the gathering, or assorting, or exchanging the wisdom we possess. If this be true of our knowledge of common things, it is overwhelmingly so of all knowledge of God and of things divine. We must be in touch with God to know Him in the true sense of knowledge. At the basis of every real advance in religion there must be an intimate vision of God impressed upon us as a religious experience which we know to be true because we have felt it; and what one has, another receives by a species of spiritual contagion. The revival under Francis of Assisi spread as it did because the fire flaming in the heart of the preacher was also kindled in the hearts of his hearers. Luther headed a Reformation because men felt and knew that he had, as he said, found a gracious God by trusting in the grace of God revealed to him in Christ Jesus. It was not the Augsburg Confession that made the Reformation; it was the expansion of a religious experience which finds very inadequate description in that or in any other statement of doctrines.

§ 2. *The universal Priesthood of Believers.*

Luther's religious experience, that he, a sinner, received forgiveness by simply throwing himself on God revealed in Christ Jesus the Saviour, came to him as an astounding revelation which was almost too great to be put into words. He tried to express it in varying ways, all of which he felt too utterly inadequate to describe it. We can see how he laboured at it from 1512 to 1517. It lay hidden in his discourse to the assembly of clergy in the episcopal palace at Ziesar (June 5th, 1512), when he declared that all reform must begin in the hearts of individual men. We can see it growing more and more articulate in his annotations, notes, and heads of lectures on the Psalms, delivered in the years 1513–1516, struggling to free itself from the phrases of the Scholastic Theology which could not really express it. His private letters, in which he was less hampered by the phraseology which he still believed appropriate to theology, are full of happier expressions.[1] *Justificatio* is *vivificatio*, and means to redeem from sins without any merit in the person redeemed; it takes place when sin is not imputed, but the penitents are reputed

[1] These annotations, glosses, and notes of lectures have been collected and published in volumes iii. and iv. of the Weimar edition of *Luther's Works.* The most important phrases have been carefully extracted by Loofs in his *Leitfaden*, pp. 345–352.

righteous. Grace is the pity (*misericordia*) of God; it manifests itself in the remission of sins; it is the truth of God seen in the fulfilment of His promises in the historical work of Christ; Jesus Christ Himself is grace, is the way, is life and salvation. Faith is trust in the truth of God as manifested in the life and work of Jesus Christ; it is to believe in God; it is a knowledge of the Cross of Christ; it is to understand that the Son of God became incarnate, was crucified, and raised again for our salvation. The three central thoughts—*justification, grace, faith*—expressed in these inadequate phrases, are always looked upon and used to regulate that estimate of ourselves which forms the basis of piety. It is needless to trace the growing adequacy of the description. Luther at last found words to say that the central thought in Christianity is that the believer in possession of faith, which is itself the gift of God, is able to throw himself on God in Christ Who is his salvation and Who has mirrored Himself for us in Christ Jesus. He had trod the weary round that Augustine had gone before him; he had tried *to help himself* in every possible way; he had found that with all his striving he could do nothing. Then, strange and mysterious as it was, the discovery had not brought despair, but rejoicing and comfort; for since there was no help whatever in man, his soul had been forced to find *all*—not part, but all—help in God. When he was able to express his experience he could say that the faith which throws itself on God, which is God's own gift, is the certainty of the forgiveness of sins. It was no adherence to doctrines more or less clearly comprehended; it was no act of initiation to be followed by a nearer approach to God and a larger measure of His grace; it was the power which gives life, certainty, peace, continuous self-surrender to God as the Father, and which transforms and renews the whole man. It was the life of the soul; it was Christianity within the believer—as Jesus Christ and His work is Christianity outside the believer.

It is manifest that as soon as this experience attained

articulate statement, it was bound to discredit much that was in mediæval theology and religious usage. Yet the striking thing about Luther was that he never sought to employ it in this way until one great abuse forced itself upon him and compelled him to test it by this touchstone of what true Christianity was. This reserve not only shows that there was nothing revolutionary in the character of Luther, nothing romantic or quixotic, it also manifests the quiet greatness of the man. Nor was there anything in the fundamental religious experience of Luther which necessarily conflicted with the contents of the old ecclesiastical doctrines, or even with the common usages of the religious life. There was a change in the attitude towards both, and an entirely new estimate of their religious value, but nothing which called for their immediate criticism, still less for their destruction. Faith, which was the Christian life, could no longer be based upon them; they were not the essential things that they had been supposed to be; but they might have their uses if kept in their proper places—aids to all holy living, but not that from which the life sprang. The thought that the entire sum of religion consists in "unwavering trust of the heart in Him Who has given Himself to us in Christ as our Father, personal assurance of faith, because Christ with His work undertakes our cause," simplified religion marvellously, and made many things which had been regarded as essential mere outside auxiliaries. But it did not necessarily sweep them away. Though the acceptance of certain forms of doctrine, auricular confession, the monastic life, communion by the laity in one "kind" only in the Sacrament of the Supper, a celibate priesthood, fasting, going on pilgrimages, not to eat meat on Friday, had nothing to do with the essentials of the Christian life; still it was not necessary to insist on eating meat on Friday, on abstaining from fasting, and so on. The great matter was the spirit in which such things were performed or left undone. What the fundamental religious experience had done was to show the liberty of the Christian man to trust courageously in

God and count all things of little moment compared with this which was the one thing needful.

"Out of a complex system of expiations, good deeds, and comfortings, of strict statutes and uncertain apportionments of grace, out of magic and blind obedience, Luther led religion forth and gave it a strenuously concentrated form. The Christian religion is the living assurance of the living God Who has revealed Himself and opened His heart in Christ—nothing more."[1]

It was a vital part of this fundamental experience that the living God Who had manifested Himself in Christ was accessible to every Christian. To quote Harnack again:

"Rising above all anxieties and terrors, above all ascetic devices, above all directions of theology, above all interventions of hierarchy and Sacraments, Luther ventured to lay hold of God Himself in Christ, and in this act of faith, which he recognised as God's work, his whole being obtained stability and firmness, nay, even a personal joy and certainty, which no mediæval Christian had ever possessed."[2]

God Himself gave the believer the power to throw himself directly on God. But this contradicted one of the most widely diffused and most strongly held religious beliefs of the mediæval Church, and was bound to come in collision with it whenever the two were confronted with each other. It was the universal conception of mediæval piety that the mediation of a priest was essential to salvation. Mediæval Christians believed with more or less distinctness that the supernatural life of the soul was *created*, nourished, and perfected through the sacraments, and that the priests administering them possessed, in virtue of their ordination, miraculous powers whereby they daily offered the true sacrifice of Jesus Christ upon the altar, forgave the sins of men, and taught the truths of salvation with divine authority. It was this universally accepted power of a mediatorial priesthood which had enslaved Europe, and which had rendered the liberty of a Christian

[1] A. Harnack, *History of Dogma*, vii. 183. [2] *Ibid.* vii. 184.

man an impossible thing. Everywhere the priesthood barred, or was supposed to be able to bar, the way to God. The Church, which ought to have shown how God Who had revealed Himself in Christ was accessible to every believer, had surrounded the inner shrine of the sanctuary of His Presence with a triple wall of defence which prevented entrance. When man or woman felt sorrow for sin, they were instructed to go, not to God, but to a man, often of immoral life, and confess their sins to him because he was a priest. When they wished to hear the comforting words of pardon spoken, it was not from God, but from a priest that the assurance was supposed to come. God's grace, to help to holy living and to bring comfort in dying, was given, it was said, only through a series of sacraments which fenced man's life round, and priests could give or withhold these sacraments. Man was born again in baptism; he came of age spiritually in confirmation; his marriage was cleansed from the sin of lust in the sacrament of matrimony; penance brought back his spiritual life slain by deadly sin; the Eucharist gave him his voyage victual as he journeyed through life; and deathbed grace was imparted in extreme unction. These ceremonies were not the signs and promises of the free grace of God, under whose wide canopy, as under that of heaven, man lived his spiritual life. They were jealously guarded doors from out of which grudgingly, and commonly not without fees, the priests dispensed the free grace of God.

During the later Middle Ages a gross abuse made the evils of this conception of a mediating priesthood emphatic. The practical evil lying in the whole thought was not so very apparent when the matter was regarded from the side of giving out the grace of God; but when it came to withholding it, then it was seen what the whole conception meant. The Bishops of Rome gave the peoples of Europe many an object lesson on this. If a town, or a district, or a whole country had offended the Pope and the Curia, it was placed under an *interdict*, and the priests were commanded to refuse the sacraments to the people. They stood between the newborn babe and the initial grace supposed to be bestowed in baptism, and to be absolutely withheld if baptism was not administered; between the dying man and the deathbed grace which was received in extreme unction; between young men and women and legal marriage blessed by God; between the people and daily worship and the bestowal of grace in the Eucharist The God of grace could not be approached, the blessings of pardon and strength for holy living could not be procured, because the magistrates of a town or the king and councillors of a nation had offended the Bishop of Rome on an affair of worldly policy. The Church, *i.e.* the clergy, who were by the theory enabled to refuse to communicate the grace of God, barred all access to the God who had revealed Himself in Christ Jesus. The Pope by a stroke of the pen could prevent a whole nation, so it was believed, from approaching God, because he could prohibit priests from performing the usual sacramental acts which alone brought Him near. An *interdict* meant spiritual death to the district on which it fell, and on the mediæval theory it was more deadly to the spiritual life than the worst of plagues, the Black Death itself, was to the body. An *interdict* made the plainest intellect see, understand, and shudder at the awful and mysterious powers which a mediatorial priesthood was said to possess.

The fundamental religious experience of Luther had made him know that the Father, who has revealed Himself in His Son, is accessible to every humble penitent and faithful seeker after God. He proclaimed aloud the spiritual priesthood of all believers. He stated it with his usual graphic emphasis in that tract of his, which he always said contained the marrow of his message—*Concerning Christian Liberty.* He begins by an antithesis: "A Christian man is the most free lord of all, and subject to none: a Christian man is the most dutiful servant of all, and subject to everyone"; or, as St. Paul puts it, "Though I be free from all men, yet have I made myself servant of all." He expounds this by showing that no outward things have any influence in producing Christian righteousness or liberty; neither eating, drinking, nor anything of the kind, neither hunger nor thirst have to do with the liberty or the slavery of the soul. It does not profit the soul to wear sacred vestments or to dwell in sacred places; nor does it harm the soul to be clothed in worldly raiment, and to eat and drink in the ordinary fashion. The soul can do without everything except the word of God, and this word of God is the gospel of God concerning His Son, incarnate, suffering, risen, and glorified through the Spirit the Sanctifier. "To preach Christ is to feed the soul, to justify it, to set it free, to save it, if it believes the preaching; for faith alone and the efficacious use of the word of God bring salvation." It is faith that incorporates Christ with the believer, and in this way "the soul through faith alone, without works, is, from the word of God, justified, sanctified, endued with truth, peace, liberty, and filled full with every good thing, and is truly made the child of God." For faith brings the soul and the word together, and the soul is acted upon by the word, as iron exposed to fire glows like fire because of its union with the fire. Faith honours and reveres Him in Whom it trusts, and cleaves to His promises, never doubting but that He overrules all for the best. Faith unites the soul to Christ, so that "Christ and the soul become one flesh." "Thus the believing soul, by the pledge of its faith in Christ, becomes free from all sin, fearless of death, safe from hell, and endowed with the eternal righteousness, life, and salvation of its husband Christ." This gives the liberty of the Christian man; no dangers can really harm him, no sorrows utterly overwhelm him: for he is always accompanied by the Christ to whom he is united by his faith.

"Here you will ask," says Luther, "'If all who are in the Church are priests, by what character are those whom we now call priests to be distinguished from the laity?' I reply, By the use of these words 'priest,' 'clergy,' 'spiritual person,' 'ecclesiastic,' an injustice has been done, since they have been transferred from the remaining body of Christians to those few who are now, by a hurtful custom, called ecclesiastics. For Holy Scripture makes no distinction between them, except that those who are now boastfully called Popes, bishops, and lords, it calls ministers, servants, and stewards, who are to serve the rest in the ministry of the word, for teaching the faith of Christ and the liberty of believers. For though it is true that we are all equally priests, yet we cannot, nor ought we if we could, all to minister and teach publicly."

The first part of the treatise shows that everything which a Christian man has goes back in the end to his faith; if he has this he has all; if he has it not, nothing else suffices him. In the same way the second part shows that everything that a Christian man does must come from his faith. It may be necessary to fast and keep the body under; it will be necessary to make use of all the ceremonies of divine service which have been found effectual for the spiritual education of man. The thing to remember is that these are not good works in themselves in the sense of making a man good; they are all rather the signs of his faith, and are to be done with joy, because they are done to the God to whom faith unites us. So ecclesiastical ceremonies, or what may be called the machinery of Church life, are valuable, and indeed indispensable to the life of the soul, provided only they are regarded in the proper way and kept in their proper place; but they may become harmful and most destructive of the true religious life if they are considered in any other light than that of means to an end. "We do not condemn works," says Luther, "nay we attach the highest value to them. We only condemn that opinion of works which regards them as constituting true righteousness." They are, he explains, like the scaffolding of a building, eminently useful so long as they assist the builder; harmful if they obstruct; and at the best of temporary value. They are destructive to the spiritual life when they come between the soul and God. It follows, therefore, that if through human corruption and neglect of the plain precepts of the word of God these ecclesiastical usages hinder instead of aid the true growth of the soul, they ought to be changed or done away with; and the fact that the soul of man, in the last resort, needs absolutely nothing but the word of God dwelling within it, gives men courage and tranquillity in demanding their reformation.

In the same way fellow-men are not to be allowed to come between God and the human soul; and there is no need that they should. So far as spiritual position and privileges go, the laity are on the very same level as the clergy, for laity and clergy alike have immediate access to God through faith, and both are obliged to do what lies in them to further the advance of the kingdom of God among their fellow-men. All believing laymen "are worthy to appear before God, to pray for others, to teach each other mutually the things that are of God . . . and as our heavenly Father has freely helped us in Christ, so we ought freely to help our neighbours by our body and our works, and each should become to the other a sort of Christ, so that we may be mutually Christs, and that the same Christ may be in all of us; that we may be truly Christians." Luther asserted that men and women living their lives in the family, in the workshop, in the civic world, held their position there, not by a kind of indirect permission wrung from God out of His compassion for human frailties, but by as direct a vocation as called a man to what by mistake had been deemed the only "religious life." The difference between clergy and laity did not consist in the supposed fact that the former were a spiritual order of a superior rank in the religious life, while the latter belonged to a lower condition. The clergy differed from the laity simply in this, that they had been selected to perform certain definite duties; but the function did not make him who performed it a holier man intrinsically. If the clergy misused their position and did not do the work they were set apart to perform, there was no reason why they should not be compelled by the laity to amend their ways. Even in the celebration of the holiest rites there was no distinction between clergy and laity save that to prevent disorder the former presided over the rites in which all engaged. At the Eucharist

"our priest or minister stands before the altar, having been publicly called to his priestly function; he repeats publicly and distinctly Christ's words of the institution; he takes the Bread and the Wine, and distributes it according to Christ's words; and we all kneel beside him and around him, men and women, young and old, master and servant, mistress and maid, all holy priests together, sanctified by the blood of Christ. We are there in our priestly dignity. . . . We do not let the priest proclaim for himself the ordinance of Christ; but he is the mouthpiece of us all, and we all say it with him in our hearts with true faith in the Lamb of God Who feeds us with His Body and Blood."

It was this principle of the Priesthood of all Believers which delivered men from the vague fear of the clergy, and which was a spur to incite them to undertake the reformation of the Church which was so much needed. It is the one great religious principle which lies at the basis of the whole Reformation movement. It was the rock on which all attempts at reunion with an unreformed Christendom were wrecked. It is the one outstanding difference between the followers of the reformed and the mediæval religion.

Almost all the distinctive principles of the Reformation group themselves round this one thought of the Priesthood of all Believers. It is sufficient for our purpose to look at Justification by Faith, the conceptions of the Holy Scriptures, of the Person of Christ, and of the Church.

§ 3. *Justification by Faith*

When Luther, oppressed with a sense of sin, entered the convent, he was burdened by the ideas of traditional religion, that the penitent must prepare himself in some way so as to render himself fit to experience that sense of the grace of God which gives the certainty of pardon. It was not until he had thoroughly freed himself from that weight that he experienced the sense of pardon he sought. This practical experience of his must always be kept in view when we try to conceive what he meant by Justification by Faith.

As has been already said, Luther recognised that there were two kinds of faith,—one which man himself begot and through which he was able to give assent to doctrines of some sort; and another which Luther vehemently asserted was the pure gift of God. The first he thought comparatively unimportant; the latter was all in all to him. Faith is always used in the latter sense when the Reformers speak about *Justification by Faith*; and the sharp distinction which Luther draws between the two is a very important element in determining what he meant when he said that we are justified by faith alone.

This faith of the highest kind, the true faith, has its beginning by God working on us and in us. It is continually fed and kept strong by the word of God. The promise of God on God's side and faith on man's side are two correlative things; "for where there is no promise, there is no faith." Luther brings out what this true faith is by contrasting it with the other kind of faith in two very instructive and trenchant passages:

"When faith is of the kind that God awakens and creates in the heart, then a man trusts in Christ. He is then so securely founded on Christ that he can hurl defiance at sin, death, hell, the devil, and all God's enemies. He fears no ill, however hard and cruel it may prove to be. Such is the nature of true faith, which is utterly different from the faith of the sophists (the Schoolmen), Jews, and Turks. Their faith, produced by their thoughts, simply lights upon a thing, accepts it, believes that it is this or that. God has no dealings with such delusion; it is the work of man, and comes from nature, from the free will of man; and men possessing it can say, repeating what others have said: I believe that there is a God. I believe that Christ was born, died, rose again for me. But what the real faith is, and how powerful a thing it is, of this they know nothing."[1]

[1] *Luther's Works* (2nd Erlangen edition), xv. 540.

He says again:

"Wherefore, beware of that faith which is manufactured or imagined; for the true faith is not the work of man, and therefore the faith which is manufactured or imagined will not avail in death, but will be overcome and utterly overthrown by sin, by the devil, and by the pains of hell. The true faith is the heart's utter trust in Christ, and God alone awakens this in us. He who has it is blessed, he who has it not is cursed."[1]

This faith has an outside fact to rest upon—the historical Christ. It is neither helped nor hindered by a doctrine of the Person of Christ, nor by a minute and elaborate knowledge of the details of our Lord's earthly ministry. The man who has the faith may know a great deal about the doctrine of the Person of Christ: that will do his faith no harm but good, provided only he does not make the mistake of thinking that doctrines about Christ, ways by which the human understanding tries to conceive the fact, are either the fact itself or something better than the fact. He may know a great deal about the history of Jesus, and it is well to know as much as possible; but the amount of knowledge scarcely affects the faith. Wayfaring men, though fools, need not err in the pathway of faith.

The faith which is the gift of God makes us see the practical meaning in the fact of the historic Christ—this, namely, that Jesus Christ is there before us the manifestation of the Fatherly love of God, revealing to us our own forgiveness, and with it the possibilities of the Kingdom of God and of our place therein. The fact of the historic Christ is there, seen by men in a natural way; but it is the power of God lying in the faith which He has given us that makes us see with full certainty the meaning of the fact of the historic Christ for us and for our salvation. Moreover, this vision of God in the historic Christ, which is the deepest of all personal things, always involves something social. It brings us within the family of the faithful, within the Christian fellowship

[1] *Luther's Works* (2nd Erlangen edition), xv. 542.

with its confirming evidences of faith and love. The power of faith comes to us singly, but seldom solitarily; the trust we have in God in Christ is faintly mirrored in the faith we learn to have in the members of the household of faith, and in their manifestations of faith and the love which faith begets.

What has been called the doctrine of Justification by Faith is therefore rather the description of a religious experience within the believer; and the meaning of the experience is simply this. The believer, who because he has faith—the faith which is the gift of God, which is our life and which regenerates — is regenerate and a member of the Christian fellowship, and is able to do good works and actually does them, does not find his standing as a person justified in the sight of God, his righteousness, his assurance of pardon and salvation, in those good works which he really can do, but only in the mediatorial and perfectly righteous work of Christ which he has learned to appropriate in faith. His good works, however really good, are necessarily imperfect, and in this experience which we call Justification by Faith the believer compares his own imperfect good works with the perfect work of Christ, and recognises that his pardon and salvation depends on that alone. This comparison quiets souls anxious about their salvation, and soothes pious consciences; and the sense of forgiveness which comes in this way is always experienced as a revelation of wonderful love. This justification is called an act, and is contrasted with a work; but the contrast, though true, is apt to mislead through human analogies which will intrude. It is an act, but an act of God; and divine acts are never done and done with, they are always continuous. Luther rings the changes upon this. He warns us against thinking that the act of forgiveness is all done in a single moment. The priestly absolution was the work of a moment, and had to be done over and over again; but the divine pronouncement of pardon is continuous simply because it is God who makes it. He says:

"For just as the sun shines and enlightens none the less brightly when I close my eyes, so this throne of grace, this forgiveness of sins, is always there, even though I fall. Just as I see the sun again when I open my eyes, so I have forgiveness and the sense of it once more when I look up and return to Christ. We are not to measure forgiveness as narrowly as fools dream."[1]

In the Protestant polemic with Roman Catholic doctrine, the conception of Justification by Faith is contrasted with that of Justification by Works; but the contrast is somewhat misleading. For the word justification is used in different meanings in the two phrases. The direct counterpart in Roman Catholic usage to the Reformation thought of Justification by Faith is the absolution pronounced by a priest; and here as always the Reformer appeals from man to God. The two conceptions belong to separate spheres of thought.

"The justification of which the mediæval Christian had experience was the descending of an outward stream of forces upon him from the supersensible world, through the Incarnation, in the channels of ecclesiastical institutions, priestly consecration, sacraments, confession, and good works; it was something which came from his connection with a supersensible organisation which surrounded him. The justification by faith which Luther experienced within his soul was the personal experience of the believer standing in the continuous line of the Christian fellowship, who receives the assurance of the grace of God in his exercise of a personal faith,—an experience which comes from appropriating the work of Christ which he is able to do by that faith which is the gift of God."[2]

In the one case, the Protestant, justification is a personal experience which is complete in itself, and does not depend on any external machinery; in the other, the Mediæval, it is a prolonged action of usages, sacraments, external machinery of all kinds, which by their combined effect are supposed to change a sinner gradually into a saint,

[1] *Luther's Works* (2nd Erlangen edition), xiv. 294.
[2] Dilthey, *Archiv für Geschichte der Philosophie*, v. iii. 358

righteous in the eyes of God. With the former, it is a continuous experience; with the latter, it cannot fail to be intermittent as the external means are actually employed or for a time laid aside.

The meaning of the Reformation doctrine of Justification by Faith may be further brought out by contrasting it with the theory which was taught by that later school of Scholastic theology which was all-powerful at the beginning of the sixteenth century. The more evangelical theory of Thomas Aquinas was largely neglected, and the Nominalist Schoolmen based their expositions of the doctrine on the teaching of John Duns Scotus.

It must be remembered that mediæval theology never repudiated the theology of Augustine, and admitted in theory at least that man's salvation, and justification as part of it, always depended in the last resort on the prevenient grace of God; in their reverence for the teaching of Aristotle, they believed that they had also to make room for the action of the free will of man which they always looked on as the pure capacity of choice between two alternatives. John Duns Scotus got rid of a certain confusion which existed between the *gratia operans* and *gratia co-operans* of Augustine by speaking of the grace of God, which lay at the basis of man's justification, as a *gratia habitualis*, or an operation of the grace of God which gave to the will of man an habitual tendency to love towards God and man. He alleged that when conduct is considered, an act of the will is more important than any habitual tendency, for it is the act which makes use of the habit, and apart from the act, the habit is a mere inert passivity. Therefore, he held that the chief thing in meritorious conduct is not so much the habit which has been created by God's grace, as the act of will which makes use of the habit. In this way the grace of God is looked upon as simply the general basis of meritorious conduct, or a mere *conditio sine qua non*, and the important thing is the act of will which can make use of the otherwise passive habit. The process of justification

—and it is to be remembered that the Schoolmen invariably looked upon justification as a process by which a sinner was gradually made into a righteous man and thoroughly and substantially changed—may therefore be described as an infusion of divine grace which creates a habit of the will towards love to God and to man; this is laid hold on by acts of the will, and there result positive acts of love towards God and man which are meritorious, and which gradually change a sinner into a righteous person. This is the theory; but the theory is changed into practice by being exhibited in the framework of the Church provided to aid men to appropriate the grace of God which is the basis for all. The obvious and easiest way to obtain that initial grace which is the starting-point is by the sacraments, which are said to infuse grace—the grace which is needed to make the start on the process of justification. Grace is infused to begin with in Baptism; and it is also infused from time to time in the Eucharist. If a man has been baptized, he has the initial grace to start with; and he can get additions in the Eucharist That, according to the theory, is all that is needed to start the will on its path of meritorious conduct. But while this exhibits the ideal process of justification according to mediæval theology, it must be remembered that there is mortal sin—sin which slays the new life begun in baptism—and the sacrament which renews the life slain will be practically more important than the sacrament which first creates it. Hence practically the whole process of the mediæval justification is best seen in the sacrament which renews the life slain by deadly sins. That sacrament is Penance; and the theory and practice of justification is best exhibited in the Sacrament of Penance. The good disposition of the will towards God is seen in confession; this movement towards God is complete when confession stimulated by the priest is finished; the performance of the meritorious good works is seen in the penitent performing the "satisfactions," or tasks imposed by the priest, of prayer, of almsgiving, of maceration; while the absolution announces that the process is complete, and that the sinner has become a righteous man and is in "a state of grace."

In opposition to all this, Luther asserted that it was possible to go through all that process prescribed by the mediæval Church, embodying the Scholastic theory of justification, without ever having the real sense of pardon, or ever being comforted by the sense of the love of God. The faith, however, which is the gift of God makes the believer see in the Christ Who is there before him a revelation of God's Fatherly love which gives him the sense of pardon, and at the same time excites in him the desire to do all manner of loving service. He is like the forgiven child who is met with tenderness when punishment was expected, and in glad wonder resolves never to be naughty again—so natural and simple is the Reformation thought. That thought, however, can be put much more formally. Chemnitz expresses it thus:

"The main point of controversy at present agitated between us and the Papists relates to the good works or new obedience of the *regenerate.* They hold that the regenerate are justified through that renewal which the Holy Spirit works *in* them, and by means of the *good works which proceed* from that renewal. They hold that the good works of the regenerate are the things on which they can trust, when the hard question comes to be answered, whether we be children of God and have been accepted to everlasting life. We hold, on the other hand, that in true repentance faith lays hold on and appropriates to itself *Christ's satisfaction*, and in so doing has something which it can oppose to the law's accusations at the bar of God, and thus bring it to pass that we should be declared righteous. . . . It is indeed true that believers have actual righteousness through their renewal by the Holy Spirit, but inasmuch as that righteousness is imperfect and still impure by reason of the flesh, all men cannot stand in God's judgment with it, nor on its account does God pronounce us righteous."[1]

Hence we may say that the difference in the two ways of looking at the matter may be exhibited in the answer to the

[1] *Examen Concilii Tridentini* (Geneva, 1641), pp. 134 f.

question, What does faith lay hold on in true repentance? The Reformation answer is—(1) not on a mechanically complete confession made to a priest, nor on a due performance of what the priest enjoins by way of satisfaction; but (2) only on what God in Christ has done for us, which is seen in the life, death, and rising again of the Saviour.

The most striking differences between the Reformation and the mediæval conception of justification are:

(1) The Reformation thought always looks at the comparative *imperfection* of the works of believers, while admitting that they are good works; the mediæval theologian, even when bidding men disregard the intrinsic value of their good works, always looks at the relative *perfection* of these works.

(2) The Reformer had a much more concrete idea of God's grace — it was something special, particular, unique—because he invariably regarded the really good works which men can do from their relative imperfection; the mediæval theologian looked at the relative perfection of good works, and so could represent them as something congruous to the grace of God which was not sharply distinguished from them.

(3) These views led Luther and the Reformers to represent faith as not merely the receptive organ for the reception and appropriation of justification through Christ, but, and in addition, as the active instrument in all Christian life and work—faith is our life; while the mediæval theologians never attained this view of faith.

(4) The Reformer believes that the act of faith in his justification through Christ is the basis of the believer's assurance of his pardon and salvation in spite of the painful and abiding sense of sin; while the mediæval theologian held that the divine sentence of acquittal which restored a sinner to a state of grace resulted from the joint action of the priest and the penitent in the Sacrament of Penance, and had to be repeated intermittently.

§ 4. *Holy Scripture.*

All the Reformers of the sixteenth century, whether Luther, Zwingli, or Calvin, believed that in the Scriptures God spoke to them in the same way as He had done in earlier days to His prophets and Apostles. They believed that if the common people had the Scriptures in a language which they could understand, they could hear God speaking to them directly, and could go to Him for comfort, warning, or instruction; and their description of what they meant by the Holy Scriptures is simply another way of saying that all believers can have access to the very presence of God. The Scriptures were therefore for them a personal rather than a dogmatic revelation. They record the experience of a fellowship with God enjoyed by His saints in past ages, which may still be shared in by the faithful. In Bible history as the Reformers conceived it, we hear twc voices—the voice of God speaking love to man, and the voice of the renewed man answering in faith to God. This communion is no dead thing belonging to a bygone past; it may be shared here and now.

But the Reformation conception of Scripture is continually stated in such a way as to deprive it of the eminently religious aspect that it had for men of the sixteenth century. It is continually said that the Reformers placed the Bible, an infallible Book, over-against an infallible Church; and transferred the *same kind* of infallibility which had been supposed to belong to the Church to this book. In mediæval times, men accepted the decisions of Popes and Councils as the last decisive utterance on all matters of controversy in doctrine and morals; at the Reformation, the Reformers, it is said, placed the Bible where these Popes and Councils had been, and declared that the last and final appeal was to be made to its pages. This mode of stating the question has found its most concise expression in the saying of Chillingworth, that "the Bible and the Bible alone is the religion of Protestants." It is quite true that the Reformers did set the authority of the Scriptures over-against that of Popes and Councils, and that Luther declared that "the common man," "miller's maid," or "boy of nine" with the Bible knew more about divine truth than the Pope without the Bible; but this is not the whole truth, and is therefore misleading. For Romanists and Protestants do not mean the same thing by *Scripture*, nor do they mean the same thing by *Infallibility*, and their different use of the words is a most important part of the Reformation conception of Scripture.

This difference in the meaning of *Scripture* is partly external and partly internal; and the latter is the more important of the two.

The *Scriptures* to which the Romanist appeals include the Apocryphal Books of the Old Testament; and the *Scriptures* which are authoritative are not the books of the Old and New Testament in the original tongues, but a translation into Latin known as the Vulgate of Pope Sixtus v. They are therefore a book to a large extent different from the one to which Protestants appeal.

However important this external difference may be, it is nothing in comparison with the internal difference; and yet the latter is continually forgotten by Protestants as well as by Roman Catholics in their arguments.

To understand it, one must remember that every mediæval theologian declared that the whole doctrinal system of his Church was based upon the Scriptures of the Old and New Testaments. The Reformers did nothing unusual, nothing which was in opposition to the common practice of the mediæval Church in which they had been born, educated, and lived, when they appealed to Scripture. Luther made his appeal with the same serene unconsciousness that anyone could gainsay him, as he did when he set the believer's spiritual experience of the fact that he rested on Christ alone for salvation against the proposal to sell pardon for money. His opponents never attempted to challenge his right to make this appeal to Scripture—at least at first. They made the same appeal themselves; they believed that they were able to meet Scripture with

Scripture. They were confident that the authority appealed to—Scripture—would decide against Luther. It soon became apparent, however, that Luther had an unexpectedly firmer grasp of Scripture than they had. This did not mean that he had a better memory for texts. It was seen that Luther somehow was able to look at and use Scripture as one transparent whole; while they looked on it as a collection of fragmentary texts. This gave him and other Reformers a skill in the use of Scripture which their opponents began to feel that they were deficient in. They felt that if they were to meet their opponents on equal terms they too must recognise a unity in Scripture. They did so by creating an external and arbitrary unity by means of the dogmatic tradition of the mediæval Church. Hence the decree of the Council of Trent, which manufactured an artificial unity for Scripture by placing the dogmatic tradition of the Church alongside Scripture as an equal source of authority. The reason why the Reformers found a natural unity in the Bible, and why the Romanists had to construct an artificial one, lay, as we shall see, in their different conceptions of what was meant by saving faith.

Mediæval theologians looked at the Bible as a sort of spiritual law-book, a storehouse of divinely communicated knowledge of doctrinal truths and rules for moral conduct —and nothing more.

The Reformers saw in it a new home for a new life within which they could have intimate fellowship with God Himself — not merely knowledge about God, but actual communion with Him.

There is one great difficulty attending the mediæval conception of the Scriptures, that it does not seem applicable to a large part of them. There is abundant material provided for the construction of doctrines and moral rules; but that is only a portion of what is contained in the Scriptures. The Bible contains long lists of genealogies, chapters which contain little else than a description of temple furniture, stories of simple human life, and details of national history. The mediæval theologian had either to discard altogether a large part of the Bible or to transform it somehow into doctrinal and moral teaching. The latter alternative was chosen, and the instrument of transformation was the thought of the various senses in Scripture which plays such a prominent part in every mediæval statement of the nature and uses of the revelation of God contained in the Bible.[1] No one can deny that a book, where instruction is frequently given in parables, or by means of aphorisms and proverbial sayings, must contain many passages which have different senses. It may be admitted, to use Origen's illustrations, that the grain of mustard seed is, *literally*, an actual seed; *morally*, faith in the individual believer; and, *allegorically*, the kingdom of God;[2] or, though this is more doubtful, that the little foxes are, literally, cubs; morally, sins in the individual heart; and, allegorically, heresies which distract and spoil the Church.[3] But to say that every detail of personal or national life in the Old Testament or New is merely dead history, of no spiritual value until it has been transformed into a doctrinal truth or a moral rule by the application of the theory of the fourfold sense in Scripture, is to destroy the historical character of revelation altogether, and, besides, to introduce complete uncertainty about what any passage was really meant to declare. The use of a fourfold sense—*literal*, *moral*, *allegorical*, and *anagogic*—enables the reader to draw any meaning he pleases from any portion of Scripture.

While mediæval theologians, by their bewildering fourfold sense, made it almost hopeless to know precisely what the Bible actually taught, another idea of theirs made it essential to salvation that men should attain to an absolutely

[1] The mediæval fourfold sense in Scripture was explained by Nicholas de Lyra in the distich:

> "*Litera* gesta docet, quid credas *Allegoria*,
> *Moralis* quid agas, quo tendas *Anagogia*."

It is expounded succinctly by Thomas Aquinas, *Summa Theologiæ*, I. i. 10.

[2] Matt. xiii. 31.

[3] Song of Songs, ii. 15.

correct statement of what the Scriptures did reveal about God and man and the relation between them. They held that faith—the faith which saves—was not trust in a person, but assent to correct propositions about God, the universe, and the soul of man; and the saving character of the assent depended on the correctness of the propositions assented to. It is the submission of the intellect to certain propositional statements which are either seen to be correct or are accepted as being so because guaranteed in some supernatural way. Infallibility is looked upon as that which can guarantee the perfect correctness of propositions about God and man in their relations to each other.

If it be necessary to employ the fourfold sense to confuse the plain meaning of the greater portion of Scripture, and *if* salvation depends on arriving at a perfectly correct intellectual apprehension of abstract truths contained somewhere in the Bible, then Lacordaire's sarcastic reference to the Protestant conception of Scripture is not out of place. He says: "What kind of a religion is that which saves men by aid of a book? God has given the book, but He has not guaranteed your private interpretation of it. What guarantee have you that your thoughts do not shove aside God's ideas? The heathen carves himself a god out of wood or marble; the Protestant carves his out of the Bible. If there be a true religion on earth, it must be of the most *serene* and unmistakable authority."[1] We need not wonder at John Nathin saying to his perplexed pupil in the Erfurt Convent: "Brother Martin, let the Bible alone; read the old teachers; reading the Bible simply breeds unrest."[2] We can sympathise with some of the earlier printers of the German Vulgate when they inserted in their prefaces that readers must be careful to understand the contents of the volume in the way declared by the Church.[3] Men who went to the Bible might go wrong, and it was spiritual death to make any mistake; but all who simply assented to the interpretation of the Bible given in the

[1] *Lettres à jeunes gens*, à Eugene l'hermite (Paris, 1863).
[2] Cf. above, p. 200. [3] Cf. above, p. 151.

Church's theology were kept right and had the true or saving faith. Such was the mediæval idea.

But all this made it impossible to find in the Bible a means of communion with God. Between the God Who had revealed Himself there and man, the mediæval theologian, perhaps unconsciously at first, had placed what he called the "Church," but what really was the opinions of accredited theologians confirmed by decisions of Councils or Popes. The "Church" had barred the way of access to the mind and heart of God in the Scriptures by interposing its authoritative method of interpretation between the believer and the Bible, as it had interposed the priesthood between the sinner and the redeeming Saviour.

Just as the Reformers had opposed their personal experience of pardon won by throwing themselves on the mercy of God revealed in Christ to the intervention of the Church between them and God, so they controverted this idea of the Scriptures by the personal experience of what the Bible had been to them. They had felt and known that the personal God, Who had made them and redeemed them, was speaking to them in this Book, and was there making manifest familiarly His power and His willingness to save. The speech was sometimes obscure, but they read on and lighted on other passages which were plainer, and they made the easier explain the more difficult. The "common" man perhaps could not understand it all, nor fit all the sayings of Scripture into a connected whole of intellectual truth; but all, plain men and theologians alike, could hear their Father's voice, learn their Redeemer's purpose, and have faith in their Lord's promises. It was a good thing to put text to text and build a system of Protestant divinity to which their intellects could assent; but it was not essential. Saving faith was not intellectual assent at all. It was simple trust—the trust of a child—in their Father's promises, which were Yea and Amen in Christ Jesus. The one essential thing was to hear and obey the personal God speaking to them as He had spoken all down through the ages to His people, promising His salvation now in direct words, now in pictures of His dealings with a favoured man or a chosen people. No detail of life was dead history; for it helped to fill the picture of communion between God and His people. The picture was itself a promise that what had been in the past would be renewed in their own experience of fellowship with a gracious God, if only they had the same faith which these saints of the Old and New Testaments enjoyed.

With these thoughts burning in their hearts, the Bible could not be to the Reformers what it had been to the mediæval theologians. God was speaking to them in it as a man speaks to his fellows. The simple historical sense was the important one in the great majority of passages. The Scripture was more than a storehouse of doctrines and moral rules. It was over and above the record and picture of the blessed experience which God's saints have had in fellowship with their covenant God since the first revelation of the Promise. So they made haste to translate the Bible into all languages in order to place it in the hands of every man, and said that the "common man" with the Bible in his hands (with God speaking to him) could know more about the way of salvation than Pope or Councils without the Scriptures.

The change of view which separated the Reformers from mediæval theologians almost amounted to a rediscovery of Scripture; and it was effected by their conception of faith. Saving faith was for them *personal trust* in a *personal Saviour* Who had manifested in His life and work the Fatherly mercy of God. This was not a mere theological definition; it was a description of an experience which they knew that they had lived. It made them see that the word of God was a personal and not a dogmatic revelation; that the real meaning in it was that God Himself was there behind every word of it,—not an abstract truth, but a personal Father. On the one side, on the divine, there was God pouring out His whole heart and revealing the inmost treasures of His righteousness and love in Christ the Incarnate Word; on the other side, on the human, there was the believing soul looking straight through all works and all symbols and all words to Christ Himself, united to Him by faith in the closest personal union. Such a blessed experience—the feeling of direct fellowship between the believer and God Incarnate, of a communion such as exists between two loving human souls, brought about by the twofold stream of God's personal word coming down, and man's personal faith going up to God—could not fail to give an entirely new conception of Scripture. The mediæval Church looked on the Jesus Christ revealed in Scripture as a Teacher sent from God; and revelation was for them above all things an imparting of speculative truth. To the Reformers the chief function of Scripture was to bring Jesus Christ near us; and as Jesus always fills the full sphere of God to them, the chief end of Scripture is to bring God near *me*. It is the direct message of God's love to *me*,—not doctrine, but promise (for apart from promise, as Luther said unweariedly, faith does not exist); not display of God's thoughts, but of God Himself as *my* God. This manifestation of God, which is recorded for us in the Scriptures, took place in an historical process coming to its fullest and highest in the incarnation and historical work of Christ, and the record of the manifestation has been framed so as to include everything necessary to enable us to understand the declaration of God's will in its historical context and in its historical manifestation. "Let no pious Christian," says Luther, "stumble at the simple word and story that meet him so often in Scripture." These are never the dead histories of the mediæval theologian,—events which have simply taken place and concern men no more. They tell how God dealt with His faithful people in ages past, and they are promises of how He will act towards us now. "Abraham's history is precious," he says, "because it is filled so full of God's Word, with which all that befell him is so adorned and so fair, and because God goes everywhere before him with His Word, promising, commanding, comforting, warning, that we may verily see that Abraham was God's special trusty friend. Let us mirror ourselves, then, in this holy father Abraham.

who walks not in gold and velvet, but girded, crowned, and clothed with divine light, that is, with God's Word." The simplest Bible stories, even geographical and architectural details, may and do give us the sidelights necessary to complete the manifestation of God to His people.

The question now arises, Where and in what are we to recognise the infallibility and authoritative character of Scripture? It is manifest that the ideas attaching to these words must change with the changed conception of the essential character of that Scripture to which they belong. Nor can the question be discussed apart from the Reformation idea of saving faith; for the two thoughts of Scripture and saving faith always correspond. In mediæval theology they are always primarily intellectual and propositional; in Reformation thinking, they are always in the first instance experimental and personal. In describing the authoritative character of Scripture, the Reformers always insisted that its recognition was awakened in believers by that operation which they called the witness of the Holy Spirit (*Testimonium Spiritus Sancti*). Just as God Himself makes us know and feel the sense of pardon in an inward experience by a faith which is His own work, so they believed that by an operation of the same Spirit, believers were enabled to recognise that God Himself is speaking to us authoritatively in and through the words of Scripture.

Their view of what is meant by the authority and infallibility of Scripture cannot be seen apart from what they taught about the relation between Scripture and the word of God. They have all the same general conception, however they may differ in details in their statement. If Luther, as his wont was, speaks more trenchantly, and Calvin writes with a clearer vision of the consequences which must follow from his assertions, both have the same great thought before them.

The Reformers drew a distinction between the word of God and the Scripture which contains or presents that word. This distinction was real and not merely formal; it was more than the difference between the word of God and the word of God written; and important consequences were founded upon it. If the use of metaphor be allowed, the word of God is to the Scripture as the soul is to the body. Luther believed that while the word of God was presented in every part of Scripture, some portions make it much more evident. He instances the Gospel and First Epistle of St. John, the Epistles of St. Paul, especially those to the Romans, to the Galatians, and to the Ephesians, and the First Epistle of St. Peter.[1] He declares that if Christians possessed no other books besides those, the way of salvation would be perfectly clear. He adds elsewhere that the word of God shines forth with special clearness in the Psalms, which he called the Bible within the Bible.

Luther says that the word of God may be described in the phrase of St. Paul, "the Gospel of God, which He promised afore by His Prophets in the Holy Scriptures, concerning His Son, who was born of the seed of David according to the flesh, who was declared to be the Son of God with power, according to the spirit of holiness, by the resurrection of the dead."[2] Calvin calls it "the spiritual teaching, the gate, as it were, by which we enter into His heavenly kingdom," "a mirror in which faith beholds God," and "that wherein He utters unto us His mercy in Christ, and assureth us of His love toward us."[3] The Scots Confession calls it the revelation of the Promise "quhilk

[1] Luther is continually reproached for having called the Epistle of James an Epistle of straw; it is forgotten that he uses the term comparatively (*Prefaces to the New Testament; Works* (Erlangen edition), lxiii. 115): "Summa, Sanct Johannis Evangelium, und seine erste Epistel, Sanct Paulus Epistel, sonderlich die zu Römern, Galatern, Ephesern, und Sanct Peters erste Epistel, das sind die Bücher, die dir Christum zeigen und alles lehren, das dir zu wissen noth und selig ist, ob du schon kein ander Buch noch Lehre nimmermehr sehest noch hörist. Darumb ist Sanct Jakobs Epistel ein recht strohern Epistel *gegen sie*, denn sie doch kein evangelisch Art an ihr hat."

[2] *De Libertate* (Erlangen edition, Latin), xxxv. 222; Rom. i. 1–3.

[3] *Genevan Catechism; Institutio*, III. ii. 6: "The word itself, *however conveyed to us*, is a mirror in which faith may behold God"; *Second Geneva Catechism.*

as it was repeated and made mair clear from time to time; so was it imbraced with joy, and maist constantlie received of al the faithful."[1] And Zwingli declares it to be "that our Lord Jesus Christ, the very Son of God, has revealed to us the will of the Heavenly Father, and, with His innocence, has redeemed us from death."[2] It is the sum of God's commands, threatenings, and promises, addressed to our faith, and above all the gospel offer of Christ to us. This word of God need not take the form of direct exhortation; it may be recognised in the simple histories of men or of nations recorded in the Scripture.

This true and real distinction between the word of God and Scripture may easily be perverted to something which all the Reformers would have repudiated. It must not be explained by the common mystical illustration of kernel and husk, which husk (the record) may be thrown away when the kernel (the word) has been once reached and laid hold of. Nor can it be used to mean that one part of the Bible is the word of God and that another is not. The Reformers uniformly teach that the substance of *all* Scripture is the word of God, and that what is no part of the record of the word of God is not Scripture. Finally, the distinction between the two need not prevent us saying that the Scripture *is* the word of God. Luther is very peremptory about this. He says that he is ready to discuss differences with any opponent who admits that the evangelical writings are the word of God; but that if this be denied he will refuse to argue; for where is the good of reasoning with anyone who denies first principles? (*prima principia*).[3] Only it must be clearly understood that the copula *is* does not express logical identity, but some such relation as can be more exactly rendered by *contains, presents, conveys, records,*—all of which phrases are used in the writings of Reformers or in the creeds of the Reformation Churches. The main thing to

[1] (Dunlop), *A Collection of Confessions of Faith*, ii. 26.
[2] *Zurich Articles of 1523*, i. ii.
[3] *Luther's Works* (Erlangen edition), lvii. 34.

remember is that the distinction is not to be made use of to deny to the substance of Scripture those attributes of authority and infallibility which belong to the word of God.

On the other hand, there is a vital religious interest in the distinction. In the first place it indicates what is meant by the infallibility of Scripture, and in the second it enables us to distinguish between the divine and the human elements in the Bible.

The authoritative character and infallibility belong really and primarily to the word of God, and only secondarily to the Scriptures,—to Scripture only because it is the record which contains, presents, or conveys the word of God. It is this word of God, this personal manifestation to us for our salvation of God in His promises, which is authoritative and infallible; and Scripture shares these attributes only in so far as it is a vehicle of spiritual truth. It is the unanimous declaration of the Reformers that Scripture is Scripture because it gives us that knowledge of God and of His will which is necessary for salvation; because it presents to the eye of faith God Himself personally manifesting Himself in Christ. It is this presentation of God Himself and of His will for our salvation which is infallible and authoritative. But this manifestation of God Himself is something spiritual, and is to be apprehended by a spiritual faculty which is faith, and the Reformers and the Confessions of the Reformation do not recognise any infallibility or divine authority which is otherwise apprehended than by faith. If this be so, the infallibility is of quite another kind from that described by mediæval theologians or modern Roman Catholics, and it is also very different from what many modern Protestants attribute to the Scriptures when they do not distinguish them from the word of God. With the mediæval theologian infallibility was something which guaranteed the perfect correctness of abstract propositions; with some modern Protestants it consists in the conception that the record contains not even the smallest error in word or description of fact—

in its inerrancy. But neither inerrancy nor the correctness of abstract propositions is apprehended by faith in the Reformers' sense of that word; they are matters of fact, to be accepted or rejected by the ordinary faculties of man. The infallibility and authority which need faith to perceive them are, and must be, something very different; they produce the conviction that in the manifestation of God in His word there lies infallible power to save. This is given, all the Reformers say, by the Witness of the Spirit; "the true kirk alwaies heares and obeyis the voice of her awin spouse and pastor."[1] Calvin discusses the authority and credibility of Scripture in his *Institutio*, and says: "Let it be considered, then, as an undeniable truth that they who have been inwardly taught of the Spirit feel an entire acquiescence in the Scripture, and that it is self-authenticated, carrying with it its own evidence, and ought not to be made the subject of demonstration and arguments from reason; but that it obtains the credit which it deserves with us by the testimony of the Spirit."[2] This is a religious conception of infallibility very different from the mediæval or the modern Romanist.

The distinction between the word of God and Scripture also serves to distinguish between the divine and the human elements in Scripture, and to give each its proper place.

Infallibility and divine authority belong to the sphere of faith and of the witness of the Spirit, and, therefore, to that personal manifestation of God and of His will toward us which is conveyed or presented to us in every part of Scripture. But this manifestation is given in a course of events which are part of human history, in lives of men and peoples, in a record which in outward form is like other human writings. If every part of Scripture is divine, every part of it is also human. The supernatural reality is incased in human realities. To apprehend the former, faith illumined by the Holy Spirit is necessary;

[1] *Scots Confession*, Art. xix.; (Dunlop), *A Collection of Confessions*, p. 73.
[2] *Institutio*, I. vii. 5.

but it is sufficient to use the ordinary methods of research to learn the credibility of the history in Scripture. When the Reformers distinguished between the word of God and Scripture which conveys or presents it, and when they declared that the authority and infallibility of that word belonged to the region of faith, they made that authority and infallibility altogether independent of questions that might be raised about the human agencies through which the book came into its present shape. It is not a matter belonging to the region of faith when the books which record the word of God were written, or by whom, or in what style, or how often they were edited or re-edited. It is not a matter for faith whether incidents happened in one country or in another; whether the account of Job be literal history, or a poem based on old traditions in which the author has used the faculty of imagination to illustrate the problems of God's providence and man's probation; whether genealogical tables give the names of men or of countries and peoples. All these and the like matters belong to the human side of the record. No special illumination of faith is needed to apprehend and understand them. They are matters for the ordinary faculties of man, and subject to ordinary human investigation. Luther availed himself freely of the liberty thus given. He never felt himself bound to accept the traditional ideas about the extent of the canon, the authorship of the books of the Bible, or even about the credibility of some of the things recorded. He said, speaking about Genesis, "What though Moses never wrote it?"[1] It was enough for him that the book was there and that he could read it. He thought that the Books of Kings were more worthy of credit than the Books of Chronicles;[2] and he believed that the prophets had not always given the kings of Israel the best political advice.[3]

But while the Bible is human literature, and as such may be and must be subjected to the same tests which are

[1] *Luther's Works* (Erlangen edition), lvii. 35.
[2] *Ibid.* lxii. 132. [3] *Ibid.* (2nd Erlangen edition), viii. 23.

applied to ordinary literature, it is the record of the revelation of God, and has been carefully guarded and protected by God. This thought always enters into the conception which the Reformers had of Scripture. They speak of the singular care and providence of God which has preserved the Scriptures in such a way that His people always have a full and unmistakable declaration in them of His mind and will for their salvation. This idea for ever forbids a careless or irreverent biblical criticism, sheltering itself under the liberty of dealing with the records of revelation. No one can say beforehand how much or how little of the historic record is essential to preserve the faith of the Church; but every devout Christian desires to have it in large abundance. No one can plead the liberty which the principles of the Reformers secure for dealing with the record of Scripture as a justification in taking a delight in reducing to a minimum the historical basis of the Christian faith. Careless or irreverent handling of the text of Holy Scripture is what all the Reformers abhorred.[1]

[1] It may be useful to note the statements about the authority of Scripture in the earlier Reformation creeds. The Lutherans, always late in discerning the true doctrinal bearings of their religious certainties, did not deem it needful to assert dogmatically the supreme authority of Scripture until the second generation of Protestantism. The Schmalkald Articles and the Augsburg Confession expressly assert that human traditions are among abuses that ought to be done away with; but they do not condemn them as authorities set up by their opponents in opposition to the word of God, only as things that burden the conscience and incline men to false ways of trying to be at peace with God (*Augsburg Confession*, as given in Schaff, *The Creeds of the Evangelical Protestant Churches*, p. 65; *Schmalkald Articles*, xv.). It was not until 1576, in the Torgau Book, and in 1580 in the *Formula Concordiæ*, that they felt the necessity of declaring dogmatically and in opposition to the Roman Catholics that "the only standard by which all dogmas and all teachers must be valued and judged is no other than the prophetic and apostolic writings of the Old and of the New Testaments" (§ 1).

The Reformed theologians, with the clearer dogmatic insight which they always showed, felt the need of a statement about the theological place of Scripture very early, and declared in the *First Helvetic Confession* (1536) that "Canonic Scripture, the word of God, given by the Holy Spirit and set forth to the world by the prophets and apostles, the most perfect and ancient of all philosophies, alone contains perfectly all piety and the whole rule of life." The various Reformed Confessions, inspired by Calvin, followed this

§ 5. *The Person of Christ.*

"No one can deny," said Luther, "that we hold, believe, sing, and confess all things in correspondence with the Apostles' Creed, the faith of the old Church, that we make nothing new therein nor add anything thereto, and in this way we belong to the old Church and are one with it." Both the Augsburg Confession and the Schmalkald Articles begin with restating the doctrines of the old Catholic Church as these are given in the Apostles', Nicene, and Athanasian Creeds, the two latter being always regarded by Luther as explanatory of the Apostles' Creed. His criticism of theological doctrines was always confined to the theories introduced by the Schoolmen, and to the perversion of the old doctrines of the Church introduced in mediæval times mainly to bring these doctrines into conformity with the principles of the philosophy of Aristotle. He brought two charges against the Scholastic Theology.

example, and the supreme authority of Scripture was set forth in all the symbolical books of the Reformed Churches of Switzerland, France, England, the Netherlands, Scotland, etc.—*The Geneva Confession* of 1536 (Art. 1), *The Second Helvetic Confession* of 1562 (Art. 1), *The French Confession* of 1559 (Arts. 3–6), *The Belgic Confession* of 1561 (Arts. 4–7), *The Thirty-nine Articles* of 1563 and 1571 (Art. 6), *The Scots Confession* of 1560 (Art. 19). It is instructive, however, to note how this is done. The key to the central note in all these dogmatic statements is to be found in the first and second of *The Sixty-seven Theses* published in 1523 by Zwingli at Zurich, where it is declared that all who say that the Evangel is of no value apart from its confirmation by the Church err and blaspheme against God, and where the sum of the Evangel is "that our Lord Jesus Christ, very Son of God, has revealed to us the will of the heavenly Father, and with His innocence has redeemed us from death and has reconciled us to God." The main thought, therefore, in all these Confessions is not to assert the formal supremacy of Scripture over Tradition, but rather to declare the supreme value of Scripture which reveals God's good will to us in Jesus Christ to be received by faith alone over all human traditions which would lead us astray from God and from true faith. The Reformers had before them not simply the theological desire to define precisely the nature of that authority to which all Christian teaching appeals, but the religious need to cling to the divinely revealed way of salvation and to turn away from all human interposition and corruption. They desire to make known that they trust God rather than man. Hence almost all of them are careful to express clearly the need for the Witness of the Holy Spirit.

It was, he insisted, committed to the idea of work-righteousness; whatever occasional protest might be made against the conception, he maintained that this thought of work-righteousness was so interwoven with its warp and woof that the whole must be swept away ere the old and true Christian Theology could be rediscovered. He also dedeclared it was sophistry; and by that he meant that it played with the outsides of doctrine, asked and solved questions which had nothing to do with real Christian theology, that the imposing intellectual edifice was hollow within, that its deity was not the God and Father revealed in Jesus Christ, but the unknown God, the God who could never be revealed by metaphysics larded with detached texts of Scripture, the abstract entity of pagan philosophy. With an unerring instinct he fastened on the Scholastic devotion to Aristotle as the reason why what professed to be Christian theology had been changed into something else. Scholastic Philosophy or Theology (for the two are practically the same) defined itself as the attempt to reconcile *faith* and *reason*, and the definition has been generally accepted. Verbally it is correct; really it is very misleading from the meanings attached to the words faith and reason. With the Schoolmen, faith in this contrast between faith and reason meant the sum of patristic teaching about the verities of the Christian religion extracted by the Fathers from the Holy Scriptures; and reason meant the sum of philosophical principles extracted from the writings of ancient philosophers, and especially from Aristotle. The great Schoolmen conceived it to be their task to construct a system of Christian Philosophy by combining patristic doctrinal conclusions with the conclusions of human reasoning which they believed to be given in their highest form in the writings of the ancient Grecian sages. They actually used the conceptions of the Fathers as material to give body to the forms of thought found ready made for them in the speculations of Aristotle and Plato. The Christian material was moulded to fit the pagan forms, and in consequence lost its most essentially Christian characteristics. One can see how the most evangelical of the Schoolmen, Thomas Aquinas, tries in vain to break through the meshes of the Aristotelian net in his discussions on merit and satisfaction in his *Summa Theologiæ*.[1] He had to start from the thought of God as (1) the Absolute, and (2) as the *Primum Movens*, the *Causa efficiens prima*, the *Intelligens a quo omnes res naturales ordinantur in finem*—conceptions which can never imprison without practically destroying the vision of the Father who has revealed Himself in the Saviour Jesus Christ. His other starting-point, that man is to be described as the possessor of free will in the Aristotelian sense of the term, will never contain the Christian doctrine of man's complete dependence on God in his salvation. It inevitably led to work-righteousness. This was the "sophistry" Luther protested against and which he swept away.

He then claimed that he stood where the old Catholic Church had taken stand, that his theology like its was rooted in the faith of God as Trinity and in the belief in the Person of Christ, the Revealer of God. The old theology had nothing to do with Mariolatry or saint worship; it revered the triune God, and Jesus Christ His Son and man's Saviour. Luther could join hands with Athanasius across twelve centuries. He had done a work not unlike that of the great Alexandrian. His rejection of the Scholastic Aristotelianism may be compared with Athanasius' refusal to allow the Logos theology any longer to confuse the Christian doctrines of God and the Person of Christ. Both believed that in all thinking about God they ought to keep their eyes fixed upon His redemptive work manifested in the historical Christ. Athanasius, like Luther, brought theology back to religion from "sophistry," and had for his starting-point an inward religious experience that his Redeemer was the God who made heaven and earth. The great leaders in the ancient Church, Luther

[1] Compare especially the discussions in the first part of the Second Book of the *Summa*.

believed, held as he did that to have conceptions about God, to construct a real Christian theology, it was necessary first of all to know God Himself, and that He was only to be known through the Lord Jesus Christ. He had gone through the same experience as they had done; he could fully sympathise with them, and could appropriate the expressions in which they had described and crystallised what they had felt and known, and that without paying much attention to the niceties of technical language. These doctrines had not been dead formulas to them, but the expression of a living faith. He could therefore take the old dogmas and make them live again in an age in which it seemed as if they had lost all their vitality.

"From the time of Athanasius," says Harnack, "there had been no theologian who had given so much living power for faith to the doctrine of the Godhead of Christ as Luther did; since the time of Cyril, no teacher had arisen in the Church for whom the mystery of the union of the two natures in Christ was so full of comfort as for Luther—'I have a better provider than all angels are: he lies in the cradle and hangs on the breast of a virgin, but sits, nevertheless, at the right hand of the almighty father'; no mystic philosopher of antiquity spoke with greater conviction and delight of the sacred nourishment in the Eucharist. The German reformer restored life to the formulas of Greek Christianity: he gave them back to faith."[1]

But if Luther accepted the old formulas describing the Nature of God and the Person of Christ, he did so in a thoroughly characteristic way. He had no liking for theological technical terms, though he confessed that it was necessary to use them. He disliked the old term *homoousios* to describe the relation between the Persons in the Trinity, and preferred the word "oneness";[2] he even disliked the term Trinity, or at least its German equivalents, Dreifaltig-

[1] Harnack, *History of Dogma*, vii. 173–174.

[2] *Luther's Works* (Erlangen edition), Latin, xxxvi. 506: "Quodsi odit anima mea vocem homoousion, et nolim ea uti, non ero hæreticus, quis enim me coget uti, modo rem teneam, quæ in concilio per scripturas definita est?" It may be remarked that Athanasius himself did not like the word that has become so associated with his name.

keit or Dreiheit—they were not good German words, he said;[1] he called the technical terms used in the old creeds *vocabula mathematica*;[2] he was careful to avoid using them in his Short and even in his Long Catechism. But Jesus Christ was for him the mirror of the Fatherly heart of God, and therefore was God; God Himself was the only Comforter to bring rest to the human soul, and the Holy Spirit was God; and the old creeds confessed One God, Father, Son, and Holy Ghost, and the confession contented him whatever words were used. Besides, he rejoiced to place himself side by side with the Christians of ancient days, who trusted God in Christ and were free from the "sophistries" of the Schoolmen.

Although Luther accepted, honestly and joyfully, the old theology about God and the Person of Christ, he put a new and richer meaning into it. Luther lets us see over and over again that he believed that the only thing worth considering in theology was the divine work of Christ and the experience that we have of it through faith. He did not believe that we have any real knowledge of God outside these limits. Beyond them there is the unknown God of philosophical paganism, the God whom Jews, Turks, pagans, and nominal Christians ignorantly worship. In order to know God it is necessary to know Him through the Jesus Christ of history. Hence with Luther, Christ fills the whole sphere of God: "He that hath seen Me hath seen the Father," and conversely: "He that hath not seen Me hath not seen the Father." The historical Jesus Christ is for Luther the revealer and the only revealer of the Father. The revelation is given in the wonderful experience of faith in which Jesus compels us to see God in Him—the whole of God, Who has kept nothing back which He could have given us. It is very doubtful whether the

[1] *Luther's Works* (2nd Erlangen edition), vi. 358: "Dreyfaltigkeit ist ein recht böse Deutsch, denn in der Gottheit ist die höchste Einigkeit. Etliche nennen es Dreyheit; aber das lautet allzuspöttisch"; he says that the expression is not in Scripture, and adds: "darum lautet es auch kalt und viel besser spräch man Gott denn die Dreyfaltigkeit" (xii. 408).

[2] *Ibid.* v. 236.

framers of the old creeds ever grasped this thought. The great expounder of the old theology, Augustine, certainly did not. The failure to enter into it showed itself not merely in the doctrine of God, but also in the theories of grace. With Luther all theology is really Christology; he knew no other God than the God Who had manifested Himself in the historical Christ, and made us see in the miracle of faith that He is our salvation. This at once simplifies all Christian theology and cuts it clearly away from that Scholastic which Luther called "sophistry." Why need Christians puzzle themselves over the Eternal Something which is not the world when they have the Father? On the old theology the work of Christ was practically limited to procuring the forgiveness of sins. There it ended and other gracious operations of God began—operations of grace. So there grew the complex system of expiations, and satisfactions, of magical sacraments and saints' intercessions. These were all at once swept away when the whole God was seen revealed in Christ in the vision of faith and nowhere else.

Like Athanasius, Luther found his salvation in the Deity of Christ.

"We must have a Saviour Who is more than a saint or an angel; for if He were no more, better and greater than these, there were no helping us. But if he be God, then the treasure is so ponderous that it outweighs and lifts away sin and death; and not only so, but also gives eternal life. This is our Christian faith, and therefore we rightly confess: 'I believe in Jesus Christ His only Son, our Lord, Who was born of Mary, suffered and died.' By this faith hold fast, and though heathen and heretic are ever so wise thou shalt be blessed."[1]

He repeats this over and over again. If we cannot say God died for us, if it was only a man who suffered on the cross, then we are lost, was Luther's firmest conviction; and the thought of the Divinity of Christ meant more to Luther than it did to previous theologians. The old theo-

[1] *Luther's Works* (Erlangen edition), xlvii. 3, 4.

logy had described the two Natures in the One Person of the God-man in such a way as to suggest that the only function of the Divine was to give to the human wor` of Christ the importance necessary to effect salvation. Luther always refused to adopt this limited way of regarding the Divinity of the Saviour. He did not refuse to adopt and use the *phraseology* of his predecessors. Like them, he spoke of the two Natures in the One Person of Christ. But it is plain from his expositions of the Creed, and from his criticisms of the current theological terminology, that he did not like the expression. He thought that it suggested an idea that was wrong, and that had to be guarded against. He says that we must beware of thinking as if the deity and humanity in Christ are so externally united that we may look at the one apart from the other.

"This is the first principle and most excellent article how Christ is the Father: that we are not to doubt that whatsoever the man says and does is reckoned and must be reckoned as said and done in heaven for all angels; in the world for all rulers; in hell for all devils; in the heart for every evil conscience and all secret thoughts. For if we are certain of this: that what Jesus thinks, speaks, and wills the Father also wills, then I defy all that may fight against me. For here in Christ have I the Father's heart and will."[1]

He brings the thought of the Person of Christ into the closest relation to our personal experience. It is not simply a doctrine—an intellectual something outside us. It is part of that blessed experience which is called Justification by Faith. It is inseparably connected with the recognition that we are not saved by means of the good deeds which we can do, but solely by the work of Christ. It is what makes us cease all work-righteousness and trust in God alone as He has revealed Himself in Christ. When we know and feel that it is God who is working for us, then we instinctively cease trying to think that we can work

[1] *Luther's Works* (Erlangen edition), xlix. 183, 184.

out our own salvation.[1] Hence the Person of Christ can never be a mere doctrine for the true Christian to be inquired about by the intellect. It is something which we carry about with us as part of our lives.

"To know Christ in the true way means to know that He died for us, that He piled our sins upon Himself, so that we hold all our own affairs as nothing and let them all go, and cling only to the faith that Christ has given Himself for us, and that His sufferings and piety and virtues are all mine. When I know this I must hold Him dear in return, for I must be loving to such a man."

He insists on the human interest that the Man Jesus Christ has for us, and declares that we must take as much interest in His whole life on earth as in that of our closest friend.

Perhaps it ought to be added, although what has been said implies it, that Luther always approached the Person of Christ from His mediatorial work, and not from any previously thought out ideas of what Godhead must be, and what manhood must be, and how they can be united. He begins with the mediatorial and saving work of Christ as that is revealed in the blessed experience which faith, the gift of God, creates. He rises from the office to the Person, and does not descend from the Person to the office. "Christ is not called Christ because He has the two Natures. What does that matter to me? He bears this glorious and comforting name because of His Office and Work which He has undertaken."[2] It is in this way that He becomes the Saviour and the Redeemer.

It can scarcely be said that all the Reformers worked out the conception of the Person of Christ in the same way as Luther, although almost all these thoughts can be found in Calvin, but the overshadowing conception is always present to their mind—Christ fills the full sphere of God. That is the characteristic of Reformation thought and of Reformation piety, and appears everywhere in the writings of the Reformers and in the worship and rites of the

[1] *Luther's Works* (2nd Erlangen edition), xii. 244.
[2] *Ibid.* xii. 259.

Reformed Church. To go into the matter exhaustively would necessitate more space than can be given; but the following instances may be taken as indicating the universal thought.

1. The Reformers swept away every contemplation of intercessors who were supposed to share with our Lord the procuring of pardon and salvation, and they declared against all attempts to distinguish between various kinds of worship which could only lead pious souls astray from the one worship due to God in Christ. Such subtle distinctions, says Calvin, as *latria*, *doulia*, and *hyperdoulia* are neither known nor present to the minds of those who prostrate themselves before images until the world has become full of idolatry as crude and plain as that of the ancient Egyptians, which all the prophets continuously denounced; they can only mislead, and ought to be discarded. They actually suggest to worshippers to pass by Jesus Christ, the only Mediator, and betake themselves to some patron who has struck their fancy. They bring it about that the Divine Offices are distributed among the saints as if they had been appointed colleagues to our Lord Jesus Christ; and they are made to do His work, while He Himself is kept in the background like some ordinary person in a crowd. They are responsible for the fact that hymns are sung in public worship in which the saints are lauded with every blessing just as if they were colleagues of God.[1]

In conformity with these thoughts, the Confessions of the Reformation all agree in reprobating prayers to the saints. The Augsburg Confession says:

"The Scripture teacheth not to invoke saints, nor to ask the help of saints, because it propoundeth to us one Christ, the Mediator, Propitiatory, High Priest, and Intercessor. This Christ is to be invocated, and He hath promised that He will hear our prayers, and liketh this worship, to wit, that He be invocated in all afflictions. 'If any man sin, we have an advocate with God, Jesus Christ the righteous' (1 John ii. 1)."[2]

[1] Calvin, *Opera omnia* (Amsterdam, 1667), viii 38 39.

[2] *Augsburg Confession*, Art. xxi.

The Second Helvetic Confession, in its fifth chapter, entitled, *Regarding the adoration, worship, and invocation of God through the One Mediator, Jesus Christ,* lays down the rule that prayer is to be through Christ alone, and the saints and relics are not to be worshipped. And no prayer-book or liturgy in any branch of the Reformed Church contains prayers addressed to any of the saints or to the Blessed Virgin.

2. The Reformers insist on the necessity of Christ and of Christ alone for all believers. Their Confessions abound in expressions which are meant to magnify the Person and Work of Christ, and to show that He fills the whole field of believing thought and worship. The brief Netherlands Confession of 1566 has no less than three separate sections on *Christ the only Mediator and Reconciler*, on *Christ the only Teacher*, and on *Christ the only High Priest and Sacrifice.*[1] The *Heidelberg* or *Palatine Catechism* calls Christ *my faithful Saviour,* and says that we can call ourselves Christians "because by faith we are members of Jesus Christ and partakers of His anointing, so that we both confess His Holy Name and present ourselves unto Him a lively offering of thanksgiving, and in this life may with free conscience fight against sin and Satan, and afterwards possess with Christ an everlasting kingdom over all creatures." The Scots Confession abounds in phrases intended to honour our Lord Jesus Christ. It calls Him *Messiah, Eternal Wisdom, Emmanuel, our Head, our Brother, our Pastor and great Bishop of our souls,* the *Author of Life,* the *Lamb of God,* the *Advocate and Mediator,* and the *Only Hie Priest.* All the Confessions of the Churches of the Reformation contain the same or similar expressions. The liturgies of the Churches also abound in similar terms of adoration.

3. The Reformers declare that Christ is the *only* Revealer of God. "We would never recognise the Father's grace and mercy," says Luther in his Large Catechism, "were it not for our Lord Jesus Christ, Who is the mirror

[1] Müller, *Die Bekenntnisschriften der reformierten Kirche*, pp. 935 f.

of the Father's heart." "We are not affrayed to cal God our Father," says the Scots Confession, "not sa meikle because He has created us, quhilk we have in common with the reprobate, as for that He has given us His onely Son." The instructions issued by the Synod which met at Bern in 1532 are very emphatic upon this thought, as may be seen from the headings of the various articles: (Art. 2) That the whole doctrine is the unique Christ (*Das die gantze leer der eynig Christus sye*); (Art. 3) That God is revealed to the people in Christ alone; (Art. 5) That the gracious God is perceived through Christ alone without any mediation; (Art. 6) A Christian sermon is entirely about and from Christ. It is said under the third article: "His Son in Whom we see the work of God and His Fatherly heart toward us . . . which is not the case where the preacher talks much about God in the heathen manner, and does not exhibit the same God in the face of Christ."[1] The Confessions also unite in declaring that the gift of the Holy Spirit comes from Christ.

4. The conception that Christ filled the whole sphere of God, which was for the Reformers a fundamental and experimental fact, enabled them to construct a spiritual doctrine of the sacraments which they opposed to that held in the mediæval Church. Of course, it was various theories about the sacraments which caused the chief differences among the Reformers themselves; but apart from all varying ideas—consubstantiation, ubiquity, signs exhibiting and signs representing—the Reformers united on the thoughts that the efficacy in the sacraments depended entirely on the promises of Christ contained in His word, and that the virtue in the sacraments consisted in the presence of Christ to the believing communicant. What was received in the sacraments was not a vague, mysterious, not to say magical, grace, but Christ Jesus Himself. He gave Himself in the sacraments in whatever way His presence might be explained.

They all taught that the efficacy of the sacraments depends upon the promise of Christ contained in their

[1] Müller, *Die Bekenntnisschriften der reformierten Kirche*, pp. 34 ff.

institution, and they insisted that word and sacrament must always be taken together. Thus Luther points out in the *Babylonish Captivity of the Church* that one objection to the Roman practice is that the recipients "never hear the words of the promise which are secretly mumbled by the priest," and exhorts his readers never to lose sight of the all-important connection between the word of promise and the sacraments; and in his Large Catechism he declares that the sacraments include the Word. "I exhort you," he says, "never to sunder the Word and the water, or to separate them. For where the Word is withheld we have only such water as the maid uses to cook with." Non-Lutheran Confessions are equally decided on the necessity of connecting the promise and the words of Christ with the sacraments. The Thirty-nine Articles declare that the sacraments are effectual because of "Christ's institution and promise." The Heidelberg or Palatine Catechism (1563) says that the sacraments "are holy and visible signs ordained of God, to the end that He might thereby the more fully declare and seal unto us the *promise* of the Holy Gospel."

Similarly the Reformers unanimously declared that the virtue in the sacraments consisted in no mysterious grace, but in the fact that in them believing partakers met and received Christ Himself. In the articles of the Bern Synod (1532) we are told that the sacraments are mysteries of God, "through which from without Christ is proffered to believers." The First Helvetic Confession (1536) says, concerning the Holy Supper, "we hold that in the same the Lord truly offers His Body and His Blood, that is, Himself, to His own." The Second Helvetic Confession (1562) declares that "the Body of Christ is in heaven at the right hand of the Father," and enjoins communicants "to lift up their hearts and not to direct them downwards to the bread. For as the sun, though absent from us in the heaven, is none the less efficaciously present . . . so much more the Sun of righteousness absent from us in the heavens in His Body, is present to us not indeed corporeally, but spiritually by a life-giving activity." The French Confession of 1557 says that the sacraments are pledges and seals, and adds, "Yet we hold that their substance and truth is in Jesus Christ." So the Scots Confession of 1560 declares that "we assuredlie beleeve that be Baptisme we ar ingrafted in Christ Jesus to be made partakers of His justice, be quhilk our sinnes ar covered and remitted. And alswa, that in the Supper richtlie used, Christ Jesus is so joined with us, that Hee becummis very nurishment and fude of our saules." In the *Manner of the Administration of the Lord's Supper* the Scottish Reformation Church directed the minister in his exhortation to say to the people: "The end of our coming to the Lord's Table . . . is to seek our life and perfection in Jesus Christ, acknowledging ourselves at the same time to be children of wrath and condemnation. Let us consider then that this sacrament is a singular medicine for all poor sick creatures, a comfortable help to weak souls, and that our Lord requireth no other worthiness on our part, but that we unfeignedly acknowledge our naughtiness and imperfection."

Everywhere in prayer, worship, and teaching the Reformers see Christ filling the whole sphere of God. Jesus was God appearing in history and addressing man.

§ 6. *The Church.*

In the Epistles of St. Paul, the Church of Christ stands forth as a *fellowship* which is both divine and human. On the side of the divine it is a fellowship with Jesus, its crucified, risen, and ascended Lord; on the human, it is a fellowship among men who stand in the same relation to Jesus. This fellowship with Jesus and with the brethren is the secret of the Church—what expresses it, what makes it different from all other fellowships. Every other characteristic which belongs to it must be coloured by this thought of a double fellowship. It is the double relation which makes it difficult to construct a conception of the Church. It is easy to feel it as an experience, but it has always been found hard to express it in propositions.

It does not require much elaborate thinking to construct a theory of the Church which will be true to all that is said about the fellowship on its divine side; nor is it very difficult to think of a great visible and historical organisation which in some external aspects represents the Christian fellowship, provided the hidden union with Christ, so prominent in St. Paul's descriptions, be either entirely neglected or explained in external and material ways. The difficulty arises when both the divine and the human sides of the fellowship are persistently and earnestly kept in view.

It is always hard to explain the unseen by the seen, the eternal by the temporal, and the divine by the human; and the task is almost greater than usual when the union of these two elements in the Church of Christ is the theme of discussion. It need not surprise us, therefore, that all down through the Middle Ages there appear, not one, but two conceptions of the Christian Church which never harmonised. On the one side, the Church was thought of as a fellowship of God with man, depending on the inscrutable purpose of God, and independent of all visible outward organisation; on the other, it was a great society which existed in the world of history, and was held together by visible political ties like other societies. Augustine had both conceptions, and the dialectical skill of the great theologian of the West was unable to fuse them into one harmonious whole.

These two separate, almost mutually exclusive, ideas of what the Church of Christ was, lived side by side during the Middle Ages in the same unconnected fashion. The former, the spiritual Church with its real but unseen fellowship with Christ, was the pre-eminently religious thought. It was the ground on which the most conspicuous mediæval piety rested. It was the garden in which bloomed the flowers of mediæval mystical devotion. The latter was built up by the juristic dialectic of Roman canonists into the conception that the Church was a visible hierarchical State having a strictly monarchical constitution—its king being the Bishop of Rome, who was the visible representative of Christ. This conception became almost purely political. It was the active force in all ecclesiastical struggles with princes and peoples, with Reformers, and with so-called heretics and schismatics. It reduced the Church to the level of the State, and contained little to stimulate to piety or to holy living.

The labours of the great Schoolmen of the thirteenth century did try to transform this political Church into what might represent the double fellowship with Christ and with fellow-believers which is so prominent a thought in the New Testament. They did so by attempting to show that the great political Church was an enclosure containing certain indefinite mysterious powers of redemption which saved men who willingly placed themselves within the sphere of their operation. They maintained that the core of the hierarchical constitution of the Church was the priesthood, and that this priesthood was a species of plastic medium through which, and through which alone, God worked in dispensing, by means of the sacraments entrusted to the priesthood, His saving grace. It may be questioned whether the thought of the Church as an institution, possessing within itself certain mysterious redemptive powers which are to be found nowhere else, was ever thoroughly harmonised with that which regarded it as a mass of legal statutes embodied in canon law and dominated by papal absolutism. The two conceptions remained distinct, mutually aiding each other, but never exactly coalescing. Thus in the sixteenth century no less than three separate ideas of the Church of Christ were present to fill the minds and imaginations of men; but the dominant idea for the practical religious life was certainly that which represented the Church as an institution which, because it possessed the priesthood, was the society within which salvation was to be found.

Luther had enjoyed to the full the benefits of this society, and had with ardour and earnestness sought to make use of all its redemptive powers. He had felt, simply because he was so honest with himself, that it had not made him a real Christian, and that its mysterious powers had worked on him in vain. His living Christian experience made him know and feel that whatever the Church of Christ was, it was not a society within which priests exercised their secret science of redemption. It was and must be a fellowship of holy and Christlike people; but he felt it very difficult to express his experience in phrases that could satisfy him. It was hard to get rid of thoughts which he had cherished from childhood, and none of these inherited beliefs had more power over him than the idea that the Church, however described, was the Pope's House in which the Bishop of Rome ruled, and ought to rule, as house-father. It is interesting to study by what devious paths he arrived at a clear view of what the Church of Christ really is;[1] to notice how shreds of the old opinions which had lain dormant in his mind every now and then start afresh into life; and how, while he had learnt to know the uselessness of many institutions of the mediæval Church, he could not easily divest his mind of the thought that they naturally belonged to a Church Visible. Monastic vows, the celibacy of the clergy, fasting, the hierarchy, the supremacy of the Pope, the power of excommunication with all its dreaded consequences, were all the natural accompaniments of a Visible Church according to mediæval ideas, and Luther relinquished them with difficulty. From the first, Augustine's thought of the Church, which consists of the elect, helped him; he found that Huss held the same idea, and he wrote to a friend that "we have been all Hussites without knowing it."[2] But while Luther and all the Reformers held strongly by this conception of Augustine, it was not of very much service in determining the conception of the Visible Church which was the more important practically; and although the definition of the Catholic Church Invisible has found its way into most

[1] Luther's gradual progress towards his final view of the Church is traced minutely by Loofs, *Leitfaden*, pp. 359 ff.

[2] Enders, *Dr. Martin Luthers Briefwechsel*, ii. 345

Protestant Confessions, and has been used by Protestants polemically, it has always remained something of a background, making clearer the conception of the Church in general, but has been of little service in giving clear views of what the Church Visible is. From the very first, however, Luther saw in a certain indefinite way that there was a real connection between the conception of the Visible Church and the proclamation of the Word of God—a thought which was destined to grow more and more definite till it completely possessed him. As early as October 1518, he could inform Cajetan that the Pope must be under the rule of the Word of God and not superior to it.[1] His discovery that the communion of the saints (*communio sanctorum*) was not necessarily a hierarchy (*ecclesia prælatorum*),[2] was made soon afterwards. After the Leipzig Disputation his views became clearer, and by 1520 they stood revealed in the three great Reformation treatises.

Luther's doctrine of the Church is extremely simple. The Church is, as the Creed defines it to be, the *Communion of the Saints*, which has come into existence through the proclamation of the Word of God heard and received by faith. He simplified this fundamental Christian conception in a wonderful way. The Church rests on the sure and stable foundation of the Word of God; and this Word of God is not a weary round of statutes issued blasphemously by the Bishops of Rome in God's name. It is not the invitations of a priesthood to come and share mysterious and indefinite powers of salvation given to them in their command over the sacraments. It is not a lengthy doctrinal system constructed out of detached texts of Holy Scripture by the application of a fourfold sense used under the guidance of a dogmatic tradition or a rule of faith. It is the substance of the Scriptures. It is the "gospel according to a pure understanding." It is the "promises of God"; "the testimony of Jesus, Who is the Saviour of souls"; it is the "consolations offered in Christ." It is, as Calvin said,

[1] Enders, *Dr. Martin Luthers Briefwechsel*, i. 253.

[2] *Luther's Works* (Weimar edition), i. 190.

"the spiritual gate whereby we enter into God's heavenly kingdom"; the "mirror in which faith beholds God." It is, according to the Westminster Confession, the sum of God's commands, threatenings, promises, and, above all, the offer of Christ Jesus. All these things are apprehended by faith. The Church comes into existence by faith responding to the proclamation of the Word of God. This is the sure and stable thing upon which the Church of Christ is founded.

The Church of Christ, therefore, is a body of which the Spirit of Jesus is the soul. It is a company of Christ-like men and women, whom the Holy Spirit has called, enlightened, and sanctified through the preaching of the word; who are encouraged to look forward to a glorious future prepared for the people of God; and who, meanwhile, manifest their faith in all manner of loving services done to their fellow-believers

The Church is therefore in some sense invisible. Its secret is its hidden fellowship with Jesus. Its roots penetrate the unseen, and draw from thence the nourishment needed to sustain its life. But it is a visible society, and can be seen wherever the Word of God is faithfully proclaimed, and wherever faith is manifested in testimony and in bringing forth the fruits of the Spirit.

This is the essential mode of describing the Church which has found place in the Reformation creeds. Some vary in the ways in which they express the thought; some do not sufficiently distinguish, in words at least, between what the Church is and what it has, between what makes its being and what is included in its well-being. But in all there are the two thoughts that the Church is made visible by the two fundamental things—the proclamation of the word and the manifestation of faith.

This mode of describing the Church of Christ defines it by that element which separates it from all other forms of human association—its special relation to the divine; and it is shown to be visible at the place where that divine element can and does manifest itself. It defines the

Church by its most essential element, and sets aside all that is accidental. It concerns itself with what the Church is, and does not include what the Church has. It therefore provides room for all things which belong to the well-being of the Church—only it relegates them to their proper place.[1]

If the proclamation of the Word of God, and the manifestation of the faith which answers, be the essence of the Church, all that tends to aid both is to be included in the thought. There must be a ministry of some sort in word and sacrament instituted within the Church of Christ in order to lead the individual to faith. God has created this ministry, and all the Reformed Churches were careful to declare that no one should seek entrance into office unless he was assured that he had been called of God thereto; and as his function is to be a minister of the Church and a servant of the faithful, no one "should publicly teach or administer the sacraments unless he be duly called (*nisi rite vocatus*)." Such a ministry has its field simply in ministering the means of grace. "The Church of Christ," says Luther, "requires an honest ministry diligently and loyally instructed in the holy Word of God after a pure Christian understanding, and without the addition of any false traditions. In and through such a ministry it will be made plain what are Christ and His Evangel, how to attain to the forgiveness of sins, and the properties and power of the *keys* in the Church."

All this is matter of administration. Some societies of believers may have different ideas about the precise form that this ministry ought to take; but such differences, while they may lead to separate administrations, do not imply any separation from the one Catholic Church of Christ to which they all belong. However outwardly they differ, all retain the essential things—the preaching and teaching of the Word of God and the due administration of the sacraments. Some may prefer to set forth a creed of one kind and others may prefer another. The French,

[1] *Luther's Works* (Erlangen edition), xii. 249.

the Scottish, and the Dutch Churches had all their own creeds, and all believed each other to be parts of the same One Catholic Church of Christ.

"When we affirm," says Calvin, "the pure ministry of the Word, and pure order in the celebration of the Sacraments, to be a sufficient pledge and earnest that we may safely embrace the society in which both these are found as a true Church, we carry the observation to this point, that such a society should never be rejected as long as it continues in these things, although it may be chargeable in other respects with many errors."[1]

Within this Christian fellowship, which is the Church of Christ, the sense by which we see God is awakened and our faith is nourished and quickened. The Word of God speaks to us not merely in the public worship of the faithful, but in and through the lives of the brethren; their deeds act on us as the simple stories of experience and providence which the Scriptures contain. God's Word speaks to us in a thousand ways in the lives and sympathies of the brethren. The Christian "receives the revelation of God in the living relationships of the Christian brotherhood, and its essential contents are that personal life of Jesus which is visible in the gospel and which is expounded by the lives of the redeemed."[2]

"The Christian Church," says Luther, "keeps all words of God in its heart, and turns them round and round, and keeps their connection with one another and with Scripture! Therefore, anyone who is to find Christ must first find the Church. How could anyone know where Christ is and faith in Him is, unless he knew where His believers are? Whoever wishes to know something about Christ must not trust to himself, nor by the help of his own reason build a bridge of his own to heaven, but must go to the Church, must visit it and make inquiry. Now the Church is not wood and stone, but the company of people who believe in Christ. With these he must unite and see how they believe, live, and teach, who assuredly have Christ among

[1] Calvin, *Institutio*, IV. i. 12.

[2] Herrmann, *Communion with God*, p. 149.

them. For outside the Christian Church there is no truth, no Christ, no blessedness."[1]

For these reasons the Church deserves to be called, and is, the Mother of all Christians.

[1] *Luther's Works* (2nd Erlangen edition), x. 162.

CHRONOLOGICAL SUMMARY

OF

THE HISTORY OF THE REFORMATION

CHRONOLOGICAL

Contemporary Events.	Lutheran Church.	Reformed Church.
1493–1519. — Jan. 12, Maximilian I. Emperor. At his death the Elector Frederick the Wise of Saxony (1480-1525), viceroy. 1499 - 1535. — Elector Joachim I. (Nestor) of Brandenburg. 1500 - 1539. — Duke George of Saxony. 1509 - 1547. — Henry VIII. of England. 1515–1547.—Francis I. of France.	1517.—Oct. 31, MARTIN LUTHER [*b.* 1483, Nov. 10, at Eisleben; 1497, at Latin School at Magdeburg; 1498, at Eisenach (Frau Cotta, *d.* 1511); 1501, at Erfurt; 1505, Master of Arts; July 17, entered the Augustinian Cloister at Erfurt; 1508, Professor at Wittenberg; 1511, at Rome; 1512, Oct. 19, Dr. of Theology] nailed 95 theses against the abuse of indulgences on the door of the Castle Church at Wittenberg. Counter-theses of John Tetzel, composed by Conrad Wimpina.	ULRICH ZWINGLI: *b.* 1484, Jan. 1, at Wildhaus, in Canton of St. Gallen; scholar of Henry Wölflin (Lupulus) at Berne; of Thomas Wyttenbach at Basel; 1499, student of Joachim Vadianus at Vienna; 1506, M.A.; 1506 - 16, pastor at Glarus; 1516 - 18, preacher at St. Mary's, Einsiedeln.
1518–1567.—Philip the Magnanimous of Hesse (*b.* 1504).	1518.—Silvester Mazzolini of Prierio: *Dialogus in præsumptuosas M. L. conclusiones de potestate Papæ*; Luther's *Resp. ad Silv. Prier.* April 26, Luther at Heidelberg Disputation. Aug.: Cited to appear at Rome. Aug. 25, Melanchthon at Wittenberg. Oct. 12–15, Luther at Augsburg before Card. Thomas Vio de Gaeta; appeals *a papa male informato ad melius informandum.* Nov.: Luther, *On the Sacrament of Penance.*	1518. — Zwingli against the indulgence preached by Bernardin Sampson (Guardian of the Franciscan Cloister at Milan). Dec.: Zwingli pastor in the Minster at Zurich.
1519. — June, *Charles V. (since 1516 King of Spain) — 1556, Aug. 27, Emperor of Germany (d. 1558).* 1519–1566.—Suliman I. Sultan.	1519. — Jan.: Luther's interview with Charles of Miltitz, papal chamberlain at Altenburg; Truce. June 27–July 8, DISPUTATION AT LEIPZIG: (1) between Eck and Carlstadt, on the Doctrine of Free Will; and (2) between Eck and Luther, *De primatu Papæ.*	1519.—Jan. 1, Zwingli delivers his first sermon in Zurich; sermons on St. Matthew's Gospel, Acts, and the Pauline Epistles; Reformation sermons, pointing out a clear

SUMMARY

Revolutionary Movements.	Roman Catholic Church.	Protestant Theology.
	1513, Mar. 11–1521, Dec. 1. —Leo x.	
	1517.—The Lateran Council grant to the Pope the tithes of all church property. Indulgence (the fifth between 1500 and 1517) for the building of St. Peter's and for the Pope's private needs. Three indulgence commissions granted for Germany, one farmed by Elector Archbishop of Mainz (consec. 1514), the Dominican John Tetzel (*d.* 1519), his commissioner. Thomas Vio de Gaeta (Card. Cajetan): "The Catholic Church is the bond-slave of the Pope"; asserts papal infallibility in the widest sense.	PHILIP MELANCHTHON (*b.* 1497, Feb. 16, at Bretten; 1509–12, at Heidelberg; 1512–14, at Tübingen; 1514, M.A., 1514–18, teaches in Tübingen; 1518, Prof. of Greek at Wittenberg; Aug. 29, Introductory Lecture, *De corrigendis adolescentiæ studiis*; 1519, Sept. 19, Bach. of Theology; *d.* 1560, April 19). Loci communes rerum Theologicarum, seu hypotyposes Theologicæ, 1521; three editions in 1521; edition of 1525 modifies absolute predestination; edition of 1535 reconstructs his theology; edition of 1543, Synergism.
... ...	1519.—The Cortes of Aragon ask three Briefs (never sent) from Leo x. to restrain the Inquisition. Similarly fruitless applications made by the Estates of Aragon, Castile, and Catalonia to Charles v. in 1516.	ZWINGLI: *Commentarius de vera et falsa religione*, 1525; *Fidei ratio ad Carolum Imperatorem*, 1530, July 3; *Sermonis de providentia Dei Anamnema*. 1530; *Christianæ Fidei expositio*, 1531.

Contemporary Events.	Lutheran Church.	Reformed Church.
1519–1521. — **Fernando** Cortez discovers and conquers Mexico.	The controversy is no longer one about a point in scholastic theology; it involves the whole round of ecclesiastical principles. Break with the Roman Christendom. The doctrine of the Priesthood of all Believers. Christian freedom and the right of private judgment. Luther's sermons on the Sacraments of Repentance and Baptism, and on Excommunication. Demand for the celebration of the Lord's Supper under both kinds.	distinction between Biblical and Romanist Christianity; Humanist study of Scripture (Pauline Epistles).
1521. — Magellan sails round the world.	1520.—April: Ulrich v. Hutten (*b.* 1488, April 21; *d.* 1523, Aug. 29); Dialogue: Vadiscus or the Roman Trinity; June 15, Bull of Excommunication against 41 propositions of Luther; 60 days for recantation; Aug.: Luther, "To the Christian Nobles of the German Nation, on the Bettering of the Christian Estate"; Oct.: *De Captivitate Eccles. Babylonic.; De libertate Christiana* (of the freedom of a Christian man); Dec. 10, Papal Bull burnt.	... ...
1521–26. — First war between Charles v. and Francis i. 1525.—Battle of Pavia. 1526.—Peace of Madrid.	1521.—April 17, 18, Luther at the Diet of Worms; April 26, leaves Worms; at the Wartburg, May 4–Mar. 3, 1522. [In Dec. begins translation of N.T.; Tracts: *On Penance, Against Private Masses, Against Clerical and Cloister Vows, The German Postille.*] May 26, Edict of Worms falsely antedated May 8. May 28, Imperial decree against Luther. June: Carlstadt against celibacy. Oct.: The Mass abolished at	In France, spread and preaching of Reformed doctrines through William Briçonnet, Bishop of Meaux from 1521. With him Le Fèvre and Farel. 1521.—Cornelius Hoën, Dutch jurist, writes *De Eucharistia* (The Lord's Supper purely symbolical); the doctrine brought to Wittenberg and Zurich by

Revolutionary Movements.	Roman Catholic Church.	Protestant Theology.
	Romanist Theologians in the first period of the Reformation.	(*a*) *Lutheran Theologians.*
	John Eck, Prof. of Theology at Ingolstadt since 1510; *b.* 1486, in the Swabian village of Eck; *d.* 1543.	George Spalatin: *b.* 1484 at Spalt, in the bishopric at Eichstädt; 1514, court chaplain to Frederick the Wise; 1525, Superintendent at Altenburg; *d.* 1545.
	Jerome Emser, court preacher to Duke George of Saxony; *d.* 1527.	Justus Jonas: *b.* 1493, at Nordhausen; 1521, Provost and Prof. at Wittenberg; 1541–46, at Halle; 1551, Superintendent at Eisfeld; *d.* 1555.
	John Cochlæus (Dobeneck), Dean at Frankfort-on-the-Maine, Canonicus in Mainz and Breslau; *d.* 1552; *Commentaria de actis et scriptis M. Lutheri* (1517-46), 1549; *Historiæ Hussitarum.*	Nicholas of Amsdorf: *b.* 1483; since 1504 at Wittenberg; 1524, at Magdeburg; 1528, at Goslar; 1542–46, Bishop of Naumburg; after 1550, at Eisenach; *d.* 1565.
	John Faber, 1518, Vicar-General at Constance; 1529, Provost at Ofen; 1530, Bishop of Vienna; *d.* 1561; 1523, *Malleus hæreticorum.*	John Bugenhagen: *b.* 1485; from 1521 in Wittenberg; 1522, pastor; 1536, General Superintendent there.
		Casper Cruciger: 1528–48, when he died, Prof. at Wittenberg.
1521.—The (Zwickau) Prophets in Wittenberg, Nicholas Storch, Marcus Thomæ Stübner; Martin Cellarius.	1521.—Henry VIII. of England: *Assertatio vii. Sacramentorum contra Lutherum* (Defender of the Faith).	Fred. Myconius, Franciscan at Annaberg, then pastor in Weimar; 1524, Court preacher at Gotha; *d.* 1546.
Andrew Bodenstein of Carlstadt: 1504, Prof. in Wittenberg; 1520, at Copenhagen; 1522, riots about images and vestments; 1523–24, in Orlamünde; then excommunicated in South Germany, East Friesland, Switzerland; *d.* Basel, 1541.	April 15, Decree of the Sorbonne condemning Luther's doctrines. May 8, Edict of Charles V. (founded on Edict of Worms) against the spread of Reformation doctrines in the Netherlands. [1522, the Augustinian cloister at Antwerp closed for heresy.]	Paul Speratus: 1521, at Vienna, then at Iglau; 1523, at Wittenberg (1524, "Salvation has come to us"); 1524, in Königsberg; 1529–51, when he died, Bishop of Pomerania in Marienwerder. John Brenz, *b.* 1499: 1520, Romanist preacher at Heidelberg; 1522-46, Lutheran preacher at Hall in Swabia; from 1563, provost at Stuttgart; *d.* 1570, Sept. 11.

Contemporary Events.	Lutheran Church.	Reformed Church.
	Wittenberg by the Augustinian monks (Gabriel Didymus). Dec.: Carlstadt's innovations. Dec. 25, Lord's Supper in both kinds. Dec. 27, The Prophets in Wittenberg.	John Rhodius, President of the Brother House at Utrecht.
... ...	1522.—Feb.: Riots in Wittenberg against images and pictures. Mar. 7, Luther back in Wittenberg. Mar. 9–16, Sermons against fanaticism. July: *Contra Henricum regem Angliæ.* Sept.: Translation of N.T. finished (whole Bible in 1534). Dec.: Diet at Nürnberg; The Hundred Grievances of the German Estates, in answer to Hadrian VI.'s Brief of Nov. 25.	1522.—April 16, Zwingli: *Von Erkiesen und Fryheit der Spysen*; Aug.: *Apologeticus Archeteles*, to the Bishop of Constance. The Zwinglian theology gradually becomes the more powerful in the Netherlands.
... ...	1522–23.—The Reformation conquers in Pomerania, Livonia, Silesia, Prussia, Mecklenburg; in East Friesland from 1519; 1523, in Frankfort-on-the-Maine, in Hall in Swabia; 1524, Ulm, Strasburg, Bremen, Nürnberg.	1523.—Jan. 29, Disputation in Zurich between Zwingli and John Faber, the Bishop's Vicar-General; Zwingli's 67 theses. Oct. 26, Disputation at Zurich about image-worship and the Mass. Nov. 17, Instruction of Zurich Council to pastors and preachers.
1523–33.—Frederick I. of Denmark. 1523-60.—Gustavus Vasa of Sweden.	1523.—July 1, Henry Voes and John Esch (Augustinians), burnt at Brussels; the first martyrs. Gustavus Vasa establishes the Reformation in Sweden (Olaf and Lorenz Petersen, Lorenz Andersen). May 7, Sickingen slain; revolt of nobles quelled by the princes. Luther: Of the Order of Public Worship; Dec.: *Formula Missæ* (Lord's Supper *sub utraque*).	1524.—Thorough reform of church at Zurich; pictures taken down; Friars' convents closed. Victory of the Reformation in Berne (Berchtholdt Haller, Nic. Manuel), Appenzell, Solothurn; Romanist League of the Forest Cantons at Lucerne.
... ...	1524.—*The first German Hymn-Book.* June–May 1525, THE PEASANTS' WAR; peasants slaughtered at Frankenhausen.	

Revolutionary Movements.	Roman Catholic Church.	Protestant Theology.
... ...	1522–23. —Sept. 14, Pope Hadrian VI. (tutor to Charles V., Bishop of Utrecht), learned in the old learning; aspiration after a reform of the clergy through the hierarchy.	(*b*) *Zwinglian Theologians.* John Œcolampadius (Heusgen), *b.* 1488; 1515, pastor at Basel; 1519, in Augsburg; 1522, Prof. and preacher at Basel; *d.* 1531, Nov. 24.
	In Spain, from 1520, circulation of Lutheran writings in Spanish translations made at Antwerp.	Leo Judæus: 1523, curate in St. Peter's at Zurich; *b.* 1482; *d.* 1542.
1523.—Conrad Grebel, Felix Manz, and Stumpf in Zurich, against Zwingli's State Church.	1523.—Juan de Avila, "the Apostle of Andalusia," suffered persecution for Lutheran doctrine.	Oswald Myconius (Geisshüsler): *b.* 1488 at Lucerne; 1532–*d.* 1552, Oct. 14, Antistes at Basel.
1524.—Disturbances in Stockholm; Melchior Hoffmann.	1523–34. —Sept. 25, Pope Clement VII. (Julius Medici, natural son of Julian de Medici).	Conrad Pellican (Kürsner): *b.* 1478; 1493, Franciscan; from 1502, Lector in Franciscan Cloister in Basel; 1527, at Zurich as Prof. of Hebrew; *d.* 1556.
	1524.—Cardinal Campeggio, Pope's Legate at the Diet of Nürnberg.	(*c*) *Intermediate Theologians.* Urbanus Rhegius: *b.* 1490, at Argau on the Bodensee; 1512, Prof. at Ingolstadt; 1519, Priest at Constance; 1520–22, Preacher in Augsburg; from 1530, Reformer in Brunswick, in the service of Duke Ernest; *d.* at Celle, 1541, May 23.
1525.—Thomas Münzer at Mühlhausen; executed May 1525. Tract: *Wider das geistlose sanftlebende Fleisch zu Wittenberg*, 1522. Jan.: Rise of the Anabaptists; Jürg Blaurock, a monk from Chur.	League of South German Roman Catholic States at Regensburg (Ferdinand of Austria, the Dukes of Bavaria, and the South German bishops). Terms: A certain measure of ecclesiastical reform, and alliance with the civil power; but no further spread of the new doctrines.	Ambrose Blaurer: *b.* 1492, at Constance; 1534–38, Reformer of Würtemberg; to 1548, at Constance; *d.* at Winterthur, 1564. (1534, *Stuttgart Concord.*)

Contemporary Events.	Lutheran Church.	Reformed Church.
1525.—Albert of Brandenburg (*d.* 1568); last Grand Master of the Teutonic Knights; changed the territory of the Order into the Dukedom of Prussia.	1525.—Jan.: Luther: *Against the Heavenly Prophets.* May: Exhorts princes and peasants to keep the peace, with comments on the twelve articles. Then: *Against the robber-murdering Peasants.* June 13, Marries Catherine von Bora. Conservative tendency of Lutheran Reformation; separation from more revolutionary elements.	1525.—The Mass abolished in Zurich; public worship very simple and in German language; Lord's Supper *sub utraque.* Zwingli's Commentary and first part of Zurich translation of Bible. (First complete edition 1531.)
1525–32.—Elector John the Constant of Saxony (brother of Frederick the Wise).	1525.—Dec.: Luther, *De Servo Arbitrio* against Erasmus, *Διατριβὴ de libero arbitrio*, Sept. 1524.	Zwingli's distinctive confessional statement of his doctrine of the Lord's Supper. [Carlstadt publishes his theory of the Lord's Supper in South Germany; δεικτικῶς: This My Body, is the Body, etc.]
1526.—Aug. 29: Lewis, king of Hungary and Bohemia, falls fighting at Mohacz against the Turks. His successor, Ferdinand of Austria (Oct., chosen king of Bohemia), has to make good his claims to Hungary against the Turks.	1526.—May 4: League at Torgau between Philip of Hesse and John the Constant, joined in June at Magdeburg by other evangelical princes. June 26, League of North German Roman Catholic princes at Dessau. June and July, DIET AT SPEIER. "*In matters of religion each State shall live, govern, and behave itself, as it shall answer to God and His Imperial Majesty.*" Oct. 20, Synod at Homberg; Hessian Church Order by Francis Lambert (*b.* 1487, at Avignon; Franciscan; fled 1522 to Switzerland; 1527, Prof. in Marburg; *d.* 1530); independence of the Christian community, and strictest church discipline.	Zwingli to Matth. Alber at Reutlingen, 1524, Nov. 16, *Manducatio spiritualis*; then in his commentary. *Against* Zwingli: Bugenhagen. *For* Zwingli: Œcolampadius. The Syngramma Suevicum, 1525 (at Hall), by Brenz, Schnepf, Griebler, etc., later Calvin. Luther against Zwingli—(1) in his preface to Agricola's translation of the Syngramma Suevicum; (2) in 1527, "That the words, This is My Body, etc."

Revolutionary Movements.	Roman Catholic Church.	Protestant Theology.
Severe persecution of the Anabaptists (Manz drowned at Zurich, 1527; Balth. Hubmaier burnt at Vienna, 1528; Hetzer beheaded at Constance, 1529).		Martin Bucer: *b.* 1491, at Schlettstadt; 1505, Dominican; from 1524, pastor in Strasburg; 1549, under Edward VI. in England, and Prof. at Cambridge; *d.* 1551, Feb. 28.
		Wolfgang Fabricius Capito: *b.* 1478; 1515, in Basel; 1520, in Mainz: 1523-*d.* 1541, Dec., Provost of St. Thomas, Strasburg.
	1524.—Peter Caraffa. Bishop of Theate [Pope Paul IV.], instituted the Order of the Theatini to stay the spread of the Reformation.	(*d*) *Zwinglian Confessions.*
		1523. — Jan. 29, Zwingli's 67 Articles. Nov. 17, Instructions to the Council of Zurich.
Melchior Hoffmann: *b.* at Hall, in Swabia; 1523, in Livonia; 1527, in Holstein; 1529, at Strasburg; thence to Friesland, where he joined the Baptists; then in the Netherlands; 1533, in Strasburg; *d.* 1540. (*Ordinanz Gottes*): a strict millenarian of the more spiritual kind; spreads millenarian views among the Baptists.	1526.—May 22: League at Cognac against Charles V. (the Pope, Francis I., Venice, and Milan).	1530.—July 3, *Fidei Ratio ad Carolum V.* (Zwingli, assented to by Œcolampadius and other Reformers).
		1530.—*Confessio Tetrapolitana* (Strasburg, Constance, Lindau, Memmingen); Bucer, Capito, Hedio; during the sitting of the Diet at Augsburg.
		1534. — *Confessio Basiliensis* (Myconius) accepted by Mühlhausen in 1537, and called *Conf. Mühlhusiana.*
		1536.—*Confessio Helvetica Prior* (Basil. II.) drawn up at Basel (Jan. to March) by delegates from the Evangelical Cantons, and by their theologians, Bullinger, Myconius, Grynæus, Leo Judæus, etc.

Contemporary Events.	Lutheran Church.	Reformed Church.
	Luther.—German Mass; **Order of Public Worship.**	Zwingli's ecclesiastical and political church principles; his political reformation of Switzerland; political league of the Roman Catholic Forest Cantons to preserve their supremacy.
1527.—Sack of Rome.	Frederick I. of Denmark adheres to the Lutheran doctrine (John Tausen in Jutland from 1524).	1526.—The Roman Catholic Cantons attacking the Evangelical. May: Disputation at Baden (Eck and Œcolampadius.
1527-29.—The second war between Charles V. and Francis I.; Peace of Cambrai, Aug. 1529.	1527.—*The first Visitation of Electoral Saxony*; Gustavus Vasa proposes the Reformation to the Diet at Westerås.	
1527.—Henry VIII. of England seeks divorce from Catharine of Aragon (Charles V.'s aunt); 1529, Wolsey in disgrace; Thomas More, chancellor.	Frederick I. of Denmark, at the Diet of Odensee, gives the reformed religion the same privileges as the Roman Catholic.	
	1528.—Otto v. Pack's statement of a Roman Catholic League formed at Breslau, 1527; the Reformation spreads in Norway.	1528.—The Reformation victorious in St. Gallen (Joachim Vadianus, John Kessler); and in Berne.
1529.—Sept.-Oct. 14, Suliman lays siege to Vienna.	1529.—Feb. 26, Diet at Speier; April 12, the decision of Roman Catholic majority of Electors and Princes, "Whoever has enforced the Edict of Worms is to do so still; the others are to allow no further innovations; no one to be prevented from celebrating Mass"; April 19, agreed to by the cities. PROTEST: April 25, Appeal taken to the Emperor and Council by Saxony, Hesse, Brandenburg, Anhalt, Lüneburg, and fourteen cities.	1529.—Reformation conquers in Basel (Œcolampadius, Capito, Hedio). League of five Forest Cantons with the House of Hapsburg. June 24, Peace of Cappel; the Forest Cantons abandon the Hapsburg League and recognise liberty of conscience.

Revolutionary Movements.	Roman Catholic Church.	Protestant Theology.
Caspar Schwenkfeld: b. 1490, at Ossing, near Liegnitz; in the service of the Duke of Liegnitz; 1525, believed that he had found an explanation of the words of the institution: "Quod ipse panis fractus est corpori esurienti, nempe cibus, hoc est corpus meum, cibus videlicet esurientium animarum"; hence his doctrine of Christ, The Inner Word (*De cursu Verbi Dei, origine fidei et ratione justificationis*, 1527); of the Person of Christ (not made man, but begotten by the Divine nature: His flesh, Divine); 1528, driven from Silesia; in Strasburg, Augsburg, Speier, Ulm, persecuted from 1539 by Lutheran theologians; in many controversies; *d.* 1561, at Ulm; followers in Silesia; since 1730 in Pennsylvania.	1527.—Process of the Sorbonne against Jacques le Fêvre (*d.* 1537, on a journey to Strasburg, under the protection of Margaret of Navarre). 1527. — May 6, Charles of Bourbon storms Rome; the Pope shut up in St. Angelo till June 6; Charles v., master of most of the States of the Church, proposes to limit the temporal power of the Pope; the Pope appeals to England and France; a French army equipped by English money marches to his assistance. 1528.—June 29: Peace between Emperor and Pope at Barcelona; the Pope gets back the States of the Church and Florence; Heresy to be exterminated.	(*e*) *Lutheran Confessions.* 1529. — Luther's *Larger and Shorter Catechism* in German; appeared simultaneously. 1530.—**Confessio Augustana**; or, Augsburg Confession, framed out of—(1) the 15 Marburg Articles; (2) the 17 Schwabach. Articles drawn up by Luther; (3) Torgau Articles, compiled by Luther, Melanchthon, Justus Jonas, Bugenhagen, and presented to the Elector at Torgau in March 1530. The work of Melanchthon assisted by the evangelical theologians assembled at Augsburg, and revised by Luther. Statement of Evangelical Doctrine, "In qua cerni potest, nihil inesse, quod discrepet a Scripturis vel ab ecclesia catholica vel ab ecclesia Romana, quatenus ex scriptoribus nota est. . . . Sed dissensus est de quibusdam abusibus, qui sine certa auctoritate in ecclesiam irrepserunt." Philip of Hesse signed with protest against Article X. on the Lord's Supper in the *Invariata.* Impossible to fix the exact text of either the German or the Latin editions; Melanchthon's first printed edition, Wittenberg, 1530, in 4to. The *Variata* (variations specially in Article X.) since 1540. *The Apology for the Augsburg Confession.* — The *prima de-*

Contemporary Events.	Lutheran Church.	Reformed Church.
	Separation between the Lutheran and South German Protestants; Luther objects to armed resistance; Zwingli plans to abolish the Papacy and the Mediæval and Papal Empire; Philip of Hesse tries to bring about union.	
	Oct. 1–4, Religious conference at Marburg (Luther, Melanchthon, Zwingli, Œcolampadius, Justus Jonas, Osiander, Brenz, etc.); on Oct. 4, union on fourteen articles, division on fifteenth—Sacrament of Supper. *Zwingli*: "There are none on earth's round I would more gladly be at one with than the men of Wittenberg." *Luther*: "You have another Spirit than we." Zwingli's hand refused.	
	Oct. 16, Luther at the Convent of Schwabach; Nov. 30, at Schmalkald; Saxony breaks away from South German cities.	
1530.—Feb. 24, Charles V. crowned at Bologna by the Pope. No German princes present.	1530.—**Diet at Augsburg**: June 15, entry of Emperor; fruitless negotiations with the Evangelical princes to induce them to join the Corpus-Christi procession; June 20, Diet opened; June 25, Augs. Confess. read and given in (Aug. 3, Confutation read); July 11, Confes. Tetrapolitana read); Confutation, Oct. 17), and Zwingli's *Fidei Ratio*; Aug. 16–29, Negotiations with Melanchthon, in which he proves too pliable. Nov. 19.—Decree of Diet. Protestants to get till April 15, 1531, then suppression by force.	The Roman Catholic Cantons do not observe the terms of peace.
1531.—Ferdinand of Austria, king of the Romans; Bavaria and Electoral Saxony oppose.	1531.—Schmalkald League of Protestants—at the head, Hesse and Saxony.	1531.—May 15, at Aarau the Forest Cantons are refused provisions, Zwingli objecting. Oct. 11, Battle of Cappel; *Zwingli slain*; Second Peace of Cappel.
1532.—Aug.-1547, John Frederick the Magnanimous, Elector of Saxony; *d.* 1554.	1532.—Diet of Nürnberg: Toleration till a General Council. Dessau receives the Reformation.	Henry Bullinger, Zwingli's successor.

Revolutionary Movements.	Roman Catholic Church.	Protestant Theology.
		lineatio apologiæ by Melanchthon in Sept. 1530, at Augsburg; fully revised, Nov. 1530–April 1531; first edition, April 1531; German edition by Justus Jonas, Oct. 1531.
	1530.—Reformed congregations in *Spain*. In Seville: Rodrigo de Valero, Joh. Egidius, Ponce de la Fuente. In Valladolid, 1555, Augustin Cazalla.	*The Schmalkald Articles*, by Luther, for the Protestant Convention at Schmalkald, 1557, and with reference to the proposed General Council at Mantua. [Strictly Lutheran.]
	Francis Enzinas translates the N.T.; 1556, new translation by Juan Perez.	
1533.—*The Kingdom of Christ* in Münster.	All stamped out by Philip II. and the Inquisition.	
Bernhard Rothmann, Evangelical Superintendent in Münster, joins the Anabaptists; Henry Roll and the Wassenberg preachers from Jülich.	*Italy*.—The German Reformation awakens religious life and Augustinian theology; Contarini, Reginald Pole, Joh. de Morone (Archbishop of Modena), *Peter Paul Vergerius* (went over to the Reformation in 1548; *d.* 1565).	*Controversies in the Lutheran Church.*
Summer: Melchiorites in Münster.		1548–55. — *Adiaphoristic*: Flacius, Wigand, Amsdorf, against Leipzig Interim.
Nov.: Jan Matthiesen.	Reformation at Ferrara (Renée married, 1527, to Hercules II.); at Venice; at Naples (Juan Valdez, *d.* 1540; and Bernard Ochino); at Lucca (Peter Martyr).	
1534.—Lent: Riot, destruction of images and cloisters.		1549–66. — *Osiander*: Andrew Osiander (at Nürnberg, 1522–48; at Königsberg, 1549–*d.* 1552); 1550, *De Justificatione*; 1551, *De Unico Mediatore Jesu Christo*; "Justification is a participation in the righteousness of Christ," *cujus natura divina homini quasi infunditur*. In connection therewith his doctrine of the Divine image in man.
Easter Eve: Matthiesen overthrown; John of Leyden at the head of the Anabaptists; Theocracy.	1534–49. — Paul III. Pope (Farnese); Vergerius his legate in Germany.	
1535.—Eve of St. John: Münster taken.		In opposition: Francis Stancarus from Mantua (1551–52 in Königsberg, then in the

Contemporary Events.	Lutheran Church.	Reformed Church.
Henry VIII. divorced by Parliament from Catharine of Aragon. Nov.: Marries **Anne Boleyn.**		
1534.—Restoration of Duke Ulrich of Würtemberg by Philip of Hesse.	1534.—Lutheran Reformation gains Würtemberg, Anhalt, Augsburg, and Pomerania.	*Reformation in French Switzerland under Calvin.*
1535. — Joachim II., Elector of Brandenberg. 1536–38. — Third war between Charles V. and Francis I.	1536.—Wittenberg Concord; Melanchthon and Bucer; *Lord's Supper* in Lutheran sense only; eating of the unworthy, "of the unbelieving," avoided; *Baptism*; *Absolution*; came to nothing; difficulties concealed, not explained. Reformation victorious in Denmark.	*William Farel* (*b.* 1489, in Dauphiné; 1530, in Neufchatel; 1532, in Berne; *d.* 1565, in Geneva); and *Peter Viret* (*b.* 1511, at Orbe; 1531–59, at Lausanne; from 1561, at Nismes and Lyons; *d.* 1571); from 1534, Reformation preachers in Geneva.
1538. — Ten years' truce at Nice.	1537.—Convention at Schmalkald; the Schmalkald Articles. 1538.—Roman Catholic League at Nürnberg. 1539. — Reformation victorious in Ducal Saxony and in Electoral Brandenburg. 1540.—June; Conference at Hagenau. Nov. 25–Jan. 14, at Worms (Granvella, Melanchthon, Bucer, Capito, Brenz, Calvin, Eck, Cochlæus). Feb.: Regensburg Interim.	1536.—JOHN CALVIN at Geneva: *b.* 1509, July 10, at Noyon; studied at Orleans and Paris; 1533, joined Reformation in Paris; at Basel; 1536, **Institutio Christianæ Religionis**; then in Ferrara; strict ecclesiastical discipline; Easter, 1538, banished from Geneva, goes to Strasburg; recalled 1541; *d.* 1564, May 27

Revolutionary Movements.	Roman Catholic Church.	Protestant Theology.
1536.—Jan. 22, John of Leyden, Knipperdolling, and Krechting executed.		Siebenbürgen and in Poland; *d.* 1574; 1562, *De Trinitate et Mediatore*, "Christ our righteousness only as regards His human nature."
		1551–62. — *Majorist*: George Major (*d.* 1574, Prof. at Wittenberg); *bona opera necessaria esse ad salutem.* Against him, Amsdorf; *bona opera perniciosa esse ad salutem.*
1534.—David Joris: *b.* 1501, at Delft; joins the Anabaptists; reforms them; his influence in the Netherlands and East Friesland; 1542, his *Wunderbuch*; 1544, in Basel; a Mystical-spiritualistic speculation with a rationalist tendency.	1536.—Paul III. summons the long-promised Council to meet at Mantau; 1537, adjourned; called to meet at Vicenza; again adjourned.	1556–60.—*Synergist*: Pfeffinger, 1555, *Propos. de libero arbitrio* (in Melanchthon's synergistic sense); against him, Amsdorf (1558, *Confutatio*); and Flacius.
	1542. — Antonio Paleario (burnt 1570); *Del beneficio di Gesu Christo crocifisso verso i Christiani.*	1560.—Disputation at Weimar between Flacius and Strigel. Flacius: Original Sin is of the substance of man. The Lutheran doctrine overcomes. Heshusius: *de servo arbitrio.*
The Mennonites. Menno Simonis: *b.* 1492, at Witmarsum; 1524, priest; 1536, resigned his office, disgusted with the persecution of the Münster Anabaptists; baptized by an apostle of Jan Matthiesen; reformed and organised the Anabaptist communities in Holland and Friesland; *d.* at Oldesloe in 1559; expelled the enthusiastic fanatical elements, and increased the tendency towards Donatism.	1540.—Sept. 27, SOCIETAS JESU constituted by Paul III.; *Don Inigo* (*Ignatius*) *of Loyola*, *b.* 1491, at the Castle Loyola in the Basque Provinces; wounded (1521) at Pampelona; legends of the Saints; studies at Barcelona; from 1528 in Paris. In 1534, with six companions (Francis Xavier, Jac. Lainez, Pet. Lefevre, etc.), he took the three monastic vows and a fourth of absolute obedience to the Pope. Loyola, *d.* 1556; Lainez, *d.* 1564.	1527–40, and renewed 1556.—*Antinomian*: John Agricola, *b.* 1492, at Eisleben; *d.* 1566, Court preacher at Berlin; 1527, against Melanchthon; and 1537, against Luther. Contrition is taught not by the Law but by the Gospel. Recants 1540. From 1556 controversy about "Tertius usus legis."
	"To advance the interests of the Roman Catholic	1567.—*Crypto-Calvinist*: Melanchthon's admissions to Calvinists in doctrines of Lord's

<table>
<tr><th>Contemporary Events.</th><th>Lutheran Church.</th><th>Reformed Church.</th></tr>
<tr><td>1541-53.—Duke Maurice of Saxony; made Elector, 1546.

1541.—Diet at Regensburg; Suliman conquers the Hungarians.

1542–44.—Fourth war of Charles v. with Francis I.; Peace of Crespi.

1542.—Diet at Speier; union against the Turk.</td><td>1541.—April 27–May 22, Conference at Regensburg (Contarini, Melanchthon, Bucer, Eck), Transubstantiation the difficulty.

1542.—Nicolas v. Amsdorf Bishop of Naumburg.

1543. — Reformation in the Archbishopric of Köln; Herman v. Wied, the archbishop, advised by Bucer and Melanchthon; excommunicated, 1546; abdicates, 1547; d. 1552.</td><td>Calvin's Ecclesiastical polity in Geneva.—Worship: prayer and preaching. Organisation: Presbyterian. 1542.—Jan.; Ordonnances ecclésiastiques de l'église de Genève. Pastors, doctors, elders, deacons. Church discipline.

Reformation in France 1559-98.

Earlier: Francis I., Humanist, careless in religion, treated the Reformation as a politician; his sister Margaret, Queen of Navarre (d. 1549), protected the Reformers; severe persecution of French Protestants in spite of alliance with German Protestant princes, and an invitation to Melanchthon to settle in France, 1535.</td></tr>
<tr><td colspan="2">1544.—Diet at Speier; recognition of the Protestants; peace all round till a General Council.

1545.—Reformatio Wittenbergensis.

1546.—Second Religious Conference at Regensburg; Feb. 18, Luther dies at Eisleben; the Protestants do not appear at the Diet.

1546-47.—The Schmalkald War; June 19, league between Maurice and the Emperor; July 20, decree against John Frederick and Philip; Oct. 27, Maurice made Elector; April 24, Battle of Mühlberg, John Frederick, prisoner; Philip surrenders at Halle; Emperor breaks faith, and keeps the princes in prison.</td><td>Henry II.: Anthony of Navarre, and his wife Joan d'Albret, at the head of the Protestants in France.</td></tr>
<tr><td>1547–59. — Henry II. of France; spouse, Catherine de Medici, d. 1589.</td><td>1548.—May 15, Augsburg Interim retains Roman Catholic hierarchy, ceremonies, feasts and fasts; marriage of clergy and Lord's Supper sub utraque permitted.</td><td>1559.—May 25–29, First Reformed Synod at Paris, assembled by a Parisian pastor, Anthony Chandieu; Conf. Gallica.</td></tr>
</table>

Revolutionary Movements.	Roman Catholic Church.	Protestant Theology.
His followers, Mennonnites, tolerated in 1572 by William of Orange in the Netherlands; also found in Emden, Hamburg, Danzig, Elbing, in the Palatinate, and in Moravia; moderated the original Anabaptist spirit; rejected all dogmatic; forbade oaths and war; appealed to the letter of Scripture.	Hierarchy against Protestantism within and without the Romish Church." Xavier's mission work in East Asia. Society's Morals: casuistry. Its dogmatic: superstition systematised. 1542.—Cardinal Caraffa advises the reconstruction of the Inquisition to crush Protestantism in Italy. 1545.—*Council of Trent* opened: First period, Mar. 11, 1547, at Trent; April 21, 1547–Sept. 13, 1549, at Bologna. Second period, May 1, 1551–April 28, 1552, at Trent. Third period, Jan. 13, 1562–Dec. 4, 1563 (25 Sessions). Romanist doctrinal teaching concluded and petrified.	Supper, Christology, and Predestination. From these controversies a need for concord in the Lutheran Church; hence various forms of concord, out of all which came the *Formula Concordiæ.* (1) Swabian Concord of Jac. Andreas (from 1562 Prof. at Tübingen, *d.* 1590) in 1574; 1575, Swabian Concord of Martin Chemnitz; 1576, Maulbronn Formula of Lucas Osiander. (2) Torgau Convention with the *Torgau Book.* Thence 1577, *Formula Concordiæ.* *The principal Lutheran Theologians.* *Martin Chemnitz*: 1554–*d.* 1586, Superintendent in Brunswick; *Examen Concilii Trid.*; 1565–73, *Loci Theologici.* *Matthew Flacius*: *b.* 1520, at Albona in Illyria; 1545, at Wittenberg; 1548, at Magdeburg; 1557–61, at Jena; *d.* at Frankfort-on-Maine, 1575, March 11.

Contemporary Events.	Lutheran Church.	Reformed Church.
1547-53.—Edward VI. of England: *b.* 1537.	1548.—Leipzig Interim (Maurice of Saxony and Melanchthon).	1561.—Sept.: Religious Conference at Poissy; Theodore Beza.
	1551.—Vehement desire of the Emperor that the Protestants should submit to the Council of Trent; Secret League of Maurice of Saxony with Henry II. of France.	1562.—Jan.: Protestants gain right to worship outside the towns; Francis of Guise massacres Protestant congregation at Vassy.
1553-58. — (Bloody) Mary of England.	Oct.: Würtemburg ambassadors, and Jan. 1552, Saxon ambassadors at Trent.	
1554.—July 9, Maurice slain in battle near Sievershausen, against Albert, Margrave of Brandenburg. Ferdinand beaten by the Turks in Hungary.	1552.—Mar. 20, Maurice breaks loose; May 19, seizes Ehrenberg Castle and Ehrenberg Pass, the keys of the Tyrol; the Council breaks up; July, Treaty of Passau; John Frederick and Philip free.	1562-63.—Huguenot war. Anthony of Navarre *d.*; Francis of Guise shot before Orleans.
		1567-68 and 1569-70.—Huguenot wars.
1555-98.—Philip II. of Spain. 1556-64. — *Ferdinand I., Emperor.*	1555.—Sept. 25: *Religious Peace of Augsburg*; the Lutheran Church (Augs. Confes.) has the same legal rights as the Roman Catholic: *Cujus regio ejus religio*; the *Reservatum ecclesiasticum*; the Reformed Church not recognised.	1572.—Aug. 24, Paris massacre on eve of St. Bartholomew; Coligny and 20,000 Huguenots murdered.
1558-1603. — Elizabeth of England.	1558.—Disputes between old Lutherans (Gnesiolutherani) and Melanchthon's followers.	1574-76.—Huguenot war; Holy League of the Guises.
1559-60. — Francis II. of France (married Mary of Scotland).	1560. — Death of Melanchthon, April 19.	1588.—Henry and Louis of Guise slain.
1560-74.—Charles IX. of France.	1586-91.—Crypto-Calvinist troubles in Electoral Saxony; suppression of Calvinism; execution of Krells, 1601.	1589.—Henry III. murdered by a League fanatic, J. Clement, Aug. 1.

Anglican Church.	Roman Catholic Church.	Protestant Theology.
England, 1547–1600, under Henry VIII.: John Frith, William Tindal.	1564.—*Professio Fidei Tridentinæ*: 1566, *Catechismus Romanus* (Leonardo Marini, Egidio Foscarari, Muzio Calini).	*Catalogus Testium Veritatis*, 1556; *Ecclesi. Hist. per aliquot . . . studiosos et pios viros in urbe Magdeburgica* (the Magdeburg Centuries), 13 vols., 1560–74; *Clavis Script. Sac.*, 1567; *Glossa Compendaria in N.T.*, 1570, etc.
1534.—Act of Parliament about Royal supremacy; the King "the only supreme head on earth of the Church of England"; at the head of the Evangelical party, Thomas Cranmer [1533, Archbishop of Canterbury] and Thomas Cromwell; Translation of the Bible, 1538.	1548.—Philip Neri founds the Oratory. 1550–64.—Julius III. (del Monte). 1551.—Foundation of Jesuit Collegium Romanum. 1552.—Foundation of Collegium Germanicum. 1555–59.—Paul IV. (Caraffa) protests against the Peace of Augsburg; Inquisition.	*John Gerhard*: *b.* 1582, at Quedlinburg; 1606, Superintendent at Heldburg; 1615, General Superintendent at Coburg; 1616–*d.* 1637, Prof. at Jena. *Loci Theologici*, 1610–25; *Medit. Sac.*, etc. *Leonhard Hutter*: 1596–*d.* 1616, Prof. at Wittenberg; *Compendium Loc. Theol.* 1610; *Loci Commun. Theolog.*, 1619.
1539.—July 28, Transubstantiation; refusal of cup to the laity; celibacy of the clergy; Masses for the dead; auricular confession.	1559–65.—Pius IV. (Medici) rules under the influence of his nephew Cardinal Charles Borromeo, Archbishop of Milan, *d.* 1584. 1564.—*Index librorum prohibitorum.*	
The Reformation of Henry VIII. the act of the King, and meant only revolt from the mediæval system, with the King in the place of the Pope.	1566–72.—Pius V., a zealous Dominican. 1567.—Bull of excommunication against 79 Augustinian propositions of Michael Baius (*d.* 1589), Chancellor of University of Louvain.	*The confessional writings of the Reformed Church universally recognised.* *Catechismus ecclesiæ Genevensis*; 1541, French; 1545, Latin; Calvin. *Consensio in re sacramentaria ministrorum Tigur. Eccles. et Joh. Calvini.*
Isolation of the Church of England; no relation to the	1568.—*Breviarium.*	

Contemporary Events.	Lutheran Church.	Reformed Church.
1560–78.—Mary, Queen of Scots; executed 1587.	*The Lutheran Church loses to—*	1593.—*Henry IV. becomes a Roman Catholic.*
	(*a*) The Roman Catholic Church.	
1564–76. — *Maximilian II., Emperor.*	1558.—Bavaria.	1598.—EDICT OF NANTES: liberty of conscience; right of public worship; full civil privileges; cities given to the Huguenots as pledges.
	1578.—The Austrian Duchy (Rudolph II.).	
1574–89. — Henry III. of France.	1584.—The Bishoprics of Würzburg, Bamberg, Salzburg, Hildesheim, etc.	
1576–1612. — *Rudolph II., Emperor.*	1594.—Steiermark, Carinthia (Ferdinand II.).	
	1607.—Donauwerth.	
1588–1648. — Christian IV., King of Denmark.		1620–28.—Huguenot revolts.
	(*b*) The Reformed Church.	1629.—La Rochelle taken.
1589–1610.—Henry IV. of France; became Roman Catholic, 1593; murdered by Ravaillac, 1610, May 14.	1560.—The Palatinate; 1563, Heidelberg Catechism (Reformed under Frederick III.; Lutheran under Louis VI., 1576–83; Reformed under Frederick IV., 1583–1610.)	Edict of Nismes. *Ecclesiastical* rights guaranteed to the Huguenots.
1598–1621.—Philip III. of Spain.	1568.—Bremen.	
	1596.—Anhalt (John George, 1587–1603); repeal of Consist. Syst. and Lutheran Catechism; 1597–1628, Calvinist Articles.	

Anglican Church.	Roman Catholic Church.	Protestant Theology.
Papacy; no relation to the Reformed Churches.	1570.—*Missale Romanum.*	The **Heidelberg Catechism**: 1563, written at the suggestion of Frederick III. of the Palatinate by Zachary Ursinus (from 1561 Prof. at Heidelberg; *d.* 1583) and Caspar Olevianus (Prof. at Heidelberg; *d.* 1587).
1547.—Under Lord Protector Somerset; Peter Martyr Vermigli (*b.* 1500, at Florence; 1542, in Strasburg; *d.* 1562, in Zurich) and Bernard Ochino (*b.* 1487) brought to Oxford; Martin Bucer and Paul Fagius, to Cambridge.	1572–85. — Gregory XIII.: congratulatory letter to Charles IX. about Massacre of St. Bartholomew; *Te Deum* at Rome in honour of event.	*Confessio Helvetica Posterior*: 1566, sent by Bullinger to Frederick III. of the Palatinate.
The Book of Homilies.	1582.—Reform of Calendar.	*The Decrees of the Synod of Dort*: 1619, recognised in the Netherlands, Switzerland, the Palatinate, and in 1620 in France; not universally recognised.
1548.—The Book of Common Prayer; revised, 1552.	1582–1610.—Jesuit missions in China.	
	1585–90.—Sixtus V.: Vatican Library.	
	1588.—Baronius' *Eccl. Annales.*	
	1590.—Infallible edition of the Vulgate.	
	1592–1605.—Clement VII.	
	1592.—New edition of Vulgate (declared to be the edition of Sixtus V.).	

Contemporary Events.	Lutheran Church.	Anglican Church.
	The Lutheran Church loses to the Reformed Church—	1552.—*The* 42 *Articles.*
	1605.—Hesse-Cassel reformed, under Landgrave Maurice (1592–1627).	[1554.—Cardinal Reginald Pole, Papal Legate; 1555–58, Bloody persecutions under Mary; 1556, Mar. 21, Cranmer burnt at Oxford.]
	1613.—Dec. 25, Brandenburg reformed under the Elector John Sigismund; 1614, *Confessio Marchica.*	
	———	*Reformation restored under Elizabeth.*
		1559.—June: Act of Uniformity, Matthew Parker, Archbishop of Canterbury.
	Anti-Trinitarians.	
	Michael Servetus from Aragon; 1530, in Basel; 1531, *De Trinitatis erroribus*; 1534, in Lyons; 1537, in Paris; 1540, in Vienne; 1553, *Christianismi restitutio*; burnt at Geneva, 1553.	Book of Common Prayer revised and restored.
	Valentinus Gentilis, from Calabria; beheaded at Berne, 1556.	1562.—Jan. 23, *The* 39 *Articles*: Calvinist doctrine of Predestination; Doctrine of Lord's Supper, Calvinist.
	Laelius Socinus: *b.* 1525, at Siena; 1546, in Venice; 1547, travels in Switzerland, Germany, and Poland; *d.* 1562 in Zurich.	1567.—Puritans against Uniformity. [Puritanism; Reformation from within through the Church community; in England strict acceptance of the spiritual priesthood of all be-